The Minnesota Nonprofit Legal Handbook

650 Practical Questions and Answers for Managers, Board Members and Volunteers

Published by the Minnesota Council of Nonprofits

Copies my be ordered from:

Minnesota Council of Nonprofits
2314 University Ave. W., Suite 20
St. Paul, MN 55114
651-642-1904
651-642-1517 (fax)
www.minnesotanonprofits.org

Any corrections, revisions and digital footnotes for this publication will be posted at:
www.minnesotanonprofits.org

IMPORTANT DISCLAIMER: The materials available in this handbook are for informational purposes only and not for the purpose of providing legal advice. You should contact your attorney to obtain advice with respect to any particular issue or problem. Use of and access to this handbook or any of the links contained within the book do not create an attorney-client relationship between the user and the Minnesota Council of Nonprofits or any attorney contributors. The opinions expressed at or through this book are the opinions of the individual author and may not reflect the opinions of their firm or any individual attorney.

ISBN-13: 978-0-692-09230-9

Printed in the United States of America.

Table of Contents

Chapter 5. Charitable Donation Regulations

Chapter 6. Board of Directors

Chapter 7. Lobbying, Election-related Activity and Voter Education

Chapter 8. Financial Accountability

Chapter 9. Human Resources

Chapter 10. Insurance for Nonprofit Organizations

Chapter 11. Disclosure and Privacy Requirements

Chapter 12. Relationships with Other Entities

Chapter 13. Other Regulatory Issues

Chapter 14. Ongoing Compliance

Chapter 15. Contracts

Chapter 16. Intellectual Property

Contributors

The Minnesota Council of Nonprofits would like to extend special thanks to the many attorneys and nonprofit leaders who contributed to this creation and updating of the material in this publication. Without your vast experience and knowledge, this project would not have been possible.

David Arons
National Brain Tumor Society

Kate Barr
Propel Nonprofits

Rich Besonen
Travelers Companies, Inc.

Mary Boatright
Arizona Department of Insurance

Eve Borenstein
BAM Law Office, LLC

Susie Brown
Hennepin County Bar Association

Madeline Buck
Minnesota Supreme Court

Nina Carranco

Susan Stevens Chambers

Ryan Check
Virtual Radiologic (vRad)

Fangzhou Chen
J.D. Class of 2018,
University of Minnesota Law School

Heidi Christianson
Nilan Johnson Lewis, P.A.

Rich Cowles

Gina DeConcini
Moss & Barnett, P.A.

Sarah Duniway
Gray Plant Mooty

Kimberly Espinosa
U.S. Department of Education

Dale Evensen
Travelers Insurance

Tom Feinberg

Nancy Gaschott

Paul Godfread
Godfread Law Firm

Karen Gries
CliftonLarsonAllen, LLP

Barbara Haley

Melanie Lockwood Herman
Nonprofit Risk Management Center

Kristin Hibbard

Veena Iyer
Nilan Johnson Lewis, P.A.

Scott R. Johnson
Minnesota Department of Human Services

Gina Kastel
Faegre Baker Daniels LLP

Steve Lepinski
Steve Lepinski Consulting

Ben Lindblad
Dorsey & Whitney LLP

Kimberly Lowe
Avisen Legal, PA

Ellen McVeigh

JoMarie Morris
Jeremiah Program

Chris Mossing

Jon Nelson
Residential Services Inc.

Debra Page
Ballard Spahr LLP

Ella Phillips
Planned Parenthood Minnesota, North Dakota, South Dakota

Jon Pratt
Minnesota Council of Nonprofits

Jeff Prauer
Airport Foundation MSP

Rinal Ray
People Serving People

Ron Reed

Sondra Reis
Minnesota Council of Nonprofits

Emily Robertson
Rubric Legal, LLC

Marie Rutz
Lifeworks Services, Inc.

Margie Siegel
Center for Nonprofit Management,
University of St. Thomas

Chris Sullivan
Law Office of Chris Sullivan, PLLC

Mike Temali
Neighborhood Development Center

James Toscano
Toscano Advisors, LLC

Jenn Urban
Legal for Good PLLC

Ben Velzen
Minnesota Attorney General's Office

Maureen Ventura
Apttus Corporations

Tene Wells
Tene Wells Consulting

Ann Wilczynski
Marquette Asset Management

Kathi Wright
Gray Plant Mooty

Laura Zabel
Springboard for the Arts

Patty Zurlo
Zurlo Law Office

Introduction

You don't need to be an attorney to serve on a nonprofit board, or to help manage the organization, but every organization needs to reference legal requirements multiple times in a year. The *Minnesota Nonprofit Legal Handbook* serves as a quick reference to these matters across 16 chapters for the major areas of nonprofit regulation, structure and liability—both Federal and Minnesota.

The handbook's Q & A format is designed to be a useful tool to locate basic answers, to help identify potential related questions, and then direct the user to relevant statutes and regulatory requirements. The full list of questions within these chapters is presented in our Question by Chapter index on page 369, providing a path to explore a particular issue.

As noted in the caveat at page 2, the *Minnesota Nonprofit Legal Handbook* is not a substitute for advice from qualified legal professionals, and does not constitute the practice of law. There are many situations where professional advice from attorneys or accountants is necessary.

Nonprofit and tax-exempt organizations are increasingly seen as a specialty area, where it is advisable to seek legal counsel experienced and knowledgeable in the workings of the Internal Revenue Service, Office of the Minnesota Attorney General, County Assessors, Minnesota Department of Revenue or other agencies. A directory of many of the Minnesota law firms and accounting firms with nonprofit expertise is located at the Nonprofit SpeciaLIST website at www.nonprofitspecialist.org.

In some cases pro bono (free) legal help may be available from attorneys and organizations such as LegalCORPS.

The *Minnesota Nonprofit Legal Handbook* benefited from thousands of volunteer hours of writing, editing and review from attorneys and nonprofit managers over a period of years. MCN is grateful for their insights and commitment to assisting nonprofit organizations to succeed at their charitable missions, and we salute their role and contributions at left.

The *Minnesota Nonprofit Legal Handbook* project turned out to be a much greater and longer task than initially understood, so we have to give a special recognition to the editor who first corralled the sum of the pieces that helped make this final product possible, a great nonprofit leader and attorney at law, Rinal Ray.

While the primary regulatory structures for nonprofit organizations are well established and relatively stable, we recognize that laws and regulations are subject to change. This handbook is intended to be a useful resource and updated in print on an occasional basis—every three years on the dot.

MCN will maintain an online list of updates to the latest version of the *Minnesota Nonprofit Legal Handbook* at www.minnesotanonprofits.org, organized by chapter and question, as well as digital versions of chapter footnotes.

CHAPTER 1

INTRODUCTION TO NONPROFIT LAW

Topics

A. Brief Introduction to Nonprofit Law

Nonprofit organizations are entities that form a distinct sector of the economy, alongside business organizations and governmental units. Fundamentally, nonprofit organizations are highly regulated, mission-based organizations as is distinguished from profit-based entities, and they must meet very specific requirements for registration as set forth by the United States Internal Revenue Service (IRS)[1]. In 2012 there were over 1.44 million organizations with $320 billion in private charitable contributions and $2.16 trillion in total revenue.[2]

Nonprofit organizations in the U.S. are formed by incorporating under state law or setting up a trust. To incorporate as a nonprofit in Minnesota, the organization first files Articles of Incorporation with the Office of the Secretary of State of Minnesota. Federal nonprofit status is granted through application with the IRS Form 1023. The central and most essential requirement for nonprofit status is that the organization's purpose is mission-driven rather than profit driven. Lacking a clearly stated mission that seeks to improve some aspect of society or culture, the application will fail. Under certain circumstances, nonprofit organizations will enjoy favorable tax treatment – the ability to be free from paying various taxes, which such as exemptions from state and federal corporate income tax, local property taxes, and state sales and use taxes. The tax exemption and eligibility for tax deductible gifts, convey a significant economic benefit to the recipient organizations, and contributes to why charitable organizations in the U.S. comprise a larger segment of the economy than in other developed countries. Nonprofit status also allows donors to receive a tax deduction for their charitable gift, which is a significant incentive support.

The requirements attached to tax exemptions provide parameters that guide the behavior of nonprofit organizations in public discourse and communities, and distinguish nonprofit organizations from business and government. Generally, charitable organizations must agree to limitations on lobbying and political activity, and not distribute private benefits or profit to stakeholders.

Both federal and state laws govern nonprofit organizations, and laws vary from state to state. Tax exemption usually starts at the federal level. Organizations often apply for tax-exempt status from the IRS, and file the annual financial information return (Form 990). IRS Form 990 is available to the public directly by nonprofit organizations and on several national websites that support and encourage nonprofit transparency. IRS Form 990 also provides uniform collection of financial information and information about an organization's mission, programs, board of directors, various policies and compensation of officers. Nonprofit startups lacking the infrastructure to comply with reporting requirements can organize through a "fiscal sponsor" nonprofit organization, which, for a small fee, takes responsibility for financial reporting among other administrative details.[3]

In addition to filing IRS Form 990, most states, including Minnesota, require organizations seeking charitable contributions from public to register and make annual disclosures. In Minnesota, nonprofits comply with this requirement by submitting an annual report to the Charities Division of the Attorney General's office. In addition to enforcing tax laws and collecting revenue, state and federal governments focus on the financial aspects of nonprofits as part of their interest in protecting consumers and preventing theft and fraud; and the state attorneys general have broad powers to preserve charitable trusts and assets. A dual system of enforcement of charitable laws exists between state attorneys general and the IRS, with authority to conduct investigations and seek legal sanctions for violations of law.

1 Footnotes throughout this Chapter refer to the Internal Revenue Service as "IRS", unless the text notes otherwise.

2 Brian S. McKeever, Sarah L. Pettijohn, "The Nonprofit Sector in Brief 2014: Public Charities, Giving, and Volunteering," Urban Institute, National Center for Charitable Statistics (2014).

3 *See* I.R.C. § 501(c)(3) (2015).

While nonprofits may be exempt from paying income taxes, their employees are not, and these organizations must also comply with the full range of employment, land use, environmental, postal and credit regulations that govern every other employer, property owner, mailer and financial entity in the United States.

B. FAQs about Nonprofit Organizations

Q1. ***What is a nonprofit organization?***

A1. "Nonprofit organization" is a phrase used to describe a number of different legal situations, including unincorporated associations, but most often corporations formed under state statute, such as the Minnesota Nonprofit Corporation Act in Minnesota Statutes Chapter 317A. A "nonprofit organization" is an organization or corporate entity which is formed for the purpose of fulfilling a mission to improve the common good of society rather than to acquire and distribute profits. In order to be a legally recognized entity, organizing documents, or articles of incorporation, must be filed with the Secretary of State of Minnesota describing the purpose of the organization.[4] Nonprofit organizations are also subject to certain specific benefits as well as obligations, which are governed by Minnesota state statutes. Some types of nonprofit organizations, usually those that are charitable in nature, may qualify for "tax exempt" status by separate application to the IRS.[5] Nonprofit organizations are prohibited by law from distributing a financial return (equity), or profit. These organizations may pay employees for services rendered.

Q2. ***Why do we have nonprofit organizations?***

A2. Nonprofit organizations exist in many forms in almost every country (commonly called nongovernmental organizations, or NGOs, outside of the United States) for a common goal or mission which improves an area of the community. Nonprofit organizations provide a vehicle for people to do things that they cannot do apart, in which they are engaged in communities. Sometimes the need for these activities is explained as market failure (demand for goods or services that businesses cannot or will not provide) or government failure (government will not do it—as in prohibited from doing it in the case of religion—or cannot do it, as the community will not engage in the activities when provided by government). In any case, a common affinity brings people together for small and large causes—from coin collecting to climate changing—and the organizations they form are held in common for mutual benefits.

Q3. ***Is there a difference between a "nonprofit" organization and a "not-for-profit" organization? If so, what is the difference? Which term is more appropriate?***

A3. The phrase "not-for-profit" is used occasionally as an informal expression to refer to the same set of organizations or activities, but is not used in any of the statutes that govern nonprofit activity. "Nonprofit" is the most commonly used term, and is the legal term used throughout the Minnesota Nonprofit Corporation Act.[6]

4 Minn. Stat. § 317A.111 (2016).
5 *See* I.R.C. § 501(c)(3) (2015); I.R.S. Form 1023 (October 2013); I.R.S. Pub. 557 (2017).
6 Minn. Stat. § 317A (2016).

Q4. ***Is there a difference between a "nonprofit organization" and a charity? If so, what is the difference?***

A4. While many nonprofits are considered charitable organizations, recognized by the IRS as being formed for defined public benefit purposes set out in Internal Revenue Code (IRC)[7] § 501(c)(3), many other nonprofits are formed for other purposes and are not considered charitable—including veterans organizations, cemeteries, credit unions and political organizations.

Q5. ***Can a nonprofit organization actually make a "profit"?***

A5. Profit, commonly defined is revenue less expenses. Nonprofits are not prohibited from earning a profit, but they may not pay out net proceeds or equity to individuals or directors.[8] Nonprofits are allowed to end a year with greater revenues than expenses, and add to the organization's net assets. All revenue must be expended solely for the organization's exempt purpose as set out in its Articles of Incorporation.[9]

Q6. ***Can a nonprofit organization pay its staff members?***

A6. Despite the fact that they are sometimes referred to as "voluntary organizations," many nonprofit organizations compensate their employees with pay and benefits comparable to other areas of the workforce. Nonprofit organizations employ millions of people in the U.S., and are best positioned to attract and retain a qualified workforce if they pay market rates of wages and benefits. They may not pay "excess" compensation, though there is no set amount that would be considered excessive, and many executives of large nonprofits, including hospitals and universities, are among top earners in all fields in the U.S.

Q7. ***What does it mean to be a "nonprofit corporation"?***

A7. In Minnesota, a nonprofit corporation is an organization that has filed Articles of Incorporation with the Secretary of State, as required by the Minnesota Nonprofit Corporation Act.[10] As a recognized legal entity, this organization can own property and bank accounts, hire employees, make investments, can sue and be sued, and is subject to a variety of regulations, taxes and reporting requirements. Nonprofits incorporated in Minnesota must be governed by a board of directors whose structure and processes are defined in bylaws, and must file an annual registration with the Secretary of State to remain active.[11]

Q8. ***What does 501(c)(3) mean? From where does this term come?***

A8. The Internal Revenue Code comprises the federal tax laws enacted by the U.S. Congress, which are organized in more than 9,000 sections. Section 501(c)(3) of the Internal Revenue Code sets out the definition of charitable organizations, which are eligible to receive contributions that are deductible from the federal individual income tax, estate tax and corporate income tax.[12] This deductibility can be a powerful

---

7 Footnotes throughout this chapter refer to the Internal Revenue Code as "IRC". The use of the word "Section" in this Part's text from this point forward is a reference to Sections of the I.R.C. unless the text notes otherwise.

8 *See* I.R.C. § 501(c)(3) (2015).

9 *Croixdale, Inc. v. County of Washington*, 726 N.W.2d 483, 488 (Minn. 2007).

10 Minn. Stat. § 317A.111 (2016).

11 Minn. Stat. § 317A.823 (2016).

12 *See* I.R.C. § 170(c)(2) (2015).

incentive for charitable giving, and qualifies organizations for a variety of grant programs, including private foundations.

Q9. ***Are all nonprofit organizations tax-exempt?***

A9. Tax exemptions vary by type of organization and type of tax. To become tax exempt, nonprofit organizations that have incorporated must apply for tax exemption from the relevant taxing authority – generally the IRS (for federal corporate income tax exemption), the state Department of Revenue (for state corporate income tax and sales tax exemptions), and the county where land or buildings owned by the organization are located (for property tax exemption). To be tax-exempt under section 501(c)(3) of the Internal Revenue Code, an organization must be organized and operated exclusively for exempt purposes set forth in section 501(c)(3), and none of its earnings may inure to any private shareholder or individual.[13] In addition, it may not be an action organization, i.e., it may not attempt to influence legislation as a substantial part of its activities and it may not participate in any campaign activity for or against political candidates.[14] Each state establishes their own definition of what qualifies for sales or property tax exemptions. For more information on nonprofit tax exemption, see Chapter 3: Tax Exemptions.

Like other employers, nonprofit organizations must report and withhold a portion of employees pay and forward this to the IRS and state government. Nonprofit employers are exempt from paying the federal portion of unemployment compensation (FUTA) and are eligible to withdraw from the state unemployment compensation (SUTA), and directly reimburse the state for the actual cost of unemployment benefits used.[15] For more information about FUTA and SUTA, see Chapter 3: Tax Exemptions, Section G: Federal and State Unemployment Tax (FUTA and SUTA).

C. Differences between Various Types of Nonprofit Organizations

Q10. ***Are there different kinds of nonprofit organizations? How do they differ?***

A10. The founders of nonprofit organizations face multiple options for organizational form and structure, but tend to adopt the same structure as other organizations performing similar functions. Under the Internal Revenue Code (I.R.C.), the U.S. Congress has established specific classifications for 29 types of I.R.C. § 501(c) organizations[16], each with its own advantages and accountabilities, including:

501(c)(1) — Corporations Organized under Act of Congress
501(c)(2) — Title-Holding Corporations for Single Parent Corporations
501(c)(3) — Religious, Educational, Charitable, Scientific, Literary, Testing for Public Safety, to Foster National or International Amateur Sports Competition, or Prevention of Cruelty to Children or Animals Organizations
501(c)(4) — Civic Leagues, Social Welfare Organizations, and Local Associations of Employees
501(c)(5) — Labor, Agricultural, or Horticultural Organizations

13 *See* I.R.S., *Exemption Requirements - 501(c)(3) Organizations*, www.irs.gov/charities-non-profits/charitable-organizations/exemption-requirements-section-501-c-3-organizations (last updated Jan. 26, 2017).
14 *Id.*
15 *See* I.R.C. § 3303(e) (2014).
16 *See* I.R.S. Pub. 557 (Jan. 2017), www.irs.gov/pub/irs-pdf/p557.pdf.

501(c)(6) — Business Leagues, Chambers of Commerce, Real Estate Boards, or Professional Football Leagues
501(c)(7) — Social and Recreational Clubs
501(c)(8) — Fraternal Beneficiary Societies, Orders, or Associations
501(c)(9) — Voluntary Employees' Beneficiary Associations
501(c)(10) — Domestic Fraternal Societies, Orders, or Associations
501(c)(11) — Teachers' Retirement Fund Associations of a Purely Local Character
501(c)(12) — Local Benevolent Life Insurance Associations, Mutual Irrigation and Telephone Companies, and Like Organizations
501(c)(13) — Cemetery Companies
501(c)(14) — Credit Unions and Other Mutual Financial Organizations
501(c)(15) — Mutual Insurance Companies or Associations
501(c)(16) — Cooperative Organizations to Finance Crop Operations
501(c)(17) — Supplemental Unemployment Benefits Trusts
501(c)(18) — Employee Funded Pension Trusts (created before June 25, 1959)
501(c)(19) — Veterans' Organizations
501(c)(21) — Black Lung Benefit Trusts
501(c)(22) — Withdrawal Liability Payment Fund
501(c)(23) — Veterans Organization (created before 1880)
501(c)(25) — Title-Holding Corporations or Trusts for Multiple Parent Corporations
501(c)(26) — State-Sponsored High-Risk Health Coverage Organizations
501(c)(27) — Qualified State-Sponsored Workers' Compensation Organizations
501(c)(28) — National Railroad Retirement Investment Trust
501(c)(29) — CO-OP Health Insurance Issuers

The most common 501(c) category is a 501(c)(3) charitable organization, numbering 1,067,619 organizations in 2013 and comprising 69.3 percent of all nonprofit organizations. The next most populous category is a 501(c)(3) private foundation, numbering 102,415 in 2013, or 6.6 percent of all 501(c) organizations.[17]

Q11. ***What is an unincorporated association?***

A11. An unincorporated association is a group of people that have agreed to form a group for a common purpose, but have not incorporated under a state statute. They are typically small in size and limited in scope and purpose. Examples of unincorporated associations may include a book club, informal neighborhood, professional networking or study group. Informal or unincorporated associations allow for greater flexibility in organizational structure for very small organizations. However, because the group has no legal existence, it may be limited by the threat of personal liability for members, inability to offer tax-deductibility for donations, difficulty in securing a bank account or line of credit, and the potential for income-offsets on personal tax-returns. For more information on the advantages and disadvantages of unincorporated associations, see Chapter 2: The Nonprofit Corporation, Section C: The Nonprofit Incorporation Process in Minnesota.

17 National Center for Charitable Statistics, *Number of Nonprofit Organizations in the United States, 2003 – 2013* (2013), nccsweb.urban.org/PubApps/profile1.php?state=US (last visited June 20, 2017).

Q12. *What is a charitable trust?*

A12. A charitable trust is an arrangement where property is held and managed by a person, group of persons or organizations for a charitable purpose, the object of which is to benefit the community.[18] The person, group or organizations managing the property are called trustees. Trustees have a fiduciary responsibility to deal with the property with regard to its charitable purpose.[19] The Minnesota Attorney General has the rights, duties, and powers to enforce laws related to charitable trusts in the state and must be notified of all court proceedings.[20]

Generally, a charitable trust that has gross assets of $25,000 or more at any time during the year must register with the Minnesota Attorney General's Office by paying a $25 fee and filing either its Articles of Incorporation or the instrument that created the charitable trust within three months after the trust first receives control of the trust property.[21] Once registered, a charitable trust must annually submit or file a copy of its federal tax or information return and a $25 fee with the Minnesota Attorney General's office.[22]

The charitable trust form offers:

- Ease and swiftness of formation,
- Administration with fewer formalities than the corporate form (no audit requirement),
- Fewer housekeeping requirements,
- Perpetual or indefinite period of existence, and
- The possibility of continuing control by the grantor.[23]

While charitable trusts are not the predominant form of charitable engagement, they are often used by private foundations that are engaged solely in making grants.

Q13. *What are the differences between nonprofit corporations, unincorporated associations and charitable trusts?*

A13. The main difference between nonprofit corporations, unincorporated associations, and charitable trusts is related to corporate form and regulatory oversight. Unincorporated associations that are very small and informal are not subject to regulatory oversight (if they are not governed by 501(c)(3)), but in turn are prohibited from collecting tax-deductible donations reaping other benefits of incorporation and 501(c)(3) status.

18 Minn. Stat. § 501B.35, subdiv. 3 (2016).
19 Minn. Stat. § 501B.35, subdiv. 4 (2016).
20 Minn. Stat. §§ 501B.34-35, subdiv. 4 (2016).
21 Minn. Stat. §§ 501B.36-38 (2016).
22 Minn. Stat. § 501B.38 (2016).
23 James J. Fishman, Stephen Schwarz & Lloyd Hitoshi Mayer, *Nonprofit Organizations, Cases and Materials*, 46 (5th ed. 2015).

	Tax Exempt Nonprofit Corporation (501(c)(3) status)	Unincorporated Association (no 501(c)(3) status)	Charitable Trust
Charitable purpose	X		X
Corporate entity (personal liability protection, banking)	X		
Subject to IRS oversight (Form 990)	X		X
Must file and report to Attorney General	X		X
Must file and report to Secretary of State	X		
Must have Generally Accepted Accounting Principles (GAAP) audit	X (if above $750,000 in Minnesota)		

Q14. ***Can a nonprofit organization have members?***

A14. There are two kinds of legal entities related to membership — nonprofit organizations with members, and those without. Nonprofit organizations with members are unique in member control over organizational decisions, generally exerted through the ability to select the board of directors. True membership-based nonprofits afford members legal rights set out in organizational Articles of Incorporations and/or by-laws. Under the Minnesota Nonprofit Corporation Action, in the absence of a provision in organizational documents providing for members, a corporation has no members.[24] A voting membership model may be appropriate for organizations seeking authentic member control, such as condo or neighborhood associations and policy organizations. For these organizations, bylaws define member rights and responsibilities and act as the internal governance foundation. Membership rights include voting and electing board members, access to governance documents and enforcement power.[25] Organizational communication, member tracking and administrative burdens, election procedures and battles for control may be disadvantages of true membership based organizations.

24 Minn. Stat. § 317A.401 subdiv.1(a) (2016).
25 Minn. Stat. §§ 317A.401-467 (2016).

D. Differences between 501(c)(3) Charitable Nonprofit Organizations and Other Types of Organizations

Q15. ***What is the difference between a public charity and a private foundation if they both have 501(c)(3) tax-exempt status from the IRS?***

A15. 501(c)(3) organizations typically hold public charity status by demonstrating that their conduct or operations have one of four different characteristics:

- **Function** – Some organizations are public charities by virtue of the activities they conduct; this is the basis by which churches, educational institutions, hospitals or medical research organizations operated in conjunction with a hospital, endowment funds operated for certain educational institutions and governmental units are classified as they are specifically excluded from being private foundations.[26]
- **Public support** – Some organizations are public charities because they receive substantial financial support in the form of gifts, grants or contributions from the public or the government.[27] Examples of publicly supported organizations in this category may include museums, libraries, community centers to promote the arts and organizations such as community foundations and the United Way.[28]
- **Public support** – An additional way some groups can qualify as public charities if they receive substantial financial support comprised not only of gifts, grants or contributions from the public or the government, but also including exempt function income (i.e., fees for service) from diverse payers.[29] Examples of publicly supported organizations in this category may include theatres, instructional organizations and hockey arenas.
- **Supporting** – Some organizations are public charities because they are organized to support the activities of another organization that is a public charity by virtue of its function or receipt of public support. So-called "supporting organizations"[30] must be organized and operated exclusively to perform the functions or carry out the purpose of the public charity that it supports.[31]

Generally, a private foundation has two or more of the following three characteristics:

- It was initially funded by a single, private source (such as a family or business).
- Its income comes mostly from investments of its own or another's endowment funds.
- It makes grants to other charitable organizations rather than running its own programs.

Private foundations are highly regulated and have more restrictions on activities, expenditures, payouts, excise tax liability on investment income. Private foundations generally have a single or smaller source of funding. In general, public charities have greater latitude in expenditures, including lobbying activity, and are not subject to excise tax. For more information on the difference between private foundations and public charity, see Chapter 3: Tax Exemptions, Section C: Keeping a Federal Income Tax Exemption.

26 *See* I.R.C. § 509(a)(1) (2006). See also I.R.C. § 170(b)(1)(A) (2015).
27 *See* I.R.C. § 509(a)(2)(2006).
28 *See* I.R.C. § 509(a)(1) (2006). See also I.R.C. § 170(b)(1)(A)(vi) (2015).
29 *See* I.R.C. § 509(a)(2) (2006).
30 *See* I.R.C. § 509(a)(3) (2006).
31 Many changes were made with respect to 509(a)(3) supporting organizations by Congress in 2006. Organizations believing they need to fit under this classification should seek legal counsel experienced with exempt organizations to learn the possible limits and concerns such classification conveys.

Q16. ***What is the difference between a 501(c)(3) tax-exempt nonprofit organization (that is, a "charitable" nonprofit organization) and a 501(c)(4) tax-exempt nonprofit organization?***

A16. The difference between 501(c)(3) and (c)(4) organizations relate to their organizational purpose, abilities as limited by law, and tax implications. 501(c)(4) tax exempt organizations are "civic leagues or organizations not organized for profit but operated exclusively for the promotion of social welfare, or local associations of employees."[32] Alternatively, (c)(3) organizations are dedicated to "religious, charitable, scientific, testing for public safety, literary, or educational purpose… or for the prevention of cruelty to children or animals."[33] "Social welfare" is broadly defined as "promoting the common good and general welfare of the public in some way."[34] Both (c)(3) and (c)(4) organizations are prohibited from private or individual benefit from organizational earnings.

A key difference between charitable (c)(3) organizations and social welfare (c)(4) organizations is whether the intended beneficiaries would be considered eligible for charity. For example, a neighborhood organization that serves an impoverished community by sponsoring a food shelf may be a (c)(3), while an upper or middle class neighborhood security organization may be a (c)(4).

Another important difference between (c)(3) and (c)(4) organizations is that 501(c)(4) organizations have the ability to engage in partisan political campaigns without risking tax exempt status, as long as its partisan political activity is a secondary activity of the organization.[35] Lobbying efforts of (c)(4) organizations do not have to be limited. However, the principal disadvantage of (c)(4) status, in comparison to a (c)(3), is that contributions to the organization are not tax-deductible to the donor. See Chapter 7: Lobbying, Election-related Activity and Voter Education and Chapter 3: Tax Exemptions for more information.

Q17. ***What's the difference between churches, religious organizations and faith-based organizations?***

A17. Along with other types of charitable organizations, section 501(c)(3) of the Internal Revenue Code grants income tax exemption to organizations organized and operated for "religious purposes." Additionally, "churches, church property, and houses of worship" are constitutionally exempt in Minnesota from property taxation, as long as the property is used for religious purposes.[36]

"Church" refers to a place of worship. That is not precisely spelled out in the tax code but generally refers to temples, mosques, and synagogues, as well as traditional churches.[37] The IRS uses these criteria when deciding if an organization can be called a church[38]:

- A distinct legal existence
- A recognized creed and form of worship
- A definite and distinct ecclesiastical government
- A formal code of doctrine and discipline
- A religious history

32 *See* I.R.C. § 501(c)(4) (2015).
33 *See* I.R.C. § 501(c)(3) (2015).
34 *See* Rev. Rul. 71-530, 1971-2 C.B. 237.
35 Alliance for Justice's Bolder Advocacy, *Influencing Legislation*, bolderadvocacy.org/navigate-the-rules/influencing-legislation (last visited June 19, 2017).
36 Minn. Const. art. X, § 1. See also Minn. Stat. § 272.02, subdiv. 6 (2016).
37 Joanne Fritz, *What's the Difference Between a Church and a Religious Organization?* The Balance (Aug. 13, 2016), www.thebalance.com/church-vs-religious-organization-2501877.
38 *See* I.R.S. Pub. 1828, *Tax Guide for Churches and Religious Organizations*, (Aug. 2015), www.irs.gov/pub/irs-pdf/p1828.pdf.

- Members that are not associated with any other church or denomination
- Ordained ministers who have completed specific studies
- A literature of its own
- Established places of worship
- Regular congregations
- Regular religious services
- Sunday schools for religious teaching of children
- Schools that educate its ministers

A church is automatically considered a 501(c)(3) charity if it meets most of these standards. However, churches that are automatically considered charities must also fulfill the requirements common to the 501(c)(3) status. Those conditions include no benefit to an insider such as a staff member or director, little to no lobbying, no political advocacy, and activities that are legal.[39] In other words, churches, to be considered 501(c)(3) charities, must act like other charities. If they do so, they may qualify for tax-exemption.[40] Unlike other charities, churches do not have to register with the IRS by submitting Form 1023.

However, many do file to make their status perfectly clear to their donors and supporters. Churches that do officially register as charitable organizations are included on the IRS list of registered charities.[41] Churches that do not register with the IRS do not have to file yearly Form 990s. If the church has registered as a 501(c)(3), it does have to file a Form 990.[42]

Religious organizations exist to fulfill the needs of their members rather than the general public, but they are not referring to churches or integrated auxiliaries.[43] According to IRS Publication 1828, "religious organizations that are not churches typically include nondenominational ministries, interdenominational and ecumenical organizations, and other entities whose principal purpose is the study or advancement of religion." To be considered tax-exempt, a religious organization must register as a 501(c)(3) charity. That means filing Form 1023 (groups with income below $5000 annually are not required to file although they may wish to). Once registered, the organization must file an annual Form 990.[44]

Usually, faith-based organizations (that are not churches), need to apply for 501(c)(3) status to accept donations that are tax-exempt for their donors and to apply for foundation grants.[45] The term "faith-based" is not a legal term. It is used loosely to refer to a broad range of religiously involved groups that could be a church, a religious charity, or simply an unincorporated group based on religious values.[46] The best resource for more information about "churches, religious groups and faith-based organizations" is IRS Publication 1828, Tax Guide for Churches and Religious Organizations.

39 Joanne Fritz, *What's the Difference Between a Church and a Religious Organization?*, The Balance (Aug. 13, 2016), www.thebalance.com/church-vs-religious-organization-2501877.
40 *Id.*
41 I.R.S. Pub. 1828, *Tax Guide for Churches and Religious Organizations* (Aug. 2015), www.irs.gov/pub/irs-pdf/p1828.pdf.
42 *Id.*
43 *Id.*
44 *Id.*
45 *Id.*
46 Joanne Fritz, *What's the Difference between a Church and a Religious Organization?*, The Balance (Aug. 13, 2016), www.thebalance.com/church-vs-religious-organization-2501877.

Q18. ***How do nonprofits like social clubs and veterans' organizations fit within the universe of nonprofit organizations?***

A18. 501(c)(3) nonprofit organizations provide a public benefit. Nonprofit social clubs (501(c)(7)) and veterans' organizations (501(c)(19)) are considered "mutual benefit organizations" and exist to further the common goals of their members. Mutual benefit organizations may include labor unions, trade and professional associations, social clubs, fraternal lodges, veterans' organizations, cooperatives, and various other specialized entities.[47] Mutual benefit organizations enjoy exemption from federal corporate income tax, but most mutual benefit organizations are not eligible to receive tax-deductible contributions. Exceptions to this general rule include veterans' organizations and fraternal societies that use donated funds for charitable purposes may receive tax deductible donations.[48]

Social clubs may be exempt[49] under section 501(c)(7) of the Internal Revenue Code as "clubs organized for pleasure, recreation, and other nonprofitable purposes, substantially all of the activities of which are for such purposes and no part of the net earnings of which inures to the benefit of any private shareholder."[50] The IRS requires a "club" to have personal contacts, fellowship and a commingling of members as a material part in the life of the organization, where the members evidence an "identity of purpose."[51]

Internal Revenue Code section 501(c)(19) provides exemption from federal income tax for veterans organizations. A veterans' organization is specifically defined as "A post or organization of past or present members of the Armed Forces of the United States, or an auxiliary unit or society of, or a trust or foundation for, any such post or organization—(A) organized in the United States or any of its possessions, (B) at least 75 percent of the members of which are past or present members of the Armed Forces of the United States and substantially all of the other members of which are individuals who are cadets or are spouses, widows, widowers, ancestors, or lineal descendants of past or present members of the Armed Forces of the United States or of cadets, and (C) no part of the net earnings of which inures to the benefit of any private shareholder or individual."[52] Unlike other mutual benefit organizations, veterans' organizations are exempt from federal income tax, unrelated business tax and contributions to veterans' organization are tax-deductible.[53] Additionally, unlike 501(c)(3) organizations, veterans' organizations historically have been permitted to lobby without limitation to advance charitable purposes.[54]

A19. ***How does a nonprofit corporation differ from a for-profit corporation, like a large corporation or a business?***

A19. There are a few key ways that nonprofit corporations are different from for-profit corporations. Mainly, the distinction lies in the distribution of excess resources. Whereas a business has owners that divide any excess income, or profit, for personal financial benefit, nonprofits do not have a private owner that receives a share of the profit. Because nonprofit corporations are held for the public benefit, any excess

47 James J. Fishman, Stephen Schwarz & Lloyd Hitoshi Mayer, *Nonprofit Organizations, Cases and Materials,* 865-66 (5th ed. 2015).
48 *See* I.R.C. § 170(c)(3), (4) (2015).
49 Federal income tax exempt is limited to "exempt function income" that may include dues and charges for goods and services to members. Exemption does not extend to social club investment income or to net revenue from dealings with nonmembers. See I.R.C. § 512(a)(3) (2015).
50 *See* I.R.C. § 501(c)(7) (2015).
51 Rev. Rul. 69-635, 1969-2 C.B. 126. See also Rev. Rul. 74-30, 1974-1 C.B. 137.
52 *See* I.R.C. § 501(c)(19) (2015).
53 *See* I.R.C. § 512(a)(4) (2015). See also I.R.C. § 170(c)(3) (2015).
54 *Regan v. Taxation with Representation*, 461 U.S. 540 (1983).

income must either be held in reserves or be recycled back into the organization to support the charitable purpose. Additional basic differences include the following:

Differences	Nonprofit	Business
IRS Tax Form Filed	990, 990EZ, 990PF, 990-T	1120
Tax forms open to public inspection?	Yes	No
May pay market wages to employees?	Yes	Yes
Profits may be distributed?	No	Yes
Eligible for property tax exemption?	Yes	No
Must deduct income taxes for employees eligible	Yes	Yes
May elect to become direct reimburser on state UC systems	Yes	No
Required to pay FUTA	No	Yes

Q20. ***What are the advantages and disadvantages of being a nonprofit versus a business?***

A20. Owners and private shareholders of for-profit companies expect to materially benefit from the company's earnings and operate to maximize corporate earnings. Nonprofits fill the space between the public and private sector for the benefit of the public at large through charitable activities. The nonprofit organizations that comprise the "third," "independent," or nonprofit sector are generally committed to the public good, abide by a restraint on private financial benefit and reinvest property and resources into mission related charitable work. Nonprofits incur certain obligations and fiduciary duties related to methods of operation. For example, board members are strongly encouraged to volunteer, they hold a heightened responsibility to the good of the organization, and must disclose any conflict of interest while serving. Additionally, a nonprofit can benefit from state and federal income tax, sales tax and property tax exemptions. Individuals and entities which donate to a legally IRS recognized 501(c)(3) public charity can deduct some or all of the donation from their own income tax obligations. As nonpartisan entities generally supported by the public, nonprofits also have a unique ability to advance public understanding and support for particular issues and causes that may not be addressed by the for-profit sector.

E. Related Resources

Publication:

How Did We Get Here: The Regulatory Framework, Jon Pratt, *The Nonprofit Quarterly* (2005), www.un-ngls.org/orf/cso/cso9/Regulatory-Issue.pdf.

Websites:

I.R.S., *Tax Information for Charities & Other Non-Profits*, www.irs.gov/charities-non-profits (last updated June 05, 2017).

Minnesota Attorney General's Office, *Charities*, www.ag.state.mn.us/Charity/Default.asp (last visited July 05, 2017).

Minnesota Council of Nonprofits, *Nonprofit Resources Library*, www.minnesotanonprofits.org/nonprofit-resources (last visited July 05, 2017).

Minnesota Secretary of State Office, *Business & Liens*, www.sos.state.mn.us/index.aspx?page=3 (last visited July 05, 2017).

CHAPTER 2

THE NONPROFIT CORPORATION

Topics

A. Overview

The life of the nonprofit corporation often begins as a creative idea by a group of people agreeing on a social mission they believe would benefit their community. The potential of public service is strong enough to motivate some people to explore the legal steps involved to create a nonprofit organization to achieve this mission. At its highest level, the mission or purpose of a nonprofit corporation sets the nonprofit corporation apart from its for-profit counterpart. The purpose focuses the projects and tasks that the nonprofit corporation will undertake through the activities of its volunteers or its employees. The purpose attracts individuals, corporations and foundations to provide financial support. Finally, the purpose allows the state and federal governments to grant the nonprofit tax-exempt status, therefore minimizing the amount of money that is not used for the nonprofit's programs, services and administration.

The desire to accomplish good works through the mission of the nonprofit corporation must be carried out within the legal and procedural requirements of various state and federal agencies. Before substantial charitable fundraising activities can get underway, the nonprofit corporation must be formed and tax-exempt status should be sought. Both procedures include drafting and filing legal documents that include to purpose and programmed activities of the nonprofit.

The incorporation process begins with the filing of Articles of Incorporation with the Minnesota Secretary of State, which creates the legally recognized nonprofit corporation. The Articles of Incorporation are drafted and filed by individuals who are interested in forming the nonprofit corporation and maybe in serving as board members. Bylaws addressing governance issues are drafted and adopted by the first board of the nonprofit corporation. The leaders of the nonprofit corporation should draft a business plan that acts as a strategic guide for the organization during its first years of life. Key questions answered in a business plan include: How will the nonprofit corporation get its funding? Is the funding from individual donors, program service fees or foundations? How will the nonprofit corporation achieve its mission? What specific activities will it undertake and how much will those activities cost? Who will do the work of the nonprofit corporation – the board, volunteers or paid staff? How does the nonprofit corporation sustain itself over the first five years of existence and into the future?

With a business plan completed, the nonprofit corporation can apply for federal tax-exempt status from the Internal Revenue Service. The application requires extensive documentation of programs, services and anticipated financial activity. It is a challenging application with significant rewards: exemption from federal income tax for mission-related income and tax deductibility for donations made to the nonprofit corporation.

This chapter deals with the basic considerations of creating the nonprofit corporation, such as obtaining a name for an organization and drafting Articles of Incorporation and Bylaws. In addition, if a nonprofit corporation must end its existence for any reason, this chapter describes the dissolution process.

B. Reserving a Name for a Nonprofit Corporation

Q1. How do I check on the availability of a name for my potential organization?

A1. Checking on the availability of a name for your organization is crucial because the Minnesota Secretary of State will not allow an organization to incorporate if it has a name that is the same as or indistinguishable from other previously incorporated or registered entities.

To check on the availability of a name for a nonprofit corporation, check the Minnesota Secretary of

State's searchable database available on their website at www.sos.state.mn.us. Checking name availability is preliminary and the Minnesota Secretary of State will not guarantee the name will be available when the Articles of Incorporation are filed. To ensure that the name will be available, reserve the name with the Minnesota Secretary of State. For this process, see Question 3.

Q2. What if I want to use a name that is already being used or reserved by someone else?

A2. There are several options available to an organization that wants to use a name that is already being used or is reserved by another organization. The organization can: (1) file a consent to use the name with the Minnesota Secretary of State; (2) file a court order; or (3) file a statement of dormant business.

In order to file a consent to use the name with the Minnesota Secretary of State, written consent is required from the entity that holds the name. The Minnesota Secretary of State provides a form called "Consent to the Use of Name" to help with this process. This form is available on their website at www.sos.state.mn.us/media/1381/consent.pdf. The fee for filing the consent to use a name is $55 for expedited service in-person, $35 for mail.

To file a court order for use of a name, the applicant must obtain a court order that establishes a right to the use of the name.[1] The court's final decree should establish the prior right of the applicant to use its corporate name in Minnesota. A certified copy of the final decree must be attached to the Articles of Incorporation when the applicant files for the name.[2]

Before filing a statement of dormant business, the applicant must: (1) determine that the entity or person who holds the name has not filed any document under the name with the Minnesota Secretary of State in the past three years; (2) send a notice via certified mail to the entity or person at the last address registered with the Minnesota Secretary of State and confirm that the notice was returned by the U.S. Postal Service as "undeliverable"; (3) prove there is no telephone listing for the entity or person who holds the name in the county of its registered office; and (4) verify you have no knowledge that the entity is currently engaged in business in Minnesota.

The Minnesota Secretary of State provides a form called "Abandoned Name Affidavit" to help with this process. This form is available on their website at www.sos.state.mn.us/media/1371/abandonedname-affidavit.pdf. The fee for filing a statement of dormant business is $55 for expedited service in-person, $35 if submitted by mail.

Q3. How do I reserve a name for the organization I want to incorporate?

A3. It is a good idea to make sure the desired name for a nonprofit corporation will be available for use when the incorporator is ready to file Articles of Incorporation. To do this, reserve a name with the Minnesota Secretary of State by filing the form called "Request for Reservation of Name". This form is available on the website www.sos.state.mn.us/media/1395/namereservation.pdf. The fee for filing a name reservation request is $55 for expedited service in-person and online filings, $35 if by mail. The reservation is valid for 12 months from the date of filing, and can be renewed for an unlimited number of additional 12-month periods. To renew a name reservation, submit the "Request for Reservation of Name" form and pay a $35 fee. If you are ready to file your Articles of Incorporation, you do not need to reserve the name separately.

1 Minn. Stat. § 317A.115, subdiv. 2(a)(2) (2016).
2 *Id.*

Q4. What is an "assumed name" and when do I need to register one?

A4. If an entity conducts or transacts business under a name different than the name under which it is incorporated (also known as its legal name), it is using an assumed name. For example, if the nonprofit corporation "Association of Pet Owners" began selling a product or a service under the name "Petlovers," it would need to register "Petlovers" as an assumed name.

State Consumer Protection law requires the registration of all assumed names. The registration of an assumed name helps consumers identify the true identity of a business owner. There is a multi-step process for registering an assumed name. First, check to make sure the assumed name is available, as registration for an assumed name will not be accepted if it is indistinguishable from other previously incorporated or registered entities.

Next, complete and submit a form called "Certificate of Assumed Name Registration" to the Minnesota Secretary of State. This form is available on their website at www.sos.state.mn.us/media/1373/assumed-nameregistration.pdf. The fee for filing this form is $50 for expedited service in-person and online filings, $30 if submitted by mail.

The Office of the Minnesota Secretary of State will process the form and send a notification indicating whether or not the assumed name was accepted. If the assumed name is accepted, a Certificate of Assumed Name must be published in the legal notices section of a qualified legal newspaper for two consecutive issues (a list of qualified legal newspapers is available from the Office of the Minnesota Secretary of State). If the notice is not published, filing of the assumed name becomes invalid.

Once filed, a certificate of assumed name is valid for ten years from the date of filing.

Q5. Once our organization has filed forms with the Minnesota Secretary of State, does our name exclusively belong to our organization?

A5. Once the organization's name has been registered with the Minnesota Secretary of State, the organization has exclusive rights to use that name within the state of Minnesota. Under the name registration procedure, there is no protection against another organization in a different state using the same name, unless they want to do business in Minnesota as a foreign corporation. More substantial protection of the name is available under federal trademark law. A trademark is any word, symbol, or device used to identify a source or origin of a good or service. In order to qualify for federal trademark protection, the organization would have to be the first to use the name as a mark in interstate commerce. Minnesota State trademark legislation offers similar protection in the form of injunctive relief and money judgment for trademark infringement beyond that provided by name registration.[3]

3 Minn. Stat. § 333.29 (2016).

C. The Nonprofit Incorporation Process in Minnesota

Q6. Do I have to incorporate an organization?

A6. No. There are other options available if you choose not to form a nonprofit corporation. These options include:

- Creating a charitable trust (See Chapter 4: Charitable Solicitation Registration, Section D: Registering a Charitable Trust);
- Forming an unincorporated association (See Question 7);
- Finding an incorporated nonprofit that is willing to serve as a fiscal sponsor for the organization (See Chapter 8: Financial Accountability, Section E: Fiscal Agency or Sponsorship);
- Working with an existing organization to develop a new program or project.

There are several types of acceptable legal forms that may be eligible for tax-exempt status. If the organization does not desire to be a nonprofit corporation, it can be a charitable trust, an unincorporated association or (in very limited circumstances) a limited liability company. An individual or partnership cannot operate an exempt organization. See Question 7 for the differences between unincorporated associations and nonprofit corporations.

Q7. What are the differences between an unincorporated association and an incorporated nonprofit corporation?

A7. An unincorporated association is two or more people joined together to achieve a common purpose. Unincorporated associations are typically small in size. Unincorporated associations are often formed for the following reasons: the entity is newly formed and is still in the incorporation process, the future prospects of the organization are uncertain or the organization is expected to operate either for a short period of time or on an informal basis.

The differences between these two types of entities can be found in the advantages and disadvantages inherent in their legal structures.

Advantages of being an unincorporated association instead of a nonprofit corporation:

- They are informal and flexible structures, as no governmental approvals are needed to form or dissolve an unincorporated association.
- They can still apply for and receive tax-exempt status, but the IRS does require an unincorporated association to have a charter. The IRS does look more closely at the exemption applications from unincorporated associations.

Disadvantages of being an unincorporated association instead of a nonprofit corporation:

- Because an unincorporated association has no separate legal existence, the people who join an unincorporated association can be found personally liable for debts, injuries, contract disputes of the unincorporated association. In the case of a lawsuit, all of the people who join an unincorporated association would be defendants to an alleged liability.

- There are not many statutes or rules that legally guide unincorporated associations.[4]
- It is very difficult for an unincorporated association to hold and receive property and donations. An individual member of the group would have to hold the property in their name and open a bank account.
- Unincorporated associations cannot form a legal contract with another entity.
- Because vendors and creditors are more familiar with doing business with nonprofit corporations, they may be reluctant to deal with unincorporated associations.

Advantages of being a nonprofit corporation instead of an unincorporated association:

- The liability arising from the actions of the organization falls onto the nonprofit corporation and not on the individuals involved in the organization.
- A nonprofit corporation can enter into binding contracts.
- A nonprofit corporation can hold and own property in its own name.

Disadvantages of being a nonprofit corporation instead of an unincorporated association:

- Because it is a legal entity, it has specific legal requirements, including disclosures and filing documents and fees when forming or dissolving.

Q8: What is a public benefit corporation? How is it different from a nonprofit corporation?

A8: A public benefit corporation is a for-profit corporation formed under Minnesota law that has elected to pursue a social mission as well as a business mission. Public benefit corporations intentionally blend the pursuit of profit with a social motivation. Public benefit corporations operate like any other for-profit business with shareholders, investors, business operations, and a revenue generating goal. In addition to revenue generation, a public benefit corporation takes into account its declared social mission that must be at least co-equal with its profit generating activities.

A public benefit corporation cannot receive charitable donations like a tax-exempt nonprofit corporation and it is not subject to Minnesota Attorney General's and IRS's oversight. A public benefit corporation is a good option for an operating business. However, a public benefit corporation is not a good option for a donative organization that looks to contributors for money.

Q9. What does it cost to establish a nonprofit corporation?

A9. There are a number of fees associated with forming a nonprofit corporation. The following chart lists the purpose of the fee, the amount of the fee, whether or not the fee is mandatory and to whom the fee is submitted. Be aware that these fees change frequently, so readers should check updates of the IRS, Office of the Minnesota Secretary of State, and Office of the Minnesota Attorney General.

4 This may change because, as of May, 2017, the Minnesota State Bar Association is working on proposing a Uniform Unincorporated Associations Act.

Purpose of the fee	Amount	Mandatory?	Submit to
Request for Reservation of Name	$35 mailing; $55 for expedited service in-person and online filings	No	Office of the Minnesota Secretary of State, Business Services Division
Filing Articles of Incorporation for a Nonprofit Corporation	$70 mailing; $90 for expedited service in-person and online filings	Yes	Office of the Minnesota Secretary of State, Business Services Division
Application for Exempt Status (Form 1023 or Form 1023-EZ)	(1) If the organization's average annual gross receipts have exceeded or will exceed $10,000 annually over a four-year period, the fee is $850; (2) If gross receipts have not exceeded or will not exceed $10,000 annually over a four-year period, the user fee is $400; (3) If the organization is eligible to submit Form 1023-EZ, the user fee is $275.1	Yes (if you want to be a tax-exempt organization)	Internal Revenue Service
Charitable Organization B Registration Statement	$25	Yes if any of the following are true: (1) the organization's functions and activities are not performed wholly by volunteers; (2) the organization employs a professional fundraiser; (3) the organization intends to raise more than $25,000 in charitable contributions annually.	Office of the Minnesota Attorney General, Charities Unit
Annual Secretary of State Renewal	$0	Yes	Office of the Minnesota Secretary of State
Annual Form 990 Informational Tax Filing	$0	Yes, but the specific Form 990 differs based on gross receipts	Internal Revenue Service

A *See* I.R.S., *Form 1023. Amount of User Fee*, www.irs.gov/charities-non-profits/form-1023-amount-of-user-fee (last updated Mar. 21, 2017).

B A "charitable organization" is a person who engages in or purports to engage in solicitation for a charitable purpose. See Minn. Stat. § 309.50, subdiv. 4. "Solicit" and "solicitation" have the meanings set forth in Minn. Stat. § 309.50, subdiv. 10 and include oral or written requests. An organization must register before it solicits contributions. Solicitation prior to registration may result in the imposition of civil penalties up to $25,000 for each violation of Minn. Stat. § 309.

Q10. Why would I want to incorporate my organization?

A10. The traditional reason that people incorporate any sort of business is to have an entity to hold property and to minimize personal liability. Corporations have legal standing to engage in business transactions, such as contracts, financial transactions and loans. This means that the risk of such transactions is shifted away from the incorporators, directors or employees of a corporation onto the corporation itself. In cases of extreme wrongdoing, individuals responsible for the corporation could still be held financially or even criminally liable for the actions of the corporation, but for the most part the corporation acts to shield individuals.

In the case of nonprofit corporations, however, the benefits are far more substantial. Federal and state tax-exempt status is generally predicated on the organization being incorporated as a nonprofit entity except in certain limited situations. Donations that are tax deductible for the donor can only be solicited by organizations that have been granted 501(c)(3) charitable status by the Internal Revenue Service. The process of obtaining charitable status is less cumbersome for a nonprofit corporation. Incorporation is the first step toward taking advantage of the benefits that come with being a tax-exempt nonprofit corporation.

Q11. What is the process to incorporate under the Minnesota Nonprofit Corporation Act?

A11. To incorporate under the Minnesota Nonprofit Corporation Act,[5] you must:

- Choose an incorporator or incorporators. In Minnesota, one or more persons can incorporate a nonprofit corporation.[6]
- Choose a name. A nonprofit corporation's name must be distinguishable from other entities. Check with the Minnesota Secretary of State to see if the name is already being used. (See Question 1 and Question 3.)
- Draft Articles of Incorporation. (To learn about the necessary elements of these Articles of Incorporation, see Question 27.)
- File Articles of Incorporation with the Minnesota Secretary of State. An incorporator must sign the Articles of Incorporation.
- Pay a filing fee to the Minnesota Secretary of State. The filing fee is $70 for mailing, $90 for expedited in-person or online filings.
- Choose a board of directors (minimum of three people). The Articles of Incorporation may list the members of the first board of directors, but this is not required. The incorporator(s) appoint the first board if the directors are not named in the Articles of Incorporation.
- Hold an organizational meeting. At this meeting the incorporator can formally elect the board of directors and then the directors can approve the Bylaws.

Q12. Who can be an incorporator and what does the incorporator do?

A12. Any natural person (i.e., not a corporation, limited liability company or partnership) over the age of 18 can be an incorporator of a nonprofit corporation. By signing the Articles of Incorporation, the incorporator requests that the state recognize the organization as a separate legal entity.[7]

5 Minn. Stat. § 317A.051 (2016). The Minnesota Nonprofit Corporation Act (Minnesota Statutes Chapter 317A) does not apply to a religious corporation authorized by Minnesota Statutes Chapter 315 unless it is formed under Chapter 317A or elects to be governed by Chapter 317A as provided in Minnesota Statutes Section 317A.021 (2016).

6 Minn. Stat. § 317A.105 (2016).

7 Minn. Stat. § 317A.105 (2016).

Q13. What are the minimum legal requirements my organization must meet to incorporate as a nonprofit corporation under Minnesota law?

A13. To be a nonprofit corporation in Minnesota an organization needs to follow a nondistribution constraint. The nondistribution constraint means nonprofit corporations cannot distribute any financial gain, or profit, to any person or for-profit entity. While nonprofit corporations can pay a reasonable salary to staff members and to contractors in return for the services they provide, a nonprofit corporation cannot pay dividends or distribute its profits to its members, directors or other individuals. This nondistribution constraint is the main characteristic that distinguishes nonprofit corporations from other for-profit entities established in the State of Minnesota. In addition, to be a nonprofit corporation in Minnesota, an organization's purpose must be legal as stated in its Articles of Incorporation.

Q14. How do I incorporate without using an attorney?

A14. It is possible to incorporate a nonprofit organization without consulting an attorney. Many of the mandatory statements and clauses in the Articles of Incorporation have been standardized into readily available boilerplate, or sample, documents. For a copy of sample Articles of Incorporation, see the *Handbook for Starting a Successful Nonprofit* from the Minnesota Council of Nonprofits.

Yet, for many organizations, careful drafting of these documents is crucial, particularly if the organization has a complex structure or proposes to undertake activities that will cause closer scrutiny by the IRS when the organization applies for tax-exempt status. Examples of such activities include those considered political or typically commercial in nature. Therefore, the organization should carefully examine the scope and purpose of its proposed activities before deciding whether or not to consult an attorney to help with the incorporation process.

Even if an organization decides to consult an attorney, there are several ways to tap into low-cost help. Prepare your Articles of Incorporation, Bylaws, and application for tax exemption and then pay an attorney only to review the final draft of these documents and propose necessary changes. Or you could seek pro bono (meaning "provided without charge") help from a local attorney. Many local law firms are committed to providing a certain amount of pro bono legal services to those who cannot otherwise afford to pay. Another option is to seek help from a nonprofit capacity building organization. For example, the Minnesota Council of Nonprofits has a publication called *Handbook for Starting a Successful Nonprofit.* See Section I: Related Resources for more information.

Q15. Should I incorporate without using an attorney?

A15. The creation process for each new nonprofit corporation is going to be a unique experience. The level of complexity of any particular incorporation is going to depend on factors such as the individuals involved, board composition, the purpose or mission of the organization, aspects of fundraising (such as major donors), the new nonprofit corporation's legal relationship to other existing corporations and so forth. On the one hand, an experienced attorney provides insight into the incorporation process and foresight into possible problems. An attorney can draft language that ensures that the Articles of Incorporation match the goals and mission anticipated by ongoing operations. Certainly, the Articles of Incorporation can be amended, but competent legal representation may prevent that need from arising. On the other hand, there are additional costs and time delays while legal counsel is found. Nothing prevents individuals from incorporating without using an attorney, and for smaller, simpler nonprofit organizations this is a reasonable low-cost option. Ultimately, the decision depends on the complexities of the situation. In addition, it is important to note that not all lawyers have the requisite experience to be of assistance to a start-up nonprofit enterprise. If the incorporators determine legal assistance is required, it is important for those incorporators to engage experienced legal counsel.

Q16. How long does it take to receive a Certificate of Incorporation from the State of Minnesota?

A16. Articles of Incorporation and the filing fee can be submitted to the Minnesota Secretary of State online, in person or by mail. Online filings are processed immediately, assuming that the corporate name is available, the required fields have been properly completed, and the payment is validly made.

Articles of Incorporation filing fee for a nonprofit corporation is $70 for mail, $90 for in-person and online.[8] The address for in-person and mail filing is Minnesota Secretary of State Business Services, 60 Empire Drive, Suite 100, St. Paul, MN 55103. The documents will then be reviewed and the Certificate of Incorporation and filed documents will be returned to you while you wait. If accepted, the effective date of incorporation will be that very same day.

Articles of Incorporation dropped off at the counter or mailed to the Minnesota Secretary of State will be reviewed within two or three days of receiving these materials. The organization's Certificate of Incorporation will be mailed to these customers about 7 to 10 days after the Articles of Incorporation have been reviewed and accepted by the Minnesota Secretary of State.

An organization's incorporation becomes effective on the day its documents are reviewed and accepted, whether by a staff person or by the computer system. The organization filing online will receive a link to download the Certificate of Incorporation along with a copy as filed of the Articles of Incorporation and a receipt for the filing fee within a day after the filing has been accepted.

Q17. What is the difference between organizations that are Chapter 315 corporations and those that are Chapter 317A corporations?

A17. A nonprofit corporations organized under Chapter 317A may have a religious or faith-based aspect to its mission. In fact, the faith component of a nonprofit can be quite significant. However, Chapter 315 corporations are religious associations that are formed by members of an unincorporated church, congregation or religious society.

Q18. What is a historical incorporation?

A18. Since January 1, 1991, the incorporation of nonprofit organizations in Minnesota has been governed by the current Minnesota Statutes Chapter 317A. Prior to that time there were other statutes—Chapters 317 and 300 --that governed nonprofit incorporations. For organizations governed by Chapter 317, the current law was amended to automatically apply to them. Organizations incorporated under Chapter 300 (prior to the year of 1951), could elect to be governed by Chapter 317 and subsequently 317A. However, it is possible that some organizations incorporated under Chapter 300 are still governed by Chapter 300.

8 The latest fee information can be found on www.sos.state.mn.us/media/2851/businessentityfees.pdf.

Q19. Our organization has a charter; does that mean it is already incorporated?

A19. Maybe. The term "charter" has several meanings, two of which could apply to incorporation, depending on circumstance. First, "charter" can refer to the corporate charter, meaning either Articles of Incorporation that are filed with the Minnesota Secretary of State or the Certificate of Incorporation that the Minnesota Secretary of State issues to indicate that an organization has been incorporated as a legal entity. A charter, however, may merely mean that an unincorporated association has a formal charter that governs its activities. To be certain, check with the Minnesota Secretary of State.

The second applicable meaning refers to an act of a legislative body that creates a corporation. In a sense, the legislature acts as the incorporator of the organization. The American Red Cross is an example of such an organization created by federal charter. In the case of either of these meanings of the word "charter," the organization has already been incorporated.

Q20. If my organization is already incorporated in another state, can its incorporation be transferred to Minnesota?

A20. Organizations incorporated in a different state wishing to do business in Minnesota are called foreign corporations. The technical procedure for obtaining permission to conduct business in Minnesota does not involve a transfer by itself. Rather, the foreign nonprofit corporation must file a form seeking a certificate from the Minnesota Secretary of State for authority to transact business in Minnesota. The foreign nonprofit corporation must provide details regarding its original incorporation and where it proposes to be located in Minnesota. Also, the name of the foreign nonprofit corporation cannot conflict with the obligations for naming an organization in Minnesota (i.e., not already in use, distinct, etc.). A form for registering a foreign nonprofit corporation in Minnesota is available at www.sos.state.mn.us/media/1559/foreigncorpregistration.pdf.

Q21. During the incorporation process, does it matter whether a membership-based or a non-membership-based organization is being formed?

A21. Yes. The universe of tax-exempt entities can be broadly divided into two categories: public benefit and mutual benefit charities. The typical public benefit nonprofit organization (as opposed to a for-profit benefit corporation) is focused on improvement of social welfare through charitable, religious, educational or other purposes, as well as public burying grounds. This category includes the charities and private foundations granted tax-exempt status under I.R.C. § 501(c)(3) as well as those social welfare organizations granted tax-exempt status under I.R.C. § 501(c)(4). Examples include most art, educational, environmental, human service and health-related charities. These organizations do not generally have members unless the structure dictates membership (charter schools are statutorily required to have members).

Mutual benefit organizations, on the other hand, are not organized to benefit society at large; instead they are organized for the mutual benefit of the members of the organization. These members may be individuals, or a labor union, or corporations, or a chamber of commerce. While the organizations serve a beneficial purpose and are therefore tax-exempt under the Internal Revenue Codes, donations or dues paid to mutual benefit organizations are not tax deductible as charitable contributions. This includes organizations under:

- I.R.C. § 501(c)(6)—Business leagues, boards of trade and chambers of commerce ;

- I.R.C. § 501(c)(7)—Social and recreational clubs;
- I.R.C. § 501(c)(8)—Fraternal beneficiary societies and associations;
- I.R.C. § 501(c)(9)—Voluntary employees' beneficiary association; and
- I.R.C. § 501(c)(10)—Domestic fraternal societies and associations.

Q22. During the incorporation process, does it matter what the organization's stated purposes are?

A22. If the organization's goal is to be considered a charitable organization eligible to receive deductible contributions, then its stated charitable purpose does matter. From the very beginning, the purpose of the organization as written in the Articles of Incorporation must reflect a charitable, educational or religious purpose. The language recommended for inclusion in the Articles of Incorporation is:

> "This corporation is organized exclusively for charitable, religious, educational and scientific purposes as specified in Section 501(c)(3) of the Internal Revenue Code, including for such purposes, the making of distributions to organizations that qualify as exempt organizations under Section 501(c)(3) of the Internal Revenue Code, or the corresponding section of any future federal tax code."

Since the organization's Articles of Incorporation will be included with its application for tax-exempt status with the IRS, inclusion of this language may prevent problems during the application process. The Articles of Incorporation should also include specific language briefly describing the purpose, activities or mission of the organization.

Q23. Once I file my organization's Articles of Incorporation with the Minnesota Secretary of State, is the organization automatically tax-exempt?

A23. No. A nonprofit corporation is not automatically tax-exempt. After incorporation, the nonprofit corporation must apply to the Internal Revenue Service to become tax-exempt. To do so, complete and file IRS Form 1023 (Application for Recognition of Exemption Under Section 501(c)(3) of the Internal Revenue Code) or IRS Form 1023-EZ. The IRS publishes a guide "Tax-Exempt Status for Your Organization", also known as I.R.S. Publication 557, to help with the tax-exempt application.[9] After the organization receives its federal exemption from corporate income tax, its exemption from state corporate income tax is automatic. See Chapter 3: Tax Exemptions for more information.

Q24. Can an organization be incorporated as a nonprofit corporation and not file for tax-exempt status?

A24. Yes. Becoming a tax-exempt nonprofit organization is a two-step process involving both the state and federal government. First, the organization must incorporate by filing Articles of Incorporation with the Minnesota Secretary of State. Then the organization must file for tax-exempt status with the federal government through the Internal Revenue Service. Without filing for and receiving approval of federal tax-exempt status, an organization is technically a "C corporation"[10] that must file an annual tax return and will be subject to corporate income tax liability for any income generated and is prohibited from

9 *See* I.R.S. Pub. 557 (Jan. 2017), www.irs.gov/pub/irs-pdf/p557.pdf.

10 "A C corporation, under United States federal income tax law, refers to any corporation that is taxed separately from its owners. A C corporation is distinguished from an S corporation, which generally is not taxed separately. Most major companies (and many smaller companies) are treated as C corporations for U.S. federal income tax purposes." Wikipedia, C corporation, en.wikipedia.org/wiki/C_corporation (last visited June 21, 2017).

soliciting and collecting tax-deductible donations. See Question 25 for more information.

Q25. ***What if we incorporate but never file for the tax exempt status? Do we file the regular corporate tax return?***

A25. Incorporating as a nonprofit is a state law concept that indicates that a corporation is formed for a purpose not involving the distribution of any pecuniary gain for any individuals and paying no dividends to its members. It may be formed for any lawful purpose, including the conduct of commercial activities. Nonprofit incorporation under the Minnesota Nonprofit Corporation Act may allow an organization to benefit from certain state sales tax exemptions[11]. State level incorporation does not exempt an organization from federal or state corporate income tax. The nonprofit corporation that has not been determined to be tax exempt must file federal and state corporate income tax returns, pay taxes if gross income exceeds deductions on the IRS Form 1120, and advise donors that contributions are not deductible (unless an organization has a 501(c)(3) fiscal sponsor. See Chapter 8: Financial Accountability, Section E: Fiscal Agency or Sponsorship for more information.

Q26. ***If an organization can incorporate as a nonprofit corporation and not apply for tax-exempt status, why and when would we want to apply for tax-exempt status?***

A26. If an organization does not file for tax-exempt status with the IRS, it will not be able to take advantage of several key aspects of being a tax-exempt organization. First, without federal tax exemption, a nonprofit corporation will have to pay both federal and state taxes on its income. Secondly, without receiving a determination of being tax-exempt as a 501(c)(3) charitable organization, the organization will not be able to offer income tax deductibility to the individuals and businesses that give charitable donations (unless the organization utilizes a 501(c)(3) fiscal sponsor). Finally, most private foundations will be reluctant to give the organization a grant because the IRS requires that they provide special oversight to non-501(c)(3) tax-exempt grantees.

Therefore, if an organization: (1) hopes to receive charitable donations from individuals, businesses, corporations and private foundations; and (2) expects a positive net income, or surplus, and wants to take advantage of the income tax exemption for nonprofit organizations, it should apply for tax-exempt status. To do so, use IRS Form 1023, the Application for Recognition of Exemption under Section 501(c)(3) of the Internal Revenue Code, or IRS Form 1023-EZ. This form must be filed within 27 months after the date of incorporation for contributions during that time to be considered deductible.

Q27. ***Is it necessary for non-charitable tax-exempt organizations (like social clubs and veterans' organizations) to incorporate? If so, what differences apply when incorporating these types of organizations versus charitable (i.e., 501(c)(3) tax-exempt) organizations?***

A27. The same benefits of incorporation (limiting liability, ability to enter into contracts, etc.) would accrue to social clubs and other non-charitable tax-exempt organizations if they incorporate. For incorporation of such an organization, there would be very little difference from the incorporation of a charitable organization. The purpose language in the Articles of Incorporation would not include the reference to "charitable, educational or religious" purposes, but would describe their own activity. If the organization sought tax-exempt status from the IRS under section 501(c)(4) or certain other 501(c) status, filers would use IRS Form 1024 (available at www.irs.gov/pub/irs-pdf/k1024.pdf).

11 Minn. Stat. § 297A.70, subdiv. 13, 14 (2016).

Q28. Once a nonprofit corporation is incorporated, who is responsible for calling its first official meeting?

A28. If the first board of directors is specified in the Articles of Incorporation, then a majority of the members of the board of directors is responsible for calling the first meeting within in a reasonable time of the issuance of the Certificate of Incorporation from the Minnesota Secretary of State. Otherwise, the responsibility is that of a majority of the incorporators or the incorporator if there is just one.

Q29. If the members of the board of directors are not named in the nonprofit corporation's Articles of Incorporation, who is responsible for electing them?

A29. In cases where the first board is not named in the Articles of Incorporation, either the incorporators can act as the board with all the rights and responsibilities, or they can elect the first board.[12]

Q30. Can an organization begin fundraising or receive charitable donations before it receives a Certificate of Incorporation?

A30. The organization is created when the Articles of Incorporation are filed with the Minnesota Secretary of State and the fee is paid. Once the organization is incorporated, it is a good policy to file the registration to solicit charitable contributions with the Minnesota Attorney General. After the charitable solicitation registration, the organization can legally solicit funding in Minnesota.

D. Articles of Incorporation

Q31. I am preparing Articles of Incorporation for a new nonprofit corporation. What should and should not be included in this document?

A31. Preparing an organization's Articles of Incorporation is an important process, as this is the document that establishes the organization as a legal entity. An organization is restricted to behaving within the limits of its Articles of Incorporation unless the Articles of Incorporation are formally amended (which involves filing amendments with the Minnesota Secretary of State and paying an amendment filing fee and, if holding exempt status from the IRS, notifying the IRS of changes). Therefore Articles of Incorporation should contain all of the elements needed to both become a nonprofit corporation and to receive tax-exempt status (if desired) while not including elements an organization may want to change in the future.

In Minnesota, the Articles of Incorporation for a nonprofit corporation must contain four elements:

- The name of the nonprofit corporation.
- The address of the nonprofit corporation's registered office.
    - While this does not have to be the same address as the nonprofit corporation's principal place of business, it cannot be a post office box. A registered agent is not required, but if the nonprofit corporation has a registered agent, its registered address must be the same as the address of the registered agent. A registered agent is a person or organization who is designated to receive official documents.

12 Minn. Stat. § 317A.201 (2016).

- The names and addresses of the incorporator(s).
- A statement that the corporation is organized under Minnesota Statute Chapter 317A (the Minnesota Nonprofit Corporation Act).

To receive 501(c)(3) tax-exempt status from the IRS, the following elements should also be included in the Articles of Incorporation:

- A statement that the organization is organized and operated exclusively for one or more of the following purposes: charitable, religious, educational, scientific, literary, testing for public safety, fostering national or international amateur sports competition or the prevention of cruelty to children or animals.
- A statement that the assets of the organization are permanently dedicated to an exempt purpose and that if the organization dissolves, its assets will be distributed only for an exempt purpose as outlined in Chapter 501(c)(3) of the Internal Revenue Code. (See Section G: Dissolving a Nonprofit Corporation and Disposing of its Assets for more information.)

In addition, the Articles of Incorporation must not empower an organization to engage in activities, other than as an insubstantial part of its overall activities, that do not further one or more of these purposes: charitable, religious, educational, scientific, literary, testing for public safety, fostering national or international amateur sports competition or the prevention of cruelty to children or animals.

For sample Articles of Incorporation, visit www.minnesotanonprofits.org and search for "Sample Articles of Incorporation."

Q32. What is the difference between Articles of Incorporation and Bylaws?

A32. An organization's Articles of Incorporation establish the organization as a legal entity. Once the Articles of Incorporation are filed with the Secretary of State, the organization receives a certificate and is recognized by the State of Minnesota as a nonprofit corporation. By filing Articles of Incorporation, the organization agrees to be governed by the laws in the Minnesota Nonprofit Corporation Act (Chapter 317A).

The Bylaws are the internal procedures and rules that govern an organization. They provide the additional rules (other than those found in the articles) by which an organization will act. They commonly address the rights of members (if applicable), the powers of the board of directors, the term length and limits for directors, the names and responsibilities of board committees and the minimum and maximum number of directors. Bylaws are not required but they are recommended.

In addition to being more detailed than Articles of Incorporation, Bylaws are also more flexible, as they are more easily amended. Article amendments need to be filed with the Secretary of State and submitted with the annual information return (Form 990). Bylaw amendments, along with other changes to governing documents, also need to be indicated on the Form 990, but do not need to be filed with the Secretary of State.[13]

Altogether, the organization's Articles of Incorporation and Bylaws, along with the Minnesota Nonprofit Incorporation Act, provide the rules and regulations by which the organization must obey.

---

13 *See* I.R.S., *Form 990 Return of Organization Exempt from Income Tax*, pt VI, question 4 (2016).

Q33. How are Articles of Incorporation amended?

A33. The method a nonprofit corporation uses to amend its Articles of Incorporation may be found in its own documents, specifically its Articles of Incorporation or Bylaws. So before a nonprofit corporation amends its Articles, it should check these two documents to see if either contains information about the procedure an organization uses to amend its Articles of Incorporation.

If the procedure for amending Articles of Incorporation cannot be found in the nonprofit corporation's Articles of Incorporation or Bylaws, the Minnesota Nonprofit Corporation Act, Chapter 317A, spells out the procedure that governs this action. The procedure varies according to whether or not a nonprofit corporation has "members with voting rights".[14] If a nonprofit corporation does not have members with voting rights, amendments to the Articles of Incorporation are made by the board and must be approved by a majority of the members of the board of directors. Before the vote, board members must be given a copy of the proposed amendment and notice of the meeting at which the amendment will be considered.

If a nonprofit corporation does have members with voting rights, the amendment must be approved by both a majority of the members with voting rights and a majority of the members of the board of directors. If the board proposed the amendment, the members must be invited to a meeting at which the amendment will be considered. If the members proposed the amendment, the members can request a special board meeting at which the amendment will be considered. In some organizations with members with voting rights, the members may give the board of directors authority to amend the Articles of Incorporation without seeking approval from the members.[15]

After an amendment to the Articles of Incorporation has been adopted, the nonprofit corporation needs to prepare an instrument called the "Articles of Amendment."[16] This document needs to contain three elements: the name of the nonprofit corporation, a statement of the adopted amendment, and a statement that the amendment was adopted under the Minnesota Nonprofit Corporation Act. For clarity, a notation at the end of the Articles of Incorporation should state "as amended as of [insert date]," since multiple versions of organizational documents sometimes get confused.

Finally, the Articles of Amendment must be filed with the Minnesota Secretary of State. (See Question 34 for this procedure.)

Q34. When should we send in amendments to our Articles of Incorporation to the Minnesota Secretary of State and what is the process for doing so?

A34. Amendments to a nonprofit corporation's Articles of Incorporation are not effective until they are filed with the Minnesota Secretary of State. Therefore a nonprofit corporation should file its Articles of Amendment as soon as possible after they are approved by the board or members (as applicable). If a nonprofit corporation wants the amendment to be effective on a date after the Articles of Amendment are filed, the Articles of Amendment must state its effective date. This effective date can be no more than 30 days after the Articles of Amendment are filed. The Minnesota Secretary of State provides a form called "Amendment to Articles of Incorporation" to help with this process. This form is available on their website at www.sos.state.mn.us/media/1387/dcnpamendment.pdf. The fee for filing amendments is $55 for expedited service in-person and online filings, $35 for mail.

---

14 "Members with voting rights' means members or a class of members that has voting rights with respect to the purpose or matter involved." Minn. Stat. § 317A.011 (2017).

15 Minn. Stat. § 317A.133 (2016) for more information about amending the articles of an organization with members with voting rights.

16 Minn. Stat. § 317A.139 (2016).

E. Bylaws

Q35. Are nonprofit corporations required to submit Bylaws or Bylaw amendments to the Secretary of State?

A35. No. A nonprofit corporation does not have to submit its Bylaws to the Secretary of State or any other state or federal government agency. In fact, Bylaws are not required.[17] However, there are several reasons to develop and adopt Bylaws. First, Bylaws provide the rules governing an organization's internal operations. Second, if a nonprofit corporation does not spell out certain provisions (like the definition of a quorum, the method for removing directors and filling board vacancies and whether or not the organization has members) in its Bylaws, it will be governed by the relevant provisions outlined in the Minnesota Nonprofit Incorporation Act.[18] Third, both funders and organizations with which the nonprofit corporation contracts may request to see Bylaws before approving a grant or contract. Additionally, Bylaws have legal authority, and if the courts are asked to settle a dispute over organizational purpose or control, they will look into the nonprofit corporation's Bylaws. See Chapter 3 Tax Exemptions for more information about IRS's requirements on Bylaws.

Q36. Our board of directors is preparing Bylaws for our new nonprofit corporation. What should and should not be included in the Bylaws?

A36. Bylaws are more detailed than Articles of Incorporation. A strong set of Bylaws includes all of the internal procedures and rules that will govern a nonprofit corporation. The following matters are often addressed in the Bylaws of a nonprofit corporation[19]:

- Procedures for selecting and electing members of the board of directors;
- Procedures for removing members from the board of directors;
- Term length and limits for directors;
- The officers and their responsibilities;
- Quorum requirements for conducting board meetings;
- Number of board meetings required in a fiscal year;
- The board committees and their responsibilities;

- Procedures for amending the Articles of Incorporation and Bylaws; and
- The nonprofit corporation's fiscal year.

If a nonprofit corporation has members, these additional topics should be addressed:

- The definition of a member;
- The voting rights of members;
- The date of the annual meeting of the membership; and
- Notice requirements for meetings of the membership.

There are numerous procedures and rules outlined in the Minnesota Nonprofit Corporation Act that will govern an organization unless an alternate procedure or rule is included in Articles of Incorporation or Bylaws.[20] When crafting Bylaws, be sure to review these state provisions. If a nonprofit corporation does

17 Minn. Stat. § 317A.181, subdiv. 1. (2016).
18 Minn. Stat. § 317A.111, subdiv. 3. (2016).
19 Minn. Stat. § 317A.181 (2016).
20 Minn. Stat. § 317A.111, subdiv. 3 (2016).

not wish to be governed by one or more of these provisions, include alternative provisions in the Bylaws. These provisions are listed in the Minnesota Nonprofit Corporation Act Section 317A.111, subdivision 3.

Q37. What are unique Bylaw provisions that apply to nonprofit corporations with members with voting rights?

A37. Without a specific provision to the contrary, state law presumes that nonprofit corporations *do not* have members. In order to operate a nonprofit corporation with members either with or without voting rights, the Articles of Incorporation or the Bylaws must specifically designate members. There are provisions regarding membership in the Minnesota Nonprofit Corporation Act that the nonprofit corporation can modify in its Articles of Incorporation or Bylaws:

- Whether all members are of one class. If voting and non-voting membership[21] categories are contemplated, these different rights should be specified;
- Whether membership transfers are permitted;
- What constitutes a quorum of members entitled to vote;
- Methods through which (voice, mailed ballot or electronic communication) members may vote; and
- Minimum number of days for notification of a meeting of the members.[22]

Q38. What is the procedure for amending the Bylaws of a nonprofit corporation?

A38. Generally, a nonprofit corporation's own Bylaws or Articles of Incorporation will outline the procedure a nonprofit corporation should use to amend its Bylaws. Before a nonprofit corporation amends its Bylaws, it should check these two documents to see if either contains the procedure that should be used.

If the procedure for amending Bylaws is not in the Articles of Incorporation or Bylaws, the Minnesota Nonprofit Corporation Act Section 317A.181 provides some directions about Bylaw amendment. If a nonprofit corporation does not have members with voting rights, the power to amend Bylaws belongs to the board of directors.[23] If the nonprofit corporation does have members with voting rights and the Articles of Incorporation do not restrict the right to amend the Bylaws to the members with voting rights, the board of directors has the power to amend the Bylaws, except with respect to Bylaws about defining quorums for member meetings, removing directors or filling board vacancies, decreasing the mandatory number of directors or setting board qualifications, classifications, or term limits.[24]

Be sure to keep copies of original Bylaws and all Bylaw amendments for reference and historical documentation, noting the last date amended.

21 Minn. Stat. § 317A.011, subdiv. 13 was revised on April 21, 2017. Prior to these revisions, Chapter 317A used the terms "members with voting rights" and "voting members" to describe the same set of person. The use of two separate terms to the same term created an opportunity for misinterpretation, so Revised 317A removes "voting members" from the definition of "members with voting rights" (as shown above) and substitutes "members with voting rights" throughout Chapter 317A where the phrase "voting members" was used.

22 Minn. Stat. § 317A.181 (2016).

23 Minn. Stat. § 317A.181, subdiv. 1(a) (2016).

24 Minn. Stat. § 317A.181, subdiv. 2 (2016).

Q39. What should our organization do with its original Articles of Incorporation and Bylaws?

A39. Copies of the Articles of Incorporation and the Bylaws will be needed for reference or official submissions throughout the life of the nonprofit corporation. As a result, copies of the signed and dated originals should be made shortly after they are adopted or filed. The originals should be kept in a safe place along with the Certificate of Incorporation from the Secretary of State and other key legal and financial documents. Amendments should also be copied and stored safely to preserve a historical record of the governing documents of the organization.

F. Keeping your Nonprofit Corporation in Good Standing

Q40. What annual registrations are required to maintain a nonprofit corporation's corporate status?

A40. To maintain entity status, a nonprofit corporation must submit a corporate renewal form each calendar year to the Minnesota Secretary of State.[25] The renewal can be filed online at mblsportal.sos.state.mn.us/Business/Search. The Secretary of State encourages online filing, which takes less than a minute.

Alternatively, a paper renewal can be filed. The form is available at: www.sos.state.mn.us/media/1534/nonprofitrenewal.pdf. The form must be signed and returned to the Secretary of State by December 31 of each year. This form must include the name of the nonprofit corporation, the address of its registered office, the name of its registered agent (if applicable) and the name and business address of the nonprofit corporation's president.

Failure to file can trigger loss of entity status and name protection. To learn more about the consequences of failing to return the organization's annual corporation renewal form, see Question 41 and Question 42.

Q41. I have just received a notice from the Secretary of State that says my nonprofit corporation has been involuntarily dissolved. What does this mean?

A41. Most likely, the nonprofit corporation was involuntarily dissolved because a responsible party failed to return or electronically file its annual corporate renewal form. See Question 40. This form must be filed online or completed, signed and returned by December 31 of each calendar year. If it is not, the nonprofit corporation is automatically involuntarily dissolved. The nonprofit corporation's name is protected for a one-year period after dissolution, in case the corporation reinstates, but after this time the nonprofit corporation's name is not protected and someone else could file to use this name.

Q42. If a nonprofit corporation has been involuntarily dissolved, can it get a retroactive reinstatement of its nonprofit corporation status? How?

A42. To retroactively reinstate corporate existence, a nonprofit corporation needs to submit a corporate registration form. The Secretary of State provides a form called "Minnesota Nonprofit Corporation Annual Business Renewal" to help with this reinstatement process. This form is available on their website

25 Minn. Stat. § 317A.823 (2016).

at www.sos.state.mn.us/media/1534/nonprofitrenewal.pdf. The filing of the renewal form reinstates the nonprofit corporation retroactively to the time of the administrative dissolution.[26]

G. Dissolving a Nonprofit Corporation and Disposing of its Assets

Q43. Why would a nonprofit corporation voluntarily dissolve?

A43. Dissolution is the formal term for the termination of the nonprofit corporation's legal existence as well as the process leading up to that termination. A nonprofit corporation dissolves for many of the same reasons that a for-profit corporation dissolves: money, market and purpose. A nonprofit corporation can experience financial insolvency if its debts exceed its revenue and assets. While some debts, such as a mortgage or short-term cash flow loans, can be a responsible part of financial management, excessive debt or cash out-flow shortages can force the board of directors to cease operations. Determining excessive debt is a case-by-case decision, based on the totality of operations, assets, pledges, revenue, fixed and variable expenses, etc. Directors of the nonprofit corporation should undertake the decision to cease operations for financial reasons with great care and objectivity.

Related to the issue of financial dissolution is the notion of dissolution due to changes in the marketplace. For nonprofit organizations, the marketplace can mean both the services they provide as well as their sources of donations. Nonprofits face as competitive an environment as for-profit organizations. New service providers may come on the scene whose presence in the market decreases demand for a nonprofit's services. A foundation that had been a key source of funds may shift their giving priorities to focus on another area of giving. Donors may give less or not at all. None of these factors is dispositive for deciding if the nonprofit should dissolve. In fact, innovative nonprofits may adapt to changes in the market and take the opportunity to develop new services.

Perhaps a more appealing reason for dissolving a nonprofit corporation is the successful completion of its mission. A group that comes together to work on a particular issue or to stage a particular event may find that their work has been completed to everyone's satisfaction. Some nonprofit corporations may include language in their Articles of Incorporation that triggers dissolution after the occurrence of a specific condition or the passage of a certain number of years.

Q44. Who can dissolve a nonprofit corporation?

A44. There are four methods for dissolving a nonprofit corporation.[27] First, if the first board of directors has not been elected, appointed, or named in the Articles of Incorporation, then the incorporator(s) may dissolve the nonprofit corporation.[28] This method can only occur very early in the life of the nonprofit corporation. As a result, this method can be used to remedy flaws in the initial structure of the nonprofit corporation.

The second and third methods of dissolution involve the board of directors, in conjunction with any members that have voting rights, voluntarily dissolving the nonprofit corporation.[29] The substantive difference

26 Minn. Stat. § 317A.827 subdiv. 2 (2016).
27 Minn. Stat. § 317A.701 (2016).
28 Minn. Stat. § 317A.711 (2016).
29 Minn. Stat. § 317A.721 (2016).

between the two methods involves court supervision. In the first case, the nonprofit corporation notifies regulatory agencies of its intent to dissolve and performs the dissolution. In the second case, a portion of the members with voting rights, the Minnesota Attorney General or a creditor with good cause can ask the court to conduct or supervise the dissolution. In this situation, the dissolution is still voluntary, but the court imposes additional scrutiny on the dissolution process. Finally, failure to file annual corporate registrations can trigger a form of involuntary dissolution that nonprofit corporations must take care to avoid. Failure to file the annual corporation registration with the Secretary of State's office for three consecutive years can result in involuntary dissolution. If a nonprofit corporation is involuntarily dissolved, a single filing of the "Annual Renewal of Reinstatement" corporation registration form can reinstate the nonprofit corporate entity.[30]

Q45. What is the procedure used to voluntarily dissolve a nonprofit corporation?

A45. While the method of voluntary dissolution has been simplified in recent years, the process continues to involve a number of steps that must be followed.

First, a majority of the board of directors must adopt a resolution to dissolve.[31] The resolution must include a plan for distributing the assets of the nonprofit corporation after dissolution.

Second, if the nonprofit corporation has members with voting rights, the next step is to notify these members of a membership meeting regarding the dissolution of the nonprofit corporation.[32] The meeting notice must comply with the requirements of time and manner of notification of member meetings in general. If the dissolution is approved by the membership, the dissolution must proceed.

Third, the nonprofit corporation must file its intention to dissolve with the Secretary of State's office.[33] Notification of intent to dissolve must include the name of the nonprofit corporation; if applicable, the date and place of the meeting of the board of directors and membership that approved the dissolution resolution; and a statement that the required approval was received.

Fourth, most nonprofit corporations will also have to notify the Minnesota Attorney General of their intentions to dissolve.[34] This is required of nonprofit corporations that hold assets for charitable purposes or are tax-exempt under Internal Revenue Code 501(c)(3). This notice is more involved and reflects the regulatory concerns of the Minnesota Attorney General's office. The notice must include:

- The purpose of the corporation;
- A list of assets held for charitable purposes;
- A description of restricted assets and the purpose for which each asset was received;
- A description of debts or other liabilities of the organization;
- A description of tangible assets that are going to be sold for cash and the manner of their sale;
- Anticipated expense of the transaction, including attorney's fees;

30 Office of the Minnesota Secretary of State, *Annual Renewal Form*, www.sos.state.mn.us/media/1386/dcrenewal.pdf (last visited June 21, 2017).

31 Minn. Stat. § 317A.721, subdiv. 2 (2016).

32 Minn. Stat. § 317A.721, subdiv. 3(a) (2016).

33 Minn. Stat. § 317A.723 (2016). See also Office of the Minnesota Secretary of State, *Minnesota Business Corporation Forms*, www.sos.state.mn.us/business-liens/business-forms-fees/minnesota-business-corporation-forms/ (last visited June 21, 2017).

34 Minn. Stat. § 317A.811 (2016). See also Office of Minnesota Attorney General, *Minnesota Non-Profit Corporation Forms*, www.sos.state.mn.us/business-liens/business-forms-fees/minnesota-non-profit-corporation-forms (last visited June 21, 2017).

- List of persons or corporations to whom assets are going to be transferred;
- The purposes of the persons or corporations receiving the assets; and
- Any conditions that will be imposed on the transferred assets.

An authorized signer for the nonprofit corporation must sign this notification.

The Attorney General's office has consolidated these information requirements into a single form that can be completed and filed with their office. The form is available at www.ag.state.mn.us/Charity/Forms/NoticeOfIntentToDissolve.pdf.

After filing notification with the Attorney General's office, the nonprofit corporation must wait 45 days before it may transfer or convey any assets. It is during this period that the Attorney General or other interested party may, with good cause, request court supervision of the dissolution process. If needed, the Attorney General may also request one extension of the waiting period for an additional 30 days.

Fifth, once the nonprofit corporation has filed the notice of intent to dissolve, it should cease functional activities and begin the process for winding up. This involves the collection of outstanding debts owed to the corporation, payment of obligations and liabilities owed by the organization, voluntary public notice to potential creditors and claimants, transfer and distribution of assets and finally, the filing of articles of dissolution.[35]

Sixth, depending on the extent of obligations to creditors and claimants, the nonprofit corporation will have to wait between 90 days and two years before it can file its Articles of Dissolution.[36] This allows time for anyone with a financial interest in the dissolution to come forward. After this period the organization files Articles of Dissolution with the Secretary of State's office stating:

- Whether or not public notice was given and that payments or plans for payments to creditors have been made.
- Remaining assets have been properly distributed.
- There are no pending legal actions against the corporation, or that plans have been made for satisfaction of any pending judgment.
- Indication of notification of the Attorney General and expiration of the waiting period.

Finally, in response to the Articles of Dissolution, the Secretary of State issues a Certificate of Dissolution indicating that the nonprofit corporation has been dissolved.[37]

Q46. What happens to assets when a nonprofit corporation dissolves?

A46. The law provides for priorities in the distribution of assets of the nonprofit corporation.[38] First and foremost, those assets that were received and held for a special use or purpose must be distributed with the expressed or implied intentions of the original donor. This means that assets held for a specific charitable purpose must not be diverted from that charitable purpose. Normally, this means that the assets will be distributed to a similar charitable organization for the continuation of their restricted purpose, if such an organization can be identified. These assets would include all restricted donations and grants.

35 Minn. Stat. §§ 317A.725, 727, 735, 733 (2016).
36 Minn. Stat. §§ 317A.730, 733 (2016).
37 Minn. Stat. § 317A.763 (2016).
38 Minn. Stat. § 317A.735 (2016).

After those assets are distributed, the priority order of the assets is as follows: (1) payment of costs or expenses associated with the dissolution; (2) payment of debts and other liabilities; and (3) distribution pursuant to specifications in the Articles of Incorporation or the Bylaws.

Finally, if there are any remaining assets, they must also be distributed for charitable purposes to a similar organization. This is known as the *cy pres* doctrine, providing that charitable assets and donations approximate the intentions of the donor as closely as possible. The main idea being that once a donation is made for charitable purposes, then that asset should remain restricted to the charitable purpose.

Q47. Who can receive the assets of a charitable nonprofit corporation when it dissolves?

A47. If an individual or for-profit business is a creditor of the nonprofit corporation, then some of the assets may be used to satisfy those debts. Assets restricted for charitable purposes may be transferred to either nonprofit or for-profit operations, but because the dissolution process requires notification to the Attorney General of planned distributions, there will be a heightened burden to show that transfers of assets to a for-profit business will remain for their original charitable purpose. In general, a similar 501(c)(3) organization will be the optimal solution. If property is sold it must be for market value – the value that an independent third party would pay for such property.

Q48. Is voluntary dissolution reversible or revocable?

A48. Yes. Up to the point that the Articles of Dissolution are filed, the board and members with voting rights, if any, may adopt a resolution revoking the dissolution.[39] Notification of the revocation of dissolution must be filed with the Minnesota Secretary of State and with the Minnesota Attorney General if the notice of intent was required. After the Articles of Dissolution are filed, the corporation no longer exists and dissolution is final.

Q49. What procedure must a charitable nonprofit corporation use to transfer its assets?

A49. Requirement of notification of the Attorney General is the same as under dissolution. If a nonprofit corporation plans to transfer all or substantially all of its assets, then it must notify the Minnesota Attorney General of the specific nature of those transfers. The same notification form is used (www.ag.state.mn.us/Charity/Forms/NoticeOfIntentToDissolve.pdf).

39 Minn. Stat. § 317A.731 (2016).

H. Related Resources

Publications:

A Guide to Starting a Business in Minnesota, Charles A. Schaffer et al., Minnesota Department of Employment and Economic Development (Jan. 2017), mn.gov/deed/assets/guide-starting-business-minnesota-35th-ed-2017_tcm1045-155254.pdf. (A physical copy may be ordered at apps.deed.state.mn.us/Publications/index.shtml.)

Guide for the Voluntary Dissolution of Minnesota Nonprofit Corporations (Nov. 2009), LegalCORPS, www.legalcorps.org/wp-content/uploads/2012/03/LegalCorps-Nonprofit-Dissolution-Guidelines.pdf.

Handbook for Starting a Successful Nonprofit (2012), Minnesota Council of Nonprofits, www.minnesotanonprofits.org.

More information from the Minnesota Department of Employment and Economic Development is available at mn.gov/deed/business/starting-business/.

Nonprofit Organizations (5th ed. 2015), James J. Fishman, Stephen Schwarz & Lloyd Hitoshi Mayer.

Tax-Exempt Status for Your Organization (Jan. 2017), I.R.S. Publication 557, www.irs.gov/pub/irs-pdf/p557.pdf.

Trainings:

Center for Nonprofit Management
University of St. Thomas
1000 LaSalle Avenue
Minneapolis, MN 55403
Phone: 517-290-4220
www.stthomas.edu/cnm
Offers graduate education and executive education and professional development.

Minnesota Council of Nonprofits
See www.minnesotanonprofits.org/events-training/management for management training events.
See www.minnesotanonprofits.org/nonprofit-resources/start-a-nonprofit for additional resources, including an online library.

Propel Nonprofits
One Main Street, Suite 600
Minneapolis, MN 55414
612-278-7180
www.propelnonprofits.org
Offers training and consultation services to help nonprofits.

Organizations:

Alliance for Nonprofit Management
1732 First Avenue #28522
New York, NY 10128
Phone: 1-800-397-2034 (Monday - Friday, 11 a.m. - 3 p.m. ET)
www.allianceonline.org

Office of the Minnesota Secretary of State
Business and Nonprofit Services
Metro Area: 651-296-2803 (9 a.m. - 4 p.m. CT)
Greater MN: 1-877-551-6767 (9 a.m. - 4 p.m. CT)
business.services@state.mn.us
Learn more about starting a business or nonprofit, please visit:
www.sos.state.mn.us/business-liens/start-a-business/how-to-start-a-business-in-minnesota/,
www.sos.state.mn.us/business-liens/business-forms-fees/minnesota-non-profit-corporation-forms/.
Registers businesses and corporations (including nonprofit corporations) in Minnesota and also serves as the public record for almost all businesses and corporations in the state.

Springboard for the Arts
308 Prince Street, Suite 270
St. Paul, MN 55101
Phone: 651-292-4381
Nonprofit incorporation consultations for arts organizations, including a fiscal sponsorship program designed for arts groups and projects that have a nonprofit purpose and are looking at becoming their own tax-exempt nonprofit organizations.
springboardforthearts.org
www.springboardforthearts.org/incubator-program

CHAPTER 3

TAX EXEMPTIONS

Topics

A. Overview

Nonprofit organizations may be eligible for a wide range of tax exemptions, depending on their primary purpose, activities, and sources of support and service recipients. The primary exemption that a nonprofit organization may seek to qualify for is federal corporate income tax exemption.

Corporate Income Tax Exemption. A nonprofit organization must select the section of the Internal Revenue Code (IRC)[1] under which it believes it holds a basis for federal income tax exemption; this will vary based on its exempt purpose and the particular activities it will undertake. The section of the IRC under which the organization is ultimately described will describe limits on the organization's activities, as well as the level of tax exemption and benefits of such status. Organizations seeking tax-exempt status under IRC Section 501(c)(3)—the section that covers organizations organized and operated exclusively for charitable, religious, educational or scientific purposes—typically need to apply to be recognized by the Internal Revenue Service (IRS) as qualifying for exemption under Section 501(c)(3). They do so by filing IRS Form 1023—the Application for Recognition of Exemption under Section 501(c)(3) of the Internal Revenue Code, or IRS Form 1023-EZ.[2] Organizations seeking tax-exempt status under almost all other sub-paragraphs of Section 501(c) may file IRS Form 1024—the Application for Recognition of Exemption under Section 501(a)—to receive a determination letter reflecting their exempt status. The IRS provides detailed descriptions of the various types of Section 501(c) organizations as well as an overview of the application process at www.irs.gov/charities-non-profits/application-for-recognition-of-exemption. More detailed information on applying for federal income tax exemption has been posted by the IRS (and is continuously updated) at www.irs.gov/charities-non-profits/applying-for-tax-exempt-status.

If a nonprofit corporation receives an IRS determination letter that indicates it is exempt from federal corporate income tax in accord with any of the paragraphs under Section 501(c), it will also be exempt from Minnesota income tax.

Minnesota Property Tax Exemption. At the state level, Minnesota nonprofit organizations may apply for a property tax exemption with the assessor in the county and/or city where the property is located. They may be approved for an exemption on property used as any of the following, among others:

- Academy, college, university or seminary of learning;
- Church, church property or house of worship;
- Public hospital;
- Public school;
- Public property used exclusively for public purposes;
- Public burying ground; and
- Institution of purely public charity.

Nonprofit corporations with Section 501(c)(3) status may apply for property tax exemption as "institutions of purely public charity" and may be required to substantiate their claim for tax exemption to a greater extent than organizations that claim exemption in another category. Not all Section 501(c)(3) organizations will qualify.

Minnesota Sales Tax Exemption. Some nonprofit organizations are eligible for Minnesota state sales tax exemption. However, not all 501(c)(3) organizations are qualified for sales tax exemption. In addition to churches,

---

1 Footnotes throughout this Chapter refer to the Internal Revenue Code as "I.R.C."; the use of the word "Section" in this Part's text from this point forward is a reference to Sections of the I.R.C. unless the text notes otherwise.

2 *See* I.R.S., *Form 1023: Application for Recognition of Exemption under Section 501(c)(3) of the Internal Revenue Code* (Jan. 2017), www.irs.gov/pub/irs-pdf/f1023.pdf. See also See I.R.S., *Form 1023-EZ: Streamlined Application for Recognition of Exemption Under Section 501(c)(3) of the Internal Revenue Code*, https://www.irs.gov/uac/about-form-1023ez (last visited July 17, 2017).

schools and hospitals, Minnesota grants sales tax exemption for purchases made by qualifying groups organized for charitable, religious or educational purposes and groups formed to support senior citizens and youth. Such organizations may apply for a sales tax exemption for their purchases as described in this Chapter under Section F: Sales Tax Exemption. The exemption does not apply to all purchases made by the nonprofit; for example, meals and lodging are still subject to sales tax. To apply for a Minnesota sales tax exemption, an organization must file Form ST16 with the Minnesota Department of Revenue, available at www.revenue.state.mn.us/forms_and_instructions/st16.pdf. Once a nonprofit organization has been granted an exemption from state sales tax, it must use Form ST3, Certificate of Exemption with the Minnesota Department of Revenue, available at www.revenue.state.mn.us/forms_and_instructions/st3.pdf, to make tax-free purchases. The nonprofit organization must give a completed Form ST3 to the seller.

Note that this exemption from paying sales tax, where granted, does not automatically allow the nonprofit group to sell items without collecting sales tax—it only applies to purchases made by the nonprofit group. Most sales of taxable property made by nonprofit organizations to the public are subject to sales tax, although there are some limited exceptions for limited sales made by qualifying organizations at fundraising events for fundraising purposes.

Payroll Taxes. Nonprofit corporations are still responsible for withholding federal and state income tax from employee compensation as well as tax under the Federal Insurance Contributions Act (FICA)[3]. The belief that "tax exemption" extends to employment tax withholding is wide spread, and results in the greatest number of avoidable tax audits and assessments for nonprofit organizations.

Unemployment Tax. Nonprofit corporations with 501(c)(3) determination letters are exempt from tax under the Federal Unemployment Tax Act (FUTA). Nonprofit organizations with tax-exempt status under a different IRC provision must pay FUTA tax for an employee unless the employee is paid less than $50 in a calendar year. 501(c)(3) organizations are not exempt from the obligation to pay tax under the State Unemployment Tax Act (SUTA) for covered employees, but they may opt to reimburse the state for the actual cost of unemployment benefits used by covered employees, rather than paying a calculated unemployment tax. Opting out requires that the organization send a written notice to Unemployment Insurance Minnesota (UIMN) by December 1 of the previous year.

B. Obtaining Federal Income Tax Exemption

Q1. ***I have recently incorporated a nonprofit organization and am now applying to the IRS for tax-exempt status. What are the differences between the types of 501(c) tax-exempt statuses and how do I decide what type of tax-exempt status the organization should apply for?***

A1. An organization is eligible for tax exemption when its purposes and activities are in line with those described by Congress in Internal Revenue Code Section[4] 501(c) and its more than 20 sub-sections. Accordingly, an organization's ability to qualify for tax-exempt status will be based on its purpose and the particular activities it undertakes. For example, if the organization is organized for a "charitable" and/or "educational" purpose(s), it would likely be seeking classification as a 501(c)(3) organization, but if it exists to lobby and conduct other activities to improve business conditions for a particular industry

3 FICA tax is the money that is taken out of workers' paychecks to pay senior Americans' Social Security and Medicare benefits. It is a mandatory payroll deduction. FICA tax is paid by both workers and their employers. See I.R.S. Topic 751 - Social Security and Medicare With holding Rates (Apr. 2017), https://www.irs.gov/taxtopics/tc751.html.

4 Footnotes throughout this Chapter refer to the Internal Revenue Code as "I.R.C."; the use of the word "Section" in this Part's text from this point forward is a reference to Sections of the I.R.C. unless the text notes otherwise.

or profession, it would be described in Section 501(c)(6). Similarly, recreational and social groups are described in Section 501(c)(7), and so-called "social welfare" and "community benefit organizations" are described in Section 501(c)(4).

Organizations seeking qualification under Section 501(c)(3) need to be aware that taking exemption under that section imposes further limits on the organization's activities, while at the same time allowing an increased level of tax benefits. For example, 501(c)(3) organizations may influence legislation only to an insubstantial degree[5] and may not to any degree "participate or intervene" in candidate elections. At the same time, 501(c)(3) organizations will have contributions made to them be tax-deductible for their donors. Organizations whose activities would have qualified for 501(c)(3) classification but not for 501(c)(3)'s legislative lobbying limits and/or the candidate election prohibition are still eligible for exemption under 501(c)(4), which describes organizations who work to better the "social welfare" or to provide "community benefit." 501(c)(4) organizations may influence legislation without limit, and they may even endorse or assist candidates (the latter still subject to federal, state and local campaign and election laws) so long as those political activities are not the primary aim of the organization.[6] However, donors to 501(c)(4) organizations will find that their contributions are not tax deductible.

Detailed information on qualifying for federal income tax exemption under 501(c)(3) is available at https://www.irs.gov/charities-non-profits/charitable-organizations, and also at www.irs.gov/charities-non-profits/types-of-tax-exempt-organizations. Readers can find links to information on all exemption categories under 501(c), mini-courses on exemption rules, and links to the application forms. IRS Publication 557, *Tax-Exempt Status for Your Organization*, is also useful on these topics.[7]

Q2. How does an organization apply for federal tax-exempt status?

A2. If an organization seeks federal income tax-exempt status as a 501(c)(3) organization, it must file IRS Form 1023 Application for Recognition of Exemption. Smaller organizations meeting certain requirements may use the shorter IRS Form 1023-EZ.[8] Organizations must complete the Form 1023-EZ Eligibility Worksheet in the Instructions for Form 1023-EZ to determine if the organization is eligible to file this form.[9] Please note that Form 1023-EZ is filed electronically only on Pay.gov.[10] If an organization seeks tax-exempt status under another paragraph of section 501(c), it will usually be required to apply by filing IRS Form 1024 (note though that some of the more unusual 501(c) subsections need to apply by letter). The IRS provides detailed information on the different types of 501(c) organizations in Chapter 4 of IRS Publication 557,[11] as well as a variety of resources at www.irs.gov/charities-non-profits/charitable-organizations, and also at www.irs.gov/charities-non-profits/types-of-tax-exempt-organizations.

Regardless of whether Form 1023, Form 1023-EZ, Form 1024 or a letter is used to apply, the organization must have an employer identification number (EIN) (also called a "taxpayer identification number"(TIN)) in place prior to applying for exempt status. An application for an EIN/TIN may be made online (and

5 Organizations can influence legislation to an insubstantial degree or agree to meet the expenditure limits that come with a so-called "election" to play by the rules set out in Section 501(h). See Chapter 7: Lobbying, Election-related Activity and Voter Education.

6 The contours of what makes a I.R.C. § 501(c)(4) efforts "community benefit" versus "political," and the extent to which the latter can be conducted by I.R.C. § 501(c)(4) organizations, is at the heart of the concern that the I.R.S. is insufficiently policing this area of law, a topic that surfaced in May and June of 2013 when the I.R.S. was accused of improperly vetting groups based on political party connection.

7 *See* I.R.S. Pub. 557 (Jan. 2017), www.irs.gov/pub/irs-pdf/p557.pdf.

8 *See* I.R.S., Form 1023-EZ (2017), www.irs.gov/pub/irs-pdf/f1023ez.pdf.

9 *See* I.R.S., *Instructions for Form 1023-EZ* (Jan. 2017), www.irs.gov/pub/irs-pdf/i1023ez.pdf.

10 See www.irs.gov/form1023ez for additional filing information.

11 *See* I.R.S. Pub. 557 (Jan. 2017), www.irs.gov/pub/irs-pdf/p557.pdf.

the number immediately procured) at www.irs.gov/businesses/small-businesses-self-employed/apply-for-an-employer-identification-number-ein-online. Alternatively, Form SS-4, *Application for Employer Identification Number*, may be completed and filed with the IRS via fax or mail.[12]

Every application for exemption must include:

- A conformed copy of the applicant's organizing documents (for incorporated entities this will be the organization's Articles of Incorporation, as initially filed and thereafter showing any and all amendments and/or restatements). Conformed copies of such document(s) will show filing with appropriate authorities (in the case of Articles of Incorporation) or certification under oath by an officer that the documents are exact copies of the originals.
- Current Bylaws, if any. (Note that it is not a requirement of law that Bylaws have been adopted prior to making an application for exemption.)
- Description of the organization's actual activities undertaken to date as well as those proposed over the next several years. If the nonprofit's organizing documents and/or Bylaws do not set the purposes of the organization with specificity, the description of its activities will need to also state to what purposes these are being undertaken.
- Summary of the organization's actual (if in existence for more than one year) finances showing receipts and expenditures for the current year and all preceding years (up to three), as well as the most recently completed year's balance sheet. Applicants for 501(c)(3) exempt status are required to show receipts and expenditures for at least three or four years (including projected years).[13] Applicants for exemption under non-501(c)(3) status who have been in existence for less than one year will also need to show projected receipts and expenditures for the upcoming two years.
- The appropriate "user fee." User fee for Form 1023 is $850 (this amount unchanged since Jan. 2010), but small organizations who can certify that their gross receipts will not exceed $10,000 in any of the first four years of operation pay only $400.

If an organization applies for tax-exempt status under the wrong subsection of Section 501(c), it may be recognized as exempt under another subsection if the applicant agrees to redirect the application. In such cases, the IRS will advise the organization and will provide the appropriate application form's signature page and relevant parts (if any) so the application may be reactivated under the appropriate 501(c) subsection.

After an initial review of the application, the IRS will either issue a favorable determination letter or written letter request for additional information to clarify the nature of operations and purposes of the organization. All submissions made by applicants are part of the entire application package **and are open to the public once a successful determination is issued.** Note that any documents submitted with the application will not be returned, so you should not submit original documents with your application.[14]

Q3. Where can organizations get help with applying for federal tax-exempt status?

A3. The IRS directs applicants who need help with preparing their applications for tax-exempt status to call Exempt Organization Customer Account Services at 1-877-829-5500. However, that call center is only infrequently staffed by tax law specialists from the IRS's Exempt Organizations Division and callers' questions are thus scribed and sent onto the Division. Detailed information on qualifying for

12 *See* I.R.S., *Form SS-4* (2010), www.irs.gov/pub/irs-pdf/fss4.pdf.
13 *See* I.R.S., *Notice 1382: Changes for Form 1023* (Oct. 2013), www.irs.gov/pub/irs-pdf/n1382.pdf.
14 *See* I.R.S. Pub. 557, 5 (Jan. 2017), www.irs.gov/pub/irs-pdf/p557.pdf.

federal income tax-exemption (including a sub-page on "types of tax-exempt organizations," a mini-course on exemption overall, and links to the application forms) has been posted by the IRS as noted in the last paragraph of Answer to Question 1. IRS has useful instructions for Form 1023 Application for Recognition of Exemption under Section 501(c)(3) and Form 1024 (Application for Recognition of Exemption under Section 501(a)).[15] See related resources in Section H for help from local organizations.

Q4. ***Does it make a difference if an organization's stated purpose in its forming documents is "charitable" or "educational" (so-called "public benefit" purposes) or "mutual benefit"? Why?***

A4. Internal Revenue Code Section 501(c) addresses specific exemption categories that vary depending on what purpose a nonprofit group has been organized to accomplish. Thus, an organization whose stated purpose is "charitable" rather than "mutual benefit" will be eligible for 501(c)(3) exempt status, whereas a "mutual benefit" group operating for the benefit of its members cannot qualify for that status. Examples of mutual benefit organizations are labor unions (such groups are typically described in Section 501(c)(5)); trade associations, chambers of commerce and boards of trade (typically described in Section 501(c)(6)); and social clubs (typically described in Section 501(c)(7)).

Public benefit groups, a category that includes schools, hospitals, museums and grant-making foundations, operate for the benefit of the general public.

Nonprofit Tip

To qualify for 501(c)(3) exemption, one or more of the specific purposes listed in that subsection ("charitable," "educational," "religious," etc.) will need to be included in the organizing document.

All public benefit organizations seeking recognition of exemption are prohibited from providing "private inurement" (i.e. benefiting the organization's insiders, see discussion of private inurement in Question 12). In addition, both 501(c)(3) and 501(c)(4) organizations are further required to operate for public benefit rather than private benefit.[16]

501(c)(3) organizations have more rigorous prohibitions, as contributions made to these groups are tax-deductible[17] in recognition of the fact that these groups operate in favor of purely public purposes. Conversely, since contributions made to mutual benefit organizations are not tax-deductible (indeed, since mutual benefit organizations exist to benefit their members), they have more broad authority to convey private benefit.

15 *See* I.R.S., *Instructions for Form 1023* (2006), www.irs.gov/pub/irs-pdf/i1023.pdf. See also I.R.S., *Instructions for Form 1024* (2016), www.irs.gov/pub/irs-pdf/i1024.pdf.

16 *See* I.R.C. § 1.501(c)(3) (2015) for the private inurement prohibition imposed upon 501(c)(3) organizations. See I.R.C. § 1.501(c)(3)(d)(1)(ii) (2015) for the public benefit requirement.

17 *See* I.R.C. § 170(c)(2) (2015) sets out the income-tax deductibility of contributions made to virtually the same groups described in I.R.C. § 501(c)(3) (2015).

Q5. What are the minimum legal requirements an organization needs to meet in order to be recognized as a 501(c)(3) tax-exempt organization?

A5. Generally speaking, an organization's application and attachments must show that the following three statements are true:

- The organization is organized and operated for one or more of the following: charitable, religious, educational or scientific purpose(s). (Or, less commonly, for one of the other four purposes note in IRC Section 501(c)(3): literary, preventing cruelty to animals or children, fostering national or international amateur sports competition or testing for public safety. But note that being organized solely for the last purpose will result in contributions not being eligible for income tax deduction.)
- The organization will be operated for benefit of the public and not for the benefit of private parties or interests (this is the so-called "private benefit" prohibition) **and** no part of the organization's earnings or assets will benefit private shareholders or individuals (this is the so-called "private inurement" prohibition).
- The organization will not, to a substantial degree, attempt to influence legislation (though lobbying within limits is allowed), or participate or intervene to any extent in favor of or opposition to candidates for elective office (including work with political parties).[18] *See* Chapter 7: Lobbying, Election-related Activity and Voter Education for more information.

Q6. What is the difference between a 501(c)(3) private foundation and a 501(c)(3) public charity?

A6. Every organization that qualifies for tax-exempt status under Section 501(c)(3) is classified as either a "private foundation" or a "public charity." Indeed, 501(c)(3) applicants are assumed to be private foundations until they show the IRS that they meet certain requirements and properly notify the IRS that they are **not** falling within the definitions fitting private foundations.[19] Typically, an organization makes this notification to the IRS by stating in the relevant part of the Form 1023 (Part X) the basis by which they are **not** a private foundation. The most common distinction between public charities and private foundations is in the organization's funding sources. The vast majority of public charities are those that are supported by gifts and contributions from diverse funders (or, if not, by earning fees for service from a wide array of service users).

Generally speaking, a private foundation has two or more of the following three characteristics:

- It was initially funded by a single, private source (such as a family or business).
- Its income comes mostly from investments or its own or another's endowment funds.
- It makes grants to other charitable organizations rather than running its own programs.

501(c)(3) organizations typically hold public charity status by pointing to their conduct or operations as having one of four different characteristics:

- Function – Some organizations are public charities by virtue of the activities they conduct; this is the basis by which churches, educational institutions, hospitals or medical research organizations operated in conjunction with a hospital, endowment funds operated for certain educational institutions, and governmental units are classified as they are specifically excluded from being private foundations.[20]

18 *See* I.R.C. § 501(c)(3) (2015). See also I.R.S. Pub. 557 (Jan. 2017), www.irs.gov/pub/irs-pdf/p557.pdf.
19 *See* I.R.S. Pub. 557, Chapter 3 (Jan. 2017), www.irs.gov/pub/irs-pdf/p557.pdf.
20 *See* I.R.C. § 509(a)(1) (2006). See also I.R.C. §§ 170(b)(1)(A)(i)-(v) (2015).

- Public support – Some organizations are public charities because they receive substantial financial support in the form of gifts, grants or contributions from the public or the government.[21] Qualification as a publicly supported organization requires the organization to have either one-third "public support" or meet a facts and circumstances test. To achieve one-third public support, an organization must show that it receives at least one-third of its total support from governmental units, from contributions made directly or indirectly by the general public or from a combination of these sources over the two most recent prior five-year periods. If an organization does not have one-third public support, it may still qualify under the facts and circumstances test. Under this test, an organization must have no less than "ten percent public support" (again, measured over the prior five-year periods) and meet an "attraction of public support" requirement. Examples of publicly-supported organizations in this category may include museums, libraries, community centers to promote the arts and organizations such as community foundations and the United Way.
- Public support – Some organizations do not receive many contributions, or their contributors are not diverse enough to constitute sufficient "public support" to meet the prior standard's requirements. These groups can qualify as public charities if they receive substantial financial support comprised not only of gifts, grants or contributions from the public or the government, but also including exempt function income (i.e., fees for service) from diverse payers.[22] Qualification as a publicly supported organization in this way requires the organization to have both one-third "public support" (using differing definitions for this classification) and **not** have more than one-third of the "total support" come from investment income and net unrelated business income. Testing of an organization's support is made, as with the prior standard, over recent prior five-year periods. Regulations issued in 2008 allow public charities to move year to year from one of the two public support tests (this or the standard set out in the preceding bullet point) on their annual Form 990 filing, with no need to seek specific permission from the IRS to change between the two classifications. Examples of publicly-supported organizations in this category may include theatres, instructional organizations and hockey arenas.
- Supporting – Some organizations are public charities because they are organized to support the activities of another organization that is a public charity by virtue of its function or receipt of public support. So-called "supporting organizations" [23] must be organized and operated exclusively to perform the functions or carry out the purpose of the public charity that it supports.[24]

Classification as a private foundation rather than a public charity carries several disadvantages. Most importantly, deductibility of contributions to private foundations are more limited than contributions to public charities: while donors to public charities may deduct contributions up to 50 percent of their adjusted gross income, donors to private foundations may only deduct contributions up to 30 percent of their adjusted gross income.[25] Furthermore, under the rules applied, private foundations have more administrative difficulties making grants to other private foundations than to public charities, so classification as a private foundation will narrow one's ability to get grants from private foundations. Other disadvantages include assessment of a two percent tax on investment income, a different rule with respect to limits on attempts to influence legislation (such activity is NOT permitted at all for private foundations) and the requirement to file a vastly more complex annual return with the IRS, Form 990-PF.

---

21 *See* I.R.C. § 509(a)(1) (2006). See also I.R.C. §§ 170(b)(1)(A)(i)-(vi) (2015).

22 *See* I.R.C. § 509(a)(2) (2006).

23 *See* I.R.C. § 509(a)(3) (2006).

24 Many changes were made with respect to I.R.C. § 509(a)(3) supporting organizations by Congress in 2006. Organizations believing they fit under this classification as their "primary basis" for being other than a private foundation should seek legal counsel experienced with exempt organizations to learn the possible limits and concerns such classification conveys.

25 *See* I.R.S. Pub. 526, *Charitable Contributions* (2016), https://www.irs.gov/pub/irs-pdf/p526.pdf.

Q7. What does an organization need to include on Form 1023 to ensure the IRS will approve its application to be tax exempt under IRC Section 501(c)(3)?

A7. Organizations must have an employer identification number (EIN) **prior to** applying for exempt status. An application for an EIN/TIN may be made online (and the number immediately procured) by following the procedures at www.irs.gov/businesses/small-businesses-self-employed/apply-for-an-employer-identification-number-ein-online/. Alternatively, Form SS-4, Application for Employer Identification Number, may be completed and filed with the IRS (the Form is available at www.irs.gov/businesses/small-businesses-self-employed/how-to-apply-for-an-ein.)

Form SS-4, Application for Employer Identification Number, may NOT be submitted with the application for tax-exempt status.

Every Form 1023 exemption application must include:

- A conformed copy of the applicant's organizing documents (nonprofit corporations' organizing documents will be the "Articles of Incorporation" as initially filed and subsequently altered by all amendments and/or restatements which will also need to be attached).
    - A conformed copy of Articles of Incorporation and further amendments and/or restatements is a set of documents that reflects proof of filing with appropriate authorities.
- Unincorporated entities' documents will need be attested to by an officer (under oath) stipulating that the documents are exact copies of the originals.
- Current Bylaws, if any. (Note that it is not a requirement of law that Bylaws have been adopted prior to making an application for exemption.)
- Description of the organization's activities undertaken to date as well as those proposed for upcoming periods. If the organization's organizing documents and/or Bylaws do not set out the purposes of the organization with specificity, the description here will need to also state to what purposes the activities are undertaken.
- Completion of the exemption application's Part IX columns detailing receipts and expenditures for the years in existence plus projected current and upcoming full years so that a total of three years of information is provided (for entities who at time of application have yet to complete one tax year) or four years (for entities who have completed one tax year but not in existence five or more years) or the five most recently completed five full years (for entities who have completed five tax years or more).[26]
- The appropriate user fee. As of July 2017, the user fees are:
    - $400 for organizations that have had gross receipts of less than $10,000 annually during preceding four years, or new organizations that anticipate gross receipts averaging not more than $10,000 during their first four years;
    - $850 for organizations whose actual or anticipated gross receipts exceed $10,000 annually.

26 Applying organizations that have not completed one tax year need to show financial projections for three years; those that have completed one tax year (but not been in existence for five years) need to show financial projections for four years. An applicant who has finished five or more tax years must supply completed years' financial statements for the most recently completed five years. See I.R.S., *Notice 1382: Changes for Form 1023* (Oct. 2013), www.irs.gov/pub/irs-pdf/n1382.pdf. See also I.R.S., *Instructions for Form 1023* (June 2006), www.irs.gov/pub/irs-pdf/i1023.pdf.

The application and attachments in total must reflect and confirm that the following three statements are true in order for the IRS to issue a determination letter that the organization is described in Section 501(c)(3):

- The organization has been, is and will be organized and operated for one or more of the eight purposes noted in Section 501(c)(3) (the most common: charitable, religious, educational or scientific).
- The organization will not be operated for the benefit of private parties or interests and no part of the organization's earnings or assets will inure to the benefit of private shareholders or individuals.
- The organization will not, to a substantial degree, attempt to influence legislation, nor will it participate or intervene to any extent in a political campaign.[27]

The last two pages of the Form 1023 application package provide a checklist of all materials an organization will need to submit with the Form 1023 for it to be complete. This checklist is required to be included (with payment) atop the fully completed Form 1023 submitted to the IRS.

Q8. What are the differences between Form 1023 and Form 1023-EZ?

A8. Organizations can submit Form 1023-EZ "Streamlined Application for Recognition of Exemption Under Section 501(c)(3) of the IRC" to apply for recognition as a tax-exempt organization under Section 501(c)(3).[28] To submit Form 1023-EZ, you must:

- Read the Instructions for Form 1023-EZ[29] and complete its Eligibility Worksheet found at the end of the instructions. (If you are not eligible to file Form 1023-EZ, you can still file Form 1023.)
- If eligible to file Form 1023-EZ, register for an account on Pay.gov. (There are 26 eligibility questions listed on Form 1023-EZ, you must answer "NO" to all 26 questions to be eligible to file Form 1023-EZ.)
- Enter "1023-EZ" in the search box.
- Complete the form.[30]

The chart below lists several main differences between Form 1023 and Form 1023-EZ[31]:

IRS Form 1023 (Long Form)	IRS Form 1023-EZ (Short Form and Online Only)
12 pages (100+ questions)	3 pages (41 questions)
Submit electronically at www.irs.gov/form1023 or you may print and mail	Submit electronically at www.pay.gov
May take 60+ hours to complete	May take 10-15 hours to complete
Many organizations can complete on their own; some require legal consultation	Designed for you to complete on your own

27 *See* I.R.C. § 501(c)(3) (2015). See also I.R.S. Pub. 557, 24 (2017), www.irs.gov/pub/irs-pdf/p557.pdf.
28 *See* I.R.S., *About Form 1023-EZ* (Feb. 2017), www.irs.gov/uac/about-form-1023ez.
29 *See* I.R.S., *Instructions for Form 1023-EZ* (Jan. 2017), www.irs.gov/pub/irs-pdf/i1023ez.pdf.
30 *See* I.R.S., *About Form 1023-EZ* (Feb. 2017), www.irs.gov/uac/about-form-1023ez.
31 See Paul Masiarchin & Biftu Takele, Address at the Minnesota Council of Nonprofits: How to Start a Successful Nonprofit (June 22, 2017).

IRS Form 1023 (Long Form)	IRS Form 1023-EZ (Short Form and Online Only)
Includes an $850 fee payable to the IRS: • $400 if gross receipts are/will be under $10,000 annually • $200 if you use the IRS Cyber-Assistant (when available)	Must be filed electronically and payment of $275 must be made at pay.gov via credit/ debit card or directly from your bank account. Can only be used if annual gross receipts are projected at/below $50,000.
Items needed (same as 1023-EZ): • EIN • List of officers/directors • "Necessary organizing documents" (i.e. Articles of Incorporation) • NTEE Code (your activity area) and basic information about your activities • Various decisions about pay, lobbying public support, etc. Items needed (beyond 1023-EZ): • Narrative description of activities • Compensation figures for officers / directors • Membership information (if any) • Your history (successor organizations, especially) • Fundraising plans • Statement of revenue & expenses (3 years of data) • Plus, lots of additional information	Items needed: • EIN • List of officers/directors • "Necessary organizing documents" (i.e. Articles of Incorporation) • NTEE Code (your activity area) and basic information about your activities • Various decisions about pay, lobbying public support, etc.

The IRS reminds every nonprofit organization to choose the correct foundation classification on Form 1023-EZ. Most organizations described in section 501(c)(3) are classified as public charities rather than private foundations.[32] In choosing your foundation classification, carefully review Part IV of the instructions for Form1023-EZ to ensure that you are correctly identifying your status based on your expected sources of funding.[33] Always be honest and truthful when filling out Form 1023 or Form 1023-EZ. The IRS will check on the accuracy and honesty of your answers.

If you submitted a Form 1023-EZ application, you can expect to be contacted within 90 days from the date you submitted the application.[34] After 90 days, if you haven't been contacted, you can call the toll-free Customer Account Services number, Monday through Friday, 8 a.m. – 5 p.m. (local time), at 877-829-5500 to check on the status.[35] If any part of this answer is unclear to you or your organization, see an attorney.

32 *See* I.R.S., *Choose Your Foundation Classification on Form 1023-EZ Carefully* (Feb, 2017), www.irs.gov/uac/rda-20170224-2017-f1023ez.
33 *Id.*
34 *See* I.R.S., *Where's My Exemption Application?* (Jan. 2017), www.irs.gov/charities-non-profits/charitable-organizations/wheres-my-application.
35 *Id.*

Q9. What do I need to include on Form 1024 to ensure the IRS will approve my organization's non-501(c)(3) tax-exempt application?

A9. Organizations must have an employer identification number (EIN) *prior to* applying for exempt status. An application for an EIN/TIN may be made online (and the number immediately procured) by following the procedures at www.irs.gov/Businesses/Small-Businesses-&-Self-Employed/Apply-for-an-Employer-Identification-Number-(EIN)-Online. Alternatively, Form SS-4, Application for Employer Identification Number, may be completed and filed with the IRS (the form is available at www.irs.gov/Businesses/Small-Businesses-&-Self-Employed/How-to-Apply-for-an-EIN.)

Note that Form SS-4, Application for Employer Identification Number, may not be submitted with the application. Every Form 1024 application must also include:

- A conformed copy of the applicant's organizing documents, usually the Articles of Incorporation, along with all amendments to the original document (for nonprofit corporations these will be the organizations Articles of Incorporation, as initially filed and subsequently altered by all amendments and/or restatements which will also need be attached). A conformed copy of Articles of Incorporation and further amendments and/or restatements is a set of documents that reflect proof of filing with appropriate authorities.
- Current Bylaws, if any. Note that it is not a requirement of law that Bylaws have been adopted prior to making an application for exemption.
- Description of the purposes and activities of the organization. If the articles contain a description of the purposes and activities, a separate statement is not necessary.
- Financial statements showing the organization's receipts and expenditures for the current year and the preceding three years, as well as a balance sheet for the current year. If the organization has been in existence for fewer than four years, include financial statements for all the years that the organization has existed.
- If the organization has been in operation for less than one year or has not yet begun operations, include a proposed budget for the next two accounting periods and a current statement of assets and liabilities.[36]
- Form 8718, and appropriate user fee. As of July 2017, the user fee is $400 or $850, depending on the new organization's anticipated gross receipts. Form 8718 requires filers certify eligibility for the lower fee based on either having total annual gross receipts for the last four completed tax years be under $10,000 per year or, if not in existence over such full period, projected gross annual receipts being below $10,000 per year in each of the upcoming four years. Such certification must be signed by an officer.

Q10. How long does it take to receive notification of federal tax-exempt status?

A10. The IRS handles received exemption applications in two pools. Those falling within the first pool (for applications that can be approved immediately OR that are missing minor information OR applicants who have used the wrong form or failed to have the application be complete) are told that they will hear back from the IRS in 90 days. Those in the second pool (applications with substantive issues or problems, when additional information will need to be sought to determine whether the organization indeed qualifies) must wait for an agent to be assigned, at which time they will be contacted. Very substantial wait times have been in place when an application requires a "higher grade" agent. The longest wait time

36 *See* I.R.S., *Form 1024*, 5 (1998), www.irs.gov/pub/irs-pdf/f1024.pdf.

is posted on the IRS website along with information on these pools at www.irs.gov/charities-non-profits/charitable-organizations/wheres-my-application. Be aware that it is not uncommon for the wait time for agent assignment to be more than a year. In addition, the IRS website has a list of the top tips to avoid delay in an exemption application on its website, available at www.irs.gov/charities-non-profits/top-ten-reasons-for-delays-in-processing-exempt-organization-applications. Applicant organizations may consult this list prior to submitting their own applications to avoid common application problems.

2010 Tax Year and Later (filed in 2011 and later)	**Form to File**
Gross receipts normally ≤$50,000	990-N (e-postcard)
Gross receipts > $50,000 and < $200,000, and Total assets < $500,000	990-EZ or 990
Gross receipts ≥ $200,000, or Total assets ≥ $500,000	990
Private foundation - regardless of financial status	990-PF[38]

C. Maintaining Federal Income Tax Exemption

Q11. Once an organization is recognized as tax exempt under a Section 501(c) subsection, what additional filings does the IRS require?

A11. Most tax-exempt organizations will be required to file an "annual information return" (technically NOT a tax return, as no income tax is assessed by it) with the IRS. Some tax-exempt organizations are exempt from this annual filing requirement, for example, churches and certain other religious institutions, and organizations having gross receipts each year that normally do not exceed $50,000. A complete list of tax-exempt organizations that are not required to file annual information returns is posted by the IRS at www.irs.gov/charities-non-profits/annual-exempt-organization-return-who-must-file.

Those organizations who must make an annual information return filing will find that the Forms vary depending on status and/or size of receipts and assets. As of tax years begun in 2007, organizations excepted from filing a Form 990 or 990-EZ because of size of receipts and assets are subject to an annual registration requirement using the Form 990-N (which is filed electronically and is thus also called the "e-postcard"). All private foundations (regardless of size) file Form 990-PF. Exempt organizations subject to an annual filing requirement who are NOT private foundations file either Form 990, Form 990-EZ or Form 990-N, as follows.[37]

If an exempt organization has $1,000 or more of gross income from the conduct of trade or business activities that are regularly carried on and not substantially related to the purpose that is the basis for the organization's exemption, the organization must also file a true "tax return," the Form 990-T, to report and pay "unrelated business income tax." See Question 12 for more information on unrelated business income.

37 In 2008, the I.R.S. revised the I.R.S. Form 990 at which time the filing thresholds for this form, its alternative (990-EZ) and the 990-N were established as indicated in the above table.

38 *See* I.R.S., *Form 990-PF Return of Private Foundation* (2016), www.irs.gov/pub/irs-pdf/f990pf.pdf.

This requirement is in addition to the obligation to file a Form 990, 990-EZ, the annual notice when below the filing thresholds for either of the prior returns (the Form 990-N) or the Form 990-PF.

Some organizations (e.g., 501(c) organizations that paid premiums on certain life insurance, annuity or personal benefit contracts or organizations participating in abusive tax shelters) must also file other forms with the IRS annually. See I.R.S. Publication 557 for a list of such filing requirements.[39]

Q12. What is "unrelated business income tax" (UBIT) and when is an exempt organization subject to it?

A12. UBIT is a tax (applied at the same rate that taxable corporations are subject to) on the net income a tax-exempt organization has each year from trade or business activities it regularly conducts that are not substantially related to its exempt mission. The fact that funds raised or achieved by such a trade or business will be used to support the mission of the organization does not make for a "substantial relationship." Three conditions must exist before UBIT applies to revenues received by a 501(c) exempt organization in the conduct of its activities: the income must come from the conduct of a "trade or business," such activities must be "regularly carried on," and they must lack a "substantial relationship" to accomplishing the organization's exempt purpose.[40] See Chapter 8: Financial Accountability, Question 55 for more information on UBIT and the underlying conditions summarized here.

If gross receipts from the conduct of unrelated businesses total $1,000 or more in a year, the organization must file a Form 990-T to report their receipts that are subject to unrelated business income tax and to calculate tax due and payable. The requirement to file the Form 990-T is in addition to the obligation to file the annual information return on the Form 990, 990-EZ or 990-PF, as applicable, or to make the annual notice filing if available (i.e. Form 990-N).[41]

Q13. What is private inurement and why can't 501(c)(3), 501(c)(4), 501(c)(5), 501(c)(6), and 501(c)(7) tax-exempt organizations have it?

A13. Private inurement is the transfer of an organization's assets or income to an individual, group or shareholder in their private capacity. "An organization is not operated exclusively for one or more exempt purposes if its net earnings inure in whole or in part to the benefit of private shareholders or individuals."[42]

While for-profit organizations exist specifically to benefit their owners or shareholders through the distribution of earnings, nonprofit organizations overall are prohibited from such distribution. Organizations described in or otherwise qualifying under Sections 501(c)(3), 501(c)(4), 501(c)(5), 501(c)(6), and 501(c)(7), unlike other types of Section 501(c) organizations, are explicitly prohibited from transferring their assets and income to insiders because their purposes are specific to outcomes that are public or group based, not personal to those managing the organization. These organizations exist to promote the general public's benefit, even if members of the public are those who might join a 501(c)(7) social club or be members of an industry promoted by a 501(c)(6) trade association or a 501(c)(5) agricultural association. Additionally, 501(c)(3) and 501(c)(4) organizations need be dedicated to narrow public purposes (e.g., charitable or

39 *See* I.R.S. Pub. 557, 10-11 (2017), www.irs.gov/pub/irs-pdf/p557.pdf.
40 *See* I.R.C. §§ 511-513 (2015).
41 *See* I.R.S., *Unrelated Business Income Tax*, www.irs.gov/charities-non-profits/unrelated-business-income-tax (last updated Nov. 07, 2016). The specifics of the tax are further addressed in the I.R.S. Publication 598 (Jan. 2017), www.irs.gov/pub/irs-pdf/p598.pdf.
42 Treas. Reg. § 1.501(c)(3)-1(c)(2).

religious) and social welfare purposes, respectively and not provide more than incidental private benefit.[43] Certain other 501(c) organizations are organized specifically to distribute benefits to their members to the exclusion of others. For example, a 501(c)(9) VEBA (Voluntary Employee Beneficiary Association) is not subject to the "no private inurement" rule, as it exists to distribute employee benefits and the employees financially benefit from the organization's operation. That operation is different from that of a 501(c)(4) social welfare organization (to whom the rule applies, amongst the others cited in the preceding paragraph), because while such groups often offer benefits or services to their members, these benefits are also available to the general public.

Q14. What additional legal restrictions must 501(c)(3) organizations observe in their daily operations specific to avoiding undue private benefits and maintaining only charitable operations?

A14. 501(c)(3) organizations are explicitly prohibited from transferring the organization's assets to "insiders," that is, individuals with a special relationship to the organization, such as a director, officer or trustee. This is known as the "private inurement" doctrine (explained in Question 12). Issues related to the application of that doctrine to 501(c)(3) organizations are further examined in Question 14.

In addition, 501(c)(3) organizations must be operated for "purely public benefit,"[44] a condition that requires they not provide more than incidental "private benefit." An oft-cited example of undue private benefit is having a Board of Directors comprised of the individuals who are being paid for services they provide to the organization (no matter that their compensation is "reasonable" for the services they provide as employees or contractors). In these cases, the cure (to allow exemption) is to situate the governance of the organization under individuals who are NOT related to those who are providing services. To safeguard against even incidental private benefit situations, organizations should consider adopting a Conflict of Interest Policy. See Chapter 6 Boards of Directors, Section E: Conflicts of Interest. Situations of "private benefit" are evaluated on a case–by-case basis, as the circumstances are highly factually specific; more egregious examples are subject to characterization in line with Supreme Court Justice Potter Stewart's famous quote about obscenity: "you know it when you see it."

And finally, 501(c)(3) organizations may conduct unrelated trade or business activities (these may be subject to the "unrelated business income tax" (UBIT)), so long as their primary purpose is to conduct appropriate exempt operations.[45] If gross receipts from a regularly conducted unrelated business activity total $1,000 or more, the organization is required to report and calculate UBIT by filing a Form 990-T.[46] For more information on UBIT, see Question 12.

Q15. What are the legal restrictions on hiring insiders or engaging in transactions with insiders that 501(c)(3) and 501(c)(4) tax-exempt organizations must observe?

A15. 501(c)(3) public charities and 501(c)(4) organizations (along with certain insiders, personally) are subject to an excise tax scheme set out in Section 4958 that is designed to do two things: (1) prohibit unreasonable compensation to insiders (as well as any other below–fair market value advantage, such as acquiring below–fair market loans or using the organization's property with

43 Treas. Reg. § 1.501 (c)(3)-1(d)(1)(ii) applies this mandate to 501(c)(3) organizations. The I.R.S. has in multiple letter rulings cited its application to 501(c)(4) organizations.

44 Treas. Reg. § 1.501-(c)(3)-1(d)(1)(ii).

45 Treas. Reg. § 1.501-(c)(3)-1(c)(1).

46 *See* I.R.S., *Unrelated Business Income Tax*, www.irs.gov/charities-non-profits/unrelated-business-income-tax (last updated Nov. 07, 2016).

out fairly paying for such use) and (2) require, in instances where prohibited advantage has been provided, the insiders to provide full restitution to the organization. The Internal Revenue Code does not use the term "insider" but instead refers to those who are (or have been) in "substantial influence" over the affairs of the organization now (at the time of the transaction) or at any time in the prior 60 months. Certain individuals with a special relationship to the organization are automatically in "substantial influence" positions. These include all Board members, the individual(s) acting and/or holding title as President and Treasurer, others who are found to factually have held such influence (e.g., highly-compensated employees, substantial contributors), family members of those individuals, other persons connected to those found to be in influence (for example, certain owners of companies that are substantial contributors), and entities under the control of more than 35 percent of those parties.[47]

No individual or group of individuals may profit (aside from reasonable compensation for services they provide that are necessary to the organization's operations) from a 501(c)(3) or 501(c)(4) organization's income. At issue for purposes of this excise tax scheme is whether a transaction conveys "excess benefit." Excess benefit exists when individuals receive unreasonable compensation. As such, organizations need to establish that they are paying no more than "reasonable compensation" for services rendered.[48] Neither the IRS nor the State of Minnesota require nonprofit corporations to follow a particular process to determine reasonable compensation, but Congress, in establishing the excise tax scheme, did give advantages to organizations that follow certain business practices in having their boards establish terms of transactions with those in "substantial influence."[49] In Minnesota, a nonprofit corporation's Board of Directors has both the authority to fix compensation and the responsibility to do so (although the task may be delegated).[50] Courts and the IRS rely on specific factors in their determination of whether compensation arrangements, rental or sales agreements or borrowing arrangements are unreasonable. What is evaluated with respect to compensation is generally:

- Compensation of other individuals in similar positions within the same company;
- Compensation of individuals in similar positions within the same geographic region;
- The length of time the individual will be providing services;
- The individual's experience, education, and any other relevant background that qualifies them for the position;
- The size and complexity of the organization;
- The organization's need in the position or contract for the particular experience, education and skills of the individual; and
- How and by whom was the compensation package approved.

An example of when these factors likely show compensation to be "unreasonable" would occur when the compensation package of an incoming director far exceeded that of the outgoing director and that of other similar directors in the region, the incoming director had little or no relevant education or experience usually associated with individuals in this type of position, and the compensation package was approved by a board that included the incoming director.[51]

47 The so-called "rebuttable presumption" procedures. See Treas. Reg. § 53.4958-6.
48 Treas. Reg. § 4958-4(b)(1)(ii).
49 Treas. Reg. § 53.4958-6(a)(1)(ii) (defining "rebuttable presumption of reasonableness").
50 Minn. Stat. § 317A.211 (2016).
51 Bruce R. Hopkins, *The Legal Answer Book for Nonprofit Corporations*, 61 (John Wiley & Sons, Inc. 1st ed. 1996).

As stated above, the IRS does not require organizations to follow a particular process in setting the terms of an insider transaction. However, the Form 990 disclosure requirements ask filers if they are following practices that mirror the "rebuttable presumption" safe-harbor set out by Congress in its enactment of the excise tax scheme that applies to 501(c)(3) and 501(c)(4) organizations.[52] This safe-harbor is found in Treasury Regulations Section 53.4958-6(a), which sets out that:

> "Compensation payments are **presumed to be reasonable** if the compensation arrangement is **approved in advance** by an authorized body composed entirely of individuals who **do not have a conflict of interest** with respect to the arrangement, the authorized body obtained and relied upon **appropriate data as to comparability** prior to making its determination, and the authorized body **adequately documented the bases for its determination concurrently** with making the determination."

Organizations should consider adopting an Executive Compensation policy and procedures to set reasonable compensation and help ensure that the organization is not susceptible to private inurement allegations. For more information on Executive Compensation Policies, see www.minnesotanonprofits.org/nonprofit-resources/management-hr#execcomp.

It is not just compensation that could convey excess benefit and be subject to the excise tax scheme under IRC Section 4958. A loan to an insider is unreasonable if the terms of the loan provide the organization with less than fair market value interest back. The amount of the loan, the rate of interest, the amount of any security, and the zealousness of the organization in securing payments on loans are factors that are examined in determining whether a loan is reasonable. For example, if an organization offers a non-interest loan or does not require the insider's signature on a loan agreement binding the insider to repay the loan, the loan is likely improper.[53] A rental arrangement may also be considered to convey excess benefit if the agreement is unreasonable. The amount of rent, the need of the organization for use of the particular property offered by the insider (versus similar property available from a non-insider at a similar or reduced rate), and the length and terms of the rental agreement are all factors to examine in determining whether the rental agreement is reasonable. For example, if an organization could rent a similar piece of property for less money or under more beneficial terms from a non-insider, the rental arrangement with the insider may be questioned.[54]

Q16. What are the legal restrictions that limit the amount of lobbying and electioneering that 501(c)(3) tax-exempt nonprofit organizations may undertake?

A16. 501(c)(3) organizations are allowed to engage in lobbying activities (i.e., attempting to influence the passage of laws) on a limited basis, that is, one that is "not substantial." Certain 501(c)(3) organizations may elect a bright-line test to measure their lobbying activities (and thus determine "insubstantiality") solely based upon actual dollars expended in favor of lobbying. That elective test, set out in Section 501(h), provides that lobbying expenditures (defined as communications that constitute "attempts to influence legislation"[55]) may not exceed a certain percentage of the organization's budget each year without the imposition of excise tax or eventual loss of exemption.

52 This inquiry is made upon the I.R.S. Form 990's Part VI, at Line 15a (with respect to the top management official) and Line 15b (with respect to all other "officers or key employees").

53 Lawrence M. Brauer & Leonard J. Henzke, Intermediate Sanctions (IRC 4958) Update, *Exempt Organizations Technical Instruction Program For FY 2003*, www.irs.gov/pub/irs-tege/eotopicc03.pdf (last visited June 28, 2017).

54 Bruce R. Hopkins, *The Legal Answer Book for Nonprofit Corporations*, 69 (John Wiley & Sons, Inc. 1st ed. 1996).

55 Treas. Reg. § 56.4911.

Election-related and voter-education activities, such as candidate debates and voter registration drives, must be conducted on a basis that does not comprise participation or intervention in candidate elections. Under that limitation, 501(c)(3) organizations are required to not even appear to support (or oppose) a candidate for elective office. The application of these rules require pure nonpartisan efforts, whereas the term "nonpartisan election efforts," when applied to other exempt categories, typically refers to neutrality. It is important to note that while non-501(c)(3)s, such as 501(c)(4) organizations, may produce voter guides that score incumbents, that activity would not meet the 501(c)(3) limit.

501(c)(3) organizations that engage in lobbying activities must report the extent of these activities to the Internal Revenue Service. If an organization's efforts are "substantial," the organization may lose its tax-exempt status and be subject to excise tax as a financial penalty. Lobbying activities of 501(c)(3) organizations are reported with one of two tests, the 501(h) expenditure test or the insubstantial part test:

- The 501(h) expenditure test provides specific dollar limits for lobbying activities based on a calculated percentage of an organization's budget, as well as definitions of and exceptions to lobbying activities that are unavailable under the insubstantial part test. Organizations may opt to come under the 501(h) test by filing Form 5768 with the IRS (be careful to retain a copy of Form 5768 after it is filed). These organizations must report every year (even if no lobbying expenditures have been incurred in the year) on IRS Form 990, Schedule C, Part II-A.
- Organizations that do not file Form 5768 are automatically subject to the less clearly defined insubstantial part test, which holds that lobbying activities can make up no substantial part of an organization's activities. As of the 2008 Form 990, these organizations report their lobbying expenditures on IRS Form 990, Schedule C, Part II-B. That Part requires the organization to provide a detailed description of the activities actually undertaken, in addition to disclosing expenditures by categories specified on the Form.

Under the 501(h) test, the IRS distinguishes between two forms of lobbying: direct lobbying and grassroots lobbying. Direct lobbying occurs generally, when an organization's representative or agent communicates with a legislator or legislative staff, or governmental officials who formulate legislation, and reflects a preference for or against a specific legislative proposal. Grassroots lobbying occurs, in general (exceptions exist), when a communication is made to third parties encouraging them to contact legislators, staff, or governmental officials regarding specific legislative proposals. Electing 501(h) organizations may use only 25 percent of their total lobbying limit for grassroots lobbying (the balance available for direct lobbying. This is a complicated area that is designed to allow 501(c)(3) organizations more leeway to effectively lobby. See Chapter 7: Lobbying, Election-related Activity and Voter Education for more information.

Q17. Can a 501(c)(3) tax-exempt organization be legally connected to a 501(c)(4), 501(c)(5) or 501(c)(6) tax-exempt organization?

A17. Yes, A 501(c)(3) organization may create an affiliated 501(c)(4) organization. (In the reverse direction, it is not uncommon for 501(c)(4), 501(c)(5), or 501(c)(6) organizations to create affiliated 501(c)(3) organizations, as addressed in the next paragraph.) The unique rules and restrictions that 501(c)(3) organizations are subject to may not be directly or indirectly subverted by such affiliations. Unlike 501(c)(3) organizations, 501(c)(4) organizations may conduct unlimited lobbying activities as long as the lobbying is related to the exempt purpose of the organization. A 501(c)(4) organization may also support or oppose political candidates, so long as such actions remain secondary to the organization's primary social welfare activities. Those activities (unlimited lobbying and any opposition or support of political candidates) are not permitted to 501(c)(3) organizations. Accordingly, if a 501(c)(3) does create an affiliated 501(c)(4), the organizations must be separately incorporated. The boards may overlap, but same should be kept to a minimum, with some assuredly independent directors on the 501(c)(3) side. Both entities must keep separate minutes. Most importantly, the organizations must keep records to demonstrate that the 501(c)(3) is not subsidizing the 501(c)(4)—the 501(c)(4) must pay for its portion of any costs the organizations share, such as staff salaries and overhead, as well as paying for its own activities.[56]

501(c)(4), 501(c)(5) or 501(c)(6) organizations may also be interested in forming related 501(c)(3) organizations. These organizations may wish to retain their own tax-exempt status while taking advantage of the benefits associated with 501(c)(3) organizations. 501(c)(3) organizations formed in such a way can accept tax-deductible donations and conduct activities at the direction of their parent non-501(c)(3) organization, but the 501(c)(3)s may only engage in qualified charitable undertakings, and their operations must provide no more than incidental private benefit to their non-501(c)(3) affiliates. For more information, see Chapter 12: Relationships with Other Entities. In either case, a tax-exempt organization interested in establishing a related organization should consult an attorney.

Q18. What is a "supporting organization?"

A18. A "supporting organization" is the name given to a type of 501(c)(3) public charity. As discussed at Question 6, all 501(c)(3) organizations are presumed to be private foundations unless they can show that they are public charities. One of the four ways to hold public charity status is to qualify as a "supporting organization." Supporting organizations are organized and operated "exclusively for the benefit of, to perform the functions of, or to carry out the purposes" of churches, educational, medical or hospital care, research or education, government supported, governmental unit, or other publicly supported organizations.[57]

A supporting organization must have one of three relationships with the supported organizations:

- Type I supporting organizations are *operated, supervised or controlled by* the supported organization (in essence, akin to a parent-subsidiary relationship).
- Type II supporting organizations are *supervised or controlled in connection with* the supported organization (in essence, akin to a brother-sister relationship with a shared controlling entity or group).
- Type III supporting organizations are *operated in connection with* the supported organization. Type III organizations are now (by Congressional action in 2006), further classified into subcategories: functionally integrated or non-functionally integrated. Under Regulations in place prior to 2006, these groups were required to meet a *responsiveness* test and an *integral part* test; those Regulations have been altered by the effected bifurcation into subcategories and the additional constraints on Type III "non-functionally integrated" supporting organizations mandated by the 2006 enactment.[58]

---

56 B. Holly Schadler, *The Connection: Strategies for Creating and Operating 501(c)(3)s, 501(c)(4)s, and Political Organizations*, 37-47, Alliance for Justice (2012), www.bolderadvocacy.org/wp-content/uploads/2012/10/The_Connection_paywall.pdf. See also Rosemary E. FEI et al., *The Rules of the Game: An Election Year Legal Guide for Nonprofit Organizations,* Alliance for Justice (2010), bolderadvocacy.org/wp-content/uploads/2012/10/Rules_of_the_Game_paywall.pdf for more information on 501(c)(3) organizations' participation with non-501(c)(3)'s that do election work.

57 *See* I.R.C. § 509(a)(3) (2006). See also I.R.C. § 170(b)(1)(A)(i)-(vi) (2015).

58 *See* I.R.S., *Section 509(a)(3) Supporting Organizations*, www.irs.gov/charities-non-profits/section-509a3-supporting-organizations (last updated Apr. 13, 2017). This site provides a central resource and summary of supporting organization types and the various requirements each organization is subject to.

This area of law is extremely complicated given both the 2006 law changes and the fact that the initiation of final and temporary regulations on Type III supporting organizations were only issued at the end of calendar 2012.[59] Organizations classified as supporting organization must each year certify upon their Form 990 both what "Type" (I-III) they qualify under, and name all their "supported organizations." Type III's have further 990 disclosures. Tax professionals knowledgeable with these areas should be consulted for guidance as to these and other ramifications.

Q19. Can a 501(c)(3) tax-exempt organization be legally connected to a PAC (political action committee)?

A19. The term "political action committee" has different meanings under federal election versus local (including State) jurisdictions. In general usage (including federal election law), it refers to organizations who are conducting political and/or electioneering activities in favor of political candidates or committees. A 501(c)(3) organization may neither create a PAC that is working to those ends, nor conduct activities in concert with such organizations. A 501(c)(4) organization affiliated with a 501(c)(3) may create a PAC that will work to those ends, but great care must be taken to firewall away from the 501(c)(3) affiliate the entirety of the goals and activities of that PAC. See Chapter 12, Relationships with Other Entities, Question 12 for more information; 501(c)(3)'s needing guidance as to sharing resources with affiliated 501(c)(4)s that conduct political and/or electioneering activities with candidates or political parties should consult tax professionals knowledgeable with these arenas.

Q20. What are the legal restrictions that private foundations must follow regarding payout requirements, grants to individuals, self-dealing and lobbying?

A20. A series of six excise taxes are in place which enforce specific requirements upon private foundations.[60] Three of these affect not only private foundation operations, but directly or indirectly affect public charity grantees:

1. In each tax year, private foundations must expend five percent of the average value of their prior year's assets for charitable purposes. If a foundation fails to do so, it must pay a tax equal to 15 percent of the undistributed amount.

2. Private foundations may not make "taxable expenditures." A taxable expenditure is money spent by a private foundation that is not consistent with the foundation's charitable purposes.

   Private foundations are generally prohibited from making grants **to individuals** for travel, study or other similar purposes, unless the process for selecting award recipients has been approved in advance by the IRS[61] and the grant qualifies as one of the following:

   - A scholarship or fellowship grant used for study at an educational institution;
   - A prize or award, where the recipient is selected from the general public; or

59 These were consummated in March 2013 by publication of Treasury Decision 9605 in Internal Revenue Bulletin 2013-11 and accompanying I.R.S. notice of withdrawal of proposed rulemaking and reliance on temporary regulations.

60 *See* I.R.S., *Life Cycle of a Private Foundation*, www.irs.gov/charities-non-profits/private-foundations/life-cycle-of-a-private-foundation (last updated Oct. 25, 2016).

61 *See* I.R.S., *Advance Approval of Grant-Making Procedures*, www.irs.gov/charities-non-profits/private-foundations/advance-approval-of-grant-making-procedures (last updated Aug. 16, 2016).

62 *See* I.R.S., *Grants to Individuals*, www.irs.gov/charities-non-profits/private-foundations/grants-to-individuals (last updated Aug. 16, 2016).

- A grant to achieve a specific objective, produce a report, or improve an artistic, literary, musical, scientific, teaching or other similar skill or talent of the recipient.[62]

The taxable expenditure rules also set out that a private foundation may make a grant to **an organization** that is NOT a 501(c)(3) public charity (or an exempt operating foundation) only if it "exercises expenditure responsibility." Expenditure responsibility involves exerting reasonable efforts and procedures to ensure that funds are used for the purpose for which they were granted through detailed reports.[63]

And finally, a variety of other operations are prohibited by being characterized as taxable expenditures. Chief among these are attempts to influence legislation. Unlike public charities, private foundations are not allowed to lobby unless they are invited to testify by a legislative body, or the result of the legislation in question would affect the organization's powers or responsibilities (lobbying in such cases is called "self-defense"). Because of this prohibition, it is also the case that in grant-making to organizations, private foundations may not earmark funds for use in lobbying (general purpose grants to a charity that engages in policy work through advocacy, lobbying and civic engagement does not violate this prohibition). In addition, private foundations may provide grant funding for a specific project that includes lobbying, as long as the grant does not exceed the project's budgeted amount for non-lobbying purposes.[64]

3. Private foundations may not engage in "self-dealing." This requirement is similar to the prohibition against "unreasonable compensation" or unfair dealings that public charities face, but here all transactions (except for reasonable compensation) are completely prohibited. Self-dealing occurs when there is a transaction between the foundation and one of its "disqualified" persons, generally someone with a special relationship to the organization, such as a director, officer, trustee, key employee or substantial contributors (along with their family members and parties connected to any of the foregoing). The intent of the excise tax is to prohibit not only unreasonable compensation, but also any lease or sale of property, loans or the provision of goods or services. If a private foundation engages in self-dealing, a tax equal to 5 percent of the amount involved in the transaction is levied against the individual. A foundation manager who participated in the prohibited transaction may also be assessed a tax if he or she participated with the knowledge that the act was self-dealing. If these initial taxes are imposed and the offense is not then corrected by the self-dealer, that individual is then subject to additional taxes (as would be foundation managers who stood in the way of the correction). There are several exceptions to the self-dealing rules. Given the inherent conflict that is behind contemplation of insider transactions, along with the adverse tax consequences in this arena, it is advisable for organizations to seek legal guidance if they are unsure of whether they are entering into a prohibited transaction.

The three remaining excise taxes are:

- Private foundations must pay out 2 percent of the foundation's net investment income.
- Private foundations cannot jeopardize investments.
- Private foundations are prohibited from excess business holdings.

63 *See* I.R.S., *Grants by Private Foundations: Expenditure Responsibility*, www.irs.gov/charities-non-profits/private-foundations/grants-by-private-foundations-expenditure-responsibility (last updated Jun. 10, 2016).

64 *See* I.R.S., *Political and Lobbying Activities – Private Foundations*, www.irs.gov/charities-non-profits/charitable-organizations/political-and-lobbying-activities-private-foundations (last updated Mar. 09, 2017).

D. State Income Tax Exemption

Q21. Is my organization automatically exempt from Minnesota's state income tax if it is exempt from federal income tax?

A21. Yes. Minnesota Statute provides that an organization exempt under Subchapter F of the Internal Revenue Code (which encompasses all 501(c) organizations) is exempt from the state's corporate (franchise) income tax.[65] Note that Minnesota does reserve the right to revoke exempt 501 status for state income tax purposes if it believes that an organization has violated the federal requirements for exemption qualification under Subchapter F of the IRC, regardless of whether the federal government has acted to revoke the federal exemption. This is rare, but could apply, for example, where the state believes that a church has engaged in impermissible political activity such that it would lose its nonprofit status if it were reviewed by the IRS.

Q22. Does an organization need to apply for and receive a state tax identification number in addition to its federal Employer Identification Number (EIN)?

A22. Each organization will need a state tax identification number to complete state payroll tax withholdings and information, forms such as 1099s. In order to apply for a state tax identification number, an organization will need to have already received a federal Employer Identification Number. An organization may apply for a federal Employer Identification Number by filing Form SS-4, available on the IRS website at www.irs.gov/pub/irs-pdf/fss4.pdf?portlet=3. You must have an EIN prior to filing your application for tax-exempt status.

Once an organization has received an EIN, it may apply for a state tax identification number on the website of the Minnesota Department of Revenue (www.revenue.state.mn.us/businesses/pages/business-registration.aspx). The organization will also need to provide the organization's name and address, names and social security numbers of the officers, and the name and email address of a contact person.

Note that a state tax identification number is not required on Form ST16, Application for Exemption from Minnesota Sales Tax.

D. Property Tax Exemption

Q23. Which types of nonprofit organizations qualify for a property tax exemption?

A23. The Minnesota State Constitution exempts real property from property tax if it is used in the following ways:

- Academy, college, university or seminary of learning
- Church, church property or house of worship
- Public hospital
- Public school
- Public property used exclusively for public purposes

65 Minn. Stat. § 290.05, subdiv. 2 (2017).

- Public burying ground
- Institution of purely public charity[66]

There is also a list of dozens of very specific organization types, such as shelters for battered women, which can be found in the Minnesota Statutes Section 272.02 (2016).

Nonprofit organizations applying as "institutions of purely public charity" generally must substantiate their claim to a tax exemption to a greater extent than organizations that claim exemption in the other categories. 501(c)(3) status alone does not guarantee property tax exemption or status as an institution of purely public charity.

Applications for exemption must be filed with the assessor in the county (or in some cases, the city) where the property is located. All applicant organizations must have a 501(c)(3) determination letter from the IRS and be exempt from federal income taxation. Additionally, all applicants must typically show that they meet each of the following factors to receive the exemption:

1. The stated purpose of the organization is to be helpful to others without immediate expectation of material reward.
2. The organization is supported by material donations, gifts or government grants for service to the public, in whole or in part.
3. A material number of recipients of the organization receive benefits or services at reduced or no cost, or the organization provides services to the public that alleviate burdens or responsibilities that would otherwise be borne by the government.
4. Any income the organization receives, including material gifts and donations, does not produce a profit that can be distributed to private interests.
5. The organization's beneficiaries are unrestricted or if restricted, the restriction has a reasonable relationship to the charitable objectives.
6. The organization does not distribute any dividends to private interests in form or substance and does not make assets available to private interests upon dissolution.[67]

An organization is generally required to satisfy all of the factors outlined above unless there is a reasonable justification for failing to meet factors 2, 3 or 5 and the organization provides the assessor with the factual basis for such reasonable justification.[68]

Once a Minnesota property tax exemption is approved under this statute, it will remain in effect unless there is a material change in facts.[69] Nonprofits must re-apply every three years, and may be asked for proof that no material changes have occurred.

Q24. How are "government grant" defined for an organization to qualify for property tax exemption?

A24. Minnesota Statute Section 272.02 subdivision 7(b) (2016) defines "government grant" as "a written instrument or electronic document defining a legal relationship between a granting agency and a grantee when the principal purpose of the relationship is to transfer cash or something of value to the grantee to support a public purpose authorized by law in a general manner instead of acquiring by professional or

66 Minn. Const. art. X § 1.; Minn. Stat. § 272.02 (2016).
67 *Id.* subdiv. 7.
68 *Id.*
69 *Id.* subdiv. 7(a).

technical contract, purchase, lease, or barter property or services for the direct benefit or use of the granting agency." This definition of government grant distinguishes between government contracts that benefit a third party member of the general public, as opposed to a direct benefit to the granting agency through a technical contract. An example of a technical contract that directly benefits the government granting agency may be a contract for technology services or office supplies. Whereas, under this definition of government grant, a per diem for a bed filled in a homeless youth shelter or Medicaid reimbursement for a person with a traumatic brain injury is a grant, as is a lump sum designated ahead of an environmental cleanup project.

Q25. What does "material" mean in terms of donations and gifts that are required as part of meeting factor 2 described above for institutions of purely public charity?

A25. The word "material" appears in factors 2, 3, and 4 of the statute that defines purely public charity for property tax exemption purposes. As former Hennepin County Assessor Tom May testified during legislative hearings in 2009, "material" is somewhere in between "some" and "substantial." Although it is not defined in Minn. Stat. § 272.02, subdivision 7 (2016) or elsewhere in Minnesota tax statute, it does have a commonly accepted legal understanding as a word used to indicate relational value and not quantitative value. Whereas the word *substantial* may have a certain threshold percentage required for the factor to be satisfied, *material* is relational to an organization's particular facts and circumstances. The Minnesota Department of Revenue issued a Bulletin to County Assessors statewide in 2010, and updated in 2012 to provide context and examples to aid in the determination of exemption application for the institutions of purely public charity law. See the Bulletin for examples of "material gifts or donations" and "a material number of recipients" at www.minnesotanonprofits.org/mcn-at-the-capitol/Property-Tax-Final-Revenue-Bulletin.pdf/. In July 2015, Minnesota Department of Revenue also published "Module #5—Exempt Property" in Minnesota Property Tax Administrator's Manual to provide types of exempt properties. This publication is available at www.revenue.state.mn.us/local_gov/prop_tax_admin/education/ptamanual_module5.pdf.

Q26. If an organization that applies for property tax exemption as an institution of purely public charity does not receive material gifts, donations or government grants, will it fail the second required factor? What is a reasonable justification for failing this factor?

A26. If an organization does not receive government grants, gifts or donations, it is likely to fail the second factor. However, if the organization has a reasonable justification on a factual basis for this failure, it can nonetheless qualify for exemption.[70]

Although the term "reasonable justification" is used elsewhere in statute, the definition of reasonable justification is not articulated in Minnesota statutes. Rather, the legal standard is commonly used in the judicial system as a threshold burden of proof. It is generally a standard that is satisfied with a fact-and circumstances-based explanation to indicate an excuse or substantiation for an action or lack of action that would be acceptable to a reasonable person.

For example, an organization on its face fails factor 2 because it does not receive material donations, gift or government grants. The organization is a 501(c)(3) nonprofit whose mission is to support emerging artists. The organization's primary revenue is generated by renting space to other 501(c)(3) nonprofit

70 Minn. Stat. § 272.02, subdiv. 7 (2016).

organizations with similar charitable missions and to emerging artists at below-market rents. The rental income is sufficient to cover the majority of the organization's operating costs, and the organization has sufficient interest income from its substantial endowment to cover the remainder of its expenses. The organization's sustainable income and operational structure fulfills its foundational purpose and mission. Because the organization is able to be sustainable without soliciting donations, it does not receive material donations during the year. In this situation, the organization would have a factual basis for its reasonable justification for failing factor 2.

Q27. How much needs to be given away for free or reduced cost for an organization to meet factor 3? What is a "material number of recipients"?

A27. The Minnesota Supreme Court held in the *Under the Rainbow* case that it is mandatory that organizations provide goods or services for free or below cost in order to receive exemption as a purely public charity.[71] This fixed rule was somewhat lightened by the legislature in 2009 when it added the ability to prove the lack of such gifts based on "reasonable cause." Neither the Minnesota Supreme Court in that case nor the legislature in the subsequent 2009 statute answered the "how much" question with a percentage of operating budget or a specific number, other than to state that the amount must be "material." As former Hennepin County Assessor Tom May testified during legislative hearings in 2009, "material" is somewhere in between "some" and "substantial." Although it is not defined in the Minn. Stat. § 272.02, subdivision 7 (2016) or elsewhere in statute, it does have a commonly accepted legal understanding as a word used to indicate relational value and not quantitative value. Whereas the word *substantial* may have a certain threshold percentage required for the factor to be satisfied, *material* is relational to an organization's particular facts and circumstances.

Many nonprofit organizations provide services and programs for free or reduced cost. Some organizations do this through scholarship programs for classes, events or daycare services. Some organizations may charge beneficiaries based on a sliding scale for medical or dental services, or even let patrons determine how much they can contribute for a performance, show or exhibit. Many organizations host free events or seminars, allow free access to museum or educational space on set days every month or provide a free space to emerging artists or other nonprofits to host events. Some organizations travel to schools or community centers to conduct free training or teach classes related to their mission. When applying for property tax exemption, consider and list and quantify the various concrete, documented ways the applying organization benefits the community for free or reduced cost.

Some organizations, such as group homes and long-term care facilities, may be prohibited from providing services for free or reduced cost. These organizations are required to charge rates set by the state and cannot deviate from them. This would be an example of organizations that may not meet factor 3 but which have a reasonable justification for failing to satisfy the requirement.

Q28. What does "profit" mean for the fourth requirement for property tax exemption as an institution of purely public charity?

A28. In the statute that defines purely public charity for property tax exemption purposes, "profit" is defined as earnings distributed to private interests. This enunciation of "profit" is based in I.R.C. § 501(c)(3) and I.R.S. Publication 557, which discusses the rules and procedures for organizations that seek recognition

71 *Under the Rainbow Child Care Ctr., Inc. v. Cty. of Goodhue*, 741 N.W.2d 880, 883 (Minn. 2007).

of exemption from federal income tax. "No part of the organization's net earnings will inure to the benefit of private shareholders or individuals."[72] A federally determined § 501(c)(3) organization generally fulfills the statute's factor 4 requirement.

Q29. Does an organization have to operate in the red, or at a loss, to satisfy factor 4?

A29. As long as surpluses and reserves are not distributed to private interests, a nonprofit will properly satisfy factor 4. In order to qualify for property tax exemption as an institution of purely public charity, among other requirements, profits produced to a Minnesota nonprofit organizations are not allowed **to be distributed** to private interests.[73] As the Minnesota Supreme Court wrote, *North Star* factor 4 (on which the bill factor 4 is modeled) is "not intended to discourage charitable institutions from engaging in financial planning with an eye toward long-term viability."[74] In fact, the *Principles and Practices for Nonprofit Excellence*, an MCN publication based on the fundamental values of quality, responsibility and accountability, advises that nonprofits should practice good fiscal management and "should work diligently to avoid recurring deficits and to secure appropriate levels of funding to carry out their missions and activities."[75]

Q30. What can an organization do if it loses its property tax exemption?

A30. If an organization loses its property tax exemptions, it has some options. The organization may ultimately appeal the exemption denial to Board of Equalization or Minnesota Tax Court. An organization may also consider contacting the Minnesota Department of Revenue to appear before a non-binding, advisory Review Board. The Review Board is made up of the Department of Revenue, the Minnesota Association of Assessing Officers and the Minnesota Council of Nonprofits. The goal of the Review Board is to help create consistency and set norms in assessment practices statewide. The Review Board began reviewing denied or questionable exemption requests, beginning in February 2010. Note that the Department of Revenue has indicated that in Revenue Notice 07-12 organizations that are denied property tax exemption will also be deemed to be taxable for sales tax purposes.

Q31. How does a nonprofit organization apply for a property tax exemption?

A31. Churches; houses of worship; property used solely for educational purposes by academies, colleges, universities or seminaries; and property owned by the state of Minnesota or any political subdivision are exempt from applying for property tax both in the Minnesota Constitution and statute,[76] so long as such property is used in the organization's mission.

Other nonprofit organizations claiming exemption from property tax must file an application for exemption with the assessor in the county (or in some cases, the city) where the property is located as an institution of purely public charity. Re-filing is required every three years for most properties. 501(c)(3) organizations who believe they qualify as institutions of purely public charity should file for property tax exemption using the Institution of Purely Public Charity Application for Property Tax Exemption, usually available through county websites. If the county follows the requirements for the standard state

72 *See* I.R.C. § 501(c)(3) (2015).
73 Minn. Stat. § 272.02, subdiv. 7 (2016).
74 *Croixdale, Inc. v. Cty. of Washington*, 726 N.W.2d 483, 485 (Minn. 2007).
75 Minnesota Council of Nonprofits, *Principles and Practices for Nonprofit Excellence*, 17 (2014), www.minnesotanonprofits.org.
76 Minn. Const. art. X § 1. See also Minn. Stat. § 272.02 (2016).

application forms, an organization must submit:

- The IRS letter granting 501(c)(3) status to the applying organization;
- The organization's Articles of Incorporation; and
- Financial statements or other documents showing total income, total expenditures and donations for the past three years. (This information may be submitted using the IRS Form 990 and accompanying schedules.)

Nonprofit organizations exempt under a different paragraph of IRC Section 501 must file using the basic Application for Property Tax Exemption, which does not require attachment of the documents listed above.

These applications may be available from the appropriate county's website. If you cannot locate the county application online, call the assessor's office to request an application for the applying organization and to determine if the application requirements in the county differ from those in the rest of the state.

Q32. Where can organizations get help with applying for a property tax exemption?

A32. Questions about the application for property tax exemption should be directed to the assessor's office of the county or city in which the property is located. Organizations may also find it helpful to look through the Minnesota Department of Revenue Bulletin to Assessors regarding the law change related to institutions of purely public charity. Also, visit the MCN website for background information on the law change and for other information.

Q33. What is a PILOT (payment in lieu of taxes)?

A33. A payment in lieu of taxes, or PILOT, may be requested from a nonprofit that has been granted a state level exemption from property taxes. PILOTs are sometimes extra-legal fees used by localities "in order to obtain revenue from private, nonprofit organizations that are currently exempt from paying property taxes" including the "suggestion" that permits or variances will not be approved unless the organization agrees to make a payment.[77]

Q34. How and when can a local government "require" a PILOT from a tax-exempt organization?

A34. Local governments may seek PILOTs of tax-exempt organization in order to recoup a portion of the cost they expend to provide services to the tax-exempt organization. For example, an organization that has been approved for an exemption in its county may be required to pay or requested to volunteer to pay a set amount or a reduced percentage of the property tax from which they are exempt in order to cover the cost of police, fire or other publicly provided services in the area. Some municipalities may conditionally approve a building permit or zoning request for a voluntary payment.

In deciding whether to make a payment, nonprofits should take into consideration public relations, civic duty/goodwill, coercion and compromise.[78] Organizations that do make PILOTs may do so because they

77 National Council of Nonprofits, *Tool Kit: Facing Challenges to Property Tax Exemptions*, 2 (2003), faculty.cbpa.drake.edu/frank/mpa_215_3754_qcgc_fall_2013/outlines_3754/part_10_taxes-challenge/property_tax_tool_kit.pdf.

78 *Id.*

are unwilling to publicly or legally contest the payment request because it would hold up a new building project, capital campaign or expansion.[79] Some organizations may refuse to make a PILOT for reasons that include:

- Nonprofit property is constitutionally not includable in the tax base.
- Most local government expenses are general and not directly in service of property.
- Nonprofit cannot afford it.
- Lost revenues diminish services that can be provided to the community.
- Donors did not intend money to be spent on taxes.
- Nonprofits provide so many other public benefits.[80]

F. Sales Tax Exemption

Q35. When can nonprofit organizations qualify for sales tax exemption on their purchases?

A35. Some nonprofit organizations are eligible for Minnesota state sales tax exemptions. In addition to churches, schools and hospitals, Minnesota grants sales tax exemption for purchases made by qualifying groups organized for charitable, religious or educational purposes and to groups formed to support senior citizens and youths.

The exemption does not apply to all purchases made by the nonprofit; for example, meals and lodging are still subject to sales tax. To apply for a Minnesota sales tax exemption, an organization must file Form ST16 with the Minnesota Department of Revenue, available at www.revenue.state.mn.us/forms_and_instructions/st16.pdf. Once a nonprofit organization has been granted an exemption from state sales tax, it must use Form ST3, Certificate of Exemption, available at www.revenue.state.mn.us/forms_and_instructions/st3.pdf, to make tax-free purchases. The nonprofit organization must give a completed Form ST3 to the seller.

The Minnesota Department of Revenue has indicated in Revenue Notice #07-12, "Sales and Use Tax—Charitable Organization Exemption—Exempt Status Revocation After Adverse Property Tax Exemption Determination,"[81] its belief that organizations whose property tax exemption is denied or revoked will also not qualify for sales tax exemption.

Q36. When can nonprofit organizations qualify for sales tax exemption on their sales?

A36. The exemption from paying sales tax, where granted, does not automatically allow the nonprofit group to sell items without collecting sales tax—it only broadly applies to purchases made by the nonprofit group.

Most sales of taxable property made by nonprofit organizations to the public are subject to sales tax, although there are some exceptions for limited sales made by qualifying organizations at fundraising

---

79 *See* Abby R. Levine & Jon Pratt, "Navigating PILOTs Increased Pressure for 'Voluntary' Nonprofit Tax Payments," 51-52 (*Nonprofit Quarterly* 2002).

80 *See* Abby R. Levine & Jon Pratt, "Navigating PILOTs Increased Pressure for 'Voluntary' Nonprofit Tax Payments," 51-52 (*Nonprofit Quarterly* 2002).

81 Minnesota Department of Revenue, Revenue Notice # 07-12: *Sales and Use Tax – Charitable Organization Exemption – Exempt Status Revocation after Adverse Property Tax Exemption Determination* (Oct. 15, 2007), www.revenue.state.mn.us/law_policy/revenue_notices/RN_07-12.pdf.

events for fundraising purposes. For the most part, these fundraising exceptions are limited to fundraising events that are carried on by nonprofits for fewer than 24 days per year[82], and do not include regular income that is earned by the organization for rents, passive income, membership dues, ticket sales or other commercial activity not meeting the definition of a "fundraising event." There are also special exemptions and limitations for sales activities and other fundraising activities by youth and senior groups. See *Nonprofit—Organizations and Fundraising Sales Tax Fact Sheet* (2016) published by Minnesota Department of Revenue at www.revenue.state.mn.us/businesses/sut/factsheets/FS180.pdf.

Q37. Why don't all nonprofit organizations qualify for a Minnesota sales tax exemption?

A37. As with property tax, not all organizations that qualify for 501(c)(3) status are granted sales tax exemption in Minnesota. The qualifications for sales tax exemption are set by state law. In Minnesota, only enumerated entities—such as schools, hospitals, churches, senior citizen groups, youth groups and groups organized for a charitable, religious or educational purpose—may apply for and receive a sales tax exemption. Although many other organizations enjoy federal tax-exempt status, those groups typically operate for the benefit of a much smaller segment of the population. For example, some of these organizations exist to collect and distribute life, sickness or retirement benefits to their members. Similarly, some organizations that are sufficiently "charitable" to meet 501(c)(3) standards may not meet Minnesota's definition of a charity for sales tax purposes.

Q38. How does a nonprofit organization apply for a sales tax exemption?

A38. To apply for a sales tax exemption, an organization must file Form ST16 with the Minnesota Department of Revenue, available at www.taxes.state.mn.us/sales/Documents/forms_st16.pdf. Organizations must include certain documents substantiating their claim to the exemption. For example, churches may include a photocopy of their IRS exemption letter, while senior citizen groups must enclose a copy of their articles and Bylaws. A complete list of the required attachments is listed on the form's instructions.

Once a nonprofit organization has been granted an exemption from state sales tax, it must use Form ST3, Certificate of Exemption to make tax-free purchases. Form ST3 is available online at www.revenue.state.mn.us/Forms_and_Instructions/st3.pdf. The nonprofit organization must give a completed Form ST3 to the seller. The seller must retain the form for their records and will not charge sales tax.

Q39. Where can organizations get help with applying for a sales tax exemption?

A39. Organizations that need help filing their Form ST16 "Application for Nonprofit Exempt Status—Sales Tax". Organizations can contact the Minnesota Department of Revenue at 612-282-5225 for more information.

82 "All nonprofit organizations – Sales from up to 24 days of fundraising events each year are exempt from sales tax." (Other requirements may apply.) See Minnesota Department of Revenue, *Nonprofit—Organizations and Fundraising*, 3 (2016), www.revenue.state.mn.us/businesses/sut/factsheets/FS180.pdf.

Q40. What types of purchases are not covered by a nonprofit organization's sales tax exemption?

A40. Nonprofit organizations cannot claim a sales tax exemption for the following purchases:

- Prepared food, candy, soft drinks, and alcoholic beverages, including catered food.
- Lodging.
- Gambling equipment and supplies.
- Purchases, leases, and rentals of most motor vehicles.
- 9.2 percent car rental tax and 5 percent car rental fee.
- Waste collection and disposal services.
- Building, construction or reconstruction materials purchased by a contractor or subcontractor as part of a lump-sum contract covering both labor and materials.
- Construction materials purchased by exempt organizations or their contractors for use in facilities that will not be primarily used by the exempt organization.[83]

Q41. If an organization is exempt from Minnesota's sales tax, how can it get a refund on the sales taxes it has inadvertently paid on purchases during the previous three and a half years?

A41. The organization must request a refund either from the seller or from the Minnesota Department of Revenue, depending on the amount requested. If the claimed refund will be for more than $500 in tax, the organization may file Form ST11-PUR with the Minnesota Department of Revenue, available at formupack.com/pdf-Forms/SalesUseTax/MN-Minnesota/SalesUseTaxMN_st11pur_20131021.pdf. If the claimed refund will be for less than $500 in tax, the claim must be made directly to the seller.

Practice Resources

Minnesota Department of Revenue published a booklet on Minnesota sales and use tax that might be helpful to nonprofit organizations. See *Sales and Use Tax Instruction Booklet*, www.revenue.state.mn.us/Forms_and_Instructions/sales_tax_booklet.pdf.

Minnesota Department of Revenue also provides additional guidance to helpful materials regarding sales tax, for example, see *Sales Tax Fact Sheet 180*, www.revenue.state.mn.us/businesses/sut/factsheets/FS180.pdf.

G. Federal and State Unemployment Tax and Payroll Taxes

Q42. Are nonprofit organizations exempt from federal unemployment tax (FUTA)?

A42. 501(c)(3) organizations are exempt from the federal unemployment tax (FUTA). Nonprofit organizations with tax-exempt status under Internal Revenue Code other than 501(c)(3) must pay FUTA tax for an employee unless the employee is paid less than $50 in a calendar year.[84]

---

83 Minn. R. 8130.6200 (2009). See also www.revenue.state.mn.us/businesses/sut/factsheets/FS180.pdf.

84 *See* I.R.S. Pub. 15-A (2017), www.irs.gov/pub/irs-pdf/p15a.pdf.

Q43. Are nonprofit organizations exempt from state unemployment tax (SUTA)?

A43. Nonprofit organizations are not exempt from the obligation to pay state unemployment tax (SUTA) for covered employees, but they may opt to reimburse the state for the actual cost of unemployment benefits used by covered employees, rather than paying a calculated unemployment tax. For more information on direct reimbursement, see Question 45.

Q44. Do nonprofit organizations have to participate in the state's unemployment compensation fund?

A44. Nonprofit organizations have two options with regard to state unemployment tax. First, they may make payments to the state's unemployment insurance fund at the rate calculated by the state on a quarterly basis. Alternately, they may opt to directly reimburse the state for only the claims benefits paid out to their former employees. For details on direct reimbursement, see Question 45.

Q45. What does it mean to be a direct reimburser?

A45. Nonprofit organizations may choose to opt out of payment of a calculated unemployment tax. Instead, these organizations directly reimburse the state for only the claims benefits paid to their former employees.

An organization may elect to become a direct reimburser within 30 days after it is determined to have covered employees. An established organization that has had covered employees for more than 30 days will be allowed to become a direct reimburser only if it has paid state unemployment taxes greater than or equal to 125 percent of the unemployment benefits used by its former employees. Any organization that elects to become a direct reimburser must make reimbursements for a minimum of 24 calendar months and will continue to be liable for reimbursements until it files a notice terminating its election.[85]

Q46. What are the legal implications of opting out of the state's unemployment insurance fund?

A46. An organization that opts out of the state's unemployment insurance fund and directly reimburses the state for benefits actually paid to former employees must retain its direct reimburser status for a minimum of 24 calendar months. If the organization wants to cancel its direct reimburser status and return to paying estimated state unemployment tax, it must give notice to the state at least 30 calendar days before the beginning of the calendar year for which the termination will be effective.

Direct reimburser organizations may face cash-flow problems when their former employees make successful claims. Organizations that anticipate cash-flow problems may choose to contribute to an unemployment insurance trust, explored in Question 46.

85 Minn Stat. § 268.053 (2016).

Q47. What is an unemployment insurance trust? How does it work?

A47. An unemployment insurance trust such as UST (www.chooseUST.org), allows an organization to become a direct reimburser while guarding against the cash-flow risks associated with direct reimbursement.

Direct reimburser organizations pay nothing until a former employee makes a successful claim, at which point they may owe thousands of dollars in unplanned expenditures. Instead, direct reimburser organizations may choose to join an unemployment insurance trust. The organization makes quarterly contributions to their trust account at a rate based on their history of employee claims. When unemployment claims are made against the organization, the trust reimburses the state.

Though functionally an unemployment insurance trust resembles quarterly payment of estimated state unemployment tax, the quarterly contribution rate paid by participating organizations is typically much lower than the state's unemployment tax rate. In addition, many unemployment insurance trusts offer services, such as the audit of all unemployment claims or the investment of excess funds, which make participation worthwhile.

Q48. Are nonprofit organizations exempt from federal and state income tax withholding from employee's wages and for FICA?

A48. No. Nonprofit organizations are generally required to withhold state and federal income tax and FICA (social security plus Medicaid) under the same rules or regulations applicable to taxable employers. Failure to comply with payroll tax compliance rules are by far the most commonly audited issues for nonprofit organizations, and organizations should not assume that "tax exempt" extends to payroll taxes.

H. Related Resources

Publications

I.R.S. Publication 557 (Jan. 2017).
www.irs.gov/pub/irs-pdf/p557.pdf

I.R.S. Publication 598 (Jan. 2017).
www.irs.gov/pub/irs-pdf/p598.pdf

I.R.S., *Life Cycle of an Exempt Organization* (Apr. 13, 2017).
www.irs.gov/charities-&-non-profits/life-cycle-of-an-exempt-organization

Statutes

Minnesota Statutes
www.revisor.mn.gov/pubs

Organizations

Internal Revenue Service
1111 Constitution Ave NW
Washington, DC 20224
www.irs.gov

LegalCORPS
1000 LaSalle Avenue, SCH 335
Minneapolis, MN 55403
legalcorps.org
Phone: 612-206-0780
Email: info@legalcorps.org

Minnesota Department of Revenue
www.revenue.state.mn.us/pages/default.aspx

Minnesota State Legislature
www.leg.state.mn.us/leg/legislators.aspx

Mitchell Hamline School of Law Self-Help Clinic
875 Summit Avenue, Saint Paul, MN 55105
mitchellhamline.edu/self-help-clinic
Phone: 651-227-9171

Propel Nonprofits
One Main Street SE, Suite 600
Minneapolis, MN 55414
www.propelnonprofits.org

University of Minnesota Law School Clinics
Walter F. Mondale Hall
229 19th Avenue South
Minneapolis, MN 55455
www.law.umn.edu/academics/experiential-learning/clinics
Phone: 612.625.1000

CHAPTER 4

CHARITABLE SOLICITATION REGISTRATION

Topics

A. Overview

The Minnesota Attorney General is the Minnesota's principal agent for oversight and law enforcement authority in the area of charity regulation. Minnesota statutes assign the Minnesota Attorney General the responsibility to register, regulate, enforce and supervise the state's charitable organizations and trusts. The Minnesota Attorney General's responsibility is to protect Minnesota donors who contribute to charitable organizations intended to benefit the community at large, to ensure that solicitations are legitimate and that funds are expended appropriately.

A charitable solicitation is an indirect or direct request for a contribution for a charitable purpose. The Minnesota Charitable Solicitation Act[1] requires nonprofit organizations that hold or solicit charitable funds to register and annually report to the Minnesota Attorney General. Each organization must register with the Minnesota Attorney General unless (1) the organization does not employ paid staff or a professional fundraiser *and* (2) the organization does not receive more than $25,000 in fiscal year contributions.[2] If an organization does employ paid staff but does not receive more than $25,000 in fiscal year contributions, the organization should register with the Minnesota Attorney General. Organizations located outside of Minnesota that raise funds in the state are also subject to this requirement. Failure to register within 30 days of receipt of total contributions over $25,000 may lead to criminal charges as a misdemeanor. Once an organization registers with the Minnesota Attorney General, it is required to submit an annual report to the Minnesota Attorney General and pay a $25 annual fee.[3] These reports are public information and are open to public inspection at the Minnesota Attorney General's Office at the 14th floor, Bremer Tower in St. Paul.

A charitable trust is property designated for a charitable purpose and use by a donor and named to the special care of a trustee. Minnesota Statutes Section 501B.33 to Section 501B.45, referred to as the Supervision of Charitable Trusts and Trustee Acts, governs charitable trusts. Specifically, it requires registration of all charitable trusts with gross assets over $25,000 within 30 days of receipt of the trust property.[4] Similar to the requirements for charitable organizations, charitable trusts require the trustee to file an annual filing with the Minnesota Attorney General and pay a $25 annual registration fee to ensure the property is managed appropriately.[5] These reports are also open to public inspection.

A professional fundraiser is a person or entity paid by a charitable organization to either solicit charitable contributions for the organization or provide consultation, advice or help planning, preparing or managing a campaign to solicit charitable contributions. All professional fundraisers must register with the Minnesota Attorney General and pay a $200 annual fee.[6] An organization's own paid employees, board members and volunteers who conduct fundraising activities do not fall within the definition of a professional fundraiser and so are not required to register with the Minnesota Attorney General. In addition to the initial registration requirement, professional fundraisers also have ongoing obligations to the Minnesota Attorney General. They must submit copies of contracts with organizations with which they work, provide notice of new clients or campaigns, report solicitation outcomes and give notice of completion of a campaign, and renew registration annually before May 1.[7] Similarly, these reports are open to public inspection.

---

1 Minn. Stat. § 309 (2016).

2 Minn. Stat. § 309.515 (2016).

3 Minn. Stat. § 309.53 (2016). See also Office of Minnesota Attorney General, *Charitable Organization Annual Report From Instructions*, www.ag.state.mn.us/charity/Forms/Char_AnnRepForm.pdf (last visited July, 2017).

4 *See* Minn. Stat. §§ 501B.36–501B.38 (2016).

5 Minn. Stat. § 501B.38 (2016).

6 *See* Minn. Stat. § 309.531 (2016). See also Office of Minnesota Attorney General, *Registration and Reporting—Professional Fundraisers*, www.ag.state.mn.us/Charity/InfoProfessionalFundRaisers.asp (last visited July, 2017).

7 Minn. Stat. § 309 (2016).

B. The Role of the Minnesota Attorney General

Q1. Why are certain charitable organizations required to register with the Minnesota Attorney General?

A1. In Minnesota, the Minnesota Attorney General has the primary responsibility for regulating, enforcing and supervising charitable organizations and charitable trusts. To help the Minnesota Attorney General with this task, the Minnesota Charitable Solicitation Act requires all organizations that hold or solicit funds for charitable purposes to both register with[8] and submit an annual report to the Minnesota Attorney General.[9]

The goal of the Minnesota Charitable Solicitation Act and its registration and reporting requirements is to ensure organizations that hold and solicit funds for charitable purposes are financially accountable to the public, and to prevent or prosecute fraud. In doing this, it ensures that prospective and current donors are informed about the use of charitable donations and protected from fraud and misrepresentation.

Q2. Where does the Minnesota Attorney General's authority for charitable oversight come from?

A2. The Minnesota Nonprofit Corporation Act[10], the Minnesota Charitable Solicitation Act, and the Minnesota Supervision of Charitable Trusts and Trustees Act give this authority to the Minnesota Attorney General. Therefore, the Office of the Minnesota Attorney General regulates charities, enforces charitable solicitation laws and supervises the management and governance of charitable organizations and charitable trusts.[11]

Practice Tip

From the Minnesota Attorney General's recent actions and compliance reports, nonprofit organizations should pay attention to these compliance issues:

Declining Governance

1. Lack of fiduciary duty. Board of directors and officers should:
    a. Ensure their active duty of honesty, with loyalty, in the best interests of the corporation, and with the care of an ordinary and good faith.
    b. Adequately monitor the management of its charitable assets and disclose the amount or percentage of its revenue expended for fundraising and overhead costs.
    c. File reports to the government and the donating public to disclose the expenditure of a charity's revenue into three basic categories: (1) fundraising; (2) management (e.g., overhead and administration, and (3) programming (e.g., funds used for a charitable purpose).
2. Some board of directors improperly monitored the financial management, including:
    a. Lack of oversight—did not maintain board meeting minutes; board meetings are not held frequently; lack of internal reviews and controls; lack of external auditing;
    b. Lack of transparency—did not disclose required information to the government and general public. (See Chapter 6: Board of Directors)

---

8 Minn. Stat. § 309.52, subdiv. 1 (2016).
9 Minn. Stat. § 309.53, subdiv. 1 (2016).
10 Minn. Stat. § 317A (2016).
11 Minn. Stat. § 317A.813, § 309.59, § 501B.38 (2016).

Practice Tip (continued)

From the Minnesota Attorney General's recent actions and compliance reports, nonprofit organizations should pay attention to these compliance issues:

Professional Fundraisers

1. Violated private benefit doctrine by using charitable funds for private business/benefit.
2. Charitable solicitations were not truthful and are misleading. For example, organizations put false advertisements on newspapers for soliciting donations.
3. Offered conflicting information to donors who ask about the percentage of their donation that will benefit charity. Did not disclose to contributors that the charitable programing is very limited in its scope and beneficiaries.
4. Provided misleading and inaccurate tax information to donors. For example, the charitable organization told donors that they can deduct on their tax return for the donations.
5. Operated as an unregistered professional fundraiser in Minnesota. (See Section E of this chapter for more information on Professional Fundraisers)

Vehicle Donations

1. Some organizations did not comply with the charitable vehicle donation process:
    a. Solicitation and donor contact;
    b. Vehicle pickup;
    c. Vehicle sale;
    d. Distribution of proceeds;
    e. Charity provides donor with written acknowledgment.
2. Some organizations improperly reported the revenue from vehicle donations as net, not gross, revenue on Form 990. (See Chapter 5: Charitable Donation Regulations, Section F on Donation of Vehicles for more information)

C. Registering as a Charitable Organization

Q3. What is the legal definition of a charitable solicitation?

A3. According to the Minnesota Charitable Solicitation Act, a charitable solicitation is a direct or indirect request for a contribution, regardless of which party initiates the conversation that indicates the contribution will be or may be used for charitable purposes.[12] Generally, whether or not a request is a charitable solicitation depends on the method used to ask for the contribution.[13] Several methods are included in the legal definition of a charitable solicitation, including verbal requests, oral requests,

12 Minn. Stat. § 309.50, subdiv. 10 (2016).
13 *Id.*

handbills and other printed advertisements and press announcements.[14] Also included is offering to sell items like advertisements, publications, tickets or other goods when the prospective buyer is told that part of the proceeds from the sale will support a charitable purpose.[15] The definition of a charitable solicitation is met when the solicitation is made, regardless of if or when a charitable donation is actually received.[16]

While Minnesota law does not yet specifically mention Internet-based solicitation methods, a joint statement released by the National Association of Attorneys General (NAAG) and National Association of State Charity Officials (NASCO) indicates that donation requests made using the Internet also fall within the legal definition of charitable solicitation. Since the legal definition of a charitable solicitation includes both direct and indirect methods, sending an email request for donations and posting the same request on the organization's website would both qualify as charitable solicitations.[17]

Q4. How do I decide if my organization registers as a charitable organization or a charitable trust?

A4. As defined by Minnesota law, a charitable organization means any person, corporation or entity that engages in solicitation of donations or contributions for a charitable purpose.[18] Unless your organization is exempt from the registration requirements, every charitable organization must register with the Minnesota Attorney General before requesting charitable donations.[19] To determine if your organization is exempt from this registration requirement, see Question 5. If an organization's main purpose is to seek donations to support or oppose a candidate for a public office, it is not a charitable organization.[20]

A charitable trust is money or property given to or held by a person or organization that is restricted to use for a charitable purpose.[21] Therefore, any organization that holds funds or other assets from an individual, a corporation, the government, a foundation or any other entity for a charitable purpose is a charitable trust. Generally, trusts are not actively seeking new contributions. If an organization is required to register and report as a charitable organization, it is not also required to register and report as a charitable trust.[22]

Q5. Who is exempt from charitable solicitation registration?

A5. Generally, all charitable organizations must register with the Minnesota Attorney General, unless they are qualified for exemptions.[23] Exempt charitable organizations include:

- Institutions that (1) do not employ paid staff or professional fundraisers *and* (2) do not receive or intend to receive more than $25,000 in total contributions during a fiscal year;[24]
- Religious organizations that are not required to file an IRS Form 990;[25]
- Certain educational institutions, which include those "under the supervision of the commissioner of education, the Board of Trustees of the Minnesota State Colleges and

14 Minn. Stat. §§ 309.50, subdiv. 10(1)-(3) (2016).
15 Minn. Stat. § 309.50, subdiv. 10(4) (2016).
16 *Id.*
17 National Association of State Charity Officials, *The Charleston Principles: On Charitable Solicitations Using the Internet* (Mar. 14, 2001), www.nasconet.org/wp-content/uploads/2011/05/Charleston-Principles-Final.pdf.
18 Minn. Stat. § 309.50, subdiv. 4 (2016).
19 Minn. Stat. § 309.52, subdiv. 1 (2016).
20 Minn. Stat. § 309.50, subdiv. 4 (2016).
21 Minn. Stat. § 501B.35, subdiv. 3 (2016)
22 Minn. Stat. § 501B.36(6) (2016).
23 Minn. Stat. § 309.515, subdiv. 1. (2016).
24 *Id.* subdiv. 1(a) (2016).
25 *Id.* subdiv. 1(b) (2016).

Universities, or the University of Minnesota or any educational institution that is accredited by the University of Minnesota or the North Central Association of Colleges and Secondary Schools, or by any other national or regional accrediting association;"[26]

- Institutions that solicit charitable donations only from their members who have rights to vote;[27]
- Organizations that solicit contributions for a named individual if all contributions are transferred to the named individual without restrictions and if no charitable deduction was given to the donors;[28] or
- Organizations that are private foundations and that did not solicit from more than 100 people during a fiscal year.[29]

The Minnesota Attorney General's office has provided the following examples to help clarify whether an organization pays staff that might trigger registration:

- Example 1: A charity paying someone to clean its offices, clear its parking lot of snow, or operate a server that hosts its website *does not* pay a person engaged in performing the organization's functions or activities.
- Example 2: By contrast, a charity paying a person to act as a board member or officer, oversee or provide its charitable programming, create its solicitations, websites, or publications providing information to donors, or engaging in other similar or equivalent conduct *does* pay a person who performs the organization's functions and activities.[30]

Q6. How do we register as a charitable organization with the Minnesota Attorney General?

A6. To register, your organization must submit these five items to the Charities Division of the Office of the Minnesota Attorney General[31]:

- The Charitable Organization Registration Statement and the Charitable Organization Annual Report Forms, which are both combined into one form, entitled "Initial Registration/Annual Report Form". The Office of the Minnesota Attorney General provides this form. To obtain a copy, download it from www.ag.state.mn.us/Charity/DownloadForms.asp;
- A copy of your organization's Articles of Incorporation;
- A copy of your organization's IRS determination letter (which the IRS sent to your organization to grant it tax-exempt status after reviewing your application for tax-exempt status);
- A copy of your organization's most recent financial statement (IRS Form 990, audited statement or any other statement that contains financial information about your organization for the most recent 12-month period immediately preceding the filing);[32]

---

26 *Id.* subdiv. 1(c) (2016).

27 The term "member" shall not include those persons who are granted a membership upon making a contribution as the result of a solicitation. *Id.* subdiv. 1(d) (2016).

28 *Id.* subdiv. 1(e) (2016).

29 *Id.* subdiv. 1(f) (2016). Additionally, although the Minnesota Statutes Section 309.515 is not directly applicable to all charitable organizations, the Minnesota Statutes Section 309.515 subdivision 1(g) provides that "[a]n auctioneer licensed and bonded under chapter 330 who is conducting a live auction who has no access to the proceeds of the auction is not subject to the registration and reporting requirements of this chapter, and is not considered a professional fundraiser for the purposes of subdivision 2."

30 *See* Office of the Minnesota Attorney General, *A Guide to Minnesota's Charities Laws*, www.ag.state.mn.us/Consumer/Publications/GuideCharityLaws.asp (last visited July 03, 2017).

31 For more information, visit www.ag.state.mn.us/Charity/Default.asp

32 Minn. Stat. §309.52, subdiv. 2 (2016).

- A list of the organization's officers, directors, trustees, and chief executive officer, including their titles, addresses, and total annual compensation paid to each; and
- An initial registration fee of $25 (made payable to the State of Minnesota).[33]

Additionally, the registration statement needs to be signed by two duly constituted officers of the organization who acknowledge that the statement is filed in accordance with a board resolution (or resolution of trustees or managing group) and that the governing body has been and will be responsible for policy and supervising the finances of the charitable organization.[34]

Practice Tip

Below are the most common errors the Office of Minnesota Attorney General sees regarding registration/annual reporting by charities:

1. Missing signatures on the acknowledgment page (i.e., Section C of the soliciting charity Initial Registration and Annual Report form). This form must be signed by two officers of the organization.
2. Failing to correctly identify the organization's officers, directors, trustees, and chief executive officer, including the total annual compensation paid to each on the soliciting charity Annual Report form.
3. For nonprofits who file a 990-EZ, 990-PF, or N-card, failing to complete some/all (as applicable) of Section B on the soliciting charity Annual Report form to provide to the Office the financial information missing as a result of the charity not filing a full 990.
4. Failing to pay the $50 late fee.

Q7. What are the consequences if my organization is not registered?

A7. Every charitable organization that is not exempt from the registration requirement must register within 30 days of when its total contributions exceed $25,000 for the current fiscal or accounting year.[35] Any person who willingly and knowingly does not comply with the registration and reporting requirements can be charged with a misdemeanor.[36]

In addition to the penalties and disciplinary actions the Minnesota Attorney General may impose for not registering, an organization could lose eligibility to receive grants or to participate in joint fundraising ventures, as foundations, lenders and prospective fundraising partners may require proof of charitable registration.

33 Minn. Stat. §309.52, subdiv. 2 (2016).
34 Minn. Stat. § 309.52, subdiv. 3 (2016).
35 Minn. Stat. § 309.52, subdiv. 1a (2016). See also Minn. Stat. § 309.515, subdiv. 1(a)(1) (2016).
36 Minn. Stat. § 309.581 (2016).

Q8. Do donors (including foundations, corporations and individuals) have a responsibility to require proof of registration with the Minnesota Attorney General's Office before they donate to an organization?

A8. Donors are not required to verify whether an organization is registered with the Minnesota Attorney General. However, the Minnesota Attorney General's Office advises donors to be informed before making a charitable contribution and know what the charity will do with the contribution.[37]

Donors should know that Minnesota law requires that they be provided with certain information from the soliciting organization. A charity is required to (1) identify itself by name and location; (2) tell the potential donor whether the contribution is tax-deductible; and (3) provide a description of the charitable program for which the solicitation campaign is being carried out.[38]

Q9. After my organization registers, what proof will it have of its registration?

A9. Once the Charitable Organization Registration Statement and supporting documents and fees (see Question 7) are filed with the Minnesota Attorney General's Office, the organization is considered registered. The organization will receive a confirmation letter from the Minnesota Attorney General's Office after submitting the Registration Statement and supporting documents. Additionally, organizations that are registered with the Minnesota Attorney General's Office can be found in the Office's online searchable database available at: www.ag.state.mn.us/Charity/CharitySearch.asp.

Q10. After our initial charitable registration, what are my organization's ongoing reporting requirements?

A10. To maintain your charitable organization's registration, your organization is required to file an annual report with the Office of the Minnesota Attorney General every year in which charitable contributions exceed $25,000 or in which paid staff are engaged in fundraising. This is due no later than the fifteenth day of the seventh month after the end of your organization's fiscal year (most often July 15 or January 15). The purpose of this annual report is to advise the Minnesota Attorney General and the public about your organization's financial status and to inform the public about your organization's charitable activities. To learn about what the annual report must include, see Question 12.

Q11. What organizations are required to file an annual report?

A11. All charitable organizations that have registered with the Office of the Minnesota Attorney General are required to file an annual report.[39]

---

37 Office of the Minnesota Attorney General, *Giving To Charities—Know the Facts, Avoid the Scams, and Other Tips on Charitable Giving*, www.ag.state.mn.us/Consumer/Publications/GivingToCharities.asp (last visited July 05, 2017).

38 Minn. Stat. § 309.556, subdiv. 1 (2016).

39 Minn. Stat. § 309.53 subdiv. 1 (2016). See also Office of the Minnesota Attorney General, *A Guide to Minnesota's Charities Laws*, www.ag.state.mn.us/Consumer/Publications/GuideCharityLaws.asp (last visited July 05, 2017).

Q12. What does a registered charitable organization need to file as its annual report?

A12. A registered charitable organization's annual report must contain the following:

- A completed initial registration form[40] and annual report form[41] (see Question 6);
- A list of the organization's board of directors;[42]
- A copy of the organization's IRS Form 990/IRS Form 990-EZ/IRS 990-N;
- A copy of your organization's audited financial statement (if it had $750,000 or more in total revenue)[43]; and
- An annual report filing fee of $25 (made payable to the State of Minnesota).[44]

Q13. Do all registered organizations need to submit annual audit financial statements?

A13. Only registered organization with $750,000 or more in total revenue need to submit an audited financial statement prepared in accordance with generally accepted accounting principles ("GAAP") to the Office of the Minnesota Attorney General as a part of its annual report.[45]

Q14. What is the deadline for filing an annual report with the Office of the Minnesota Attorney General?

A14. If an organization's books are kept on a calendar year basis (i.e., closed on December 31 of each year), then it shall file an annual report with the Minnesota Attorney General on or before July 15 of each year.[46] On the other hand, if an institution keeps its books on a fiscal year basis, then it shall file an annual report with the Minnesota Attorney General on or before the 15th day of the seventh month following the close of its fiscal year.[47]

If an organization does not meet its annual report deadline, it must pay a $50 late filing fee[48] in addition to the $25 annual report filing fee.[49]

Q15. Can our organization obtain an extension of time in which to file its annual report?

A15. Yes, an extension of up to four months is possible.[50] For an organization with a fiscal year closing date of December 31, the annual report filing deadline of July 15 can be extended to November 15. To obtain an extension, send a letter requesting an extension to the Office of the Minnesota Attorney General (see Section H: Related Resources for the address) or fill out an electronic extension request available at

---

40 Minn. Stat. § 309.52, subdiv. 1 (2016). See also Office of the Minnesota Attorney General, *Charitable Organization Initial Registration Form*, www.ag.state.mn.us/Charity/Forms/Char_InitRegForm.pdf (last visited July 05, 2017).

41 Minn. Stat. § 309.52, subdiv. 1 (2016). See also Office of the Minnesota Attorney General, *Charitable Organization Annual Report Form*, www.ag.state.mn.us/Charity/Forms/Char_AnnRepForm.pdf (last visited July 05, 2017).

42 Minn. Stat. § 309.53 subdiv. 3(i) (2016).

43 *Id.*

44 Minn. Stat. § 309.53 subdiv. 8 (2016).

45 Minn. Stat. § 309.53 subdiv. 3 (2016). See also Office of the Minnesota Attorney General, *A Guide to Minnesota's Charities Laws*, www.ag.state.mn.us/Consumer/Publications/GuideCharityLaws.asp (last visited July 05, 2017).

46 *See* Minn. Stat. § 309.53 subdiv. 1 (2016). See also Office of the Minnesota Attorney General, *A Guide to Minnesota's Charities Laws*, www.ag.state.mn.us/Consumer/Publications/GuideCharityLaws.asp (last visited July 05, 2017).

47 Minn. Stat. § 309.53, subdiv. 1 (2016).

48 Minn. Stat. § 309.53, subdiv. 2 (2016).

49 Minn. Stat. § 309.53, subdiv. 8 (2016).

50 Minn. Stat. § 309.53, subdiv. 1 (2016).

www.ag.state.mn.us/Charity/ExtensionRequest.aspx. After sending the letter, the organization may assume a four-month extension was granted unless otherwise notified. Be sure to ask for the extension before your organization's deadline or it will be required to pay the $50 late filing fee.[51]

Q16. What happens if my organization does not file an annual report after it registered?

A16. While extensions are available (see Question 16), if a registered organization does not file an annual report, its registration will be withdrawn.[52] If registration is withdrawn, the organization may not solicit contributions until its registration is reinstated. Registration will not be reinstated until all delinquent annual reports have been filed and an annual filing fee of $25 as well as a late filing fee of $50 for each delinquent year has been paid.[53]

Q17. If an organization's budget decreases so that it no longer meets the reporting threshold, does the organization need to notify the Minnesota Attorney General with a letter?

A17. An organization that pays employees or pays a professional fundraiser must continue to submit the Annual Reporting Form, regardless of whether or not charitable solicitations reach the $25,000 threshold.[54] Only organizations that do not employ paid staff *and* do not receive *and do not* plan to receive more than $25,000 in total contributions are exempt from registering with the Minnesota Attorney General's Office.[55] Once an organization is registered, it should continue to file the Annual Reporting Form. The organization does not necessarily have to notify the Minnesota Attorney General with a letter.

Q18. Does a charitable organization have to file an annual registration during a year when it dissolves, does not solicit or is dormant?

A18. See the answer to Question 17 regarding what should happen if an organization does not solicit or is dormant. If an organization dissolves, it should notify the Minnesota Attorney General prior to dissolution. Organizations holding assets for charitable purposes are generally required to give notice to the Minnesota Attorney General of an intent to dissolve, merge, consolidate, or convert, or to transfer all or substantially all of its assets.[56] If dissolving, organizations should file a "Notice of Intent to Dissolve, Merge, Consolidate, or Transfer Assets Pursuant to Minn. Stat. § 317A.811" with the Minnesota Attorney General, see www.ag.state.mn.us/Charity/Forms/NoticeOfIntentToDissolve.pdf. After filing the notice, the organization may not transfer or convey assets as part of a dissolution, merger, consolidation, and it may not convert until 45 days after it has given written notice to the attorney general, unless the Minnesota Attorney General waives all or part of the waiting period, or extends the waiting period.[57]

51 Minn. Stat. § 309.53, subdiv. 8 (2016).
52 Office of the Minnesota Attorney General, *A Guide to Minnesota's Charities Laws*, www.ag.state.mn.us/Consumer/Publications/GuideCharityLaws.asp (last visited July 05, 2017).
53 Minn. Stat. § 309.52, subdiv. 7 (2016).
54 Minn. Stat. § 309.53, subdiv. 1 (2016).
55 Minn. Stat. § 309.515, subdiv. 1(a) (2016).
56 Minn. Stat. § 317A.811 subdiv. 1(a) (2017).
57 Minn. Stat. §§ 317A. 811 subdiv. 2-3 (2017).

D. Registering as a Charitable Trust

Q19. When does an entity need to register as a charitable trust?

A19. Unless exempt from the registration requirements, each charitable trust and foundation with gross assets of $25,000 or more must register with the Office of the Minnesota Attorney General.[58] A charitable trust is created when a trustee (also known as a fiduciary) is named to exercise special care, good faith and loyalty in dealing with money or property that is designated to be used for a charitable purpose by the donor. A trustee can be an organization, an individual, a group of individuals, foundation or other legal entity who is vested with the control or responsibility of administering property held for a charitable purpose.[59]

Charitable trusts must file their registration with the Minnesota Attorney General within three months after first receiving possession or control of property authorized or required to be applied, either at present or in the future, for charitable purposes.[60]

Q20. What entities are exempt from registering as a charitable trust?

A20. Certain types of charitable trusts are exempt from the registration requirement. The Minnesota Supervision of Charitable Trusts and Trustees Act contains a comprehensive list of exempt charitable trusts. [61] The most common types of exempt charitable trusts include:

- Organizations that do not have at least $25,000 in gross assets at any time in the calendar year;[62]
- Organizations that have registered as charitable organizations with the Office of the Minnesota Attorney General;[63]
- Charitable trusts administered by the United States or an individual state, territory, or possession of the United States, the District of Columbia, the Commonwealth of Puerto Rico, or any of their agencies or subdivisions;[64]
- Religious associations established under the Minnesota Statutes Chapter 315 or 317A[65]; or
- Charitable trusts exclusively organized and operated by a religious association.[66]

For additional types of charitable trusts exempt from the registration requirement, see the Minnesota Statutes Chapter 501B Sections 501B.33 to 501B.45.

Q21. How does an entity register as a charitable trust?

A21. To register, the trustee(s) should submit the following to the Office of the Minnesota Attorney General within 90 days after the charitable trust receives the trust property:

---

58 Minn. Stat. § 501B.36 (2016). See also Minn. Stat. § 501B.37, subdiv. 2 (2016).
59 Minn. Stat. § 501B.35, subdiv. 4 (2016).
60 Minn. Stat. § 501B.37, subdiv. 2 (2016).
61 Minn. Stat. § 501B.36 (2016) (listing all the eight types of charitable trusts under the Minnesota law that are exempt from the registration requirements).
62 Minn. Stat. § 501B.36 (2015).
63 Minn. Stat. § 501B.36, subdiv. 6 (2016).
64 Minn. Stat. § 501B.36, subdiv. 1 (2016).
65 Minn. Stat. § 501B.36, subdiv. 3 (2016).
66 Minn. Stat. § 501B.36, subdiv. 2 (2016).

- A completed initial registration form. The Office of the Minnesota Attorney General provides this form. To obtain a copy, download it from www.ag.state.mn.us/Charity/Forms/Trust_InitRegForm.pdf.
- A copy of the trust's most recent federal tax return as submitted to the IRS (like the Form 990, Form 990-EZ, Form 990-N, or Form 990-PF).
- A copy of the charitable trust's Articles of Incorporation or trust instrument, including any amendments.[67]
- A $25 registration fee.[68]

Charities may register and make all required filings by email. Organizations may submit required materials to the Attorney General's Office at charity.registration@ag.state.mn.us. All materials submitted via email must be in **PDF format** and the subject line of the email **must contain the organization's legal name**. Emails not following these requirements may not be properly processed, which could result in noncompliant registration and reporting.[69]

If charities prefer, they may submit required materials by mail and pay required fees by check. Checks should be made payable to the "State of Minnesota." Required documents and payments should be mailed to the following address: Minnesota Attorney General's Office, Charities Division, 445 Minnesota Street, Suite 1200, St. Paul, MN 55101. Charities may contact the Minnesota Attorney General's Office at (651) 757-1496 or (800) 657-3787 with any questions about registration and reporting. For more registration information, please visit www.ag.state.mn.us/Charity/InfoCharitableorgandTrusts.asp.

Q22. What does a registered charitable trust need to file annually?

A22. Each charitable trust that has registered with the Office of the Minnesota Attorney General is required to submit an annual filing. Each registered charitable trust must file on an annual basis the following:

- A copy of the trust's federal tax return as submitted to the IRS (like the Form 990, Form 990-EZ, Form 990-N, or Form 990-PF).
- An annual filing fee of $25 (made payable to the "State of Minnesota").
- If the charitable trust does not file a federal tax or information return with the IRS, it must file a balance sheet and a statement of income and expense for the accounting year last completed.[70] A form that complies with the requirements is available on the Minnesota Attorney General's website at www.ag.state.mn.us/Charity/Forms/Trust_AnnRepForm.pdf.

Q23. What is the annual filing deadline for charitable trusts?

A23. The deadline is the fifteenth day of the fifth month following the close of the charitable trust's fiscal year. This deadline may be extended by up to six months by submitting a written request to the Office of the Minnesota Attorney General.[71]

---

67 Minn. Stat. § 501B.37, subdiv. 2 (2016).

68 Minn. Stat. § 501B.37, subdiv. 3 (2016).

69 Office of the Minnesota Attorney General, *Registration and Reporting - Charities and Charitable Trusts*, www.ag.state.mn.us/Charity/InfoCharitableorgandTrusts.asp (last visited July 05, 2017).

70 Minn. Stat. § 501B.38, subdiv. 1 (2016).

71 Minn. Stat. § 501B.38, subdiv. 1(a) (2016).

E. Registering as a Professional Fundraiser

Q24. How does Minnesota law define "professional fundraiser"?

A24. A professional fundraiser is paid by a charitable organization to either (1) solicit charitable contributions on its behalf, or (2) provide consultation, advice or help with the planning, preparation and managing of a campaign to solicit charitable contributions.[72] As defined by Minnesota law, paid officers, paid employees and volunteers are not professional fundraisers. In addition, while professionals like investment advisers, brokers, lawyers, accountants and bankers may provide advice about charitable contributions to their clients, they are not professional fundraisers in accordance with Minnesota law.[73]

Q25. Who needs to register as a professional fundraiser?

A25. Every entity (including individuals, businesses and corporations) that meets the definition of "professional fundraiser" as outlined in Question 25 needs to register with the Office of the Minnesota Attorney General on an annual basis.[74]

Q26. Do nonprofit staff members need to register as professional fundraisers?

A26. According to the definition of "professional fundraiser" as defined by the Minnesota Charitable Solicitation Act, paid staff members are not professional fundraisers and therefore do not need to register as professional fundraisers.[75] Volunteers and paid officers also do not need to register.[76]

Q27. What is the process for registering as a professional fundraiser?

A27. To register, all professional fundraisers must submit the following to the Office of the Minnesota Attorney General:

- A registration fee of $200.[77]
- A completed registration form called a "Professional Fundraiser Registration Statement." The Office of the Minnesota Attorney General provides this form.[78] To obtain a copy, download it from www.ag.state.mn.us/Charity/Forms/PFR_RegistrationStatement.pdf.
- A signed copy of the contract between the charitable organization and the professional fundraiser. The contract must be in writing and contain information about the services the professional fundraiser will provide to the charitable organization. In addition, it should mention if the professional fundraiser will, at any time, have custody of the solicited charitable contributions. If the professional fundraiser has contracts with more than one charitable organization or enters into any new contracts after the registration statement is submitted, a copy of the contracts with each of these organizations must be provided to the Office of the Minnesota Attorney General.[79]

---

72 Minn. Stat. § 309.50, subdiv. 6 (2016).
73 *Id.*
74 Minn. Stat. § 309.531, subdiv. 1 (2016). See also Minn. Stat. § 309.50, subdiv. 6 (2016).
75 Minn. Stat. § 309.50, subdiv. 6 (2016).
76 Office of the Minnesota Attorney General, *A Guide to Minnesota's Charities Laws*, www.ag.state.mn.us/Consumer/Publications/GuideCharityLaws.asp (last visited July 05, 2017).
77 Minn. Stat. § 309.531, subdiv. 1 (2016).
78 *Id.*
79 Minn. Stat. § 309.531, subdiv. 2(c) (2016).

If the professional fundraiser will be either directly or indirectly soliciting charitable contributions on the behalf of the charitable organization, there are several additional registration requirements. First, the contract between the charitable organization and the professional fundraiser must also disclose the percentage of the total amount solicited from each person that will be received by the charitable organization for charitable purposes.[80] Second, these additional documents must be attached to the registration statement:

- A completed solicitation notice.[81] The Office of the Minnesota Attorney General provides this form. To obtain a copy of the "Professional Fundraiser Solicitation Notice," download it from www.ag.state.mn.us/Charity/Forms/PFR_SolicitationNoticeForm.pdf.
- A post-solicitation campaign financial report for every campaign for which the professional fundraiser solicited charitable contributions in Minnesota during the previous registration year.[82] The Office of the Minnesota Attorney General provides this form. To obtain a copy of the "Professional Fundraiser Solicitation Campaign Financial Report" form, you can download it from www.ag.state.mn.us/Charity/Forms/PFR_FinancialReportForm.pdf.

If the professional fundraiser will, at any time, have custody of the solicited charitable contributions, a surety bond in the amount of $20,000 (which is effective for the full term of the registration) must also be attached to the registration statement.[83] To obtain a copy of the "Bond for Professional Fundraisers" form, you can download it from www.ag.state.mn.us/Charity/Forms/PFR_BondForm.pdf. The Office of the Minnesota Attorney General also provides a copy of "Bond Continuation Certificate for Professional Fundraisers" form at www.ag.state.mn.us/Charity/Forms/PFR_BondContinuationForm.pdf.

Q28. What is the deadline for registering as a professional fundraiser?

A28. No individual, business or corporation may act as a professional fundraiser without registering with the Office of the Minnesota Attorney General. Therefore, as soon as an entity signs a contract to solicit charitable contributions, provide advice or help with the solicitation of charitable contributions, it must register. All professional fundraiser registrations expire on April 30 each year.[84] Registrations may be renewed for one year by repeating the process for registration as described in Question 27.[85] There is an additional late fee of $300 if the materials are submitted after the April 30 due date, are incomplete, or are otherwise noncompliant.[86]

Q29. What are the ongoing registration and reporting requirements for a professional fundraiser?

A29. Professional fundraisers have several ongoing obligations to meet.

- After they register for a particular year, they must submit to the Office of the Minnesota Attorney General copies of any new contracts they enter into with a charitable organization.[87]

---

80 Minn. Stat. § 309.531, subdiv. 2(c)(3) (2016).
81 Minn. Stat. § 309.531, subdiv. 2(b) (2016).
82 Minn. Stat. § 309.531, subdiv. 4 (2016).
83 Minn. Stat. § 309.531, subdiv. 2(a) (2016).
84 Minn. Stat. § 309.531, subdiv. 1 (2016).
85 *Id.*
86 *Id.*
87 Office of the Minnesota Attorney General, *A Guide to Minnesota's Charities Laws*, www.ag.state.mn.us/Consumer/Publications/GuideCharityLaws.asp (last visited July 05, 2017).

- A "Professional Fundraiser Solicitation Notice" must be submitted to the Minnesota Attorney General each time the professional fundraiser begins to solicit for a new charitable contributions campaign.[88]
- For each completed solicitation campaign, a "Professional Fundraiser Solicitation Campaign Financial Report" needs to be completed, signed by the professional fundraiser and a representative from the charitable organization, notarized, and submitted to the Minnesota Attorney General within 90 days after the end of the campaign. If the campaign lasts more than one year, a "Professional Fundraiser Solicitation Campaign Financial Report" is due on the anniversary of its commencement. Professional fundraisers will be assessed a $300 late fee if they fail to file this report by the required date.[89]
- Every professional fundraiser's registration expires on April 30. Therefore, all professional fundraisers must renew their registration by repeating the process described in Question 27 by April 30 of each year. A $300 late fee will be assessed to each professional fundraiser that misses this deadline.[90]

Q30. Do nonprofit fundraising consultants need to register as a professional fundraiser?

A30. In general, yes. If your organization is paying your fundraising consultant to either (1) solicit charitable contributions on your organization's behalf, or (2) provide consultation, advice or help with the planning, preparing and managing a campaign to solicit charitable contributions, your fundraising consultant must register with the Office of the Minnesota Attorney General.[91]

Q31. Is there a penalty to the charitable organization if its professional fundraiser is not registered?

A31. The professional fundraiser is responsible to make sure their registration is properly filed. An organization is not likely to be penalized for the professional fundraiser's failure to register, but should make sure that it is registered as a charitable solicitor. While the burden to register is on the professional fundraiser, the Minnesota Attorney General's Office cannot verify its procedures and practice in every circumstance where this situation may arise.

F. Verifying an Organization's Ability to Solicit Donations

Q32. Where can a potential donor verify that a particular nonprofit organization is registered to solicit charitable contributions from in Minnesota?

A32. Each charitable organization that solicits charitable donations in Minnesota is required to register and file an annual report with the Office of the Minnesota Attorney General.[92] Its registration documents and annual reports are part of the public record and all public can inspect these statements.

88 Minn. Stat. § 309.531, subdiv. 2(b) (2016).
89 Minn. Stat. § 309.531, subdiv. 4 (2016).
90 Minn. Stat. § 309.531, subdiv. 1 (2016).
91 Minn. Stat. § 309.50, subdiv. 6 (2016).
92 Minn. Stat. § 309.52, subdiv. 1 (2016).

As a result, a member of the public can verify that a particular organization is registered to solicit charitable contributions and view its annual report by contacting the Charities Division of the Office of the Minnesota Attorney General. To do so, visit the office in person or contact it via mail or phone. (See Section H: Related Resources for contact information.) In addition, the Minnesota Attorney General's website has a searchable database containing the summaries of all registered charitable organizations at www.ag.state.mn.us/Charity/CharitySearch.asp.

While a charitable organization's annual report provides valuable information about its programs and services, financial management, and governance, registering with and reporting to the Minnesota Attorney General does not amount to an endorsement of the organization or its practices. Therefore, the public needs to use these statements to make their own judgments about particular organizations. There are some organizations that monitor charitable organizations on behalf of potential and current donors. See Question 34 for information on some of these organizations.

Q33. Where can a member of the public verify that a particular nonprofit organization is eligible to receive tax-deductible charitable donations as a 501(c)(3) tax-exempt organization?

A33. The Internal Revenue Service maintains an online search tool, the *Exempt Organizations Select Check* (*EO Select Check*) to search for organizations eligible to receive tax deductible charitable contributions. The *EO Select Check* is available at www.irs.gov/Charities-&-Non-Profits/Exempt-Organizations-Select-Check.

Q34. What organizations monitor charitable organizations on behalf of potential and current donors?

A34. Several organizations monitor charities on behalf of donors. The following two organizations are independent and nongovernmental. They have set certain financial, governance, disclosure and fundraising standards and evaluate charities against these standards. Each publishes reports on charities and makes these reports available to the public.

- The Charities Review Council of Minnesota has comprehensive, written reports on 600 nonprofit organizations. The reports evaluate these charities against the Council's Nonprofit Accountability Standards. In addition, it has detailed information on over 8,500 charities registered to solicit charitable donations in Minnesota. While the Charities Review Council does publish standards for charitable organizations, organizations voluntarily comply with their standards and participate in the Council's charity review process voluntarily.

- The BBB Wise Giving Alliance reports on nationally soliciting charitable organizations. This organization, affiliated with the Council of Better Business Bureaus, evaluates charities against its Standards for Charity Accountability Charitable Solicitations. Its reports are available directly from the BBB Wise Giving Alliance at give.org, or from all 129 local Better Business Bureaus in the United States.

For organizations' contact information, see Section H: Related Resources.

G. Other Registration and Notification Requirements

Q35. If my organization solicits donations from donors who live in other states, do we need to register as a charitable organization in those states?

A35. The answer to this question varies from state to state, as each state has specific reporting and registration requirements. If a nonprofit plans to raise funds in another state, it should investigate registration requirements in that state. This information is intended as a starting point to help organizations discern requirements in other states. For charitable organizations that solicit donations in many states, charitable registration may seem like a very time-consuming task. Fortunately, the National Association of Attorneys General (NAAG) and National Association of State Charity Officials (NASCO) have developed a Unified Registration Statement (URS) that can be completed, copied and submitted to the states that accept this form as a substitute for their own form.

Thirty states and the District of Columbia require registration of charitable organizations and accept the Unified Registration Statement: Alabama, Alaska, Arkansas, California, Connecticut, District of Columbia, Georgia, Hawaii, Illinois, Kansas, Kentucky, Louisiana, Maryland, Massachusetts, Michigan, Minnesota, Mississippi, Missouri, New Hampshire, New Jersey, New Mexico, New York, North Dakota, Oregon, Pennsylvania, Rhode Island, South Carolina, Tennessee, Virginia, West Virginia and Wisconsin.

Nine states require registration of charitable organizations but do not accept the Unified Registration Statement: Colorado, Florida, Maine, Nevada, North Carolina, Oklahoma, Ohio, Utah and Washington.

Eleven states do not require registration of charitable organizations: Arizona, Delaware, Idaho, Indiana, Iowa, Montana, Nebraska, South Dakota, Texas, Vermont and Wyoming.

You can get more information about the URS online or by contacting the Multi-State Filer Project. A downloadable document about the Unified Registration Statement and a copy of the forms associated with the URS is available at www.multistatefiling.org. Please note that requirements in this arena can change frequently and it is best to confirm requirements with the state(s) in which your organization will be conducting charitable solicitations.

Q36. Does the Minnesota Attorney General also monitor online solicitation of donations?

A36. Minnesota Statutes Chapter 309 on charitable solicitation applies to online donation solicitations as well. The Minnesota Attorney General's Office does not specifically monitor online solicitations, but they should be accounted for in the Annual Registration Form and the organization's financial documents. See Chapter 5: Charitable Donation Regulations, Question 40 for more information.

Also, while Minnesota law does not yet specifically mention Internet-based solicitation methods, a joint statement released by the National Association of Attorneys General (NAAG) and National Association of State Charity Officials (NASCO) indicates that donation requests made using the Internet also fall within the legal definition of charitable solicitation. Since the legal definition of a charitable solicitation includes both direct and indirect methods, it would seem both sending an email request for donations and simply posting the same request on the organization's website that is accessible to people in other states would both qualify as charitable solicitations.[93]

93 For more information on this statement, see NASCO, *The Charleston Principles: Guidelines on Charitable Solicitations Using the Internet* (March 14, 2001), www.nasconet.org/wp-content/uploads/2011/05/Charleston-Principles-Final.pdf.

Q37. Do we need to have a license to solicit donations door-to-door?

A37. The Minnesota Attorney General's Office does not require organizations to have a license for door-to-door charitable solicitations. Some Minnesota cities exempt nonprofit or charitable organizations from the requirement to obtain a solicitor's permit.[94] However, certain cities may require charitable solicitation permits. Check with the city in which the organization plans to solicit door-to-door for the city's ordinances and practices.

Q38. Are there other events that require notification to the Minnesota Attorney General?

A38. Yes, the Supervision of Charitable Trusts and Trustees Act (Minnesota Statutes Chapter 501B), the Minnesota Nonprofit Corporation Act (Minnesota Statutes Chapter 317A), the Uniform Prudent Management of Institutional Funds Act (UPMIFA, parts of Minnesota Statutes Chapter 309) and the Minnesota Limited Liability Company Act (Minnesota Statutes Chapter 322B) require notification to the Minnesota Attorney General's Office.

The Minnesota Attorney General must receive notices of court proceedings to: terminate a charitable trust, liquidate or distribute the assets of a charitable trust, modify or depart from the stated purposes of a charitable trust (including for the application of the doctrine of *cy pres*), construe the provisions of an instrument with respect to a charitable trust or review an accounting submitted by a trustee.[95]

UPMIFA requires notice to the Minnesota Attorney General if there is a court proceeding seeking to modify a restriction of a gift instrument of an institutional fund.[96]

Minnesota's nonprofit limited liability companies organized under the Minnesota Statutes Chapter 322B are required to provide the same notices to the Minnesota Attorney General as nonprofit corporations organized under the Minnesota Statutes Chapter 317A.[97] Accordingly, both nonprofit limited liability companies and nonprofit corporations are subject to giving notice to the Minnesota Attorney General of a nonprofit's intent to dissolve, merge, consolidate, or convert, or transfer all or substantially all of its assets.[98] A nonprofit may not transfer, convey or convert assets in connection with a dissolution or merger until 45 days after notice to the Minnesota Attorney General. The Minnesota Attorney General may extend this waiting period for one additional 30-day period by notifying the corporation in writing of the extension.[99]

Q39. Is there a maximum percentage of funds raised that can be spent on fundraising?

A39. There is not a maximum percentage of funds that can be spent on fundraising. In 1980, the U.S. Supreme Court held that a government-imposed limitation on fundraising and other non-charitable expenditures by an organization is constitutionally overbroad in violation of the First and Fourteenth Amendment.[100]

94 City of Chanhassen, *Permits/Licenses*, www.ci.chanhassen.mn.us/index.aspx?NID=739 (last visited July 07, 2017).
95 Minn. Stat. § 501B.41, subdiv. 2 (2016).
96 Minn. Stat. § 309.755(c) (2016).
97 Minn. Stat. § 322B.975, subdiv. 6 (2016).
98 Minn. Stat. § 317A.661, subdiv. 3 (2016). See also Minn. Stat. § 317A.811 (2017).
99 Minn. Stat. § 317A.811 (2017).
100 *Vill. of Schaumburg v. Citizens for a Better Env't*, 444 U.S. 620 (1980).

In this case, a local municipality required organizations to have permits to solicit funds door-to-door.[101] In order to receive a permit an organization was required to provide proof that at least 75 percent of the solicitation proceeds were expended directly for the charitable purpose of the organization.[102] The organization that brought the case failed the 75 percent requirement and was denied a permit.[103] The Supreme Court stated that organizations employing door-to-door canvassers that share information, answer question around issues and solicit funds to continue gathering and disseminating information about and advocate for positions on matters of public concern, "would necessarily spend more than 25 percent of their budgets on salaries and administrative expenses."[104] It reasoned that while the government may have an interest in protecting citizens from fraudulent solicitations, the 75 percent limitation was a "direct and substantial limitation on [free speech]."[105] The Court noted that a certain, arbitrary percentage limitation and concluded that any organization using more than 25 percent of its receipts on fundraising, salaries and overheard is not chartable, is fraudulent.[106]

The Charities Review Council mobilizes informed donors and accountable nonprofits for the greater good.[107] While there is no legal restriction, the Charities Review Council supports the philosophy that a "nonprofit should strive to efficiently and effectively use funds to achieve its mission."[108] This requires balancing program expenditures and building capacity and investing in infrastructure. One of its Accountability Standards is that "at least 65 percent of the nonprofit's three-year average annual expenses are used to directory support programming (ideal range is 70-90 percent)."[109]

H. Related Resources

Publications:

The Charleston Principles: Guidelines on Charitable Solicitations Using the Internet (Mar. 14, 2001), National Association of State Charity Officials.
www.nasconet.org/wp-content/uploads/2011/05/Charleston-Principles-Final.pdf.

A Guide to Minnesota's Charities Laws, Minnesota Attorney General's Office.
www.ag.state.mn.us/Consumer/Publications/GuideCharityLaws.asp (last visited July, 07, 2017).

Statutes:

Minnesota Statutes

- Chapter 309 – Regulation of Charitable Solicitations, www.revisor.mn.gov/statutes/?id=309
- Chapter 317A – Nonprofit Corporation Act, www.revisor.leg.state.mn.us/statutes/?id=317A
- Chapter 322B – Limited Liability Companies, www.revisor.leg.state.mn.us/statutes/?id=322B
- Chapter 501B – Trusts, www.revisor.leg.state.mn.us/statutes/?id=501B

101 *Id.*
102 *Vill. of Schaumburg v. Citizens for a Better Env't*, 444 U.S. 620, 624 (1980).
103 *Id.* at 620.
104 *Id.* at 635.
105 *Id.* at 636.
106 *Id.*
107 Charities Review Council Mission, smartgivers.org (last visited July 07, 2017).
108 Charities Review Council, Accountability Standards (Apr. 1, 2014), smartgivers.org/wp-content/uploads/2016/12/Accountability-Standards-2014.pdf.
109 *Id.*

Organizations:

BBB Wise Giving Alliance
www.bbb.org/us/charity
Standards for Charity Accountability

Charities Review Council
www.smartgivers.org
Nonprofit Accountability Standards

Minnesota Attorney General's Office
www.ag.state.mn.us

CHAPTER 5

CHAPTER FIVE

CHARITABLE DONATION REGULATIONS

Topics

A. Overview

In 2014, the largest source of charitable giving came from individuals at $258.51 billion, or 72% of total giving; followed by foundations ($53.97 billion/15%), bequests ($28.13 billion/8%), and corporations ($17.77 billion/5%).[1] While all gifts and donations are generally appreciated, they also may come with legal obligations, collateral implications and general requirements. This chapter provides some guidance on basic issues or questions that may arise when an organization receives various types of donations in Minnesota.

This chapter provides insight into the types of tax-deductible donations and donations that may not be deductible for the donor. Section B: Charitable Pledges, provides answers to common questions related to how to document or "substantiate" a donation through an acknowledgment letter. It provides information on recommended content for the letter and threshold amounts that trigger the acknowledgment. If an organization is gifted tangible property or receives a donation of services, certain regulations guide how value is determined for substantiation purposes. The chapter also outlines how long organizations should retain donor information and for what purposes.

Not only does an organization have an obligation to properly acknowledge or "substantiate" a donation for tax exemption and deduction purposes, but it also has certain responsibilities to funding sources. These responsibilities are largely defined by an organization's own policies, agreement with the funding source or donor, and/or perhaps commitment to an industry standard such as a "Donor's Bill of Rights".[2] Section C: Donor Substantiation Requirements, analyzes the differences between honoring donor requests and donor restrictions on funds. It also provides legal and practical guidelines to situations where an organization would consider changing the use of a donation or how to deal with restrictions on use of endowment proceeds.

Organizations receive contributions in many forms. Non-cash donations include in-kind donations of clothing and household items, time of volunteers with special skills, food, vehicles, real property, and stock. Donors may have tax incentives to donate these types of potentially valuable and major gifts, but recipient organizations need to be aware of potential tax, environmental, legal, long-term interest, and cost implications for their organization before accepting these gifts.

This chapter also answers questions related to general rules about recording and revocability of charitable pledges. Seeking or receiving planned gifts could be very beneficial to charitable organizations given their larger average size. Section G: Planned Giving Vehicles, defines planned giving and vehicles of giving and explains restrictions and the various types of bequests. Section H: Other Issues, includes helpful Minnesota-specific professional fundraising regulations and an overview of the laws that govern fundraising activity.

B. Charitable Pledges

Q1. What is a charitable pledge?

A1. A charitable pledge is an agreement made between a nonprofit organization and an individual or group, where the individual or group promises to pay the nonprofit organization a certain amount of money or give a certain item of property by a certain date or time.

1 *See* National Philanthropic Trust, *Charitable Giving Statistics*, www.nptrust.org/philanthropic-resources/charitable-giving-statistics/ (last visited July 07, 2017).

2 AFP, AHP, CASE, Giving Institute, *A Donor Bill of Rights* (2015), www.afpnet.org/files/contentdocuments/donor_bill_of_rights.pdf.

A charitable pledge may be enforceable, if the pledge is in writing or a pledge card is signed by a donor, and if the organization acts in reliance by incurring liabilities or expending money to further the purpose of the charitable mission for which the pledge was made.[3] If reliance on the pledge is not demonstrated by an organization, the pledge may not be enforceable, depending on the pledge instrument. If a pledge card or written pledge indicates that the donor's pledge is revocable by the donor, that the pledge is not intended to be binding, or that the charity is not entitled to rely on the pledge, the pledge may not be enforceable.[4] For more information on "reliance" see Question 4.

There may be practical concerns such as public relations and/or donor relations issues that arise if the charity attempts to enforce an unfulfilled pledge.[5]

Q2. How should a nonprofit organization handle a charitable pledge?

A2. An unconditional pledge should generally be recorded in an organization's financial statements in the period it is received (if the organization uses the accrual method of accounting and there is sufficient evidence of the pledge). It is recorded as revenue for the current period at the pledge's fair value. Most organizations use the accrual method of accounting, so pledges are generally recorded when received, not when paid.[6]

The pledge must be recorded as permanently restricted, temporarily restricted, or unrestricted. However, if the restriction is met within the same fiscal period as the contribution, the organization can report the pledge as an unrestricted asset as long as the organization consistently reports each period and discloses its accounting policy. A pledge of future payments is generally recorded as a restricted contribution unless the donor clearly indicates that the future payments are to support current activities. [7]

A pledge is conditional if the donor incurs no obligation to contribute until the occurrence or non-occurrence of a specified event, or if the occurrence or non-occurrence of a specified event allows the donor to recover the contribution. Conditional pledges are only recognized when the condition has been "substantially met," or when there is only a remote possibility that the condition will not be met.[8] Alternatively, they may be provisionally recorded as something temporary, such as a "refundable advance," until the pledge becomes unconditional.[9]

The organization should send the donor a written communication, or acknowledgment, upon receipt of a pledge. Because no actual contribution has yet been received, the written communication should not contain information about the tax deductibility of the future donation, but should serve as a courtesy to notify the donor of receipt of the pledge. The organization should then send another written acknowledgment upon receiving payment on the pledge, this time with information about the tax deductibility of the donation, which the donor may use for tax deductibility purposes. For more information about written acknowledgments, see Questions 5-13.

---

3 *Rochester Civic Theatre, Inc. v. Ramsay*, 368 F.2d 748 (8th Cir. 1966). See also *Albert Lea Coll. v. Brown*, 88 Minn. 524 (1903).

4 Thomas B. Lemann, *Enforceability of Charitable Pledges*, 2, Civil Law Commentaries (2009); see also Perlman & Perlman, LLP, *Legal Issues Related to Unfulfilled Charitable Pledges*, 1-2 (2008).

5 *See* Perlman & Perlman, LLP, *Legal Issues Related to Unfulfilled Charitable Pledges*, 3-4 (2008).

6 *See* Financial Accounting Standards Board, *Not-for-Profit Entities* (Topic 958) (Aug. 2016), asc.fasb.org/imageRoot/56/92564756.pdf.

7 *Id.*

8 *Id.*

9 *Id.*

Q3. How do auditors report charitable pledges on a nonprofit organization's audit?

A3. Under generally accepted accounting principles (GAAP), auditors must report unconditional charitable pledges at their fair value. To do this, auditors discount the future value that will be received in order to determine the present value. If the pledge is expected to be received in less than one year, it is generally valued at its net amount. A conditional pledge is not recorded until the condition has been "substantially met," or when there is only a remote possibility that the condition will not be met.[10]

Q4. What rights does a nonprofit organization have if its donors decide not to honor their charitable pledges?

A4. If the nonprofit organization has not demonstrated any sort of reliance upon the contribution, then the nonprofit organization may not have grounds to enforce the pledge.[11]

If the nonprofit organization has demonstrated reliance, such as beginning a building project, there may be grounds to enforce the promise.[12] Such reliance may be shown by the nonprofit organization beginning a large new project or purchasing new equipment, by using the pledge to induce others to make their own donations, or by the nonprofit organization taking steps to meet requirements made by the individual making the charitable pledge.[13]

If reliance has been demonstrated, then the nonprofit organization may have grounds for arguing that the pledge should be enforceable. However, no such reliance is enough to make a pledge enforceable if there is a clear, unambiguous statement included in the pledge that the pledge will be revocable by the donor and is not binding. See Question 1.

C. Donor Substantiation Requirements

Q5. Is a nonprofit organization required to provide a written acknowledgment every time it receives a donation?

A5. The Internal Revenue Services (IRS) imposes recordkeeping and substantiation rules on donors of charitable contributions and disclosure rules on charities that receive contributions.[14] A donor must have a bank record or written communication from a charity for any monetary contribution before the donor can claim a charitable contribution on their federal income tax return.[15] Moreover, a donor is responsible for obtaining a written acknowledgment from a charity for any single contribution of $250 or more before the donor can claim a charitable contribution on their federal income tax return.[16]

10 Financial Accounting Standards Board, *Not-for-Profit Entities* (Topic 958) (Aug. 2016), asc.fasb.org/imageRoot/56/92564756.pdf.

11 Perlman & Perlman, LLP, *Legal Issues Related to Unfulfilled Charitable Pledges,* 1-2 (2008), www.afpnet.org/files/ContentDocuments/Legal%20Issues%20Related%20to%20Unfulfilled%20%20Charitable%20Pledges%2012.08_1252781066437_3.pdf.

12 *Rochester Civic Theatre, Inc. v. Ramsay*, 368 F.2d 748 (8th Cir. 1966).

13 *Albert Lea Coll. v. Brown*, 88 Minn. 524 (1903). See also In re ESTATE OF STACK, 164 Minn. 57 (1925).

14 *See* I.R.S. Pub. 1771 (2016), www.irs.gov/pub/irs-pdf/p1771.pdf.

15 *Id.* at 1.

16 *Id.*

Q6. ***Is there exact language a nonprofit organization should use to substantiate a donor's contribution in its written acknowledgment?***

A6. When a donation acknowledgment letter is provided to a donor by a charitable organization, IRS Publication 1771 explains that the written acknowledgment should contain the following:

- The name of the organization.
- The amount of any cash contribution, and a description of any non-cash contribution.
- Either: (a) a statement that no goods or services were provided by the organization in exchange for the contribution; (b) a description and good faith estimate of the value of goods or services the organization provided in return for the contribution; or (c) a statement that goods or services an organization provided in return for the contribution consisted entirely of intangible religious benefits.

Intangible religious benefits are described as benefits provided by a tax-exempt organization operated exclusively for religious purposes, and are not usually sold in commercial transactions outside a donation context, such as admission to a religious ceremony and an insubstantial or *de minimus* tangible benefit like wine used in a religious ceremony.[17]

Q7. ***Under what circumstance does a nonprofit organization need to provide a donor with a written disclosure regarding goods and services provided to the donor in exchange for a charitable contribution?***

A7. A nonprofit organization is required to provide a written disclosure to a donor when the nonprofit organization provides goods or services to the donor in exchange for a charitable contribution exceeding a gift of $75 of more.[18] This is called a *quid pro quo*[19] contribution.

For *quid pro quo* contributions, the written disclosure should contain at least the following:

- A statement that the amount of the contribution that is deductible for federal income tax purposes is limited to the excess of the amount of money (and the fair market value of property other than money) contributed over the value of the goods and services provided by the nonprofit organization.
- A good faith estimate of the value of the goods or services provided by the nonprofit organization.[20]

A penalty is imposed on charities that do not meet the written disclosure requirement when receiving *quid pro quo* contributions. The penalty is $10 per contribution, not to exceed $5,000 per fundraising event or mailing. An organization may avoid the penalty if it can show that failure to meet the requirements was due to reasonable cause.[21]

17 *Id.* at 7-8.

18 *See* I.R.C. § 6115(a)(1)-(2) (2017); see also I.R.S. Pub. 1771 at 10 (2016), www.irs.gov/pub/irs-pdf/p1771.pdf.

19 In plain English, "quid pro quo" means "something for something", i.e. an action or thing that is exchanged for another action

20 *See* I.R.C. § 6115(a)(2) (2017); see also I.R.S. Pub. 1771 at 3 (2016), www.irs.gov/pub/irs-pdf/p1771.pdf.

21 For more information, see I.R.S., *Charitable Contributions—Quid Pro Quo Contributions* (Apr. 2017), www.irs.gov/charities-non-profits/charitable-organizations/charitable-contributions-quid-pro-quo-contributions.

Goods and services having an "insubstantial" value are excluded from the written disclosure requirement. Based on the Token Exception:

- Goods and services are considered insubstantial if they occur in the context of a fundraising campaign where the donor is informed how much of their donation is deductible as a charitable contribution, and either: the fair market value of the benefit received does not exceed the lesser of 2 percent of the contribution or $106.00, or
- The payment is at least $53.00, the only benefits provided are token items bearing the organization's name or logo (e.g. calendars, mugs, or posters), and the cost of these token items is equal to or less than $10.60.[22]

Q8. How does a nonprofit organization make a good faith estimate of the value of the goods and services provided for purposes of determining which portion of a donation is tax-deductible?

A8. A good faith estimate is an estimate of the fair market value of the goods and services provided by the organization. The organization may use any reasonable method in making the good faith estimate.

Q9. What information should a nonprofit organization provide to its donors about the tax deductibility of their donations?

A9. Donations are only deductible when the contribution is actually paid. In most cases, a donation is paid when the donor mails a check, delivers a piece of property, delivers a deed, or when a donor's bank or credit card account is charged. A promise or a pledge is not deductible until the donor follows through with the donation; therefore, a pledge made on December 31, 2015, but not paid until January 1, 2016, is not deductible in the year 2015.[23]

Donors are allowed to deduct the difference between the value of the amount contributed and the value of the goods and services received in return from the nonprofit organization. Therefore, the values of goods or services provided by the nonprofit organization (benefits given to a donor such as free admission, CD's, etc.) may impact the tax deductibility of a donor's gift. Nonprofit organizations are required to inform the donor that their tax deduction is less than their total contribution whenever the goods and services received by the donor cannot be disregarded.

A separate donation acknowledgment may be provided for each single contribution exceeding the threshold, or one donation acknowledgment (such as an annual summary) may be used to substantiate several single contributions exceeding the threshold. There is no IRS form for the acknowledgment. Organization-designed letters, postcards, or forms with the IRS-required information are all acceptable. Charities sending written acknowledgments to donors must do so "contemporaneously" with the receipt of the donation, but no later than January 31 of the year following the donation.

---

22 *See* I.R.S. Pub. 1771 at 5-6 (2016), www.irs.gov/pub/irs-pdf/p1771.pdf (Note that these dollar amounts are for 2016. Guideline amounts are adjusted for inflation. See IRS.gov for annual inflation adjustment information).

23 *Id.*

Q10. What does a nonprofit organization need to tell its donors about the value of the goods or services their donors purchase at events such as an auction or silent auction fundraiser?

A10. Typically, goods or services received through auction fundraisers are not deductible. In order to receive a deduction, the buyer must demonstrate that:

- The purchase price exceeded the fair market value;
- The buyer knew that before making the purchase; and
- The buyer intended to make a charitable contribution.

The organization should not send an acknowledgment stating that the amount paid is a charitable contribution.

Q11. What records does a nonprofit organization need to maintain on its donors and donations?

A11. Organizations should retain records relating to all income and expenses in order to substantiate the information submitted on the organization's annual IRS Form 990, to prove its eligibility for tax-exempt status, and to comply with grant-making procedures, in case any are called into question. [24] Organizations should document the amount and content of each contribution, the date it was received, and the donor who made it.[25]

Each contribution should be recorded for accounting purposes in one of three categories – unrestricted, temporarily restricted, or permanently restricted. Unrestricted funds are monies "free from external restrictions and available for general use."[26] Temporarily restricted funds have a donor-imposed restriction, generally a "time" restriction or a "purpose" restriction, which does not last into perpetuity.[27] Permanently restricted funds have a donor-imposed restriction, either for a designated purpose or time, that continues in perpetuity.[28] If the contribution is restricted, the organization should record the nature of the restriction, and if the restriction is temporary, the organization should also record when the donor-imposed condition will cease or be satisfied. Additionally, the conversion from restricted to unrestricted will produce a change on the organization's financial statements.[29] For more information on the management of restricted funds and accounting requirements with illustrative examples, see *Managing Restricted Funds*, a resource article authored by the Propel Nonprofits at www.propelnonprofits.org.

Moreover, when a donor receives goods or services in exchange for the contribution, and the organization provides an estimate of the value of the goods and services, the organization should retain records of what methods were used to determine the estimated value. See Question 7 regarding *quid pro quo* contributions.

24 *See* I.R.S. Pub. 4221 PC at 17-19 (2014), www.irs.gov/pub/irs-pdf/p4221pc.pdf.
25 *Id.* at 20
26 Propel Nonprofits, *Managing Restricted Funds*, 1 (2014).
27 *Id.*
28 *Id.*
29 *Id.*

Q12. What information does a tax-exempt nonprofit organization need to provide to its donors if the organization is not eligible to receive tax-deductible contributions, such as not having 501(c)(3) or (c)(17) status?

A12. If the organization is not eligible to receive tax-deductible donations, solicitations on behalf of that organization must contain an express and easily recognizable statement that donations are not deductible as charitable contributions for federal income tax purposes. While a good faith effort to meet the foregoing will suffice, the IRS has provided safe harbor rules for complying with this requirement.30

To meet the safe harbor in a written solicitation, the statement must:

- Be in at least the same size type as the primary message and readily visible.
- Be on the same page, and in close proximity to, the request for donations.
- Be the first sentence of a paragraph, or constitute the entire paragraph.
- Be worded as one of the following:
    1. "Contributions or gifts to [name of organization] are not tax deductible as charitable contributions for Federal income tax purposes."
    2. "Contributions or gifts to [name of organization] are not tax deductible."
    3. "Contributions or gifts to [name of organization] are not tax deductible as charitable contributions."

To meet the safe harbor in an oral solicitation, this statement must be made in close proximity to the request for contributions, during the same conversation or telephone call and by the same solicitor. The statement must also be worded as one of the options listed above. If a person pledges a donation during the solicitation, any written confirmation or bill sent to the donor must meet the requirements of a written solicitation as listed above.

To meet the safe harbor in a televised solicitation, a spoken statement must be in close proximity to the request for contributions. If the statement appears on the screen, it must be in large and easily readable type, and appear for at least five seconds. The statement must also be worded as one of the options listed above.

To meet the safe harbor in a radio solicitation, the statement must be made in close proximity to the request for contributions, during the same solicitation announcement, and worded as one of the options listed above.

Federal exceptions. Organizations whose annual gross receipts do not normally exceed $100,000 or that solicit only to tax-exempt organizations are exempt from this requirement. Also, solicitations that are not part of a fundraising campaign soliciting more than ten people during the calendar year are exempt.[31]

Minnesota has similar statutory requirements related to charitable solicitation, prohibition of deceptive and misleading fundraising practices, and enforcement by the state attorney general's office.[32] See Questions 34, 36, 37, and 39.

30 *See* I.R.S. Notice 88-120, 1988-2 C.B. 454 (Nov. 25, 1988). See also I.R.C. § 6113(a) (2017).
31 *See* I.R.S. Notice 88-120, 1988-2 C.B. 454 (Nov. 25, 1988).
32 Minn. Stat. § 309 (2016).

Q13. Can a nonprofit organization rely on its advance letter ruling from the IRS when it is fundraising? That is, is this advance ruling sufficient documentation of tax deductibility for donors?

A13. Yes, an advance letter ruling recognizing exempt status under the IRC Section 501(c)(3) is sufficient documentation of charitable donee status. An advance letter ruling is essentially the same as a determination letter, but is issued prior to operations.

Donors may rely on the advance letter ruling or a determination letter as long as it has not been revoked by the IRS, and organizations should maintain a copy at all times. Organizations may request a copy of their determination letter by contacting the IRS at 1-877-829-5500, and can check the state of their (or another organization's) 501(c)(3) tax exempt status by visiting www.irs.gov/charities-non-profits/exempt-organizations-select-check.

D. Responsibilities to Funding Sources

Q14. What is the "Donor Bill of Rights"? Is it legally binding?

A14. The Donor Bill of Rights[33] is a voluntary pledge and industry standard developed by various philanthropic and fundraising organizations, and has been adopted by a number of prominent nonprofit organizations. It reads as follows:

> "Philanthropy is based on voluntary action for the common good. It is a tradition of giving and sharing that is primary to the quality of life. To assure that philanthropy merits the respect and trust of the general public, and that donors and prospective donors can have full confidence in the not-for-profit organizations and causes they are asked to support, we declare that all donors have these rights:
>
> 1. To be informed of the organization's mission, of the way the organization intends to use donated resources, and of its capacity to use donations effectively for their intended purposes.
> 2. To be informed of the identity of those serving on the organization's governing board, and to expect the board to exercise prudent judgment in its stewardship responsibilities.
> 3. To have access to the organization's most recent financial statements.
> 4. To be assured their gifts will be used for the purposes for which they were given.
> 5. To receive appropriate acknowledgment and recognition.
> 6. To be assured that information about their donation is handled with respect and with confidentiality to the extent provided by law.
> 7. To expect that all relationships with individuals representing organizations of interest to the donor will be professional in nature.
> 8. To be informed whether those seeking donations are volunteers, employees of the organization or hired solicitors.
> 9. To have the opportunity for their names to be deleted from mailing lists that an organization may intend to share.
> 10. To feel free to ask questions when making a donation and to receive prompt, truthful and forthright answers."

33 AFP, AHP, CASE, Giving Institute, *A Donor Bill of Rights* (2015), www.afpnet.org/files/contentdocuments/donor_bill_of_rights.pdf.

The Donor Bill of Rights is not legally binding, but adopting it may provide a nonprofit organization's donors an extra sense of comfort.

Q15. Does a nonprofit organization need to honor an individual donor's request for the use of their donation?

A15. No, if it's an oral restriction. If the gift is not restricted in writing, or the oral restriction is not documented in some other form such as tape recordings, written contemporaneous registers, or written follow-up confirmations, as a general rule, an organization is not legally obligated to honor an individual donor's request. As a "gift," the organization's Board of Directors must have the exclusive right to determine how to use the contribution. However, there are some potential consequences to the organization (and potential recourse for the donor) should the charity decide not to honor a donor's oral restriction(s). If the gift or pledge is oral, the donor may simply decide not to fulfill the gift or to honor the pledge. In some trusts, the donor may retain the right to substitute the beneficiary charity at any time. This gives donors the opportunity to essentially take the gift away from an organization that fails to honor a request.[34] Furthermore, the donor may discontinue any future support from the organization and find a new organization to fund. In addition, Minnesota law requires that organizations use gifts in accordance with the restrictions placed by the donor, if such restriction does not threaten the tax deductibility of the donation.

Yes, if it's in writing. This general rule discussed above does not apply where the donor places written restrictions on the donation or pledge. If a donor in a written gift instrument or pledge restricts a gift, and if the organization accepts the gift, an organization must honor the individual's request. Note that some organizations have gift acceptance policies that determine situations and processes for declining acceptance of a gift, in which case they are not obligated to honor the donor's restriction. The shape and form of restrictions should be defined in the "gift instrument." The gift instrument is a record or document, including an institutional solicitation that establishes the use of the donated funds and under which funds or property is "granted to, transferred to or held" by an organization.[35] The statutory definition is intended to clarify that the "only legally binding restrictions on a gift are those that are set forth in writing."[36] Examples of legally binding gift instruments include award letters from foundations and letters from individual donors that clearly describe, in writing, the restriction on use of funds. For more information, see *Uniform Prudent Management of Institutional Funds Act* (2006), at www.uniformlaws.org.

An organization should consult legal counsel if a question exists as to whether a contribution is restricted or unrestricted.

Q16. Can an organization change the use of a donation that was given with a specified purpose? If so, how is this done?

A16. An organization may release or modify a restriction with recorded consent from the donor. If donor consent is impossible due to death, disability, anonymity, or unavailability, the organization must seek permission from the District Court to remove or relax the restrictions.[37] Additionally, if the fund is small

34 Rev. Rul. 76-8, 1976-1 C.B. 179, www.pgdc.com/pgdc/story/rev-rul-76-8; see also Rev. Rul. 76-7, 1976-1 C.B. 179, www.pgdc.com/pgdc/story/rev-rul-76-7.

35 Minn. Stat. § 309.735(3) (2016); see also Propel Nonprofits, *Managing Restricted Funds*, 1 (2014).

36 *See* Uniform Prudent Management of Institutional Funds Act, § 2 cmt. (Unif. Law Comm'n 2006).

37 Minn. Stat. § 309.755 (2016).

enough (less than $50,000), and the organization uses the fund in a manner consistent with the charitable purpose expressed and if the gift instrument was established more than twenty years ago, Minnesota law allows an organization to modify restrictions that have become unlawful, impracticable, impossible, or wasteful with sixty-day notification to the Attorney General.[38]

An organization should consult legal counsel if it desires to revise or modify a restriction on donated funds.

Q17. What are the legal restrictions placed on the use of a donation that a donor earmarked for an endowment?

A17. The Uniform Prudent Management of Institutional Funds Act (UPMIFA) is codified in the Minnesota Statutes Section 309.73 to 309.77 (2016). UPMIFA eliminated the prohibition of using the principal amount of an endowment (often referred to as the historical dollar amount) in the repealed Minnesota Statutes Section 309.63 (2008).[39] Under current Minnesota law, the person responsible for managing and investing an endowment fund is required to do so in "good faith and with the care an ordinarily prudent person in a like position would exercise under similar circumstances." [40] This person must consider the following factors, when relevant:

- The duration and preservation of the fund;
- The purposes of the fund and institution;
- General economic conditions;
- The possible effect of inflation or deflation;
- Expected investment returns;
- Other resources of the institution; and
- The investment policy of the institution.[41]

Organizations should have endowment policies that incorporate UPMIFA's factors and specifically articulate the Board of Directors' sound plans regarding endowment usage.

Endowments may be temporary or permanent. The income received on the endowment may or may not be restricted, depending on donor specifications. However, restrictions on the use of such income must be explicit.[42]

Donor consent must be received to eliminate an endowment restriction. While consent from the district court may be obtained to eliminate other restrictions when donor consent is impossible, the same is not true regarding endowments. Court consent cannot be acquired to turn endowment funds into non-endowment funds.[43]

---

38 Minn. Stat. § 309.755(c) (2016).

39 Gina Kastel, *Minnesota Adopts Model Charitable Endowment and Investment Law* (Apr. 11, 2008), www.faegrebd.com/minnesta-adopts-model-charitable-endowment-and-investment-law.

40 Minn. Stat. § 309.74(b) (2016); see also Minn. Stat. § 309.745(a) (2016).

41 Minn. Stat. § 309.74(e) (2016); see also Minn. Stat. § 309.745(a) (2016). See also Gina Kastel, *Minnesota Adopts Model Charitable Endowment and Investment Law* (Apr. 11, 2008), www.faegrebd.com/minnesota-adopts-model-charitable-endowment-and-investment-law.

42 Minn. Stat. § 309.74 (2015). See also Minn. Stat. § 309.745 (2016).

43 Minn. Stat. § 309.745 (2016).

Q18. When should a nonprofit organization report budget changes to funding sources such as foundations and corporations?

A18. Foundations and corporations often make contributions subject to applicant requests or restrictions, specifying how the contribution shall be used. If the organization wishes to amend this purpose or reallocate funds, the funder must be consulted prior to any change occurring. If the contribution comes with restrictions, organizations are legally obligated to obtain permission to divert the funds elsewhere. If the contribution is made with requests, the organization may not be obligated to obtain permission, but it is generally a good idea to do so. See Question 15 for more information on the legal obligations imposed by donor restrictions.

If a funder does not attach restrictions or requests, it may nonetheless be advantageous to report where the contribution was used, or changes to the initial allocation. Open communication between the organization and the funder fosters a good working relationship, confidence in the organization's activities, and a path toward future allocations.

E. In-kind Donations

Q19. What is an in-kind donation?

A19. An in-kind donation typically comes in the form of goods or services from donors, not cash. Examples of in-kind donations include corporations providing bottled water or protective equipment to nonprofit organizations engaging in disaster relief, individuals providing school supplies to nonprofit organizations that serve at-risk youth, or works of art given to a museum.

Q20. What documentation does a nonprofit organization need to provide to its donors when acknowledging an in-kind donation?

A20. Nonprofit organizations should provide donors who give in-kind donations a receipt similar to one provided to an individual who gives a cash donation. The only difference is that the nonprofit organization is not expected to list the actual value of the in-kind donation. However, it is important to describe what was donated. For example, "Thank you for your contribution of a used oak baby crib and matching dresser that Charity received on May 6, 2013. No goods or services were provided in exchange for your contribution."[44] See Question 5 for more information regarding acknowledgments.

Q21. Who is responsible for quantifying the value of an in-kind donation – the donor or the recipient organization?

A21. The donor is responsible for valuing the goods or services provided in non-cash contributions and reporting that amount on their own tax return if they are seeking a charitable deduction.[45]

44 *See* I.R.S. Pub. 1771 (2016), www.irs.gov/pub/irs-pdf/p1771.pdf.
45 *Id.*

Q22. Can a donor deduct the value of a donation of time or services?

A22. A donor cannot deduct the value of their time or services; however, they may be able to deduct the cost of the out-of-pocket expenses. See I.R.S. Publication 526 (2016), available at www.irs.gov/pub/irs-pdf/p526.pdf for deductibility rules regarding out-of-pocket expenses. Although nonprofit organizations cannot deduct the value of a donation of time or services, organizations can report calculation of time or services in grants reports, annual reports, or for marketing purposes. For example, the estimated value of volunteer time for 2016 is $24.14 per hour.[46]

F. Donations of Vehicles, Land, Buildings and Stock

Q23. Someone wants to donate a vehicle to our organization. What are the legal ramifications of accepting a vehicle as a donation?

A23. In 2005, federal laws changed regarding vehicle donations. A nonprofit organization's tax-exempt status should not be affected if the organization:

- Sells the donated vehicle and uses the proceeds exclusively to fund its charitable programs; or
- Regularly uses the vehicle for a significant period of time to conduct activities that substantially further its charitable programs; or
- Sells the vehicle after it makes a material improvement to the vehicle and then uses the proceeds to exclusively further its charitable programs; or
- Distributes the vehicle at a price significantly below fair market value to needy individuals in direct furtherance of the organization's charitable purpose of relieving the poor and distressed or the underprivileged who are in need of a means of transportation.[47]

Penalties exist for nonprofit organizations who knowingly furnish donors with false or fraudulent acknowledgments, or for knowingly failing to furnish acknowledgments with required information.

Q24. What is the procedure a nonprofit organization should use to accept the donation of a vehicle?

A24. The procedure a nonprofit should adopt for acceptance of a vehicle donation depends on how an organization plans to use the donation. The IRS Publication 4302 outlines requirements for written acknowledgments for various types and uses of vehicle donations.[48] The following is a summary of the written acknowledgment requirements for each type of donation and subsequent use by a tax-exempt organization.

If the vehicle is worth not more than $500, but at least $250, then the nonprofit organization should follow the same procedures as outlined in Question 2. If the vehicle is worth more than $500, then the nonprofit organization must furnish a contemporaneous written acknowledgment and report the information contained in such acknowledgment to the IRS on Form 1098-C. The contemporaneous written acknowledgment must contain the following:

46 Latest figure from 2016 Bureau of Labor Statistics data, indexed by Independent Sector in April 2017. See "The Value of Volunteer Time," www.independentsector.org/resource/the-value-of-volunteer-time/ (last visited July 17, 2017).

47 *See* I.R.S. Pub. 4302 at 2 (2015), www.irs.gov/pub/irs-pdf/p4302.pdf.

48 *See* I.R.S. Pub. 4302 (2015), www.irs.gov/pub/irs-pdf/p4302.pdf.

- Information on what the nonprofit organization did, or plans to do, with the vehicle;
- The donor's name and taxpayer identification number;
- The vehicle identification number (VIN);
- The date of the contribution, and one (1) of the following:
  a) A statement that no goods or services were provided by the charity in return for the donation, if that was the case;
  b) A description and good faith estimate of the value of the goods or services, if any, that the charity provided in return for the donation (for *quid pro quo* contributions); or
  c) A statement that goods or services provided by the charity consisted entirely of intangible religious benefits, if that was the case.

Vehicle Sale. If the nonprofit organization sells the vehicle for more than $500, the written acknowledgment must also include:

- A statement certifying that the vehicle was sold in an arm's length transaction between unrelated parties. An arm's length transaction occurs when the both parties come to an agreement, or a buyer and seller act independently, according to their respective self-interest;
- The date the vehicle was sold;
- The gross proceeds received from the sale; and
- A statement that the donor's deduction may not exceed the gross proceeds from the sale.

Significant Intervening Use. Significant intervening use by an organization is when a charitable organization actually uses the vehicle to "substantially further its regularly conducted activities." Whether a use qualifies as a significant intervening use depends on its nature, extent, frequency, and duration.

If the nonprofit organization intends to make a significant intervening use of the vehicle, in addition to the information required for all acknowledgments, the contemporaneous written acknowledgment must include:

- A statement certifying that the charity intends to make a significant intervening use of the donated vehicle;
- A detailed statement describing the intended use;
- A detailed statement of the duration of that use; and
- A certification that the vehicle will not be sold before completion of the use.

Material Improvement. A material improvement of a donated vehicle includes a major repair or improvement that results in a significant increase to the vehicle's value. Cleaning, minor repairs, and routine maintenance do not qualify as material improvements.

If the nonprofit organization intends to make a material improvement to the vehicle, in addition to the information required for all acknowledgments, the contemporaneous written acknowledgment must include:

- A statement that the charity intends to make a material improvement to the donated vehicle;
- A detailed description of the intended material improvement; and
- A certification that the vehicle will not be sold before completion of the improvement.

Means of transportation for charity beneficiaries. If the nonprofit organization, whose purpose is relieving the poor and distressed or the underprivileged who are in need of a means of transportation, intends to give or sell the vehicle to a needy individual at a price significantly below fair market value, in addition to the information required for all acknowledgments, the acknowledgment must certify:

- That the charity intends to give or sell the vehicle to a needy individual at a price significantly below fair market value; and
- That the gift or sale is in direct furtherance of the charity's charitable purpose of relieving the poor and distressed or the underprivileged who are in need of a means of transportation.

For more information regarding accepting vehicle donations, see I.R.S. Publication 4302: *A Charity's Guide to Vehicle Donations* (2015), available at www.irs.gov/pub/irs-pdf/p4302.pdf.

Q25. Someone wants to donate land or a building to our organization. What are the legal ramifications of accepting real property donations?

A25. The organization must consider whether to accept the real property donation, and then whether to keep or sell it. The organization should consider factors such as location, marketability, regular management costs, and use for the property when making this determination.

If the organization decides to sell the property, the sale may result in unrelated business income (UBI). While exempt organizations *generally* will not realize UBI on the sale of real property, it may be imposed if the organization is actively involved in the sale, and that involvement resembles the activities of a real estate broker.[49] If the sale occurs within three years of its donation, the organization must complete the "Donee Information Return," IRS Form 8282.[50] If the sale price is substantially less than the donor's deduction, the donor may find themselves subject to an audit by the IRS or need to recapture income on the difference.[51]

The donor and organization may not enter into an agreement prior to the donation for the property to be sold after the donation. The organization must retain its ability to keep or sell the property, to choose a buyer, and to negotiate the sale price. If the IRS determines that the donor controlled the sale, any gain on the sale of the property may be attributed to the donor.[52]

If the organization decides to keep and lease the property, unrelated business income tax (UBIT) may be imposed depending upon the organization's tax exempt purpose and involvement with the property. If the organization's tax exempt purpose is not substantially and importantly related to the property usage, and the entity regularly provides 'significant services' and/or incurs 'substantial costs' in its management, it may be viewed as involved in real estate management and be subject to UBIT on rental income from the property.[53] See Chapter 3: Tax Exemptions for more information.

If the property has any contamination, the organization may become liable for the resulting environmental damage or cleanup, even though the contamination was present prior to donation.[54] To reduce the likelihood of such liability, organizations should require an environmental review prior to acceptance. See Question 26 for more on environmental reviews.

---

49 Nonprofit Business Alert, 103, 8-9 (Apr. 1998).

50 *See* I.R.S. Form 8282 (2009), www.irs.gov/pub/irs-pdf/f8282.pdf.

51 "Gift Planning with Real Estate" (2013), www.endowdevelop.com/etech_pal/Content/gift_estate_planning_concepts/gift_planning_with_real_estate.htm.

52 *Id.*

53 *See* I.R.S. Pub. 598 (2017), https://www.irs.gov/pub/irs-pdf/p598.pdf. See also Giftlaw Pro, 7.1.3 Unrelated Business Income Taxation (UBIT) Exceptions, www.wwcgift.org/giftlaw/glawpro_subsection.jsp?WebID=GL1999-0001&CC=7&SS=1&SS2=3 (last visited July 10, 2017).

54 "Gift Planning with Real Estate" (2013), www.endowdevelop.com/etech_pal/Content/gift_estate_planning_concepts/gift_planning_with_real_estate.htm.

An organization should consult legal counsel when accepting donations of real estate.

Q26. What is the procedure a nonprofit organization should use to accept the donation of land or a building?

A26. The organization should first determine if the gift of real property is consistent with its acceptance policies. If it is not, the organization should question whether there is a significant reason why it should accept the donation.

Organizations should ensure that the exact legal interest in the property being donated is known. The organization should investigate, or require the donor to provide, the legal documents associated with the property, such as evidence of a clear title and the necessary qualified appraisal prior to acceptance.[55]

The organization should have an environmental review completed prior to acceptance. An environmental review is an investigation to determine if the land or property is contaminated. If contamination is found, the organization may choose not to accept the property or to pursue further testing to determine the extent of the contamination and amount of cleanup necessary. For more information on environmental reviews, see *Choosing an Environmentally Safe Site* (2006), by the U.S. Department of Housing and Urban Development, available at www.hudexchange.info/resources/documents/Choosing-an-Environmentally-Safe-Site.pdf.

Other questions that accompany the donation of real property include:

- Who will assume the cost of the environmental (or other) review? What about any necessary cleanup or remediation?
- Who will assume the debt, if there is any? The amount of the donor's deduction may differ depending on who is responsible, and the donor may even recognize gain on the donation if the debt is assumed by the organization.[56]
- Who will assume the transfer costs, such as any taxes, re-zoning, deed preparation, title insurance or review, legal fees, or repairs?
- Who will ensure that all applicable laws and regulations, such as those regarding zoning and building codes, are complied with?
- If the property is subject to a life estate, who is responsible for the costs of the property during the life tenancy?

These questions should be addressed in an organization's gift acceptance policy (for more information on gift acceptance policy, see www.councilofnonprofits.org/nonprofit-gift-acceptance-policy); if they are not, they should be discussed with and clearly communicated to the donor. While many organizations require the donor to bear most of these costs, they may be negotiated.

An organization should consult legal counsel when accepting donations of real estate.

55 *Id.*

56 *See* "Gift Planning with Real Estate" (2013), www.endowdevelop.com/etech_pal/Content/gift_estate_planning_concepts/gift_planning_with_real_estate.htm.

Q27. What procedure should a nonprofit organization use to accept donations of stock? What are the legal liabilities regarding the acceptance of a charitable donation that is received in the form of stock?

A27. The organization should first determine if the gift of stock is consistent with its gift acceptance policies.[57] If it is not, the organization should question whether there is a significant reason why it should accept the donation. If the organization accepts the stock, it must choose whether to sell or retain it. If the organization's acceptance policy provides for a particular procedure, such as immediate sale, the organization should follow that procedure. If the stock is worth $250 or more, or at the donor's request, the organization should substantiate the stock donation upon acceptance. Stock is valued by combining the high and low value per share on the date of donation, finding the average value, and multiplying that value by the number of shares donated. See Section C: Responsibilities to Funding Sources for additional information on substantiation.

If the organization chooses to retain and manage the stock, the Board of Directors must have the financial expertise to effectively manage it. Part of the fiduciary duty of care includes the prudent person rule, which requires directors to manage the organization's assets with the care that an "ordinarily prudent person in a like position would exercise under similar circumstances."[58] Directors must exercise reasonable judgment, based on reliable information, to reach sound decisions. The decisions reached are not ultimately required to produce the best possible results or the most income; they are only required to be made in good faith and in the best interests of the organization. Every decision should be evaluated in terms of its risks and benefits to the organization. If a board of directors does not have the requisite financial expertise, it should seek assistance from a qualified financial professional or delegate management responsibility to a capable board committee (if one exists). If management responsibility is delegated, the Board must use due diligence in supervising that management.[59]

Decisions made regarding the management of stock may be covered by the business judgment rule. This gives disinterested directors a certain amount of deference regarding business decisions made in good faith and upon reliable information, and does not make directors liable for losses resulting from such decisions. Decisions will not be protected if they are made without the requisite knowledge, good faith or due care, and directors may be personally liable for such decisions. What is in the best interests of an organization is determined by the facts and circumstances of the specific situation. Because most organizations lack financial expertise and seek to minimize their risks, most organizations adopt policies to immediately sell donated stocks.

Additional liabilities and considerations may also exist, such as potential depreciation in the stock's value causing a loss to the organization upon eventual sale. In addition, any gain upon sale of the stock could create unrelated business income tax implications.[60]

Organizations not experienced in accepting stock donations should consult legal counsel prior to acceptance.

57 "Gift Acceptance Policies," www.councilofnonprofits.org/tools-resources/gift-acceptance-policies.

58 Minn. Stat. § 317A.251, subdiv. 1 (2016) Minn. Stat. § 309.74(b) (2016); Minn. Stat. § 309.745(a) (2016). See Lynch v. John M. Redfield Found., 9 Cal. App. 3d 293 (1970) (trustees breached their duty of care by failing to invest funds for five years). See also James J. Fishman, Stephen Schwarz & Lloyd Hitoshi Mayer, *Nonprofit Organizations*, 46 (5th ed. 2015).

59 *Stern v. Lucy Webb Hayes, Nat'l Training Sch. for Deaconesses & Missionaries*, 381 F. Supp. 1003 (D.D.C. 1974) (trustees breached their duty of care by failing to supervise the management of assets).

60 *See* I.R.S. Pub. 598 at 14 (2017), www.irs.gov/pub/irs-pdf/p598.pdf.

Q28. If an organization receives a donation of stock, when and how should the organization dispose of the stock? What are the legal liabilities regarding the disposal of a charitable donation that is received in the form of stock?

A28. As a charitable gift, the organization must retain ultimate control over whether to retain or sell the stock. Donor restrictions requiring the stock to be sold or redeemed are not allowed, and may cause the donor to recognize the amount of the sale or redemption.[61] Donor restrictions requiring the stock to be retained, however, may be allowed.

If the organization has a gift acceptance policy that outlines the procedures to be used regarding the sale of a gift of stock, such as providing for immediate sale upon acceptance, the organization should follow that procedure. If not, the organization must decide when to sell or redeem the stock. If the stock is sold or redeemed within three years of its donation, had a claimed value at the time of donation in excess of $5,000, and is not publicly traded, the organization must complete and file Form 8282 with the IRS. [62]

Decisions regarding the sale of stock must be made according to the fiduciary duty of care and be in the best interests of the organization, which is determined by the facts and circumstances of the specific situation. Part of the fiduciary duty of care involves acting with ordinary prudence, which includes the duty to manage the organization's assets as an "ordinarily prudent person in a like position would exercise under similar circumstances." [63] Directors must exercise reasonable judgment in deciding when to sell stock. The decision must be made in good faith and based on reliable information. The ultimate decision is not required to have produced the most income possible, but must have been made in the best interests of the organization. If the Board of Directors does not possess the requisite financial expertise to decide when it is appropriate to sell the stock, it should seek assistance from a qualified financial professional or delegate the responsibility to a capable board committee (if one exists).

Directors will not be liable for losses resulting from the timing of the sale as long as the decision was made with due care and in the best interests of the organization. Directors may be held liable for losses if this standard is not met.

Many organizations' policies provide for the immediate sale of donated stock. This avoids the organization having to manage the stock according to the best interests of the organization while trying to abide by any donor requests. However, it also may cause donors who wish the stock to be retained to donate to another organization. Factors such as these should be considered when deciding whether to retain or sell stock, and whether the gift acceptance policy should outline a set procedure to be followed. For more information on gift acceptance policies, see www.councilofnonprofits.org/tools-resources/gift-acceptance-policies.

---

61 Rev. Rul. 78-197, 1978-1 C.B. 83, www.pgdc.com/pgdc/story/rev-rul-78-197.

62 *See* I.R.S., *Form 8282* (2009), www.irs.gov/pub/irs-pdf/f8282.pdf.

63 Minn. Stat. § 317A.251 (2016); Minn. Stat. § 309.74(b) (2016); Minn. Stat. § 309.745(a) (2016). See *Lynch v. John M. Redfield Found.*, 9 Cal. App. 3d 293 (1970) (trustees breached their duty of care by failing to invest funds for five years). See also James J. Fishman, Stephen Schwarz & Lloyd Hitoshi Mayer, Nonprofit Organizations 46 (5th ed. 2015).

Q29. Who is responsible for quantifying the value of a donation of land, a building, a vehicle, a work of art or shares of stock – the donor or the recipient organization?

A29. The donor is responsible for establishing the valuation of a donation, and for acquiring a qualified appraisal when needed.[64] Moreover, donors who intend to take sizable charitable deductions related to non-cash gifts (for individual donors any non-cash gift exceeding $500; for corporations, any non-cash gift exceeding $5,000), a Form 8283 must be filed with the IRS. [65]

Q30. ***Does an in-kind donor get to deduct the original price they paid for an item or its current market value at the time of the donation?***

A30. An in-kind donor will generally be able to deduct the fair market value of the property donated at the time of the contribution.[66] However, if the value of the property has increased, the donor may have to make some adjustments to the deduction amount. The deductible amount depends upon whether the property is ordinary income property to the donor (inventory, works of art created by the donor, etc.) or capital gain property (generally capital assets held for over one year, including bonds, jewelry, coins, or stamp collections).[67] According to I.R.S. Publication 526, the amount a donor can deduct from an ordinary income contribution is "fair market value ***less*** the amount that would be ordinary income . . . if you sold the property for its fair market value."[68] For capital gain property, the donor can usually deduct the entire fair market value of the gift. For examples, see I.R.S. Publication 526.

G. Planned Giving Vehicles

Q31. What is planned giving?

A31. Planned giving is a way for an organization to identify, cultivate relationships, and encourage individual or organizational donors to make larger gifts to a charitable organization. It may also be considered a method of funding a large gift rather than an end in itself. Planned gifts may be made during the donor's lifetime or at death through a variety of giving vehicles. It may be as simple as a pledge during a donor's lifetime to make an outright bequest, or a more complex arrangement that combines multiple vehicles, interests, and rights. Planned gifts can come in a variety of forms, but typically they result in a substantial financial contribution to the nonprofit organization and a hefty tax benefit for the donor.

From a donor's perspective, planned giving may be an attractive way to make a larger gift than previously thought possible. Planned giving vehicles offer flexibility and creativity through the many available options and gift structures. As an added incentive, some features of planned giving vehicles may include:

- A stream of income for life;
- A potential to increase the yield of other investments;

64 "Gift Planning with Real Estate" (2013), www.endowdevelop.com/etech_pal/Content/gift_estate_planning_concepts/gift_planning_with_real_estate.htm.

65 *See* I.R.S., *Instructions for Form 8283* (2014), www.irs.gov/pub/irs-pdf/i8283.pdf. See also I.R.S., Form 8283 (2014), www.irs.gov/pub/irs-pdf/f8283.pdf.

66 *See* I.R.S. Pub. 526 at 7-8 (Jan. 2017), www.irs.gov/pub/irs-pdf/p526.pdf.

67 *See* I.R.S. Pub. 526 at 11-12 (Jan. 2017), www.irs.gov/pub/irs-pdf/p526.pdf.

68 *Id.*

- Charitable income tax deductions;
- A possible reduction of capital gains or gift tax.

Q32. What are the types of planned giving vehicles?

A32. Planned gifts typically come in the form of bequests, trusts, life insurance policies, annuities, and gifts of stock. Each of these planned giving vehicles create unique responsibilities and requirements for the nonprofit organization. Depending on the vehicle, an organization may be required to pay a fixed income to a donor or designated beneficiary annually or more frequently for a term of up to twenty years, or may take on additional liability in terms of property maintenance or trust management. Donors will ordinarily contemplate the different types of benefits, streams of income, and/or various tax considerations (deductions, estate tax, capital gains, etc.) that best accomplish their goals. Donors and organizations should usually consult with legal counsel prior to planning a gift or accepting any sizable donation.

The following are some common types of planned giving vehicles. The descriptions are provided as an overview of technical planned giving vehicles.

Charitable Remainder Trusts. A charitable remainder trust is a gift a donor makes in their lifetime or at death through a will or revocable living trust.[69] In order to qualify as a charitable remainder trust, the trust must provide for a specified distribution, at least annually, to one or more beneficiaries, at least one of which is not a charity.[70] The distribution must be paid at least annually for life or for a term of not more than twenty years, with an irrevocable remainder interest to be held for the benefit of, or paid over to, one or more qualified charities.[71] The specified distribution must be either a fixed annual amount, which is not less than five percent (5%) and not more than fifty percent (50%) of the initial net fair market value of all property placed in trust (a charitable remainder annuity trust), or a fixed percentage, which is not less than five percent (5%) and not more than fifty percent (50%), of the net fair market value of the trust assets, valued annually (a charitable remainder trust).[72] At the expiration of the term or death of the beneficiaries, the remaining assets go to the charitable organization.

The donor receives an income tax benefit, and the charity receives an irrevocable gift to be paid after a period of time.[73] The donor's charitable income and gift tax deduction for this type of gift is the present value of the charitable remainder interest, based on the IRS's actuarial and mortality tables.[74] While the donor can take a charitable deduction, all annuity distributions or payments are taxable to the beneficiary as either ordinary income, capital gains income, other income, or trust distribution, depending on the historical income of the trust.[75] In addition, unless a charitable remainder trust has unrelated business income, the trust is exempt from all federal income taxes.[76]

Pooled Income Funds. A pooled income fund is similar to a mutual fund. It is a fund that is likely to be set up during the course of a donor's life. Pooled income funds are generally trusts created and administered by a charitable organization. A donor contributes to a common fund, receives annual (or

69 James J. Fishman, Stephen Schwarz & Lloyd Hitoshi Mayer, *Nonprofit Organizations,* 824-826 (5th ed. 2015).
70 *See* Charitable Remainder Trusts, tspf.pgdc.com/pgdc/charitable-remainder-trusts (last visited July 11, 2017).
71 *Id. See also* I.R.C. § 664(d) (2015).
72 "Charitable Remainder Trusts," tspf.pgdc.com/pgdc/charitable-remainder-trusts (last visited July 11, 2017). See I.R.C. §§ 664(d)(1)(C), (d)(2)(C) (2015).
73 *See* I.R.C. § 170(f)(2)(A) (2015); I.R.C. § 664 (2015).
74 *See* I.R.C. § 170(f)(2) (2015); I.R.C. § 7520(a) (2014).
75 *See* I.R.C. § 664(b) (2015).
76 *See* I.R.C. § 664(c) (2015).

more frequent) distributions based on their *pro rata* share of the income earned by the fund, and the remainder interest goes to a charitable organization.[77]

Pooled income funds may be a way for nonprofits to cultivate smaller donors in planned giving.[78] A pooled income fund donor receives an income tax deduction for the actuarial value of the charitable remainder interest. Similar to charitable remainder trusts, the pooled income fund is generally exempt from tax, but all distributions to a beneficiary are considered ordinary income and are taxable.

Remainder Interest in a Personal Residence or Farm. A donor may also contribute a personal residence or farm while retaining a life interest and the right to live in and/or use the property for a donor's lifetime. Similar to other planned giving vehicles, this is a planned giving option that allows a donor to make a gift during their lifetime and utilize the tax benefits and real property gift during the donor's lifetime, while benefiting a charitable organization in the long-run.

Unlike other partial interests in real property, a remainder interest in a personal residence or farm may qualify for a charitable deduction.[79] If a remainder interest in a personal residence (principal home, vacation home, cabin, etc.) or farm is donated during the donor's lifetime, the donor may take an income tax deduction based on an actuarial value of the remainder interest.[80]

Charitable Gift Annuity. Charitable gift annuities work in a similar manner to charitable remainder trusts in that the donor or designated beneficiary receives a fixed annual payment for life or a term of years as part of the gift. However, unlike a charitable remainder trust, a charitable gift annuity is most likely structured as a contract instead of a trust, with an irrevocable gift of cash or property to a charitable organization during the donor's lifetime.[81]

If a donor makes a charitable gift annuity, the donor may take a charitable deduction for the amount transferred to the charity that exceeds the present value of the annuity as actuarially determined.[82] As with all income, the amount the donor receives is includable in gross income.[83] If the donor gifts appreciated property as part of the annuity, the transfer is treated as a bargain sale for tax purposes. This means that if the donor is the person who will receive the annuity, the tax benefits may be divided between the gift portion deduction and the purchase of the annuity.[84] If the annuitant is a third-party beneficiary, the gain from the sale of the appreciated property is taxable in the year of the gift.[85]

Charitable Lead Trusts. Charitable lead trusts have been described as the "mirror image of a charitable remainder trust."[86] When a donor gives through a charitable lead trust, a trust is formed that provides income payments to at least one qualified charitable organization for a period measured by a fixed term of years; after which, trust assets are paid to either the grantor or to one or more non-charitable beneficiaries named in the trust instrument.[87] Unlike a charitable remainder trust, though also a planned giving vehicle, the charitable organization receives a gift for the life of the donor. And, at the expiration of the term, the remainder reverts to the donor or a designated family member.

77 *See* I.R.C. § 642(c)(5) (2015).
78 James J. Fishman, Stephen Schwarz & Lloyd Hitoshi Mayer, *Nonprofit Organizations*, 828 (5th ed. 2015).
79 *See* I.R.C. § 170(f)(3)(B)(i) (2015).
80 *See* I.R.C. § 170(f)(4) (2015); see also Treas. Reg. § 1.170A-12 (2011).
81 James J. Fishman, Stephen Schwarz & Lloyd Hitoshi Mayer, *Nonprofit Organizations*, 829 (5th ed. 2015).
82 *See* I.R.C. § 170(c) (2015).
83 *See* I.R.C. § 72 (2015).
84 *See* I.R.C. § 170(c) (2015); I.R.C. § 1011(b) (2015); Treas. Reg. § 1.1011-2(b) (1994).
85 James J. Fishman, Stephen Schwarz & Lloyd Hitoshi Mayer, *Nonprofit Organizations*, 82 (5th ed. 2015).
86 James J. Fishman & Stephen Schwarz, *Nonprofit Organizations*, 930 (2nd ed. 2000).
87 Charitable Remainder Trusts, tspf.pgdc.com/pgdc/charitable-remainder-trusts (last visited July 11, 2017).

There are two types of charitable lead trusts—a grantor lead trust and a non-grantor lead trust. Each trust has distinct advantages and tax consequences. A grantor lead trust bases the annual payment to the charitable organization on the actuarial value of the trust's income interest, which is also equal to the current income tax deduction.[88] A non-grantor lead trust is considered more of an estate planning technique. Unlike the grantor lead trust, a non-grantor lead trust does not provide a current income tax deduction.[89] However, it is designed to provide income to a charitable organization for a specific amount of time and pass the property to a family member at little or no wealth transfer cost.[90] This type of trust can be created during a donor's life or at the donor's death and may have gift tax advantages if properly and carefully structured.

Charitable Bequest. A charitable bequest is a gift made at death through a donor's will. It is a distribution from a donor's estate to a charitable organization. There are several types of charitable bequests that allow donors to accomplish their charitable giving goals, but careful drafting is advised to ensure final wishes are carried out without complication.

There are a number of recognized bequests. The following are some of the most common forms:

- Specific Bequest: when a donor gives a specific piece of property to an organization.
- General Bequest: typically, a gift of a sum of money.
- Contingent Bequest: a bequest made on the condition that a certain event occurs before distribution to the bequest's beneficiary.
- Residuary Bequest: a gift of the remainder of an estate after all other bequests, debts, and taxes have been paid.
- Unrestricted Bequest: a gift to be used by the nonprofit organization in any way the Board sees fit.
- Restricted Bequest: a gift to be used only for specific, restricted purposes.
- Honorary Bequest: a gift given "in memory of" an individual or group.
- Endowment Bequest: a gift in which the nonprofit organization must restrict the principal and only use the income generated by the initial gift. See Question 17 for more information regarding endowments.

See Leave a Legacy's "How to Give" (www.leavealegacy.org/how_give.asp) for examples of different types of bequests and corresponding sample language. See Question 33 for legal considerations when an organization receives a charitable bequest.

Q33. What are the legal considerations when an organization receives a charitable bequest?

A33. The most important issue when a nonprofit organization receives a charitable bequest is determining what type of bequest it has been granted. [There are a number of recognized bequests. Refer to the bulleted list in Question 32 under "Charitable Bequest."]

Typically, the unrestricted bequest is the most useful from a nonprofit organization's perspective. Nonprofit organizations should learn what type of bequest they are receiving prior to accepting the gift, and ensure that they will be able to meet any of the requirements associated with the gift. Additionally, Minnesota law requires notice to the Attorney General of certain probate proceedings in which a bequest or

88 James J. Fishman, Stephen Schwarz & Lloyd Hitoshi Mayer, *Nonprofit Organizations*, 830 (5th ed. 2015).
89 *Id.*
90 *Id.*

devise for charitable purposes is involved.[91] The Attorney General's Office must be given notice when:

- A will provides a bequest for an unnamed charitable beneficiary or for a charitable beneficiary that no longer exists; or
- A will provides a bequest for a charitable purpose in excess of $150,000; or
- A will provides a bequest to a charity that is a receivership; or
- A written request is served on the personal representative by a named charitable organization.[92]

H. Other Issues

Q34. *What laws govern fundraising practices in Minnesota?*

A34. Minnesota Statutes Chapter 309 governs solicitation of charitable funds in Minnesota.

Q35. Who needs to register as a professional fundraiser with the Attorney General's Office?

A35. Minnesota Statutes § 309.50 subdiv. 6 defines professional fundraisers as compensated persons that personally perform services connected to charitable fundraising activities and those that employ or manage people who perform such services, including grantwriters.[93] It also clearly states that bona fide officers, employees, or volunteers of an organization are not professional fundraisers.[94]

Minnesota Statutes § 309.531 requires registration with the Attorney General of all professional fundraisers. "'Professional fund-raiser' means any person who for financial compensation or profit performs for a charitable organization any service in connection with which contributions are, or will be, solicited."[95] A professional fundraiser can be an individual, organization, group, firm, partnership, corporation, church, society, league, or association, and includes a trustee, agent, or similar representative of such organization. If the professional fundraiser is going to solicit contributions in Minnesota, a registration statement must be filed with the Minnesota Attorney General, accompanied by a solicitation notice that contains written authorization from two officers of the charitable organization and (under certain circumstances) a bond. [96] The professional fundraiser must also file a financial report with the Minnesota Attorney General within 90 days of the close of the fundraising campaign. [97] If the fundraising campaign lasted over one year, a campaign report must also be filed on the anniversary of its commencement. Forms are available on the Minnesota Attorney General's website at www.ag.state.mn.us/Charity/DownloadForms.asp.

91 Minn. Stat. § 501B.41, subdiv. 5 (2016). See also Office of the Minnesota Attorney General, *A Guide to Minnesota's Charities Laws*, www.ag.state.mn.us/Consumer/Publications/GuideCharityLaws.asp (last visited July 11, 2017).
92 Minn. Stat. § 501B.41, subdiv. 5 (2016).
93 Minn. Stat. § 309.50, subdiv. 6 (2016).
94 *Id.*
95 Minn. Stat. § 309.50, subdiv. 6 (2016).
96 Minn. Stat. §§ 309.531, subdiv. 2-3 (2016).
97 Minn. Stat. § 309.531, subdiv. 4 (2016).

Q36. What is a charitable solicitation?

A36. The definition of a "charitable solicitation" is extremely broad. A solicitation includes a direct or indirect request for a contribution with the understanding that it will be used for a charitable purpose, and may include any of the following methods:

- Oral or written request.
- The distribution, circulation, mailing, posting, or publishing of any advertisement or publication.
- The making of any announcement to the press, over the radio, or by television, telephone or telegraph, concerning an event to which the public is requested to attend or make a contribution.
- The sale or attempted sale of any advertisement, advertising space, book, card, magazine, merchandise, subscription, ticket of admission or any other thing; the use of the name of any charitable person in any offer or sale as an inducement or reason to purchase such item; or the making of any statement in connection with any such sale, that the whole or any part of the proceeds from such sale will be used for any charitable purpose.

Solicitations are deemed completed when made, whether or not the person making the solicitation receives any contribution or makes a sale.[98]

Q37. Do organizations that solicit contributions need to file with the Attorney General?

A37. Charitable organizations must file a registration statement with the Attorney General prior to any solicitation, and an annual report.[99] These forms can be found on the Minnesota Attorney General's website at www.ag.state.mn.us/Charity/DownloadForms.asp. Certain organizations are exempt from this filing requirement:[100]

- Charitable organizations that are comprised *entirely* of volunteers (including no employment of a professional fundraiser) and expect to receive less than $25,000 in annual contributions from the public.
- Religious organizations exempt from filing annual IRS Form 990 returns.
- Any educational institution that is under the general supervision of the commissioner of education, the Board of Trustees of the Minnesota State Colleges and Universities, or the University of Minnesota or any educational institution that is accredited by the University of Minnesota or the North Central Association of Colleges and Secondary Schools, or by any other national or regional accrediting association.
- A fraternal, patriotic, social, educational, alumni, professional, trade, or learned society that limits its solicitation of contributions to persons who have a right to vote as a member. The term "member" does not include those who are granted a membership upon making a contribution as the result of a solicitation.
- A charitable organization soliciting contributions for any person specified by name at the time of the solicitation if all of the contributions received are transferred to that person with no restrictions on that person's use of the contributions and there are no deductions.
- A private foundation that did not solicit contributions from more than 100 people during the accounting year most recently ended.

98 Minn. Stat. § 309.50, subd. 10 (2016).
99 Minn. Stat. § 309.52 (2016).
100 Minn. Stat. § 309.515 (2016).

During both charity-driven and professional fundraiser-driven solicitations, an organization must clearly disclose the following information prior to an oral solicitation and contemporaneously with a written solicitation:[101]

- The name and location by city and state of each charitable organization on behalf of which the solicitation is being made;
- Whether the contribution is tax-deductible;
- A description of the charitable program for which the solicitation campaign is being conducted (and, if different, a description of the programs and activities of the organization on whose behalf the solicitation campaign is being conducted); and
- The identity and existence of the professional fundraiser, if one is used.

If the solicitation is made by direct personal contact, the required information shall also be disclosed prominently on a written document which shall be exhibited to the person solicited.[102] If the solicitation is made by radio, television, letter, telephone, or any other means not involving direct personal contact, the required information shall be clearly disclosed in the solicitation.[103]

If an organization violates the fundraising statute, possible penalties include injunctions, restitution, appointment of a receiver for the defendant or defendant's assets, suspension of defendant's registration, reasonable attorney fees, costs of investigation, and penalties of up to $25,000 for each violation.[104]

While federal law also regulates fundraising in Minnesota, it does so primarily through the IRS and its substantiation, disclosure, and reporting requirements of tax-exempt organizations.

Q38. Do employees of registered charities need to register as a professional fundraiser?

A38. No, the employee of a registered charity is not required to individually register as a professional fundraiser. According to the Minnesota Attorney General's Office, "true salaried officers, employees, or volunteers of a charitable organization are not professional fundraisers for the purposes of Minnesota law."[105]

Q39. What are the laws that prohibit the use of fraud or deceptive practices in fundraising?

A39. Minnesota Statute Section 309.55 establishes several rules prohibiting deceptive and misleading charitable fundraising practices. [106] Nonprofit organizations and professional fundraisers are prohibited from using the name of any person (this could be an individual or a corporation – nonprofit or for-profit) without written consent. Nonprofit organizations and professional fundraisers are not allowed to use any name, symbol, or statement so closely related or similar to that used by another charitable organization or governmental agency that the use would tend to confuse or mislead the public. Nonprofit organizations and professional fundraisers cannot use any uniformed personnel to solicit contributions. Additionally, nonprofit organizations and professional fundraisers are prohibited from engaging in fraud, false pretense,

101 Minn. Stat. § 309.556 (2016).

102 *Id.*

103 *Id.*

104 Minn. Stat. § 309.57 (2016).

105 Office of the Minnesota Attorney General, A *Guide to Minnesota's Charities Laws*, www.ag.state.mn.us/Consumer/Publications/GuideCharityLaws.asp (last visited July 11, 2017).

106 Minn. Stat. § 309.55 (2016).

false promises, misrepresentation, misleading statements, misleading names, marks or identification, and deceptive practice, methods or devices with the intent for others to rely thereon in connection with any charitable solicitation.

Q40. What laws govern the use of the Internet to solicit charitable donations?

A40. The same Minnesota laws that govern charitable solicitations in general (see Question 36) also apply to solicitations via the Internet. Additionally, organizations that solicit contributions from residents of other states, either actively or passively, may need to register with those states' charity registration office, depending on the state's registration requirements. Each state's system of fundraising regulation is different. As an alternative to completing and filing multiple state specific forms, the Unified Registration Statement (URS) may be an alternative.[107] The URS represents an effort to consolidate the information and data requirements of all states that require registration of nonprofit organizations performing charitable solicitations within their jurisdictions. In states that accept the URS, a registering nonprofit may use either the state form or the URS. However, please beware when using the URS that states accepting it may have specific addendums or additional requirements during the registration process. For more information, visit multistatefiling.org, and be sure to check with each state's charity registration office.

For guidelines regarding how to solicit charitable contributions via the Internet, see *The Charleston Principles: Guidelines On Charitable Solicitations Using The Internet* (March 14, 2001), approved by NASCO Board as advisory guidelines, at www.nasconet.org/wp-content/uploads/2011/05/Charleston-Principles-Final.pdf.

Federal laws regarding advertising and sales practices are also applicable to Internet solicitations. For example, the FTC's prohibition against "unfair or deceptive acts or practices" applies to solicitations via the Internet.[108]

An organization may encounter additional legal liability, depending on whether a hosting agent is used for their web page. Many third-party sites are technically professional fundraisers, but most may not be registered as such.[109] An organization should consult an attorney prior to initiating solicitation via the Internet.

Q41. Can a nonprofit organization ask donors to fund its efforts to enact legislative reforms, or to lobby?

A41. Contributions made to a nonprofit organization that are earmarked for lobbying efforts are not tax deductible as charitable contributions.[110] An organization may ask donors to fund its lobbying efforts, it must also inform the potential donor that such contributions would not be tax deductible. Community foundations can make charitable grants specifically for lobbying, but private foundations cannot. See Question 12 for requirements on informing potential donors of non-deductibility.

107 *See* The Unified Registration Statement, multistatefiling.org/index.html (last visited July 11, 2017).

108 Federal Trade Commission, *How to Make Effective Disclosures in Digital Advertising* (2013), www.ftc.gov/sites/default/files/attachments/press-releases/ftc-staff-revises-online-advertising-disclosure-guidelines/130312dotcomdisclosures.pdf.

109 Cheryl Chasin, et al., *Tax Exempt Organizations and World Wide Web Fundraising and Advertising on the Internet*,129 (2000), www.irs.gov/pub/irs-tege/eotopici00.pdf.

110 *See* Rev. Rul. 80-275, 1980-2 C.B. 69, www.irs.gov/pub/irs-tege/rr80-275.pdf.

Q42. Can a nonprofit organization ask candidates for public office to contribute to its organization?

A42. Yes, organizations may solicit charitable contributions from candidates for political office.[111]

Q43. Can donors choose to be anonymous?

A43. Donors may choose to be anonymous in a direct donation to a charitable organization. However, the charitable organization will be unable to provide a written acknowledgment to the donor. Recall, for donations of $250 or more, without a written acknowledgment from the organization, the donor may not take a tax deduction for the amount of the contribution.

However, if the donor makes a donation to a donor-advised fund, the donor may be able to complete their anonymous gift to the desired charitable organization as well as retain tax deductibility. Generally, a donor-advised fund is a separately identified fund or account that is maintained and operated by a nonprofit organization with 501(c)(3) tax exempt status, which is called a sponsoring organization.[112] Each donor-advised fund is composed of contributions made by individual donors.[113] Once the donor makes the contribution to the donor-advised fund, the donor-advised fund assumes legal control over it.[114] However, the donor (or the donor's representative), retains advisory privileges with respect to the distribution of monies by the donor-advised fund.[115] The donor informs the donor-advised fund about their ultimate wishes, and the donor-advised fund can choose whether to donate the monies to the donor's ultimate charity of choice. The donor is not anonymous to the donor-advised fund, and the donor receives a written acknowledgment from the donor-advised fund, but the donor-advised fund completes the donation to the desired charitable organization (so long as it is a conforming 501(c)(3)) and keeps the identity of the original donor anonymous.

Q44. Can a nonprofit organization accept cash gifts of $10,000 or more?

A44. An organization may accept cash gifts of $10,000 or more just as it would with any other monetary contribution.[116] However, if the organization receives cash of over $10,000 in a *trade or business transaction*, then it is subject to additional reporting requirements as part of the U.S. Treasury enforcement of anti-money laundering laws. See I.R.S. Publication 1544, *Report of Cash Payments over $10,000 Received in a Trade or Business* (2014), www.irs.gov/pub/irs-pdf/p1544.pdf.

Q45. If a nonprofit organization or an unincorporated association is not eligible to receive tax-deductible contributions, can it have donors contribute to an organization that is eligible and then ask that organization for the money received from its donors?

A45. Yes. This is commonly known as a fiscal agency or fiscal sponsor relationship.

---

111 *Minn. Citizens Concerned for Life, Inc. v. Kelley*, 427 F.3d 1106 (8th Cir. 2005) (Found Minn. Stat. § 211B.08 unconstitutional because it prohibited religious, charitable, and educational organizations from requesting donations from political candidates or their committees).

112 *See* I.R.S., *Donor—Advised Funds* (Apr. 2017), www.irs.gov/Charities-&-Non-Profits/Charitable-Organizations/Donor-Advised-Funds.

113 *See* I.R.S., *Donor—Advised Funds*, www.irs.gov/Charities-&-Non-Profits/Charitable-Organizations/Donor-Advised-Funds (last updated Apr. 12, 2017).

114 *Id.*

115 *Id.*

116 *See* I.R.S. Pub. 1544 (2014), www.irs.gov/pub/irs-pdf/p1544.pdf. ("Exempt organizations, including employee plans, are also 'persons.' However, exempt organizations do not have to file Form 8300 for a more-than-$10,000 charitable cash contribution they receive since it is not received in the course of a trade or business.").

Contributions made to a tax-exempt organization are tax-deductible. However, when the understanding is that such donations will be turned over to a non-qualifying organization or an unincorporated association, they are not tax deductible unless the tax-exempt organization accepts expenditure responsibly.[117] Expenditure responsibility means the tax-exempt organization exerts all reasonable efforts and establishes adequate procedures:

- To see that the charitable assets are spent only for the agreed upon purpose,
- To obtain full and complete reports from the non-qualifying organization or unincorporated association on how the funds were spent, and
- To make full and detailed reports on the expenditures to the IRS (ordinarily on its annual Form 990 filing).[118]

If the tax-exempt organization is a fiscal agent or fiscal sponsor, the donor may receive a charitable deduction. Fiscal agents or sponsors are charitable organizations that "enable the movement of resources from funders and donors to projects, activities, ideas, and organizations that share the fiscal sponsor's mission."[119] Without such a fiscal agency relationship, claiming deductions for these payments may constitute money laundering. For more information on fiscal sponsorship and agency relationships, see Chapter 8: Financial Accountability, Section E: Fiscal Agency or Sponsorship.

An organization should consult an attorney prior to initiating a fiscal agent or fiscal sponsor relationship.

Q46. If an organization is eligible to receive tax-deductible donations, do its donors who are non-itemizing taxpayers receive a charitable deduction on their federal and Minnesota tax returns?

A46. Taxpayers who do not itemize are not eligible for a tax deduction related to charitable contributions on their federal tax returns. They *are* eligible for a tax deduction on their Minnesota tax returns under the Minnesota Charitable Giving Relief Act, Minn. Stat. § 290 (2017).

Q47. What is the Minnesota Charitable Giving Relief Act, and how does it work?

A47. The Minnesota Charitable Giving Relief Act allows non-itemizers to deduct fifty percent of their charitable contributions that exceed $500. After a non-itemizing individual or couple donates over $500 to any charity or combination of charities, additional contributions are eligible for the fifty percent deduction on their Minnesota State tax return.[120]

As with itemizers, non-itemizers must now keep a record of all monetary donations, regardless of amount. Donors must be able to demonstrate that their charitable contributions exceed $500, and by how much, in order to be eligible for a Minnesota deduction. For donations under $250, the donor must retain a bank record (such as a canceled check, bank statement, or credit card statement) or obtain a receipt from the organization. For donations of $250 or more, the donor must acquire a written acknowledgment. See Question 5 for information on written acknowledgments.

117 *See* I.R.S. Rev. Proc. 82-39, section. 3.03 (1982), www.irs.gov/pub/irs-tege/rp1982_39.pdf. See also I.R.S., *Contributions Deductibility and Related Matters of Importance for Exempt Organizations Specialists* (1984), www.irs.gov/pub/irs-tege/eotopicc84.pdf.

118 *See* I.R.S., *Grants by Private Foundations: Expenditure Responsibility*, https://www.irs.gov/Charities-&-Non-Profits/Private-Foundations/Grants-by-Private-Foundations:-Expenditure-Responsibility (last updated June 10, 2016).

119 About Fiscal Sponsorship, www.tides.org/i-want-to/turn-my-vision-ideas-into-a-nonprofit-project/learn-about-fiscal-sponsorship-at-tides/ (last visited July 11, 2017).

120 Charitable Giving Relief Act, www.minnesotanonprofits.org/mcn-at-the-capitol/past-successes/charitable-giving-relief-act (last visited July 11, 2017).

I. Related Resources

Publications:

Financial Accounting Standards Board, *Not-for-Profit Entities (Topic 958)* (April 2013),
www.fasb.org/resources/ccurl/90/645/ASU%202013-06.pdf

I.R.S. *Form 8282: Donee Information Return* (2009)
www.irs.gov/pub/irs-pdf/f8282.pdf

I.R.S. *Form 8283: Noncash Charitable Contributions* (2014)
www.irs.gov/pub/irs-pdf/f8283.pdf

I.R.S. *Instructions for Form 8283* (2014)
www.irs.gov/pub/irs-pdf/i8283.pdf

I.R.S. *Publication 526: Charitable Contributions*
www.irs.gov/pub/irs-pdf/p526.pdf

I.R.S. *Publication 598: Tax on Unrelated Business Income of Exempt Organizations*
https://www.irs.gov/pub/irs-pdf/p598.pdf

I.R.S. *Publication 1544: Report of Cash Payments over $10,000 Received in a Trade or Business*
www.irs.gov/pub/irs-pdf/p1544.pdf

I.R.S. *Publication 1771: Charitable Contributions, Substantiation and Disclosure Requirements*
www.irs.gov/pub/irs-pdf/p1771.pdf

I.R.S. *Publication 4221-PC: Compliance Guide for 501(c)(3) Public Charities*
www.irs.gov/pub/irs-pdf/p4221pc.pdf

I.R.S. *Publication 4302: A Charity's Guide to Vehicle Donations*
www.irs.gov/pub/irs-pdf/p4302.pdf

I.R.S. *Publication 4303: A Donor's Guide to Vehicle Donations*
www.irs.gov/pub/irs-pdf/p4303.pdf

Propel Nonprofits, *Managing Restricted Funds* at 1 (2014),
www.propelnonprofits.org

Statutes:

Internal Revenue Code
www.law.cornell.edu/uscode/text/26

Minnesota Statutes Chapter 309
www.revisor.mn.gov/statutes/?id=309

Minnesota Statutes Chapter 317A
www.revisor.mn.gov/statutes/?id=317A

Minnesota Statutes Chapter 325E
www.revisor.mn.gov/statutes/?id=325E

Minnesota Statutes Chapter 501B
www.revisor.mn.gov/statutes/?id=501B

Websites:

Office of the Minnesota Attorney General, *Information for Nonprofit*
www.ag.state.mn.us/Charity/InfoNonProfits.asp
A list of resources for Minnesota nonprofits on registration, training, technical assistance, charity evaluations and financial information.

Office of the Minnesota Attorney General, *Charities*
www.ag.state.mn.us/Charities
Provides links to laws regarding charitable organizations, filings and forms, sample policies, and other information.

Planned Giving Design Center, *The Saint Paul Foundation*
www.pgdc.com/host/minnesota-community-foundation-and-the-saint-paul-foundation

Organizations

Association of Fundraising Professionals
www.afpnet.org
They are the national association for fundraisers that produces helpful resources like blogs, free webinars, a code of ethics, etc. and have local chapters across the United States that offer continuing education events and networking opportunities

National Council of Nonprofits' Tools for and Resources for Fundraising
www.councilofnonprofits.org/tools-resources/fundraising
They are the national association of nonprofit state associations that provide sector-wide support on topics relevant to nonprofits across the United States, including fundraising. They have great basic information about fundraising as well as lists of tools and resources covering a broad range of topics related to fundraising.

CHAPTER 6

BOARDS OF DIRECTORS

Topics

A. Overview

Boards of directors are responsible for defining an organization's mission and providing leadership and strategic direction to an organization. The Internal Revenue Service (IRS) believes that a "well-governed charity is more likely to obey tax laws, safeguard charitable assets, and serve charitable interests than one with poor or lax governance."[1] For a nonprofit organization, boards of directors provide important organizational oversight and are integral to maintaining accountability to the public and to the constituencies served by the organization. For an individual director, serving as a volunteer board member provides an opportunity for meaningful use of specialized skills and expertise for community service and for growth of personal leadership skills. For the public, well-governed organizations are more likely to reach their goals to benefit the community.

This section answers basic questions related to boards of directors, primarily based on the Minnesota Nonprofit Corporation Act (Minnesota Statutes Chapter 317A), IRS disclosure requests found in the Form 990 and nonprofit best practices. All of these authorities impose or recommend certain minimum requirements for size, structure and composition of a board of directors in order to provide sufficient organizational management and oversight.

All directors owe a fiduciary duty to the organization for which they provide service. A fiduciary duty is a legal relationship of trust, good faith or reliance between an organization and a director. A director's fiduciary responsibilities are characterized by three duties: care, loyalty and obedience. (1) The duty of care requires directors to make decisions in good faith, with a reasonable amount of information and attention in the best interest of the organization. (2) A duty of loyalty requires that directors (a) act in a manner that does not cause harm to the organization, and (b) avoid leveraging their position to obtain improper personal benefits. (3) The duty of obedience requires directors to obey and comply with federal and state laws, as well as the organization's governing documents. Written organizational governance policies, such as a conflict of interest policy or a document retention policy, often serve as mechanisms to clarify and satisfy directors' fiduciary duties and further good governance.

If a director breaches their fiduciary duty, that director may be held liable either by the organization's members or by the Minnesota Attorney General's office for financial harm suffered by the organization. Taxes and fees may also be assessed in some situations. Indemnification included within corporate organizational documents or Directors and Officers (D&O) liability insurance may shield directors from or limit directors' exposure for personal liability. And, Minnesota Statutes § 317A.257, subdivision. 1 limits a director's civil liability for acts or omissions taken in good faith without willful or reckless misconduct.

B. Board Structure and Composition

Q1. What is the recommended structure for a board of directors?

A1. Board composition and structure are critical to the success of the organization. Nonprofit boards are responsible for defining the organization's mission and for providing leadership and strategic direction. MCN's *Principles & Practices for Nonprofit Excellence* recommends that each board should:

1) Actively set policy and ensure that the organization has adequate resources to carry out its mission;
2) Provide direct oversight and direction for the executive director and be responsible for evaluating their performance; and

1 *See* I.R.S., *Governance and Related Topics - 501(c)(3) Organizations* (2008), www.irs.gov/pub/irs-tege/governance_practices.pdf.

3) Evaluate its own effectiveness as a governing body, as a group of volunteers, and as representatives of the community in upholding the public interest served by the organization.[2]

Minnesota law sets some minimum structural requirements for nonprofit boards of directors. All members of a board are entitled to vote and have equal rights unless otherwise indicated in the organization's Articles or Bylaws.[3] A board should take action based on the affirmative vote of a majority of directors present and voting unless a higher proportion is indicated in the organization's articles or bylaws.[4] Each nonprofit board of directors must have a president and treasurer, who are usually elected or appointed according to the organization's Bylaws.[5] Most nonprofit boards divide responsibilities through committees or working groups. For example, a strategic planning committee would lead the board and the organization in an evaluation of how the organization moves toward accomplishing its mission. See MCN's *Principles & Practices for Nonprofit Excellence* for further examples of board best practices.

Q2. What is the minimum number of board members that nonprofit organizations are required to have under Minnesota law?

A2. Under Minnesota law, a board of directors must consist of three or more individuals. The number of board members should be specified in the articles or bylaws.[6]

While the minimum number of required board members is three, MCN's *Principles & Practices for Nonprofit Excellence* recommends that nonprofit boards should consist of at least seven individuals to allow for adequate deliberation and diversity of perspective.[7] An odd number of directors is optimal, as it provides the greatest numerical opportunity for a majority vote in the event of disputed board actions.

Q3. Is there a maximum number of board members that nonprofit organizations are allowed to have under Minnesota law?

A3. There is no maximum number of board members required by Minnesota law. The number of board members should adequately reflect the different member constituencies and service population interests and the needs of the organization for board member participation. For most organizations, the optimum number of board members is between seven and nineteen. One disadvantage to a large board is the appearance that other board members will accomplish the work of the organization, resulting in board members with diminished participation in board meetings, committees and other activities. The minimum and maximum number of board members should be established in the Bylaws or Articles of Incorporation.

Q4. Can a husband and wife serve on the same board of directors?

A4. Yes, a husband and wife can serve on the same board of directors subject to restrictions within the Articles of Incorporation and Bylaws. Married persons should exercise special care to avoid conflicts of interest and exercise the proper fiduciary duties (see Question 5) to the organization.[8]

---

2 *See* Minnesota Council of Nonprofits, *Principles & Practices for Nonprofit Excellence*, 12 (2014).
3 Minn. Stat. § 317A.201 (2016).
4 Minn. Stat. § 317A.237 (2016).
5 Minn. Stat. § 317A.301 (2016).
6 Minn. Stat. § 317A.203 (2017).
7 Minnesota Council of Nonprofits, *Principles & Practices for Nonprofit Excellence,* 13 (2014)
8 Minn. Stat. § 317A.255 (2016).

Q5. Can members of the same family serve on a board of directors?

A5. Yes, family members can serve on the same board of directors. For example, the boards of family foundations, which are a type of nonprofit organization, are often comprised exclusively of family members. As with married persons, family members must each meet the requirements for board membership described in the Articles of Incorporation and the Bylaws. Family members are subject to the same fiduciary duties and conflict of interest provisions as other board members.

Q6. Can minors (people under 18 years of age) serve as members of the board of directors?

A6. Yes, minors can serve as members of the board of directors. Minors are prohibited from serving in officer positions and the majority of the board must be made up of adults (people 18 years of age or older).[9] Minors cannot act as incorporators of an organization.[10]

Q7. Can an employee (such as the executive director) serve as a voting member of the board of directors?

A7. There is no prohibition from a staff member such as the executive director serving on the board. The Bylaws should state whether or not employees serving on the board have voting rights. Issues such as executive compensation and performance evaluation, fundraising, program implementation, and the overall financial health of the organization can be complicated by the inclusion of staff members on the board of directors. Staff members may make presentations to the board or participate in board discussions on certain issues, but those staff members should be excused from the meeting when that presentation or topic is concluded. In its *Principles & Practices for Nonprofit Excellence*, the Minnesota Council of Nonprofits recommends that no more than one staff member serve on the board at any time and that the staff member not serve as either board chair or treasurer.

These measures, along with a substantive conflict of interest policy, minimize opportunities for abuse and wrongdoing. IRS Form 990[11] includes these questions regarding conflict of interest:

- 12a—Does the organization have a written conflict of interest policy?
- 12b—Are officers, directors or trustees, and key employees required, on an annual basis, to disclose interests that could give rise to conflicts?
- 12c—Does the organization regularly and consistently monitor and enforce compliance with the policy?

Q8. Can a staff member (like the executive director) serve as a non-voting member of the board of directors?

A8. Like the ability to serve as a voting member of the board, a staff member's ability to serve as a non-voting member is allowed under Minnesota's Nonprofit Corporation Act. This status should be described in the Bylaws. Non-voting directors do not count toward the minimum number of board members necessary to constitute a quorum. Boards should take care to excuse non-voting staff member directors from portions of board meetings concerning such staff director's performance or other employment matters.

---

9 Minn. Stat. § 317A.205 (2016).
10 Minn. Stat. § 317A.105 (2016).
11 *See* I.R.S. Form 990 (2016), Part VI, Section B, 12(a)-(c), www.irs.gov/pub/irs-pdf/f990.pdf.

Q9. What does it mean to be an ex officio member of the board of directors? What are the rights and responsibilities of ex officio members?

A9. The term "ex officio" refers to a person's status as a director by virtue of the office they hold inside or external to the organization. Regardless of the person's title who occupies such a position, they are automatically made a member of the board of directors. For example, the CEO of a corporation may be an ex officio member of the board of directors for the separately incorporated corporate foundation or giving program. Bylaws usually describe any ex officio positions and establish whether or not the position has voting rights. Since these positions involve persons who were not elected and may represent outside interests, conflict of interest policies are critical to ensure the fiduciary duties of the board as a whole.[12]

Q10. What is the maximum term length for a director?

A10. The length of time of a director's term is normally specified in the Bylaws or Articles of Incorporation. If no term is specified in the Articles or Bylaws, the default term length is one year.[13] A term of a director, other than an ex officio director, may not exceed ten years.[14] Life time terms are not allowed and terms must have a defined beginning and end. Organizations need to maintain an up-to-date roster of board members and their respective terms.

Q11. What is the maximum number of terms a director can serve?

A11. Unlike term length, there is no limitation on the number of terms a director can serve, or the number of years, unless otherwise provided in the Articles of Incorporation or Bylaws.

MCN's *Principles & Practices for Nonprofit Excellence* recommends terms of no more than nine consecutive years.[15]

C. Board Duties and Responsibilities

Q12. According to Minnesota's Nonprofit Corporation Act, what are the responsibilities of the board of directors?

A12. The board of directors has ultimate authority for the management or direction of the business and affairs of the organization.[16] This is not an indication that the board should necessarily be involved in the day-to-day management aspects of the organization. Rather, the board, by fulfilling its fiduciary obligations to the organization should be aware of the activities of the organization, provide direction and leadership, and take corrective action when necessary. For small organizations where much or all of the work is performed by volunteers, it can be useful to clarify with board members, during board training or otherwise, the different roles a single person may be asked to perform, i.e., may carry out board duties and also be a volunteer working on a fundraising event.

12 Minn. Stat. § 317A.205 (2016).
13 Minn. Stat. § 317A.207, subd. 1(a) (2016).
14 Minn. Stat. § 317A.207, subd. 1(a) (2015).
15 Minnesota Council of Nonprofits, *Principles & Practices for Nonprofit Excellence*, 14 (2014)
16 Minn. Stat. § 317A.011, subd. 4 (2016).

Q13. What are fiduciary responsibilities and how does a board of directors carry them out?

A13. The word *fiduciary* derives from the Latin *fides*, meaning "faith." A fiduciary duty is a legal relationship of trust between two or more parties, most commonly between a fiduciary or trustee and a principal or beneficiary. A corporate director's fiduciary responsibilities are the general duties of care, loyalty and obedience. In the nonprofit context, a board member is trusted to act at all times for the sole benefit and interests of the mission of the organization and not for the director's personal benefit or profit. Particular nonprofit director fiduciary responsibilities are neither specifically listed nor described in any Minnesota statute; rather they are implied in the Minnesota Statutes § 317A.251, subdivision 1 (2016). That subdivision states that "a director shall discharge the duties of the position of director in good faith, in a manner the director reasonably believes to be in the best interests of the corporation, and with the care an ordinarily prudent person in a like position would exercise under similar circumstances."[17] In order to satisfy the fiduciary duties generally, a board of directors must appoint, direct and supervise staff in their work to lawfully carry out the mission of the organization. Implicit in this obligation is regular communication between the board and the staff, which often occurs in the form of staff reports at board meetings or committee meetings.

Q14. What should directors do to ensure they are complying with the duty of care?

A14. The duty of care is a broad legal concept that requires directors to exercise the care that an ordinarily prudent person would exercise under similar circumstances. In the case of a nonprofit organization, the director should behave and act in a way that the director feels is in the best interest of the organization. To properly serve the best interests of the nonprofit, a board member should be an active participant in the management of the organization. A director should prepare for board meetings by reviewing financial statements, meeting minutes and other information about the activities of the organization. A director will be expected to discuss and vote on issues affecting the organization such as fundraising, executive compensation, insurance and leases. A director should make inquiries to ensure an understanding of the corporation's activities, particularly when the director is new to the organization or board. The board as a whole should ensure that board meeting minutes accurately reflect decisions made on board action items. Meeting minutes should indicate all votes taken with an indication of votes in favor, in opposition and in abstention of the item. Actions of the board may be delegated to staff or through the committee structure. It is important that the board act in a supervisory capacity over staff and committees to guarantee successful operations.[18]

Q15. Does a board member with specific expertise such as in law or finance, get held to a higher duty when these subjects are addressed by the board?

A15. Board members are required to act with the care of an ordinarily prudent person in a similar situation. However, if a director has some specific expertise, that board member may be held to a standard of an ordinarily prudent person with that special skill or expertise. For example, an attorney board member who is reviewing a contract or lease for the organization may be held to a higher standard of care than a non-attorney board member with the same responsibilities.[19] Also, directors with such expertise should act in accordance with the professional responsibility standards of their trade when called on to act as both

17 Minn. Stat. § 317A.251, subd. 1 (2016).

18 *See* Office of the Minnesota Attorney General, *Fiduciary Duties of Directors of Charitable Organizations* (2009), www.ag.state.mn.us/Brochures/pubFiduciaryDutiesofDirectors.pdf.

19 Adam Beaudoin, *The Fiduciary Duties of Directors of For-Profit Corporations* (Feb. 8, 2010), www.wardandsmith.com/articles/the-fiduciary-duties-of-directors-of-for-profit-corporations .

a director and advisor with special expertise. For examples, attorney directors who may provide legal advice are required to adhere to the Minnesota Rules of Professional Conduct (2017), especially Rule 1.1 "Competence" and Rule 1.7 "Conflict of Interest: Current Clients".[20]

Q16. What should a director do to ensure they are complying with the duty of loyalty?

A16. The duty of loyalty requires directors to act in a manner reasonably believed to be in the best interests of the organization.[21] A duty of loyalty requires that directors act in a manner that does not cause harm to the organization and avoid leveraging their position to obtain improper personal benefit or usurp an organizational opportunity. The duty of loyalty requires that directors make decisions objectively and look out for the best interest of the organization, rather than the director's personal interest. Directors must act objectively or refrain from participation when objectivity is not possible.

In Minnesota, the Nonprofit Corporation Act considers potential for conflict in a transaction or contract between a corporation and:

- Any of its directors;
- A director of an organization related to the corporation;
- An organization in which a director has a financial interest;
- An organization in which the corporation's director is also a director; and
- Any of the above in which a director's family member may be involved.

Minnesota Statutes § 317A.255 (2016) requires that any potential conflict transaction or contract be "fair and reasonable" to the organization when approved and that the "material facts" of the matter be fully disclosed and known to all parties to a transaction or contract and to the board or appropriate committee for good faith approval. It also requires that the vote of the potentially interested director not count in a board's authorization or ratification process.[22]

To support compliance with the duty of loyalty and state law, it is considered best practice for organizations to adopt a conflict of interest policy that requires disclosure of all relevant information to determine existing and potential conflicts of interest, and identifies procedures to follow when dealing with conflicts A nonprofit board should periodically review its conflict of interest policy to remind directors of their obligations. The board should document the dates of such reviews in its meeting minutes. Directors should periodically review their financial interests in all organizations and their close personal relationships in order to keep current on existing and potential conflicts.[23]

Organizations should document all compensation to insiders. Insiders are paid employees or unpaid individuals who have a special relationship with the organization. Insiders generally include directors, officers, trustees and any key employees with significant responsibilities.[24] Documented information regarding compensation should include the facts used to determine reasonableness, as well as the procedures used for approval. Organizations should also document transactions with related parties. Documented information regarding related-party transactions should include the names of all those considered for

20 Minn. Rules of Prof'l Conduct (2017).
21 Minn. Stat. § 317A.251, subd. 1 (2016).
22 Minn. Stat. § 317A.255 (2016).
23 *See* I.R.S., *Governance and Related Topics - 501(c)(3) Organizations* (2008), www.irs.gov/pub/irs-tege/governance_practices.pdf.
24 Bruce R. Hopkins, *650 Essential Nonprofit Law Questions Answered*, 105 (2005).

the transaction and why the related party was ultimately chosen. Detailed information on the terms of the transaction should also be documented.[25]

Q17. What should directors do to ensure they are complying with the duty of obedience?

A17. The duty of obedience requires a director to ensure that the organization is complying with all applicable laws and regulations, as well as the organization's mission and governing documents. To do this, directors must monitor the activities of the organization and the board to make sure that they are acting in accordance with such laws and documents. Directors must be familiar with the organization's documents and familiar enough with applicable laws and regulations to identify questions and hire legal counsel when necessary.[26] Directors should be provided with copies of the organization's Articles of Incorporation, Bylaws, mission statement, strategic plan and organization charts showing employee and committee reporting structures. Organizations should institute procedures for initial education and ongoing training to make sure directors have such requisite knowledge and familiarity.[27] (Note that while board members are not generally liable for the debts of the organization, they are liable for failure to pay income tax withholding and sales tax collections.)

Q18. Is there a minimum standard for attendance at board meetings and other events?

A18. There is no general minimum standard for board attendance. Each organization may adopt its own policies regarding attendance, which should be outlined in the Articles or Bylaws. However, at least one-third (or other specified proportion) of directors currently holding office by an organization's Bylaws is considered a quorum required for the transaction of business.[28] Quorum requirements vary among organizations and many commonly are fifty percent. Directors should consult the organization's Bylaws to confirm the applicable quorum requirements.

Q19. What other minimum standards must board directors meet?

A19. Board meetings should be held as provided in an organization's Articles or Bylaws. State law requires that a meeting of the board must be held at least once per year.[29] MCN's *Principles & Practices for Nonprofit Excellence* suggests that boards should hold meetings quarterly, at a minimum.[30]

Q20. What documents should the board review to ensure that the organization is in compliance with all relevant laws and statutes?

A20. Directors are responsible for fully understanding their legal and fiduciary obligations. Directors should review and understand documents related to planning, policies, annual review of the executive director's performance, setting compensation structure, fundraising and financial management.[31] Additionally, the

25 *See* I.R.S., *Governance and Related Topics - 501(c)(3) Organizations* (2008), www.irs.gov/pub/irs-tege/governance_practices.pdf.
26 Roles and Responsibilities of the Nonprofit Board, MCN, www.minnesotanonprofits.org (last visited July 31, 2017).
27 *See* I.R.S., *Governance and Related Topics - 501(c)(3) Organizations* (2008), www.irs.gov/pub/irs-tege/governance_practices.pdf.
28 Minn. Stat. § 317A.235 (2016).
29 Minn. Stat. § 317A.231, subd. 1 (2016).
30 Minnesota Council of Nonprofits, *Principles & Practices for Nonprofit Excellence*, 7 (2014).
31 *Id.* at 8.

IRS' new Form 990 inquires about whether a board of directors has reviewed the Form 990.[32] This review is implicit, given a board's obligation to approve the annual report to the Minnesota Attorney General (see Question 22 for more information on the annual report).

Q21. How can board members verify that income tax withholding is being paid?

A21. Many nonprofit organizations are exempt from federal income tax. Although they do not have to pay federal income tax themselves, they must still withhold federal income tax from the pay of their employees. Often nonprofit organizations outsource payroll functions to a payroll provider. In those instances, the payroll provider directly pays the IRS appropriate withholdings on behalf of the organization. Board members may verify that withholdings are being paid through payroll reports from the payroll provider and/or through direct verification with the IRS.

Q22. Must the board of directors officially approve and accept board meeting minutes, monthly financial reports and/or the annual audit? Are there any others?

A22. The annual report to the Minnesota Attorney General must be officially approved and accepted by the board. This approval applies to the entire annual report, which includes:

- The Minnesota Attorney General annual report form;
- IRS Form 990, 990-EZ, 990-PF or 990-N, with schedules. If an organization files a federal tax or information return with the IRS, it must also file a copy of all such returns—including all schedules except those of contributors with the Attorney General.[33]
- An audited financial statement. If a charitable organization received total revenue in excess of $750,000 for its most recent fiscal year, it must file an audited financial statement prepared in accordance with generally accepted accounting principles ("GAAP audit").[34]
- Financial statements. Organizations must submit a financial statement containing a balance sheet, a statement of income and expense and a statement of functional expenses of the organization.[35]
- Fee. The report must be accompanied by a reregistration fee of $25.00. Organizations filing a late report must submit an additional $50.00 late fee.[36]

While other documents are not technically required to be approved by the board, it may be a breach of fiduciary duties for the board not to review them. Under the duties of care and obedience, board members have an obligation to supervise the organization's activities using due care and diligence, and to ensure compliance with relevant laws and the organization's governing documents (see Questions 14 and 16 for more information on the duties of care and obedience). It is unlikely that the board can comply with these duties without reviewing board minutes, monthly or quarterly financial reports, or other of the organization's documents. In addition, some funding sources may require a board resolution, including requirements to set up bank accounts or enter into loans.

32 *See* I.R.S. Form 990, Part VI, Section B, 11(b), www.irs.gov/pub/irs-pdf/f990.pdf (2016).
33 Minn. Stat. § 309.53, subd. 2 (2016).
34 Minn. Stat. § 309.53, subd. 3 (2016).
35 Office of the Minnesota Attorney General, *A Guide to Minnesota's Charities Laws*, www.ag.state.mn.us/Consumer/Publications/GuideCharityLaws.asp#top (last visited July 12, 2017).
36 Minn. Stat. § 309.53, subd. 2, 8 (2016).

Q23. What's the difference between the board of directors and board committees?

A23. Board committees are smaller groups of people with specific tasks or goals. Committee members need not be directors unless required by the organization's Articles or Bylaws, and are often chosen by the chairperson and approved by the board.[37] Committees usually have the responsibility of investigating a particular issue or question and presenting their findings and recommendations to the board, which then votes on the proposed action. Some committees are "standing" and remain in existence indefinitely. Other committees are "ad hoc"[38] and only address limited timely issues. Committees are only authorized to perform those tasks specifically delegated by the board. The board's ability to delegate work to committees may be limited by an organization's Bylaws or Articles of Incorporation. Committees are typically formed when numerous issues must be defined for action by the entire board or when issues are of special complexity.

The board retains ultimate responsibility for the work delegated to committees and is the body that takes action on behalf of the organization.[39] Board committees may include a special litigation committee consisting of one or more independent directors or other independent persons to consider legal rights or remedies of the corporation and whether those rights and remedies should be pursued.[40] Committees other than special litigation commitees are subject at all times to the direction and control of the board.[41]

Q24. Can an organization remove a board member that is causing trouble for the organization? If so, how is this done?

A24. Unless an organization's Articles or Bylaws provide otherwise, directors may be removed with or without cause; this means removal may be for any reason or no reason at all. For example, depending on an organization's governing documents and policies, a director may be removed from a board of directors if they are not fulfilling duties or responsibilities, such as adequate attendance or lack of disclosure of a material conflict of interest. Directors may be removed by those directors who are eligible to elect a director. If the director is appointed, they may be removed with written notice by the person who appointed the director.[42]

If the organization has members with voting rights, a director may be removed by the board if:

- The director was named by the board to fill a vacancy;
- The members with voting rights have not elected directors between the time of the appointment to fill the vacancy and the time of the removal; and
- A majority of the remaining directors present affirmatively vote to remove the director.[43]

Directors may also be removed directly by those members eligible to elect the director. If Bylaws establish specific eligibility requirements, directors may be removed if they no longer meet those requirements.

The exact procedures used for the removal of directors may be developed by the organization, and should be spelled out in the organization's Articles or Bylaws.

---

37 Minn. Stat. § 317A.241 (2017).

38 This is a Latin phrase, which means "for this." In English, it generally means "formed, or done for a particular purpose only."

39 Cheryl Sorokin, *Nonprofit Governance and Management*, 55-57 (2011).

40 This change codifies the result in Janssen v. Best & Flanagan, 662 N.W. 2d 876 (Minn. 2003), where the court held that Minnesota nonprofit corporations may establish independent special litigation committees. The language tracks the language of Minn. Stat. § 302A.241.

41 Minn. Stat. § 317A.241 (2017).

42 Minn. Stat. § 317A.225 (2016).

43 Minn. Stat. § 317A.223 (2016).

Q25. Can an organization remove a board member that is not meeting minimum participation standards? If so, how is this done?

A25. Unless an organization's Articles or Bylaws provide otherwise, directors may be removed for not meeting minimum participation standards. Organizations are advised to clearly state and require regular board review of minimum participation standards, if used. See Question 24 for more information on the removal of directors.

Q26. Is the board responsible to a nonprofit corporation's members with voting rights for actions (or inactions) that trigger member complaints?

A26. A board of directors is responsible to the organization and must act in its best interest with the care of an ordinarily prudent person. If a director proceeds in such a manner, they are unlikely to be held responsible for organizational losses that result from board decisions.

However, members may have a right to vote on issues such as board elections. Minnesota law provides that, "[u]nless the Articles or Bylaws provide otherwise, each member with voting rights is entitled to one vote on each matter voted on by the members."[44] Members of an organization may also seek equitable relief for the breach of fiduciary duties.[45] An action may be brought by at least 50 members with voting rights or ten percent of the members with voting rights, whichever is less.[46]

Q27. Can regulators attack errant directors?

A27. The Minnesota Attorney General has jurisdiction to seek equitable relief for breach of fiduciary duties or violation of the Minnesota Statutes Chapter 317A by a director or an organization.[47]

D. Officers and their Duties

Q28. Are nonprofit organizations required to have certain officer positions?

A28. Yes, nonprofit organizations are required to have more than one natural person serving the functions of the offices of president and treasurer.[48] Nonprofit board officers are directors that are either elected or appointed according to an organization's Articles or Bylaws. Other officer positions, such as vice president or secretary, can be created as permitted in the Bylaws or Articles of Incorporation.

Unless otherwise specified in the Articles or Bylaws, the board president and treasurer have duties beyond those associated with other board members (see Question 30 for a full discussion of these duties). Often, some of these duties are delegated to other board members, board committees or staff members.

---

44 Minn. Stat. § 317A.441(a) (2016).

45 Minn. Stat. § 317A.467 (2016). See Ann K. Bloodhart, Address at the Minnesota Nonprofit Law Conference: The View from the Attorney General's Office (Mar. 09, 2009).

46 Minn. Stat. § 317A.467 (2016).

47 *See* Minn. Stat. § 317A.467 (2016) ("the attorney general, may grant equitable relief it considers just and reasonable in the circumstances and award expenses, including attorney fees and disbursements, to the members").

48 Minn. Stat. § 317A.301 (2016).

Q29. Are a nonprofit corporation's officers different from officers of other boards of directors?

A29. No, there is no substantive difference between a nonprofit corporation's officers and those of other boards of directors. Unlike the Minnesota Business Corporation Statute, the Minnesota Nonprofit Corporation Act uses the position names of "president" and "treasurer" instead of "chief executive officer" and "chief financial officer," respectively. Otherwise the language is identical to that requiring officers of business corporations.[49]

Q30. What are the duties of a board "president" and "treasurer"?

A30. In addition to their fiduciary duties, board officers have additional responsibilities that are named either in statute or in an organization's Articles or Bylaws. Unless otherwise indicated by organizational Bylaws, the board president shall:

1. Have general active management of the business of the corporation;
2. Preside at meetings of the board and members;
3. See that orders and resolutions are carried into effect;
4. Sign and deliver in the name of the corporation deeds, mortgages, bonds, contracts or other instruments related to the business, unless otherwise designated;
5. Maintain records of proceedings of the board and the members; and
6. Perform other duties as prescribed by the board.[50]

Similarly, the duties of a board treasurer are also outlined in statute:

1. Keep accurate financial records of the corporation;
2. Deposit money and checks in the name of and to the credit of the corporation in banks as designated by the board;
3. Endorse deposits and checks received by the corporation;
4. Disburse corporate funds and issue checks and drafts in the name of the corporation;
5. Provide the board an account of transactions by the treasurer of the financial condition of the corporation; and
6. Perform other duties as prescribed by the board.[51]

E. Conflicts of Interest

Q31. What is a conflict of interest?

A31. At its broadest, a conflict of interest exists when there is a discrepancy between the private interests of an individual and that person's role as director of an organization. Private interests can include property, contracts or service agreements, salaries, and familial relationships. Directors, as members of the community at large, will have a wide variety of personal interests. As a result, the conflict arises when the director has a personal stake in the outcome of a decision by the board of directors or some other action taken by the organization.

49 Minn. Stat. § 302A.301 (2016).
50 Minn. Stat. § 317A.305, subd. 2 (2016).
51 Minn. Stat. § 317A.305, subd. 3 (2016).

It is important to recognize that while a true conflict of interest may be addressed through proper policies and procedures, the appearance of a conflict of interest may damage the organization's reputation and ability to raise funds. Such apparent conflicts may lead to unwanted media attention and regulatory investigations.

Q32. What should directors do when they realize they have a conflict of interest?

A32. Minnesota law requires three principal actions when a director has a conflict of interest. First, the critical facts regarding the director's interest must be completely communicated to the group that is taking the action, such as the board, a committee or the membership. Second, the conflicted board member should abstain from voting and such director's presence is not counted for the purpose of determining if a quorum exists. The vote must be approved "in good faith" (meaning with integrity to the duties of the office or position) by two-thirds of the remaining members of the committee, board or members with voting rights. Finally, the overall process of bidding, negotiation, contract drafting and contract execution must be fair and reasonable from the standpoint of the organization.[52]

Failure to abide by a strict conflict of interest procedure can result in the contract being declared void (no contract ever existed) or voidable (the organization can breach the contract without repercussion).

Q33. Is a nonprofit organization required to have a conflict of interest policy?

A33. Minnesota does not require a conflict of interest policy. IRS Form 990 asks organizations to disclose whether they have a written conflict of interest policy, whether disclosure of interests is required and whether the organization monitors and enforces the policy. It is recommended practice for organizations to adopt a conflict of interest policy and to regularly review the policy with board members. Records of that review should be maintained in the board's meeting minutes. Such a policy allows each director to do a thorough examination of their own conflicts. Then, if a conflict or problem arises, the conflict of interest policy can serve as a guide for the organization. Minnesota law deals with the technical and legal aspects of dealing with conflicts of interest. A conflict of interest policy provides directors with an understanding of their role as a fiduciary of the organization.

Q34. What should a conflict of interest policy contain?

A34. A conflict of interest policy should accomplish four primary tasks:

- Define what constitutes a conflict of interest.
- Identify the individuals and activities to be covered by the policy.
- Specify procedures to be followed in managing conflicts of interest.
- Require disclosure of information that may lead to conflicts of interest.[53]

Special attention should be paid to transactions between the organization and its board members, as these can often be, or appear to be, excess benefit transactions (see Question 36 for a discussion on excess

52 Minn. Stat. § 317A.255, subd. 1(b) (2016).
53 Panel on the Nonprofit Sector, *Nonprofit Panel Makes Recommendations to Strengthen Charities* (2005), www.pgdc.com/pgdc/nonprofit-panel-makes-recommendations-strengthen-charities.

benefit transactions). There are three procedures which organizations can follow to create a rebuttable presumption that the transaction did not result in excess benefit:

- Require approval of the transaction by disinterested directors, with interested directors abstaining;
- Obtain and rely upon appropriate data before approving the transaction; and
- Sufficiently document the basis for the decision.

These procedures should be included (and followed) in the conflict of interest policy.

For sample conflict of interest policies, see the IRS sample policy at www.irs.gov/instructions/i1023/ar03.html, and the Minnesota Attorney General sample policy at www.ag.state.mn.us/pdf/charities/ConflictInterestPolicy.pdf.

Q35. Can a conflict of interest arise when a director is also an elected or appointed official that provides funding to the organization, or is a trustee or staff member of a grantmaking foundation that provides funding?

A35. Where a board member works for a funding source for the organization, a conflict could arise if the organization was being considered for a grant from that source and the two organizations are not related.[54] Accepting a grant where such a conflict of interest exists may or may not violate an organization's conflict of interest policy depending on the language in the policy. Generally, if the organization is receiving funding and not expending money, and the potential conflict or perception of it is disclosed according to the conflict of interest, it will not be considered a conflict for the nonprofit.[55]

It is probably a good idea for the director who is also a staff member, trustee or elected official of a corporation or grantmaking foundation to think about the perception of the potential conflict from the corporate/grantmaking foundation's perspective as well. An organization may want to consider other factors prior to acceptance, such as the possibility of negative publicity, the appearance of impropriety, or disproportionate influence (including over other board members) in the hands of a board member that is also a significant funder.

Q36. How can conflicts of interest lead to charges of private inurement and/or intermediate sanctions?

A36. The Internal Revenue Code describes the conditions under which private inurement or intermediate sanctions apply. Pursuant to the Code, a disqualified person is any person who within a five-year period prior to a particular transaction had substantial influence over the affairs of an organization or is a member of that person's family.[56] Additionally, an entity which is owned 35 percent or more by such a person is also deemed to be disqualified.[57] Some people are automatically disqualified by reason of the "influential" position they hold within the organization, but disqualification is generally determined by the specific facts of each individual.[58] See I.R.C. § 4958 (2017) for more specific information on "disqualified person," available at www.law.cornell.edu/uscode/text/26/4958.

If a disqualified individual or entity appears to have a conflict of interest and enters into a transaction with

54 Minn. Stat. § 317A.255 subd. 3 (2016).
55 Bruce R. Hopkins, *650 Essential Nonprofit Law Questions Answered*, Chapter 27 (2005).
56 *See* I.R.C. § 4958(f)(1) (2017).
57 *See* I.R.C. § 4958(f)(1) (2017).
58 Lawrence M. Brauer and Leonard J. Henzke, *Intermediate Sanctions* (IRC 4958) Update (2003), www.irs.gov/pub/irs-tege/eotopicc03.pdf.

a charitable organization, the transaction may be scrutinized for objective fairness or an improper benefit due to the disqualified person's influence over the organization. A transaction where the disqualified person receives an improper benefit is defined to be an excess benefit transaction, which results in the private inurement of the individual.

In an excess benefit transaction, the individual involved receives a greater benefit than the organization. The amount of benefit received by the individual that exceeds the benefit received by the organization is considered private inurement. Private inurement occurs when resources are transferred from a charitable organization to a disqualified individual due to the individual's influential relationship with the organization, and not in furtherance of the organization's exempt purposes.[59]

Not every transaction between a charitable organization and a disqualified person results in private inurement; the test is whether the transaction was reasonable under the circumstances.[60] Traditionally, the transaction was required to involve a disbursement of the organization's net earnings to result in private inurement. But the modern view is much more comprehensive, and includes essentially any transaction from which the disqualified individual receives an improper benefit, monetary or otherwise.[61]

Intermediate sanctions may be imposed in excess benefit transactions. Intermediate sanctions are penalties less severe than the revocation of exempt status, and generally come in the form of excise taxes. These taxes can be substantial and are imposed on both the disqualified person and, often, on officers and directors who had knowledge of the impropriety yet participated in the transaction.[62]

F. Board Liability

Q37. Can board members be personally sued for actions of the organization?

A37. Yes, under certain circumstances. Board members will generally not be personally sued for actions of the organization. However, they may be sued personally for approving an action which violated their fiduciary duties (see Questions 13-16 for information on fiduciary duties). For example, directors would be in violation of their duty of care by approving an action without being reasonably informed about that action, or would be in violation of their duty of obedience by approving an action that they reasonably should have known was against the law. Directors may also be personally liable for approving actions that violate federal law, whether or not fiduciary duties had been breached.[63]

Q38. What are the personal and financial liabilities that can be incurred as a result of serving on a board of directors?

A38. Directors may be personally liable for breach of their fiduciary duties (see Questions 13-16 for information on fiduciary duties). If a director fails to fulfill an obligation, such as providing effective supervision as required by the duty of care, that director may be held personally liable for the resulting consequences. Likewise, if directors engage in an activity that they are prohibited from doing, such as obtaining an

59 Bruce R. Hopkins, *The Law of Tax-Exempt Organizations*, page 429 (2004).
60 Bruce R. Hopkins, *The Law of Tax-Exempt Organizations*, page 429 (2004).
61 Bruce R. Hopkins, *The Law of Tax-Exempt Organizations*, pages 430-31 (2004).
62 *Second Legal Answer Book*, Q1.1, page 2.
63 Minn. Stat. § 317A.257 (2016).

improper personal benefit in violation of the duty of loyalty, they may be held personally liable. Directors may be financially liable for harm suffered by the organization due to their breaches of fiduciary duties, and taxes or fees may also be assessed in some situations, such as excise taxes being imposed in cases of private inurement. One of the most common situations of personal board liability is the organization's failure to pay withholding taxes for its employees.

Directors may be personally liable for actions based on federal law, such as violations of the Employee Retirement Income Security Act of 1974 ("ERISA") or anti-discrimination statutes. Personal liability may also exist for violation of an individual director's express contractual obligation and for an individual director's actions that have directly caused injury to another.[64]

Q39. How can a nonprofit organization prevent board members from being sued?

A39. There is nothing organizations can do to provide a complete bar against directors being sued. There are, however, certain actions organizations can take to reduce the likelihood of a lawsuit and/or the success of that action. First, an organization can incorporate, that is, become a corporation. Directors of a nonprofit corporation enjoy much greater immunity than those of an unincorporated association, and are generally not personally liable for actions taken as a director unless fiduciary duties are breached (see Questions 13-16 for information on fiduciary duties). Second, an organization can choose not to compensate its directors. Under Minnesota law, uncompensated directors are entitled to somewhat greater immunity than paid directors and less likely to be exposed to a lawsuit.[65] Compensation is defined as "anything of value received for services rendered" except expense reimbursements actually incurred, a per diem (not more than authorized in Minn. Stat. § 15.059, subd. 3 (2016)), or organizational payments for D&O (Directors and Officers) insurance premiums or other liability protection for directors.[66]

An organization can also reduce the vulnerability of directors being financially liable when lawsuits occur. Indemnification clauses and D&O insurance coverage are two ways that an organization can accept the financial burden of defense. Indemnification clauses are provisions in the Articles or Bylaws assuring that the organization will reimburse its directors or pay for the cost of defending against certain lawsuits. D&O insurance provides coverage for defense of certain claims against the individuals covered by the policy. Practically speaking, organizations generally would not want to provide indemnification unless the organization was being reimbursed with D&O insurance. Standard homeowner's insurance policies may also offer some liability protection for an individual's volunteer commitments.

Q40. What laws protect board members from being sued?

A40. Minnesota Statutes Section 317A.257 (2016) provides some protection for unpaid directors. Essentially, the law provides immunity for actions (or inactions) taken in good faith and on behalf of the organization.[67] It does not provide immunity for actions brought by the Attorney General for breaches of fiduciary duties, actions based on federal law or actions based on contractual obligations. Nor does it provide immunity for willful or reckless misconduct, wrongful death or physical injury caused to another. Minnesota Statutes Chapter 317A (2016) also provides protection for directors who do not approve an action.

64 Minn. Stat. § 317A.257, subd. 2 (2016).

65 Minn. Stat. § 317A.257 (2016).

66 Minn. Stat. § 317A.257, subd. 3 (2016).

67 While Minn. Stat. §317A.257 (2016) provides immunity for actions "within the scope of the person's responsibilities," the MN Supreme Court has stated that "a director acting outside the specific scope of his or her duty as members of the board will receive the statute's protection so long as the director is acting on behalf of the nonprofit corporation." Rehn v. Fischley, 557 N.W.2d 328, 335 (1997).

If a board action results in the personal liability of directors, those who dissented to such action, or were forced to abstain from voting due to a conflict of interest, will not be liable. (NOTE: such dissent must be affirmative; assent is presumed in the absence of an affirmative dissent.)[68] Personal liability is only applied to actions of that particular board member; if a director dissents, that director will have not acted or participated in the action. For this reason it is especially important for board meeting minutes to reflect which directors assented or dissented to a particular motion.

The Federal Volunteer Protection Act provides immunity to volunteers in certain situations. Under this law, unpaid directors are immune from liability when acting within the scope of their responsibilities, so long as the directors are properly licensed if necessary, the action does not constitute gross negligence or willful or reckless conduct, and the damage was not caused by operation of a motor vehicle.[69]

Q41. Does a nonprofit organization need to pay the costs associated with defending its board of directors?

A41. Minnesota law provides a standard for the indemnification of directors.[70] It states that organizations shall indemnify past/present directors who have been made a party or have been threatened to be made a party, to a legal or administrative proceeding based on their conduct as a past or present director. It states that organizations shall indemnify directors for judgments, fines, settlements, reasonable expenses (including attorneys fees) and excise taxes imposed against that director with respect to an employee benefit plan. Such indemnification will occur as long as:

- The director has not been indemnified elsewhere for the same conduct.
- The person acted in good faith.
- The person received no improper personal benefit from the conduct.
- If the person had a conflict of interest, the transaction was fair to the organization or the conflict was fully disclosed to the board prior to approval of the transaction.
- In the case of acts or omissions occurring in the official capacity, the person reasonably believed the conduct was in the best interests of the organization.
- If a criminal proceeding, the person did not have reasonable cause to believe the conduct was unlawful.

This standard is prescribed by the Minnesota Statutes Section 317A.521 (2016), which also states that organizations may condition, limit or prohibit indemnification in their Articles or Bylaws.[71] Therefore, organizations may indemnify their directors to extent the organization specifies in its documents.

Q42. What is indemnification?

A42. Indemnification is the process of creating legal protection against loss. The process involves an insurance company or other individual or corporation agreeing to compensate for damages or injuries.

68 Minn. Stat. § 317A.251 subd. 3 (2016).

69 Astho Legal Preparedness Series Emergency Volunteer Toolkit, *Volunteer Protection Acts and Good Samaritan Laws Fact Sheet* (2012), www.astho.org/Programs/Preparedness/Public-Health-Emergency-Law/Emergency-Volunteer-Toolkit/Volunteer-Protection-Acts.

70 Minn. Stat.. § 317A.521 subd. 2 (2016).

71 Minn. Stat. § 317A.521, subd. 4 (2016).

Q43. If someone resigns from a board, is that person immune as a target regarding decisions that were made while that person was still on the board?

A43. No. A person remains liable for their actions and the actions taken by the board during the time that person served as a director.

Q44. What documentation is required to resign from the board?

A44. A board director may resign at any time by giving written notice to the corporation. The resignation is effective without acceptance when the notice is given to the corporation, unless a later effective time is specified in the notice.[72] Each organization may provide additional rules and procedures for resignation within its Articles or Bylaws. Board resignation should be recorded in board meeting minutes, and the board roster should be promptly updated.

G. Board Meetings, Minutes and Notices

Q45. What type of notice is required to inform board members about meetings?

A45. Unless different requirements are outlined in the Articles or Bylaws, notice must be given at least five days prior to the meeting and include the date, time and location of the meeting, but need not include the purpose of the meeting. Such notice may be given via electronic communication (fax, email or posting on an electronic network) if the individual director had consented to receiving notice in such a form.[73]

If the date, time and location of the meeting has been specified in the Articles or Bylaws, or announced at a previous meeting, notice is not required.

Q46. What should be included in board meeting minutes?

A46. The required content of meeting minutes is not specifically regulated. However, it is recommended that they be complete and accurate, containing enough information for the reader to know what took place. [74]

Generally, meeting minutes should contain:

- The date, time and location of the meeting.
- The name of the meeting chair.
- The names of the directors who are present and who are absent.
- The time the meeting ended.
- Whether or not a quorum was present.
- A summary of any actions taken (whether there was a vote, the outcome of the vote, etc.).
- The names of who moved and seconded the motions.

---

72 Minn. Stat. § 317A.221(a) (2016).

73 Minn. Stat. § 317A.231 subd. 4 (2016).

74 Melanie L. Herman, *Ready in Defense: A Liability, Litigation and Legal Guide for Nonprofits* (2003).

- The names of who assented and dissented to the motions, and who abstained from voting. It is especially important to note who dissented or abstained; one is presumed to have assented unless they affirmatively dissent or are prohibited from voting due to a conflict of interest, which may provide immunity for any liability created as a result of the approved action.
- Any documents that were presented to the board. Some organizations may also want to attach a copy of the documents to the meeting minutes.
- A concise summary of what was discussed.

While it is important that meeting minutes contain enough information to convey what took place, organizations should keep in mind that the IRS may review all minutes in the event of an audit. Meeting minutes are legal documents and should be kept in a secure location permanently.

Q47. Can a nonprofit organization's board meetings be closed to the public?

A47. Generally, yes; a nonprofit's board meetings may be closed to the public. However, meetings must be open to the public if the organization's Articles or Bylaws require, or if the organization is subject to Minnesota's Open Meeting Law.

The Open Meeting Law applies to nonprofit organizations created by political subdivisions, and organizations specifically created by a law which states that the organization will be subject to the Open Meeting Law. It applies to both board and committee meetings where at least a quorum is present. An organization may be found in violation of the law, however, if it purposefully has less than a quorum in attendance in effort to circumvent the Open Meeting Law.[75] For more information on the Open Meeting Law, see the information brief published by the Minnesota House of Representatives, at www.house.leg.state.mn.us/hrd/pubs/openmtg.pdf.

Q48. Can a nonprofit organization's board meetings be closed to members with voting rights?

A48. Yes. Unless the organization's Articles or Bylaws require meetings to be open to members with voting rights, they need not be. The meeting minutes, however, must be made available to the members. See Question 46 for information on the availability of meeting minutes.

Q49. What types of technology are allowable for conducting board meetings? For example, can a board meet in an Internet chat room?

A49. The board may conduct its meetings using any means of remote communication it has authorized, which are often specified in the Bylaws or Articles of Incorporation. Remote communication may be electronic communication, conference telephone, video conference, the internet or other means that allow people not physically present to communicate substantially simultaneously.[76] Organizations are advised to have board meeting minutes reflect the manner of remote communication and the parties so involved.

75 Minnesota House of Representatives, *Minnesota Open Meeting Law* (Oct. 2014), at www.house.leg.state.mn.us/hrd/pubs/openmtg.pdf.

Q50. Can members with voting rights access the minutes from board meetings? If so, how?

A50. Yes, members can access the minutes from board meetings. Minutes must be kept at the organization's registered office for at least six years, and may be kept in paper or electronic form. During this time, the minutes must be made available to members upon request, as long as the purpose of the access is reasonably related to the member's interest in the organization as a member. [77]

Q51. Are the minutes from board meetings considered public documents?

A51. No, meeting minutes are not considered public documents. Organizations must make minutes available to members and directors, but not to the public at large.[78] The exception to this rule is nonprofit organizations subject to the Minnesota Statutes Section 13D.01 (2016) (the Open Meeting Law), which are required to make records involving director voting available to the public.[79] The Open Meeting Law applies to nonprofit organizations created by political subdivisions, and organizations specifically created by a law which states that the organization will be subject to the Open Meeting Law. For more information on the Open Meeting Law, see the information brief published by the Minnesota House of Representatives, at www.house.leg.state.mn.us/hrd/pubs/openmtg.pdf. Though not legally required, some organizations choose to have their board meeting minutes available to the public. The increased transparency may lead to increased participation or honesty in governance. Other organizations keep their minutes as internal documents, to protect any discussion of future plans or internal workings of the organization, or any private information that the minutes may contain.

H. Voting Rights and Requirements

Q52. Can proxies be used to vote on a board action?

A52. No, board members may not vote by proxy on an item of board action.[80] The fiduciary duty of care requires that board members deliberate issues before making a decision, that may be more nuanced than a simple "yes" or "no" vote. Boardsource warns that "allowing proxies in the boardroom could also have a negative effect on board attendance and diminish board members' adherence to their legal requirements under the duty of care."

Q53. What are the differences between taking a board action by proxy voting versus by writing?

A53. A proxy is someone that is authorized to act for another as an agent or substitute. With properly granted authority, proxies can vote on behalf of another.[81] If an action may be taken at a board meeting and is so allowed in organizational Bylaws, the action may be taken by "written action signed, or consented to by authenticated electronic communication, by all directors."[82] Whereas a proxy vote is cast by an agent of a director or member, a vote by writing is cast by the actual director. A vote by writing allows a director to fulfill their personal fiduciary duties to the organization.

76 Minn. Stat. § 317A.231 subd.3 (2016). See also Minn. Stat. § 317A.011 subd. 18a (2016).
77 *See* Minn. Stat. § 317A.461 (2016).
78 Minn. Stat. § 317A.461, subd. 2 (2016) ("A member or a director, or the agent or attorney of a member or a director, may inspect all documents").
79 Minn. Stat. §§ 13D.01 subd. 4-5 (2016).
80 Minn. Stat. § 317A.237 (2016).

Q54. Can board members vote on board actions by phone or email?

A54. Directors may participate in board meetings via conference telephone or other forms of interactive remote communication if authorized.[83] Directors participating by such means are considered present at the meeting and may vote.

Q55. Are faxed or electronic signatures allowable? Is any type of legal documentation required when a faxed or electronic signature is used?

A55. Yes, faxed or electronic signatures are allowed, and no documentation need be attached. Minnesota law specifies that where a signature is required, an electronic signature is sufficient.[84]

I. Other Issues

Q56. Can board members receive compensation?

A56. Yes, the board may fix reasonable compensation for its members, subject to any limitations set forth in the Articles of Incorporation or Bylaws.[85] The amount of compensation cannot exceed the benefit that the director reasonably provides for the organization; excessive compensation may result in excess benefit transactions, which may subject the board and the individual director to intermediate sanctions. See Question 36 for more information on excess benefit transactions and intermediate sanctions. See Question 57 for more information related to director reimbursement for board-related expenses.

Much argument exists over whether organizations *should* compensate its directors. Some feel that providing compensation is inappropriate in a nonprofit organization because donors want their contributions to go toward services, not administrative costs, and board compensation may deter donations. Some feel that providing compensation will also discourage volunteerism and jeopardize volunteer protection and immunity.[86] Alternatively, others feel that providing compensation promotes professionalism, improves performance and increases accountability. Each organization must decide whether to compensate its directors based on the particular circumstances of that organization.[87] MCN's *Principles & Practices for Nonprofit Excellence* indicates that in accordance with best practices, board members should not receive monetary compensation for their board duties other than for board-related expense reimbursements.[88]

Q57. Can board members receive reimbursement for organization-related travel or other expenses?

A57. Yes, board members may receive reimbursement for expenses incurred while carrying out their duties as a director, subject to any limitations and/or expenses specifically identified in the Articles of Incorporation or Bylaws. Reimbursement for these expenses does not qualify as "compensation"; an unpaid director may receive reimbursement without becoming a paid director.[89]

81 Minn. Stat. § 317A.453 (2016).
82 Minn. Stat. § 317A. 239, subdiv. 1 (2016).
83 Minn. Stat. § 317A.231 (2016) (participation via telephone or remote communication constitutes presence). Also Minn. Stat. § 317A.237 (2016).
84 Minn. Stat. § 317A.015, subdiv. 2, (4) (2016).
85 Minn. Stat. § 317A.211 (2016).
86 Minn. Stat. § 317A.257 (2016).

Q58. Can a nonprofit organization make a loan to a board member?

A58. An organization may make a loan to a board member only when the loan is reasonably expected to provide a benefit to the organization. This benefit often comes in the form of interest payments received from the borrower. If the organization receives no benefit because the terms are favorable to the borrower, or the chance of repayment is small, the transaction may involve private inurement. See Question 36 for information on private inurement. The loan must be approved by two-thirds of the board (not including the borrower board member), or two-thirds of members with voting rights if the organization has members with voting rights.[90]

While it is often legal to make a loan to a director, it is discouraged, so organizations should always consider the appearance of the transaction. Organizations should try to avoid the appearance of impropriety, and may want to avoid making loans to directors where it may be viewed in a negative or questionable light by the public.

Q59. Is a nonprofit organization legally obligated to train its board?

A59. No, a nonprofit is not legally obligated to train its board. It is nonetheless a good idea. Board members should be given adequate education and training so they are aware of their fiduciary duties, what is required of them, and the tools and procedures available to help fulfill those duties and requirements.

Q60. How should an organization deal with a board member that is engaging in illegal behavior?

A60. Articles of Incorporation or Bylaws should outline when a board member may be removed from a board of directors. If these documents do not so provide, directors may be removed without cause by the person appointing the director.[91] The person removing the director shall do so by giving written notice of the removal to the director and either the presiding officer of the board or the corporation's president or secretary.[92] See Question 24 for more information.

An organization may also want to adopt a "whistleblower policy" that sets out procedures to follow when someone has knowledge of another's illegal conduct or financial mismanagement. See Form 990 for additional information.

Q61. Can those who start an organization restrict the board from taking actions of which they don't approve?

A61. The founders may structure the organization in such a way that allows them more decision-making authority than the board. For example, the founders may create two classes of directors, one class of the founders and one class of all other directors, and require certain issues to be voted on only by the class of founders. However, under Minnesota law, directors may not vote by class except where the Articles or

87 *See* Should Board Members of Nonprofit Organizations be Compensated? (Dec. 21, 2015), www.asaecenter.org/Resources/whitepaperdetail.cfm?ItemNumber=22981.
88 Minnesota Council of Nonprofits, *Principles & Practices for Nonprofit Excellence*, Chapter 8 (2014).
89 Minn. Stat. § 317A.257, subd. 3 (2016).
90 Minn. Stat. § 317A.501 (2016).
91 Minn. Stat. § 317A.225 (2016).
92 Minn. Stat. § 317A.225 (2016).

Bylaws provide that only one class of directors may vote on a particular matter.[93] An organization could also be structured as a member organization with two classes of members: one class of founders and one class of all other members. The Articles or Bylaws can then provide the class of founder-members with increased rights or preferences.[94]

Q62. ***Is parliamentary procedure or Robert's Rules of Order required?***

A62. Robert's Rules of Order Newly Revised, commonly referred to as Robert's Rules of Order (or simply Robert's Rules), is the most widely-used manual of parliamentary procedure in the United States.[95] Minnesota statute does not require that a board follow Robert's Rules of Order. Each board will function differently depending on its size and board culture.

J. Related Resources

Publications:

Directors & Officers: Key Facts about Insurance and Legal Liability
Published by Nonprofits Insurance Alliance of California (NIAC), Alliance of Nonprofits for Insurance, RRG (ANI), and Member Companies in the Nonprofits Insurance Alliance Group,

Office of the Minnesota Attorney General, *Guide for Charity Board Members*
www.ag.state.mn.us/Consumer/Publications/FiduciaryDuties.asp (last visited July 13, 2017).
Guide providing recommendations to help directors act in accordance with their fiduciary duties.

Office of the Minnesota Attorney General, *Charities*
www.ag.state.mn.us/Charity/Default.asp (last visited July 13, 2017).
Guide providing information on the relevant Minnesota law regarding charitable organizations.

Principles & Practices for Nonprofit Excellence
Published by the Minnesota Council of Nonprofits

Statutes:

Minnesota Statutes Chapter 317A: *The Nonprofit Corporation Act*
Published by the Minnesota Office of the Revisor of Statutes,
www.revisor.mn.gov/statutes/?id=317A

93 Minn. Stat. § 317A.213 (2016).

94 Minn. Stat. § 317A.401 (2016). "The articles or bylaws may establish criteria or procedures for admission. . . Members are of one class unless the articles establish, or authorize the bylaws to establish, more than one class. . . Members are entitled to vote and have equal rights and preferences except to the extent that the articles or bylaws have fixed or limited the rights and preferences of members or different classes of members or provide for nonvoting members. The articles or bylaws may fix the term of membership."

95 Jim Slaughter et al., *Notes and Comments on Robert's Rules, 4th Edition* (2012).

CHAPTER 7

LOBBYING, ELECTION-RELATED ACTIVITY AND VOTER EDUCATION

Topics

A. Overview

Federal Tax Restrictions on Lobbying

Internal Revenue Code (IRC) Section[1] 501(c)(3) public charities are allowed to engage in lobbying. Public Charities may do so on a limited basis, and must report the extent of these activities to the Internal Revenue Service (IRS). If these organizations exceed the limits established by the IRS, they may lose their tax-exempt status or be subject to financial penalties. Lobbying activities of 501(c)(3) organizations are evaluated with one of two tests, the "no substantial part" test or the section 501(h) expenditure test:

- The no substantial part test is the default rule on lobbying activities. The applicable tax laws provide simply that no substantial part of the activities of a 501(c)(3) organization may consist of lobbying. There is uncertainty about how much lobbying is "substantial" under this test. The IRS never defined how much money a charity may spend on lobbying in a given year, nor did they clearly define what are and what are not lobbying activities. Organizations subject to the no substantial part test report their lobbying activities and expenditures on IRS Form 990, Schedule C, part II-B.

- Public charities other than churches can avoid the uncertainties of the no substantial part test by making the 501(h) election. Doing so results in the organization's lobbying activities being measured against the Section 501(h) expenditure test, which provides specific dollar limits for lobbying activities based on a percentage of the organization's budget. The applicable regulations also define lobbying and exceptions to lobbying. Organizations may make the 501(h) election by filing Form 5768 with the IRS. These organizations report their lobbying expenditures on IRS Form 990, Schedule C, Part II-A.

- Under the 501(h) test, the IRS distinguishes between two forms of lobbying: direct lobbying and grassroots lobbying. Direct lobbying occurs when the lobbyist contacts a legislator or legislative staff member personally concerning specific legislation. Grassroots lobbying occurs when the lobbyist encourages members of the public to contact their legislator. Electing 501(h) organizations may use only 25 percent of their total lobbying limit for grassroots lobbying.

Registration of Lobbyists

In addition to annually reporting expenditures to the IRS, organizations may be required to register with and report on their legislative activities to other federal and state agencies. The federal Lobbying Disclosure Act (LDA) requires lobbyists, lobbying firms and organizations with in-house lobbyists to register and report their activities to the United States Congress if they meet certain minimum requirements. Lobbyists meeting a separate set of requirements are also required to register and report to the Minnesota Campaign Finance and Public Disclosure Board.

Reporting Obligations

To comply with the reporting requirements of the IRS, United States Congress and the State of Minnesota, 501(c)(3) organizations and their lobbyists must keep track of their lobbying activities and expenditures. These agencies require varying levels of detail in their reports and have adopted different definitions of lobbying, so it is necessary for 501(c)(3) organizations to be aware of all three sets of requirements.

The definition of lobbying varies between state and federal agencies and even within the IRS. Organizations that elect to come under the 501(h) expenditure test must classify their lobbying activities according to the prescribed

1 Footnotes throughout this Chapter refer to the Internal Revenue Code as "IRC"; the use of the word "Section" in this Part's text from this point forward is a reference to Sections of the Internal Revenue Code unless the text notes otherwise.

definitions of grassroots and direct lobbying, but organizations that do not make the 501(h) election do not have a precise definition of lobbying available to them when reporting to the IRS and therefore must report a broader range of activities.

The 501(h) election also impacts the definition of lobbying used to report to Congress under the LDA for organizations required to report under the LDA. Organizations that have made the 501(h) election have the option of using those definitions of lobbying, while non-electing organizations must use the LDA's definitions of lobbying. Most significantly, organizations using the LDA definitions must report on communications regarding not just federal legislation, but also federal rules and regulations, which are exempt from reporting under the Section 501(h) expenditure test.

Lobbying at the state level includes attempts to influence legislative action, administrative action (changes to administrative rules), or the official actions of a metropolitan governmental unit.[2] Lobbying must be reported at the state level only if an individual meets very specific requirements that obligate the individual to register with the Minnesota Campaign Finance and Public Disclosure Board. Certain individuals are exempt from registration and reporting even if they meet these requirements. The Minnesota Campaign Finance and Public Disclosure Board provides the applicable definitions as well as a list of those individuals for whom registration is not required in the Lobbyist Handbook.[3]

Election-related Activities

Section 501(c)(3) organizations are prohibited from intervening in political campaigns either in support of or opposition to a candidate for public office and cannot coordinate with a candidate or political party. Public charities may engage in certain nonpartisan election-related activities, however, such as candidate debates and voter registration drives. Social welfare organizations, which are exempt from tax under Section 501(c)(4), have more flexibility. They may endorse or coordinate with a candidate or party as long as such efforts do not constitute their primary activities. Section 501(c)(4) organizations may also conduct nonpartisan lobbying on an unlimited basis. Contributions to these organizations are not tax deductible as charitable contributions. Political Action Committees, or PACS, may conduct partisan electioneering on an unlimited basis, and, like 501(c)(4)s, contributions made to these organizations are not tax deductible.

This chapter will primarily address the limits and requirements on lobbying for 501(c)(3) public charities. Organizations exempt from federal income tax under other subsections of Section 501(c) have less restrictive lobbying limitations.

B. Legal Opportunities and Limits on Lobbying for 501(c)(3) Nonprofit Organizations

Q1. What is and is not considered lobbying for the purpose of IRS reporting?

A1. Generally speaking, lobbying involves communication with a legislator or employee of a legislative body in an attempt to influence specific legislation. Lobbying must be contrasted with "advocacy," which covers a much broader category of activities directed at influencing public policy. Activities that do not meet all of the required elements of lobbying may be advocacy, which is not subject to the limitations applicable to lobbying activities.

2 Minnesota Campaign Finance and Public Disclosure Board, www.cfboard.state.mn.us/lob_overview.htm (last visited July 18, 2017).

3 Minnesota Campaign Finance and Public Disclosure Board, *Lobbyist Handbook*, 4-5 (Apr. 2017), www.cfboard.state.mn.us/handbook/hb_lobbyist.pdf.

Whether a specific action constitutes lobbying depends in part on whether the organization has elected to come under the 501(h) expenditure test. See Section C: The 501(h) Election: The Expenditure Test. If an organization does not make a 501(h) election, it may not take advantage of the definitions of (and exceptions to) lobbying available under the Section 501(h) test. These non-electing organizations may operate without a clear idea of whether or not their activities constitute lobbying.

- Section 501(h) and its implementing regulations define two forms of lobbying: direct and grassroots, which are explored in greater detail in Section D: Direct versus Grassroots Lobbying. Direct lobbying involves communication with an official who participates in the formulation of legislation, such as a legislator or legislative staff member. Grassroots lobbying involves encouraging the public to contact a legislator. An action must meet every element of a five-part test to be considered grassroots lobbying.

The 501(h) test excludes the following activities from the definition of lobbying even though they may otherwise meet the requirements for either direct or grassroots lobbying:

- Communications with legislators or executive branch employees stating a position on proposed *regulations*. Regulations are rules established for the purpose of implementing legislation. For example, the Food and Drug Administration issues specific rules governing the distribution and sale of prescription drugs based on a general law passed by Congress. Regulations carry the force of law, but they are not passed through a legislative process.
- Communications with an organization's own members, as long as the organization does not encourage its members to lobby.
- A response to a written request from a legislative body for technical advice on pending legislation.
- Communications with legislators while acting in self-defense of the organization, that is, regarding legislation that may affect the organization's very existence, tax exempt status, powers or similar matters. This exception does not apply to lobbying on issues related to a charity's mission.
- Preparation and distribution of a nonpartisan analysis of a legislative issue or proposal, even if the organization takes a position on the merits of the proposal, as long as the pertinent facts are presented fully and fairly so as to enable the audience to form an independent opinion, and the document does not include a direct call to the reader to contact legislators (direct and indirect calls are discussed in Section D: Direct versus Grassroots Lobbying).
- Discussion of broad policy issues whose resolution would require legislation, as long as the discussion does not deal with specific legislation; for example, a white paper stressing the need to stop global warming, which does not mention a specific bill.
- Use in grassroots lobbying of materials not created for the purpose of lobbying, as long as the organization can show that the materials were not created for the primary purpose of lobbying (perhaps through a substantial non-lobbying distribution of the material), or if at least six months have passed between the creation of the materials and their use in lobbying.[4]

Q2. What is the difference between advocacy and lobbying?

A2. "Lobbying" refers to activities to influence legislation, and may be engaged in by 501(c)(3) public charities on a limited basis. "Advocacy" covers a much broader category of activities related to public policy, including education of the public and government officials, and attempts to influence non-

4 Bob Smucker, *The Nonprofit Lobbying Guide*, 53-54 (1999). See also Elizabeth Kingsley, et al., *E-Advocacy for Nonprofits: The Law of Lobbying and Election-Related Activity on the Net,* 15 (2011).

legislative policymaking. Unlike lobbying, advocacy is not restricted for 501(c)(3) organizations.[5]

Q3. Can all nonprofits lobby?

A3. All nonprofits, except for private foundations, can lobby. The tax classification of the particular nonprofit determines the lobbying restrictions (if any) to which that organization is subject. Most of the questions in this chapter address the limits that apply to 501(c)(3) organizations.

Section 501(c)(3) public charities can lobby subject to the limitations defined by one of two IRS tests: the no substantial part test and the Section 501(h) expenditure test. By filing IRS Form 5768, the organization may elect to use the 501(h) expenditure test, which provides specific dollar limits for lobbying activities based on a percentage of an organization's budget, as well as specific definitions of and exceptions to lobbying activities. Organizations that do not file Form 5768 are automatically subject to the less clearly defined no substantial part test, which limits lobbying activities to an insubstantial part of an organization's overall activities.

Private foundations are generally not allowed to lobby. Congress imposed more stringent rules on private foundations because private foundations are typically funded by a single source and therefore are less subject to public scrutiny. However there are some exceptions to this rule that include acting in "self-defense" regarding legislation that may affect the foundation's existence, tax exempt status, powers or similar matters. There is a set of legislation-related activities that private foundations can do that are not considered lobbying. These activities include, but are not limited to:

- Funding or producing nonpartisan analysis, study or research that does not include a call to action regarding legislation;
- Providing technical assistance to government bodies or the legislature;
- Jointly funding a project with the government;
- Funding advocacy, which is a wider range of activities, permitted by law; or
- Providing support for nonpartisan voter registration and other voter engagement activities.[6]

Q4. Given the legal restrictions on lobbying that nonprofit organizations face, why would they want to do it?

A4. Many nonprofits see participation in public policy matters as critical to their missions. Lobbying on legislation of interest to the organization is an important means to influence public policy and further their charitable purposes. Active participation in lobbying can help ensure the success of legislation the organization favors and defeat of legislation it opposes.[7]

Q5. What are the budgetary limits on spending for lobbying activity and what is the difference between the 501(h) election and its expenditure test versus the no substantial part test?

A5. The spending limits for a 501(c)(3) organization's lobbying activity depend on whether the organization has made the 501(h) election (see Section C: The 501(h) Election: The Expenditure Test). If the

5 Thomas R. Asher, *Myth v. Fact: Foundation Support of Advocacy* (2003).
6 David F. Arons, *Power in Policy: A Funders Guide to Advocacy and Civic Participation,* 169-205 (2007).
7 Bob Smucker, *The Nonprofit Lobbying Guide*, 7 (1999).

organization has not made the 501(h) election, "no substantial part" of its activities may consist of lobbying. The IRS has not defined "substantial part" but all of the facts and circumstances must be analyzed including "the importance of the lobbying efforts to the organization, the time and effort of the organization (including its volunteers) in legislative activities, the frequency of those activities, and the degree of attention of the leadership of the organization to the activities."[8] Note that for purposes of the no substantial part test, activities and not just expenditures are considered in determining whether the amount of lobbying is excessive.

The lobbying nontaxable amount for any organization for any taxable year is the lesser of (A) $1,000,000 or (B) the amount determined under the following table[9]:

If the exempt purpose expenditures are—	**The lobbying nontaxable amount is—**
Not over $500,000	20 percent of the exempt purpose expenditures.
Over $500,000 but not over $1,000,000	$100,000, plus 15 percent of the excess of the exempt purpose expenditures over $500,000.
Over $1,000,000 but not over $1,500,000	$175,000 plus 10 percent of the excess of the exempt purpose expenditures over $1,000,000.
Over $1,500,000	$225,000 plus 5 percent of the excess of the exempt purpose expenditures over $1,500,000.

An organization's exempt purpose expenditures are its expenditures related to the charitable purpose for which it received tax-exempt status.[10] The expenditure limitations under Section 501(h) are discussed in more detail in Section C: The 501(h) Election: The Expenditure Test.

The no substantial part test is the default rule for 501(c)(3) organizations. It provides simply that no substantial part of the organization's activities may consist of lobbying, but does not provide specific definitions of what constitutes lobbying or precise limits on the amount of lobbying that will be deemed insubstantial.

The 501(h) test measures two forms of lobbying: direct and grassroots, which are discussed in greater detail in Section D: Direct versus Grassroots Lobbying. Direct lobbying involves communication with an official who participates in the formulation of legislation, such as a legislator or legislative staff member. Grassroots lobbying encourages the public to contact a legislative body. Grassroots lobbying expenditures are limited to 25 percent of the organization's total lobbying limit.[11]

---

8 Minnesota State Bar Association Continuing Legal Education, *Minnesota Nonprofit Deskbook*, 8-17 (1st ed. 2011).

9 *See* I.R.C. § 4911(c)(2) (2016).

10 *Id.* at 55. See also Alliance for Justice, *Worry-Free Lobbying for Nonprofits: How To Use the 501(h) Election to Maximize Effectiveness*, 4-5 (2011), www.bolderadvocacy.org/wp-content/uploads/2012/02/worry_free_lobbying.pdf.

11 *See* I.R.C. § 4911 (2016). See also Alliance for Justice, *Worry-Free Lobbying for Nonprofits: How To Use the 501(h) Election to Maximize Effectiveness,* 6 (2011), www.bolderadvocacy.org/wp-content/uploads/2012/02/worry_free_lobbying.pdf.

Q6. Can a nonprofit organization raise funds to be specifically used for lobbying?

A6. Nonprofit organizations may raise funds specifically for lobbying. However, if a donation is earmarked for lobbying, the donor cannot take a charitable deduction for that donation. For more information see Chapter 5: Charitable Donation Regulations.

Q7. Can religious organizations lobby?

A7. Religious organizations are permitted to lobby; however, churches and certain organizations affiliated with churches are not permitted to make the 501(h) election. Subject to that limitation, religious organizations may engage in nonpartisan lobbying. Like other 501(c)(3) organizations, religious organizations are barred from engaging in partisan electoral activities.

Q8. Can foundations fund lobbying activity?

A8. Private foundations may not earmark grants for use in lobbying, but they may make a general purpose grant to an organization that lobbies, regardless of whether or not the nonprofit has made a 501(h) election (see Section C: The 501(h) Election: The Expenditure Test). Private foundations may also make grants to support a specific project that includes lobbying, as long as the grant does not exceed the project's budgeted amount for non-lobbying purposes.

Foundations that are classified as public charities, such as community foundations, may lobby directly and make grants for lobbying purposes.[12]

Q9. Can volunteers lobby on behalf of a nonprofit organization?

A9. Volunteers may lobby on behalf of a nonprofit. For organizations that are subject to the no substantial part test, the activities of volunteers will be considered a lobbying activity of the nonprofit. In the case of organizations making a 501(h) election, the use of volunteers can be advantageous because such activities generally do not involve the expenditure of funds that would count toward the expenditure test. If the organization expends funds in connection with its volunteer activities, such as expense reimbursement, those payments are considered lobbying expenditures.[13]

Q10. Can 501(c)(4) organizations undertake more and/or different lobbying activities than 501(c)(3) organizations?

A10. Section 501(c)(4) organizations are not subject to the lobbying limitations that apply to 501(c)(3) organizations. In addition, 501(c)(4) organizations may undertake partisan electoral activity (support or opposition of a candidate) as long as it is not their primary function.[14]

---

12 Bob Smucker, *The Nonprofit Lobbying Guide*, 60, 118 (1999).
13 Bob Smucker, *The Nonprofit Lobbying Guide*, 51, 53-54 (1999).
14 Bob Smucker, *The Nonprofit Lobbying Guide*, 68-69 (1999).

Q11. *If a nonprofit organization receives grants or contracts from the federal government, can it lobby?*

A11. Recipients of federal grants or contracts are prohibited from using those particular funds for lobbying. Most nonprofits are covered by Office of Management and Budget guidance on lobbying, which has been incorporated into the Code of Federal Regulations.[15] Improper use of federal funding by grantees can result in suspension of the grant, ineligibility for future grants and repayment of grant funds. Improper use by contractors can result in other financial penalties.

Grantees and contractors may NOT use federal funds to:

- Lobby at the federal or state level.
  - Contractors are also prohibited from using such funds to lobby at the local level.
- Liaison with legislators in preparation for lobbying.
  - Contractors are also prohibited from using such funds to prepare for lobbying at the local level.
- Influence elections at the federal, state or local level, including referenda and initiatives.
- Establish or subsidize a political party, campaign, Political Action Committee (PAC) or other organization for the purpose of influencing a federal, state or local election.

In addition to avoiding lobbying, federal grantees must use funds consistently with the purpose of the grant, and should contact the awarding federal agency to determine if particular activities are permitted.

The following activities are exempt from the prohibitions listed above and may be undertaken by the recipient of a federal grant or contract:

- Providing a technical or factual presentation of information on a topic directly related to the performance of a grant or contract in response to a documented request, provided such information is easily obtainable and can be readily put in deliverable form.
- Lobbying at the state level to directly reduce the cost, or to avoid material impairment of the organization's authority to perform the grant or contract.
- Any activity specifically authorized by statute to be undertaken with funds from the grant or contract.[16]

Grantees of federal grants should understand that there are other sets of rules, such as "appropriations riders"[17] and the "Byrd Rule"[18] that restrict lobbying.

Q12. *If a nonprofit organization receives grants or contracts from the State of Minnesota or a local government, can it lobby?*

A12. Yes, an organization may lobby if it receives grants or contracts from the State of Minnesota, unless it is otherwise stated in the agreement. Frequently, organizations are prohibited from using the grant funds given by the state for lobbying purposes. Organizations may nonetheless use other revenue sources

---

15 *See* 2 C.F.R. §§ 200.70, 200.450 (2013).

16 Bob Smucker, *The Nonprofit Lobbying Guide*, 70-72 (1999). See also 2 C.F.R. § 200.450 (2013).

17 Rider is an "informal term for a nongermane amendment to a bill or an amendment to an appropriation bill that changes the permanent law governing a program funded by the bill." See Riders – U.S. Senate, www.senate.gov/reference/glossary_term/rider.htm

18 "Under the Byrd rule, the Senate is prohibited from considering extraneous matter as part of a reconciliation bill or resolution or conference report thereon." *Summary of The Byrd Rule, U.S. House of Representatives*, archives.democrats.rules.house.gov/archives/byrd_rule.htm.

or general operating funds to lobby. Minnesota nonprofits that receive funding from the state that was pass-through funding from a federal block grant, should understand that they must follow the grant rules related to lobbying laid out by the state agency administering the grant.

C. The 501(h) Election: The Expenditure Test

Q13. What is the 501(h) election?

A13. Section 501(h) provides definitions of lobbying and a means to measure lobbying by a 501(c)(3) organization based on expenditures. Section 501(c)(3) organizations can elect to have their lobbying activities measured under Section 501(h) by filing IRS Form 5768. As described above, 501(c)(3) organizations that do not make the 501(h) election are governed by the no substantial part test.[19]

Q14. Why would a 501(c)(3) nonprofit organization choose to make the 501(h) election?

A14. Unless a 501(c)(3) organization makes the 501(h) election, it will be subject to the no substantial part test, which does not clearly define either the activities that are treated as lobbying, or the amount of lobbying an organization may undertake. The 501(h) election gives more certainty to electing nonprofits because the definition of lobbying is clearly defined and lobbying is measured based on expenditures.

In addition to providing a clear test of an organization's compliance, the 501(h) election provides the following benefits over the no substantial part test:

- The tax exempt status of electing organizations may be revoked if the organization exceeds its lobbying limits by at least 50 percent averaged over a four-year period, while non-electing organizations can lose their exempt status by engaging in excessive lobbying in a single year.
- Because Section 501(h) includes clear definitions and exemptions of certain activities, fewer activities count toward an electing organization's lobbying limits.
- For electing organizations, there is no limit on lobbying activities that do not involve expenditures.
- Individual managers of an electing charity cannot be personally penalized by the IRS if the organization exceeds its lobbying limits, while managers of a non-electing charity may be personally penalized.[20]

Q15. How does a 501(c)(3) nonprofit organization make the 501(h) election?

A15. To make the election, an organization must file IRS Form 5768, which is available at www.irs.gov/pub/irs-pdf/f5768.pdf. The only information required on the form is the organization's name, address and the first tax year to which it wants the election to apply. The form must be signed by an authorized officer of the organization, and must be submitted within the first taxable year for which the organization wants

19 Alliance for Justice, *Worry-Free Lobbying for Nonprofits: How To Use the 501(h) Election to Maximize Effectiveness*, 2 (2011), www.bolderadvocacy.org/wp-content/uploads/2012/02/worry_free_lobbying.pdf.

20 Alliance for Justice, *Worry-Free Lobbying for Nonprofits: How To Use the 501(h) Election to Maximize Effectiveness*, 2, 5 (2011), www.bolderadvocacy.org/wp-content/uploads/2012/02/worry_free_lobbying.pdf.

the election to apply.[21]

The IRS does not send an acknowledgment when Form 5768 is received, so the organization should maintain documentation of the filing.

Q16. When would a 501(c)(3) nonprofit organization choose to not make the 501(h) election?

A16. Some organizations, such as churches and private foundations, are not eligible to make the election. In addition, very large organizations may find the $1 million per year limitation on lobbying under 501(h) too restrictive. Similarly, if the organization is part of a group of affiliated organizations that are required to aggregate their lobbying expenditures for purposes of the 501(h) test, their joint budgets may exceed $20 million. Organizations deciding against the 501(h) election for this reason should examine their activities to see if the exemptions under the 501(h) test, such as the use of volunteers at no cost to the organization, would be substantial enough to make the 501(h) election preferable.[22]

Q17. If a 501(c)(3) nonprofit organization wants to revoke its 501(h) election, how does it do so?

A17. The 501(h) election may be revoked by filing another IRS Form 5768 and completing the section on revocation. The form must specify the tax year for which the revocation is effective, be signed by an officer or trustee of the organization and be filed before the first day of the fiscal year to which the revocation applies.[23]

D. Direct Versus Grassroots Lobbying

Q18. What is the difference between direct and grassroots lobbying?

A18. Only organizations that make a 501(h) election need to track direct and grassroots lobbying (discussed in Section C: The 501(h) Election: The Expenditure Test). Organizations subject to the no substantial part test are not required to track these expenses separately.

Direct Lobbying

Direct lobbying involves communication with an official who participates in the formulation of legislation, such as a legislator or legislative staff member. An action must meet every element of a four-part test to be considered direct lobbying. There must be:

- A communication;
- With a legislator or other official;
- Expressing a view; and
- On specific legislation.

If any one of these elements is missing, the activity is not lobbying and does not count against the

21 *Id.* at 2. See I.R.S., Form 5768, *Election/Revocation of Election by an Eligible Section 501(c)(3) Organization To Make Expenditures To Influence Legislation* (2016), www.irs.gov/pub/irs-pdf/f5768.pdf.

22 Gregory L. Colvin & Lowell Finley, Seize the Initiative, 13-14 (1996).

23 *See* I.R.S., Form 5768, *Election/Revocation of Election by an Eligible Section 501(c)(3) Organization To Make Expenditures To Influence Legislation* (2016), www.irs.gov/pub/irs-pdf/f5768.pdf.

organization's lobbying limits. An organization may spend 100 percent of its total lobbying limit on direct lobbying.[24]

Communications to the public on ballot measures or referenda are treated as direct lobbying because voters act as legislators in casting their vote on the measure. In certain circumstances, if an organization urges its members (but not the general public) to contact legislators, those communications are also treated as direct lobbying.[25]

Grassroots Lobbying

Grassroots lobbying involves encouraging the public to contact a legislator. An action must meet every element of a five-part test to be considered grassroots lobbying. There must be:

- A communication;
- With the general public;
- Expressing a view;
- On specific legislation; and
- Which contains a "call to action."

If any one of these elements is absent, the action is not lobbying and does not count against the organization's lobbying limits. Grassroots lobbying expenditures are limited to 25 percent of the organization's total lobbying limit.

The "call to action" requirement of grassroots lobbying simply means that the communication must somehow encourage the public to contact a legislator or legislative body. There are four ways to include a call to action. The first three are considered "direct" calls to action, while the fourth is considered an "indirect" call to action:

- Explicitly asking the recipient to contact a legislator;
- Providing a legislator's contact information (address, telephone number, etc.); or
- Providing a means for the reader to communicate with a legislator (postcard, petition, etc.).
- Identifying one or more legislators who will vote on the legislation as the recipient's legislator, being on the relevant committee, undecided about the legislation, or opposed to the organization's position.[26]

If an organization uses any of these four methods to encourage the public to contact a legislator, the call to action element of grassroots lobbying is satisfied.

There are several categories of activities that warrant special attention:

- Production and distribution of a nonpartisan analysis that discusses a legislative proposal, even if it comes to a conclusion in support of or opposition to the proposal, is not considered lobbying as long as it does not include a direct call to action.
- Under certain circumstances, paid mass media advertisements must be treated as grassroots lobbying even if they do not contain a call to action. Mass media advertisements must be treated as grassroots lobbying if they:

24 Alliance for Justice, *Worry-Free Lobbying for Nonprofits: How To Use the 501(h) Election to Maximize Effectiveness,* 11 (2011), www.bolderadvocacy.org/wp-content/uploads/2012/02/worry_free_lobbying.pdf.

25 Elizabeth Kingsley et al., *E-Advocacy for Nonprofits: The Law of Lobbying and Election-Related Activity on the Net*, 14 (2011).

26 Elizabeth Kingsley et al., *E-Advocacy for Nonprofits: The Law of Lobbying and Election-Related Activity on the Net*, 13 (2011).

  - Appear within two weeks of a legislative vote on highly publicized legislation;
  - Express a view on the general subject of the legislation; and
  - Refer to the specific legislation, or encourage the public to communicate with legislators on the general subject of the legislation.

  If an organization can show that the advertisement was not intentionally timed to coincide with the vote (for example, if it was part of an ongoing series of advertisements), it is not required to treat the advertisement as grassroots lobbying.
- If materials not created for the purpose of lobbying are subsequently used in grassroots lobbying, the cost of creating the original material will not be counted as a lobbying expenditure, as long as the organization can show that the materials were not created for the primary purpose of lobbying, or if at least six months have passed between the creation of the materials and their use in lobbying.[27]

Q19. For the purposes of lobbying, who is considered a member of the nonprofit organization?

A19. According to the IRC, a member of a 501(c)(3) organization is anyone who contributes more than a "nominal" amount of time or money to an organization. Volunteering, paying member dues or making other financial contributions to the organization would satisfy this definition.[28]

E. Lobbying Registration and Reporting at the State and Federal Level

Q20. How does someone find out about the lobbying registration requirements at the federal, state, county and city level?

A20. Registration is required for lobbyists at the federal level according to the provisions of the Lobbying Disclosure Act. The United States Senate maintains a webpage with information about the act, available at www.senate.gov/pagelayout/legislative/g_three_sections_with_teasers/lobbyingdisc.htm. The United States House of Representatives provides a site from which lobbyists may register and file their required reports at lobbyingdisclosure.house.gov.

Registration and reporting requirements are governed at the state level by the Minnesota Campaign Finance and Public Disclosure Board. The Board publishes a guide giving an overview of registration and reporting requirements, available online at www.cfboard.state.mn.us/handbook/hb_lobbyist.pdf. Lobbyists may also visit the Board's website to download the lobbyist registration form and file their required reports.

Lobbyists should contact their county attorney's office to ask if there are any county or city level lobbyist registration requirements or other restrictions for their area. The Minnesota County Attorneys Association maintains a list of links to the various county attorney offices across the state at mcaa-mn.org/?links.

27 *Id.* at 13-15.
28 *Id.* at 14.

Q21. When is someone required to register as a lobbyist at the federal level?

A21. Some organizations and lobbyists may be required to report their federal lobbying activities to the United States Congress under the Lobbying Disclosure Act. After a lobbyist first makes a lobbying contact or is employed or retained to make a lobbying contact, registration is required no later than 45 days if the lobbyist meets the requirements for registration.

Under the Lobbying Disclosure Act, a lobbying contact is:

- Any written or oral communication;
- Made to a covered official;
- On behalf of an employer or client;
- Regarding federal legislation, federal rules or regulations, administration of a federal program or policy (including the award or administration of a federal contract, grant, loan, permit or license), or nomination or confirmation for an appointment requiring Senate confirmation.[29]

Covered officials include, in the executive branch, the President, Vice President, employees of the Executive Office of the President, generals and admirals of the military, and a broad range of senior officials holding positions in the Executive Schedule pay system. In the legislative branch, covered officials include members of Congress, their employees, employees of committees, and Congressional working groups and caucuses.

If a nonprofit hires or contracts with a lobbyist external to the organization, rather than employing that lobbyist, the contract lobbyist is responsible for registering and reporting under the Act if all three of the following thresholds are reached:

- The outside lobbyist makes more than one lobbying contact on behalf of the organization.
- The outside lobbyist spends at least 20 percent of his or her time on lobbying activities for the organization.
- The outside lobbyist receives or expects to receive more than $3,000 from the organization during a quarterly period.[30]

Lobbying activities include lobbying contacts and efforts in supporting such contacts, including preparation and planning, research, and other background work, as well as coordination of lobbying activities with others. Grassroots lobbying, as defined for purposes of Section 501(h), is not a lobbying activity for purposes of the Lobbying Disclosure Act.

Lobbying firms, including self-employed individuals, must file a separate registration for each of their clients.

Organizations that hire lobbyists as employees file a single registration. Organizations are only required to register if one or more of their employees meet all three of the following requirements:

- The employee makes more than one lobbying contact.

29 *See* 2 U.S.C. § 1602 (2017).

30 U.S. House of Representatives, *Lobbying Disclosure Act Guidance*, lobbyingdisclosure.house.gov/amended_lda_guide.html (last visited July 19, 2017).

- The employee spends at least 20 percent of his or her time on lobbying activities for a client or the organization.
- The organization spends or expects to spend more than $12,500 on lobbying activities by the covered employee in the quarter in which registration would be made.[31]

If such organizations do not meet these requirements, they do not need to register and report under the Act.

Organizations and lobbyists that are required to register must file Form LD-1. This form is available online at lda.congress.gov/LD. Lobbying firms must obtain a Senate ID and password to access the form and must submit the form online.

Q22. When is someone required to register as a lobbyist with the State of Minnesota?

A22. A lobbyist must register in Minnesota within five days after meeting one or more of the following definitions, or after being engaged by a new client or employer:

- The individual is engaged, for pay or other consideration, to influence legislative or administrative action or the official action of a metropolitan governmental unit by communicating or urging others to communicate with public officials and receives more than $3,000 for lobbying activities from all sources in any year.
- The individual is an appointed local official or an employee in a political subdivision acting in an official capacity who spends more than 50 hours in any month attempting to influence legislative or administrative action or the official action of a metropolitan governmental unit by communicating or urging others to communicate with public officials.
- The individual spends more than $250 of his or her own funds in any year, not including travel expenses and membership dues, for the purpose of attempting to influence legislative or administrative action or the official action of a metropolitan governmental unit by communicating or urging others to communicate with public officials.[32]

Certain individuals, such as public officials, state employees and elected local officials, are exempt from registration requirements. Other individuals are exempt only to the extent that their occupations or activities have been identified by the legislature as exempt, for example, a journalist engaged in publishing or broadcasting of news items. The Minnesota Campaign Finance and Public Disclosure Board provides a list of those individuals for which registration is not required in the *Lobbyist Handbook*.[33]

Lobbyists must select the appropriate reporting option when they register. There are three options for registration:

- Authorizing lobbyist – these lobbyists authorize another lobbyist who lobbies for the same organization to report their lobbying disbursements for them.
- Reporting lobbyist – these lobbyists indicate that they will be reporting lobbying disbursements for themselves and other lobbyists who lobby for the same organization.
- Self-reporting lobbyist – these lobbyists report only their own disbursements.

31 *Id.*
32 Registration & Reporting Requirements for Lobbyists, www.minnesotanonprofits.org (last visited July 19, 2017).
33 Minnesota Campaign Finance and Public Disclosure Board, *Lobbyist Handbook* 4, 5 (2017), www.cfboard.state.mn.us/handbook/hb_lobbyist.pdf.

"Lobbyist principals" also must register. A lobbyist principal is an individual or association that hires a lobbyist or spends a total of at least $50,000 per year to influence legislative action, administrative action, or the actions of metropolitan governments.[34] Lobbyist principals must also choose one designated lobbyist to be responsible for filing the annual Report of Lobbyist Principal. The designated lobbyist must indicate the lobbyist's status on the report. If the designated lobbyist for an organization changes, the lobbyist must amend the registration within 10 days and the organization must name a new designated lobbyist.[35]

Q23. Does a 501(c)(3) nonprofit organization need to register its board members, clients and volunteers if they lobby on behalf of the organization in Minnesota?

A23. Only individuals who meet the definitions listed above must register. For example, at the state level, an unpaid volunteer would not be required to register unless he or she spent more than $250 of his or her own funds in any year for the purpose of lobbying.[36]

Q24. How should a 501(c)(3) nonprofit organization keep track of its lobbying expenses, activities and hours? How does this differ in order to meet federal and Minnesota state requirements?

A24. At the federal level, the Lobbying Disclosure Act requires a good faith estimate of the expenditures for lobbying activities incurred by organizations employing in-house lobbyists. For an outside lobbying firm, including self-employed individuals, the Act requires a good faith estimate of all income received from the client. The Act does not prescribe any special record-keeping requirements as long as the system in place allows the organization or firm to give a good faith estimate. Records of the costs specific to certain activities, such as mailings or events, should be maintained. Detailed records must also be kept of the use of staff time and the corresponding portion of overhead costs. Such records may be based on time cards or a sampling taken if the sample period is generally representative of how the organization's staff uses their time.

Section 501(c)(3) organizations must also track their expenditures and activities for reporting to the IRS. Organizations that make the 501(h) election should track their expenditures, including salaries for staff time spent lobbying, costs specific to certain lobbying activities and a portion of overhead costs, and make note of the expenditures that qualify as grassroots lobbying. In addition to providing the amount spent on lobbying, organizations that have chosen not to file the 501(h) election must also provide detailed descriptions of these activities[37]:

- Work by volunteers;
- Work by paid staff;
- Media advertisements;
- Mailings to legislators and members or the general public;
- Publications or published or broadcast statements;
- Grants to other organizations for lobbying purposes;
- Direct contact with legislators, their staffs, government officials or a legislative body;

34 *Id.* at 4.
35 *See* 2 U.S.C. § 1602 (2017).
36 Minnesota Campaign Finance and Public Disclosure Board, *Lobbyist Handbook*, 4 (2017), www.cfboard.state.mn.us/handbook/hb_lobbyist.pdf.
37 Historic Lobbying Disclosure Act Guidance, www.senate.gov/legislative/common/briefing/lobby_disc_briefing.htm#6.

- Rallies, demonstrations, seminars, conventions, speeches, lectures or any other lobbying activities.[38]

The State of Minnesota has very specific requirements for the recording of lobbying expenses. The lobbyist must maintain separate records for administrative lobbying, legislative lobbying and the lobbying of a metropolitan governmental unit. Organizations must track spending in the following categories[39]:

- Disbursements for:
    - Preparing and distributing lobbying materials;
    - Media advertising;
    - Telephone and communication services;
    - Postage and distribution costs associated with lobbying activities;
    - Fees, allowances, public relations campaigns including consulting and other expenses related with those services;
    - Entertainment, food and beverages;
    - Travel and lodging;
    - Salary and administrative costs of support staff attributable to lobbying;
    - All other disbursements including general administration and overhead and any other lobbyist disbursements not reported in other categories.
- Gifts or benefits paid or given to local or public officials.
- Other sources of funds of more than $500 in a calendar year given for purposes of lobbying, including the fees or salary paid to a lobbyist as compensation.

Note that Minnesota Statutes Section 10A.071, prohibits most gifts from lobbyists or organizations to public or local officials, or to employees of the legislature, unless the lobbyist or organization receives something of equal or greater value in return. See the Minnesota Campaign Finance and Public Disclosure Board's *Lobbyist Handbook*, page 14, available at www.cfboard.state.mn.us/handbook/hb_lobbyist.pdf, for an overview of the gift ban, or *Guide to Interpretation of Minnesota Statutes 10A.071* (2013), available at www.cfboard.state.mn.us/lobby/GIFTPRIM.pdf, for more detailed information about interpretation of the gift ban.

Lobbyists must also keep records of disbursements from their personal funds used toward lobbying in the same categories listed above. In addition, if a lobbyist or other person solicits contributions for a candidate or legislative caucus, the person is required to keep records of and file reports of donations that exceed $5,000 in the aggregate.[40] The report must include the name of each contributor, the amount of the contributions, and the name and registration number of the candidate or caucus to whom each contribution was given.

A lobbyist principal must keep separate records of administrative lobbying, legislative lobbying and the lobbying of a metropolitan governmental unit in the State of Minnesota in the following categories[41]:

- All direct payments by the principal to lobbyists;
- All expenditures for advertising, mailing, research, analysis, compilation and dissemination of information, and public relations campaigns;
- All salaries and administrative expenses attributable to the activities of the principal.

38 *See* Bob Smucker, *The Nonprofit Lobbying Guide*, 75 (1999). See also Elizabeth Kingsley et al., *E-Advocacy for Nonprofits: The Law of Lobbying and Election-Related Activity on the Net*, 16 (2011).

39 Minn. R. 4511.0600, subp. 5 (2016).

40 Minnesota Campaign Finance and Public Disclosure Board, *Lobbyist Handbook*, 12 (2017), www.cfboard.state.mn.us/handbook/hb_lobbyist.pdf.

41 Minn. Stat. § 10A.04, subd. 6 (2016).

Both the principal and lobbyist must keep records of all accounts in the organization's files for four years.[42]

Q25. How should lobbying activities be reported to the federal government?

A25. Organizations that lobby are required to report their lobbying expenditures annually to the IRS on Form 990. Organizations that make the 501(h) election must also calculate and report their lobbying ceiling (based on the formula detailed in Section C: The 501(h) Election: The Expenditure Test) and report how much of their lobbying is grassroots. Non-electing organizations are required to include detailed descriptions of their lobbying activities.

In addition to IRS reporting requirements, if the organization or lobbyist was required to register under the federal Lobbying Disclosure Act (detailed in Question 21), the organization or lobbyist must file reports under this Act quarterly. Form LD-2 is available online from lda.congress.gov/LD. Like with LD-1 forms, lobbying firms must obtain a Senate ID and password to access the form and must submit the form online. The reports are due on the twentieth of January, April, July, and October for each prior quarter. Once registration has been completed, quarterly reporting is required, even if no lobbying occurred during the reporting period, until registration is terminated.[43]

Organizations that have made the 501(h) election can use those definitions of lobbying to make their reports under the Lobbying Disclosure Act. Non-electing organizations must use the Lobbying Disclosure Act's definitions of lobbying activities, which are different than the IRS definitions. Most significantly, organizations using the Lobbying Disclosure Act definitions must report on communications regarding not just federal legislation, but also federal rules and regulations, which are exempt from reporting under the 501(h) expenditure test.[44]

Q26. How should lobbying activities be reported to the Minnesota government?

A26. Both organizations and individuals that lobby and are required to register with the Minnesota Campaign Finance and Public Disclosure Board must report regularly regarding those activities to the State of Minnesota.

- Organizations that had a lobbyist registered with the Minnesota Campaign Finance and Public Disclosure Board during the previous calendar year (January 1 through December 31) must file their annual Report of Lobbyist Principal annually by March 15.[45]
- Individual lobbyists must file two reports each year. The report on their activity for the period from January 1 through May 31 is due on June 15, and the report for the period from June 1 through December 31 is due on January 15.[46]

These reports may be filed by mail, fax, personal delivery, email or electronically at www.cfboard.state.mn.us.

---

42 Minnesota Campaign Finance and Public Disclosure Board, *Lobbyist Handbook*, 12 (2017), www.cfboard.state.mn.us/handbook/hb_lobbyist.pdf.

43 Lobbying Disclosure Notice and Announcements, lobbyingdisclosure.house.gov (last visited July 19, 2017).

44 Bob Smucker, *The Nonprofit Lobbying Guide*, 74-76 (1999). See also Lobbying Disclosure Notice and Announcements, lobbyingdisclosure.house.gov (last visited July 19, 2017).

45 Minn. Stat. § 10A.04, subd. 6 (2016).

46 Minn. Stat. § 10A.04, subd. 2 (2016).

Lobbyists who make disbursements not attributable to a principal must file a Report of Lobbyist's Disbursements from Personal Funds twice annually by January 15 and June 15.[47] Persons who solicit campaign contributions in excess of $5,000 must file a Contribution Solicitor Report prior to each primary and general election, and by January 31 of each year.

The annual Report of Lobbyist Principal must be made by the organization's designated lobbyist. The individual Lobbyist Disbursement Reports may be filed by individual self-reporting lobbyists, by one or more reporting lobbyists, or by a combination of self-reporting and reporting lobbyists.

Q27. Are 501(c)(4) organizations subject to the same registration and reporting requirements as 501(c)(3) organizations at the federal and state level?

A27. Like 501(c)(3) organizations, 501(c)(4) organizations are required to file IRS Form 990 annually. 501(c)(4) organizations, however, are not required to complete Schedule A.

The federal Lobbying Disclosure Act applies to 501(c)(4) organizations just as it does to 501(c)(3) organizations. If the organization or lobbyist was required to register under the Lobbying Disclosure Act (detailed in Question 22), the organization or lobbyist must file reports under this Act quarterly.

State registration and reporting requirements apply identically to 501(c)(3) organizations and 501(c)(4) organizations.

Q28. Are religious organizations that are exempt from filing Form 990 subject to other registration and reporting requirements?

A28. Religious organizations exempt from filing Form 990 must still register their lobbyists and report on their lobbying activities both to Congress under the federal Lobbying Disclosure Act, and to the Minnesota Campaign Finance and Public Disclosure Board. These religious organizations are subject to the same definitions and registration and reporting requirements as other 501(c)(3) organizations.

F. Election Activity and Voter Education

Q29. What is election-related activity?

A29. Election-related activities include a wide range of nonpartisan activities, such as efforts to educate and enable the public to participate in the voting process, educate candidates about public policy issues, and advocate for particular positions on public policy issues. In addition, election-related activity includes work on behalf of candidates and political parties, though such partisan activity may not be undertaken by 501(c)(3) organizations.

47 Minn. Stat. § 10A.04, subd. 2 (2016).

Q30. What types of election-related activities can a 501(c)(3) nonprofit organization undertake?

A30. Section 501(c)(3) public charities can only engage in nonpartisan election-related activities. They are not allowed to influence elections or coordinate activities with a political candidate or party. Not only must the substance or purpose of their activity be nonpartisan, but it must be presented to the public on a nonpartisan basis. For example, a 501(c)(3) organization may not conduct a voter registration drive targeted to register members of only one political party. Nonpartisan issue advocacy (ads or newsletters regarding a specific issue and not supporting a candidate), voter education activities, voter registration and get-out-the-vote drives, as well as nonpartisan candidate education are all permissible types of activities for a 501(c)(3) organization. Note that in addition to Section 501(c)(3) restrictions, Federal Election Commission rules may apply to some election-related activities.

Q31. What is voter education?

A31. For purposes of this guide, "voter education" describes nonpartisan activities nonprofits undertake to bring information about candidates and issues to the voters. Voter education is one type of election-related activity.

Q32. What types of voter education activities can a 501(c)(3) nonprofit organization undertake?

A32. Section 501(c)(3) organizations can use candidate questionnaires, candidate debates and forums, voting records and scorecards to educate voters, but only if the information is presented in a fair and nonpartisan way.

Q33. Can religious organizations that are exempt from filing Form 990 support or oppose candidates?

A33. Religious organizations are subject to the same prohibitions against partisan electioneering that apply to other 501(c)(3) organizations. These organizations are not allowed to support or oppose candidates, or coordinate with a candidate or party. The IRS has identified some categories of religious organizations which are exempt from filing Form 990, however these organizations are still prohibited from supporting or opposing candidates.

Individuals or leaders of a religious organization, like all individuals associated with nonprofit organizations, are free to personally endorse or oppose a candidate, but they must make it clear that they are speaking for themselves and not on behalf of their organization. The individuals are prohibited from using the organization's resources in their work for or against a candidate's campaign.

Q34. Does a 501(c)(3) nonprofit organization need to be nonpartisan in its election-related activities and voter education activities?

A34. Yes. Section 501(c)(3) organizations may not intervene in political campaigns in support of or opposition to candidates for office. All election-related activities must be nonpartisan. In determining whether the activity is nonpartisan, the activity itself as well as the context in which it was performed is examined. For example, the timing relative to an election, history of similar activities by the organization, or ongoing nature of the activity will be considered. If the IRS determines the activity evidences a bias or preference with respect to a candidate, the activity will be viewed as inappropriate. Organizations should be mindful of perceptions that may be created regardless of whether there was an actual endorsement.

Q35. For the purpose of the federal tax rules regulating 501(c)(3) organizations, who is considered a candidate?

A35. A candidate includes anyone who is:

- Officially running for public office (has filed paperwork);
- Considering running for public office (has not filed paperwork, but has organized a committee to examine the field);
- Being drafted by the public or the press to run for public office.[48]

The definition for purposes of the Federal Election Commission rules is somewhat narrower.[49]

Q36. What positions are considered to be public offices?

A36. Any position filled by a vote of the public is a public office. Section 501(c)(3) organizations are not prohibited from supporting or opposing the appointment of a public official; however, efforts to influence a legislative body on a confirmation vote is counted as a lobbying activity.

Q37. Can a 501(c)(3) nonprofit conduct voter registration and other get-out-the-vote activities?

A37. A 501(c)(3) organization can conduct nonpartisan voter registration drives. Organizations can target particular groups based on factors that are not partisan, such as historic voting rates or economic disadvantage. It is crucial that the organization does not attempt to influence the individual's vote in favor of a particular candidate or political party.[50] Further, special requirements apply to private foundations that engage in voter registration.

Q38. Can a 501(c)(3) nonprofit organization produce and distribute legislative scorecards?

A38. A 501(c)(3) organization can use legislative scorecards that indicate whether a particular legislator voted consistently or inconsistently with the position of the organization, and voting records that indicate how the legislator voted on various bills. Section 501(c)(3) organizations may limit the scope of the legislation reported on in a legislative scorecard to issues important to the organization, should carefully word the bill or issue decided, and may even include commentary, but it can only distribute this information to its own members. Voting records that are distributed to the general public must report on a broad range of issues and cannot include commentary. Both types of reports must include all legislators, and their distribution cannot be timed to coincide with an election. This can be problematic if the end of a legislative session coincides with the beginning of campaign season. If this is the case, the organization should make

48 *See* I.R.C. § 501(c)(3) (2017).

49 Alliance for Justice, *The Rules of the Game – A Guide to Election-Related Activities for 501(c)(3) Organizations* (2012), www.bolderadvocacy.org/wp-content/uploads/2012/01/Rules-of-the-Game.pdf.

50 *Id.*

every effort to publish the report as soon as possible after the end of the session.[51]

Q39. Can a 501(c)(3) nonprofit organization produce and distribute candidate questionnaires?

A39. It is permissible for a 501(c)(3) organization with a broad range of concerns to send questionnaires to candidates and publish the results if the purpose is to educate voters in a nonpartisan manner. The questionnaires must be given to all candidates for office, including independent candidates, and questions should cover a broad range of subjects and be framed without bias. Each candidate must be given equal space to respond. If space is limited, word limits may be imposed, but responses should not otherwise be edited. Questions must cover a broad range of subjects. Organizations must avoid questions with such a narrow focus that, as a whole, they imply endorsement of the candidate whose responses are favorable.[52]

If a nonprofit has narrower focus, such as an organization that only focuses on education, awareness and research on the effects of tobacco use on youth, the questionnaire may pose a problem.[53] The IRS may take the position that a nonprofit's narrowness of focus implies endorsement of a candidate whose replies are favorable to the nonprofit's position on the topic covered in the questionnaire.[54] The Center for Lobbying in the Public Interest suggest that unless an organization "clearly qualifies as covering a broad range of issues," it should avoid disseminating replies from questionnaires.[55]

Q40. Can a 501(c)(3) nonprofit organization host a candidate forum or debate?

A40. As with candidate questionnaires discussed in Question 40, organizations should consider whether the organization's focus is too narrow in order to avoid an implied, or even the appearance of an implied, endorsement of a particular candidate. It may be a good idea to co-host a candidate forum with multiple organizations.

A 501(c)(3) organization may host a forum or debate if all viable candidates are invited. Candidate viability should be determined based on some nonpartisan criteria, for example, the top two or three candidates based on polling data or fundraising amounts. Questions must cover a broad range of issues and should be phrased in a neutral manner. Candidates should be given equal time to respond, and it is often a good idea to get a moderator who is not affiliated with the organization. The moderator should also make clear that the views expressed are not those of the nonprofit. The audience should be unbiased, or at least populated with supporters of each candidate. It may be helpful to give each candidate an equal number of tickets to distribute to their supporters.[56]

51 Alliance for Justice, *The Rules of the Game – A Guide to Election-Related Activities for 501(c)(3) Organizations* (2012), www.bolderadvocacy.org/wp-content/uploads/2012/01/Rules-of-the-Game.pdf. See Bob Smucker, The Nonprofit Lobbying Guide 67 (1999).

52 *Id.*

53 Organizations may consider engaging the League of Women Voters and/or United Way, which have been found by the IRS to be sufficiently broad such that if they do a questionnaire on a broad range of issues, it will be permissible.

54 *See* I.R.S., *Technical Advice Memo 200908050* (2009), www.capdale.com/files/upload/TAM.pdf.

55 Center for Lobbying in the Public Interest, *Nonprofits and Election-Related Activities* (2011), www.nonprofitvote.org/documents/2011/04/nps-and-election-related-activites.pdf.

56 Alliance for Justice, *The Rules of the Game – A Guide to Election-Related Activities for 501(c)(3) Organizations* (2012), www.bolderadvocacy.org/wp-content/uploads/2012/01/Rules-of-the-Game.pdf.

Q41. Can a 501(c)(3) nonprofit organization solicit candidate pledges to support particular issues?

A41. Yes, a 501(c)(3) organization may urge candidates to go on record in support of the nonprofit's position on particular issues. However, the nonprofit may not publish or distribute the candidate's statement as such until after the election, unless the statement was given in a nonpartisan questionnaire or in a statement to the media or public. The candidate themselves may distribute their responses or pledges both to the nonprofit organization and to the general public.[57]

Q42. Can a 501(c)(3) nonprofit organization endorse candidates?

A42. A 501(c)(3) organization cannot endorse candidates for political office. Individuals associated with a 501(c)(3) organization may endorse, support or oppose a particular candidate, but only if they do so in their individual capacities. The individual cannot use the nonprofit's funds or other resources and must clearly state that the individual speaks for him/herself and not the organization.[58]

Q43. Can a 501(c)(3) nonprofit criticize incumbents?

A43. Nonprofits can criticize incumbents, but they must do so while focusing on the issues and the incumbent's performance in their official capacity. Organizations may not promote the incumbent's opponent, focus on the incumbent as a candidate or compare candidates' positions. Organizations must not start or intensify criticism during the election season. If the position from which the organization is criticizing the incumbent represents a defining or divisive issue in the election or could be identified with one or more of the incumbent's opponents, the criticism could be construed as support of the opponent.[59]

Q44. Can a 501(c)(3) nonprofit produce and distribute issue ads that target candidates?

A44. Section 501(c)(3) organizations are prohibited from coordinating with a candidate or party, and this includes production or distribution of issue ads that target candidates. There is an exception made for criticism of incumbents, however, 501(c)(3) organizations cannot criticize incumbents *as candidates*. They may target an incumbent's prior voting record on a particular issue, but they must not mention the election or compare the incumbent's position with another candidate. Organizations must not start or intensify criticism during the election season, and if the position from which the organization is criticizing the incumbent represents a defining or divisive issue in the election or could be identified with one or more of the incumbent's opponents, the criticism could be construed as support of the opponent.[60]

501(c)(4) organizations are allowed to produce and distribute issue ads that target candidates, because unlike 501(c)(3) organizations, they may engage in limited partisan election-related activities. This partisan electioneering must remain secondary to the organization's primary purposes.[61]

---

57 Bob Smucker, *The Nonprofit Lobbying Guide*, 67 (1999).

58 Alliance for Justice, *The Rules of the Game – A Guide to Election-Related Activities for 501(c)(3) Organizations* (2012), www.bolderadvocacy.org/wp-content/uploads/2012/01/Rules-of-the-Game.pdf.

59 *Id.*

60 *Id.*

61 *Id.* at 33.

Q45. Can a 501(c)(3) nonprofit organization produce and distribute issue ads that do not target candidates?

A45. Issue advocacy is permissible if it does not target a candidate. The advertisement must be related to the organization's purpose and it is a good idea to include a disclaimer stating that the organization does not support or oppose candidates or political parties. Organizations should avoid using the image of a candidate or coordinating with a political party or candidate. Advertisements should avoid focusing on issues that are closely associated with a particular candidate and should not mimic candidate advertisements.[62]

Q46. Can a 501(c)(3) nonprofit organization allow a candidate to visit an organization's offices?

A46. An organization may invite candidates to appear at its office or another location. If the individual is invited because of the individual's candidacy, all candidates for that office must be invited. If candidates are invited to appear at different times, the times should be similarly prominent and accessible for all attendees. For example, one candidate should not be invited for lunch on a weekday and another for an early morning breakfast on a Saturday. If the candidate is being invited for some other reason, for example, to receive an award for the candidate's past support of the organization or its causes, equal opportunity is not required. However, the organization and the candidate should not mention the candidacy, the appearance should not be timed to coincide with an election, and it should be clear to the candidate that he or she must not campaign at the event.[63]

Q47. Can a 501(c)(3) nonprofit organization raise funds for or donate money to a candidate?

A47. A 501(c)(3) nonprofit organization cannot support or oppose a candidate for public office by making contributions or otherwise. The payment of campaign contributions could also violate federal election laws. A nonprofit may sell, trade, or rent its membership list to a candidate, but if it does so, all candidates must be offered access to the list on the same terms. If a nonprofit does give a candidate access to its membership list, the candidate must pay fair market value for the list. A nonprofit may donate, loan money or provide mailing lists to a ballot measure campaign because this is considered lobbying, not political campaign activity.[64]

Q48. Can a 501(c)(3) nonprofit educate candidates about public policy issues?

A48. Candidate education is allowed if the information is being offered to all candidates, and the provided information has already been gathered. Educational materials cannot be created for candidates at their request.[65]

---

62 Alliance for Justice, *The Rules of the Game – A Guide to Election-Related Activities for 501(c)(3) Organizations* (2012), www.bolderadvocacy.org/wp-content/uploads/2012/01/Rules-of-the-Game.pdf.

63 *Id.*

64 Bob Smucker, *The Nonprofit Lobbying Guide*, 68 (1999). See also Alliance for Justice, *The Rules of the Game – A Guide to Election-Related Activities for 501(c)(3) Organizations* (2012), www.bolderadvocacy.org/wp-content/uploads/2012/01/Rules-of-the-Game.pdf.

65 Alliance for Justice, *The Rules of the Game – A Guide to Election-Related Activities for 501(c)(3) Organizations* (2012), www.bolderadvocacy.org/wp-content/uploads/2012/01/Rules-of-the-Game.pdf.

Q49 Can the staff and board members of a 501(c)(3) organization undertake election-related and voter-education activities in their private lives?

A49. Yes, but the individuals must make it clear that they are acting as private citizens and not as spokespersons for the organization. They are prohibited from using organization resources in their personal activities. Campaign literature listing or quoting organization representatives should indicate that their position in the organization is listed for identification purposes only.[66]

Q50. Can the staff and board members of a 501(c)(3) nonprofit organization run for public office?

A50. The staff and board members of a 501(c)(3) organization may run for or hold public office. These individuals must make it clear that they are acting as private citizens and not as spokespersons for their organization. They are prohibited from using organization resources in their political activities.

Q51. Can 501(c)(4) organizations undertake more and/or different election-related and voter-education activities than 501(c)(3) organizations?

A51. Yes. A 501(c)(4) organization can engage in the same nonpartisan election-related activities as a 501(c)(3) organization, but it can conduct these activities on an unlimited basis. A 501(c)(4) organization may also engage in partisan electioneering—supporting or opposing a candidate for public office—as long as such activity is not the primary function of the organization.[67]

Nonprofit Tip

Note that 501(c)(3) organizations are prohibited from creating a connected PAC.

G. Differences between Restrictions on 501(c)(3) and 501(c)(4) Tax Exempt Organizations

Q52. What is a 501(c)(4) organization?

A52. A Section 501(c)(4) organization is exempt from income tax based on its social welfare activities. Social welfare organizations are not as limited as 501(c)(3) organizations in terms of the activities they may conduct, but contributions to them are not deductible as charitable contributions. Section 501(c)(4) organizations may conduct unlimited lobbying activities. They may also support or oppose political candidates, so long as such actions are not the organization's primary activities.[68]

66 Bob Smucker, *The Nonprofit Lobbying Guide*, 66 (1999).

67 Alliance for Justice, *The Rules of the Game – A Guide to Election-Related Activities for 501(c)(3) Organizations* (2012), www.bolderadvocacy.org/wp-content/uploads/2012/01/Rules-of-the-Game.pdf.

68 Alliance for Justice, *The Rules of the Game – A Guide to Election-Related Activities for 501(c)(3) Organizations* (2012), www.bolderadvocacy.org/wp-content/uploads/2012/01/Rules-of-the-Game.pdf.

Q53. What is a Political Action Committee (PAC)? Are there different types of PACs? If so, what are they?

A53. Political Action Committees (PACs) described in IRC Section 527 are created to influence the nomination or election of candidates for public office. Electioneering may be their sole activity.

"Connected" PACs are created and sponsored by another organization, for example, a 501(c)(4). The connected PAC may only solicit funds from the connected organization's members and qualifying employees; however, the sponsoring organization may pay certain costs for the connected PAC.

A connected PAC and its affiliated organization must be functionally separate. The two organizations must:

- Be separately incorporated, with unique bylaws;
- Have unique organization names (names may be similar but not identical);
- Have different boards of directors (though there may be some overlap);
- Use different letterhead;
- Keep separate bank accounts and financial records; and
- Have different employer identification numbers.[69]

"Non-connected" or independent PACs are not sponsored by any other organization. These organizations are created by individuals. They are permitted to solicit funds from the general public, but they must pay their own expenses.[70]

Q54. Can a 501(c)(3) organization establish a parallel organization – like a 501(c)(4) or a PAC – expressly for the purpose of lobbying or influencing elections?

A54. A 501(c)(3) organization may set up a 501(c)(4) affiliate for the purpose of lobbying, but a 501(c)(3) organization may not set up a PAC. The affiliated 501(c)(4) organization may establish a PAC if the PAC's goals and activities of the PAC are kept separate from those of the 501(c)(3) organization.[71] Individuals may also establish PACs.

Q55. How does a 501(c)(3) organization establish a parallel organization for the purpose of lobbying or election-related activity?

A55. If a 501(c)(3) organization sets up a 501(c)(4) affiliate, the organizations must be separately incorporated and must observe corporate formalities such as maintaining separate bank accounts, financial records and corporate records. The same individuals may serve on both boards, but each board must meet separately and keep separate minutes. The organizations must also ensure that the 501(c)(3) organization is not subsidizing the 501(c)(4) organization financially. The 501(c)(4) organization must pay for its share of all costs to the organizations, such as staff salaries and overhead, as well as paying for its own activities.[72]

69 Bolder Advocacy, *The Practical Implications of Affiliated 501(c)(3)s and 501(c)(4)s (2012)*, bolderadvocacy.org/wp-content/uploads/2012/05/The_Practical_Implications_of_Affiliated_501c3s_andc4s.pdf.

70 Elizabeth Kingsley et al., *E-Advocacy for Nonprofits. The Law of Lobbying and Election-Related Activity on the Net*, 25 (2011).

71 Alliance for Justice, *The Rules of the Game – A Guide to Election-Related Activities for 501(c)(3) Organizations (2012)*, www.bolderadvocacy.org/wp-content/uploads/2012/01/Rules-of-the-Game.pdf. See also Bob Smucker, *The Nonprofit Lobbying Guide* 68-69 (1999).

72 Alliance for Justice, *The Rules of the Game – A Guide to Election-Related Activities for 501(c)(3) Organizations* (2012), www.bolderadvocacy.org/wp-content/uploads/2012/01/Rules-of-the-Game.pdf.

While the 501(c)(4) organization may lobby and conduct other non-partisan activities on an unlimited basis, any partisan activity must remain secondary to the organization's primary activities.[73]

A 501(c)(3) organization interested in establishing a parallel organization should consult an attorney.

Q56. Can a 501(c)(3) organization establish a parallel organization – like a 501(c)(4) or a PAC – expressly for the purpose of election-related activity?

A56. Yes. A 501(c)(3) organization may establish a 501(c)(4) affiliate, which is allowed to conduct nonpartisan election-related activity on an unlimited basis, and may conduct partisan activity so long as such activity is not the organization's primary activity. A 501(c)(3) organization may not establish a PAC.

A 501(c)(3) organization interested in establishing a parallel organization should consult an attorney.

H. Ballot Measures

Q57. Can nonprofits do work on ballot measures like referendums and bond initiatives?

A57. Yes. Section 501(c)(3) organizations may lobby for or against a ballot measure. Ballot measures are treated as direct lobbying activities because the public acts as a deciding or legislative body in voting on the measure. Ballot measure activities therefore count toward lobbying limits.

Q58. In addition to the federal lobbying, election-related activities and voter education limitations described in this chapter, are there state and local laws of which 501(c)(3) nonprofit organizations need to be mindful?

A58. State-level rules and restrictions on lobbying are administered by the Minnesota Campaign Finance and Public Disclosure Board. The Board publishes a guide giving an overview of registration and reporting requirements, which is available online at www.cfboard.state.mn.us/handbook/hb_lobbyist.pdf. The guide also lists contact information for individuals on the Board who can assist organizations and lobbyists with specific questions. Lobbyists may also visit the Board's website at http://www.cfboard.state.mn.us/ to download the lobbyist registration form and file their required reports.

73 Alliance for Justice, *The Rules of the Game – A Guide to Election-Related Activities for 501(c)(3) Organizations* (2012), www.bolderadvocacy.org/wp-content/uploads/2012/01/Rules-of-the-Game.pdf.

I. Related Resources

Organizations:

Alliance for Justice
11 Dupont Circle NW
Suite 200
Washington, DC 20036
www.afj.org

Independent Sector
1602 L Street NW, Suite 900
Washington, DC 20036
Phone: (202) 467-6100
Fax: (202) 467-6101
www.independentsector.org

Internal Revenue Service
1111 Constitution Ave NW
Washington, DC 20224
Phone: (202) 622-5000
www.irs.gov

National Council of Nonprofits
1001 G Street NW
Suite 700 East
Washington, DC 20001
Phone: (202) 962-0322
www.councilofnonprofits.org/everyday-advocacy

Publications:

E-Advocacy for Nonprofits: The Law of Lobbying and Election-Related Activity on the Net (2000), by Elizabeth Kingsley, Gail Harmon, John Pomeranz, and Kay Guinane.

"Election Year Issues", I.R.S. (article on IRS website)
www.irs.gov/pub/irs-tege/eotopici02.pdf

Guide to Interpretation of Minnesota Statutes 10A.071
Published by the Minnesota Campaign Finance and Public Disclosure Board
Available from the Minnesota Campaign Finance and Public Disclosure Board online at www.cfboard.state.mn.us.

Lobbyist Handbook
Published by the Minnesota Campaign Finance and Public Disclosure Board
Available from the Minnesota Campaign Finance and Public Disclosure Board online at www.cfboard.state.mn.us.

Myth v. Fact: Foundation Support of Advocacy, by Thomas R. Asher.
Published by the Alliance for Justice, 1995.

The Nonprofit Lobbying Guide, 2nd Ed., by Bob Smucker.
Published by Independent Sector

Power in Policy: A Funder's Guide to Advocacy and Civic Participation, by David F. Arons.
Published by Fieldstone Alliance, 2007.

The Rules of the Game: An Election Year Legal Guide for Nonprofit Organizations, by Gregory L. Colvin and Lowell Finley.
Published by the Alliance for Justice, 1996.

Seize the Initiative, by Gregory L. Colvin and Lowell Finley.
Published by the Alliance for Justice, 1996.

Tax Guide for Churches and Religious Organizations
Published by the Internal Revenue Service
www.irs.gov/pub/irs-pdf/p1828.pdf

Worry-Free Lobbying for Nonprofits: How to Use the 501(h) Election to Maximize Effectiveness
Published by the Alliance for Justice, 1999.

Websites:

Minnesota Code
www.leg.state.mn.us/leg/statutes.asp

Minnesota Legislature
www.house.leg.state.mn.us/leg/faqtoc.asp?subject=8

Registration Thresholds
www.senate.gov/pagelayout/legislative/one_item_and_teasers/Registration_thresholds_page.htm

United States Senate
Historic Lobbying Disclosure Act Guidance
www.senate.gov/legislative/common/briefing/lobby_disc_briefing.htm

CHAPTER 8

FINANCIAL ACCOUNTABILITY

Topics

A. Overview

Financial accountability is an essential responsibility for any nonprofit organization. A nonprofit organization has limited resources with which to advance its mission, whether it be a charitable mission (in the case of 501(c)(3) organizations), a social welfare mission (in the case of 501(c)(4) organizations), or any other kind of mission. Any money lost to mismanagement or misappropriation translates into a loss of impact in carrying out this mission. Thus, it is essential for a nonprofit organization to have quality financial information, diligent financial oversight and solid internal controls.

The organization itself is not the only party with an interest in its finances. The federal government forgoes corporate income tax on certain kinds of nonprofits in recognition of their service to the public, and thus requires some assurance that its investment is not misplaced. For this reason, the Internal Revenue Service (IRS) requires most tax-exempt organizations to submit an annual report of their incomes and expenditures, subdivided by category (the Form 990 information return). Institutional and individual donors also desire assurances that their money is serving their intended purpose, which is why these organizations are also required to share their Form 990 returns with the general public.

Though taking simple precautions should allow an organization to avoid mismanagement or misappropriation, it is nonetheless important to be aware of the penalties. The legal consequences of accidental error are generally minor—if an audit reveals an accounting mistake, for example, the remedy can be as simple as correcting it. The state or federal government, however, can intervene in cases of deliberate financial mismanagement, such as embezzlement or private inurement (the diversion of organization funds for an insider's personal benefit). The IRS is authorized to punish an insider involved in private inurement with substantial monetary fines, and can revoke the tax-exempt status of an organization if the offense is sufficiently egregious. A detailed conflict of interest policy can help an organization's managers, directors and employees avoid both private inurement and its consequences.

The questions and answers in the remainder of this chapter deal with the basic financial considerations of a nonprofit organization, including the steps an organization should take to achieve sound financial practices and the taxes that even a corporate-income-tax-exempt organization must pay. It explains how to comply with donor-imposed restrictions on funds and also with government reporting and audit requirements. Finally, it describes the process of "fiscal sponsorship," and the implications this relationship has for both the sponsoring and sponsored organizations.

B. Legally Sound Financial Practices

Q1. What financial statements should a nonprofit organization keep?

A1. A nonprofit organization should keep a statement of financial position (i.e., a balance sheet), a statement of activities (i.e., an income statement) and a statement of cash flows. A balance sheet lists organization's assets and liabilities (divided in two parts, which must equal each other). The income statement tracks the organization's expenses and revenues for a set period of time and the cash flow statement tracks an organization's aggregate cash inflows from operations, donations and investment and its aggregate outflows for program activities and infrastructure.

Q2. What internal financial controls are required to maintain legally sound financial practices?

A2. Strictly speaking, no specific internal controls are specifically required by law to maintain sound financial practices. Financial controls are the procedures by which an organization ensures that it is making appropriate use of its resources (i.e., preserving its assets from mismanagement or misappropriation). Rather than adopting a set of "stock" procedures for internal control, an organization should implement those tailored to its specific needs. An organization that frequently accepts donor-restricted gifts, for example, an organization should have more detailed internal controls in place to ensure compliance with its donors' wishes than would an organization that accepts restricted gifts only rarely.

Some procedures, on the other hand, are commonly applicable to most nonprofit organizations. Requiring written budgets and subjecting them to periodic review will help an organization's board of directors make informed financial decisions. Involving multiple people in each financial transaction, especially cash transactions, will reduce the risks of bookkeeping error, fraud, or misappropriation. Hiring an outside auditor will help ensure the accuracy of an organization's financial records and the sufficiency of its system of internal controls.

Q3. What is the legal role of the finance committee in the financial management of a nonprofit organization? How does it differ from the legal role of the board of directors?

A3. Minnesota law requires a nonprofit organization to have a president and a treasurer.[1] If a nonprofit chooses to create a finance committee, however, the board would begin by appointing certain board members to the committee and assigning staff members to provide the committee with accurate and timely financial information. The finance committee would then review this information in detail and provide the full board with the information it needs to make informed financial decisions.

The specific duties of a finance committee vary depending on the specific needs of the organization. Organizations can create a separate committee for each function (e.g., audit, investment, budget and strategic planning committees) or can combine all functions within a general finance committee. Whatever form the finance committee takes, its primary responsibility is to review the financial information staff members provide it and to make recommendations regarding financial matters to the full board.

The board in turn has a legal duty of care, which the Minnesota Attorney General's Office interprets to require a certain minimum knowledge of the organization's financial state. To exercise reasonable care in financial dealings, a board must stay apprised of the financial information it is provided, whether by a committee or by the staff directly, and make an effort to understand this information. Among other things, the board must also have a general knowledge of its organization's books and financial records and take reasonable steps to assure that these books and records are accurate. Additionally, the board has a duty of loyalty (an obligation to act in the organization's best interests) and a duty of obedience (an obligation to abide by both the laws, federal and state, governing nonprofit organizations and the rules and procedures set forth in its organization's founding documents).[2]

1 Minn. Stat. § 317A.301 (2016).

2 Office of the Minnesota Attorney General, *Guide for Charity Board Members*, www.ag.state.mn.us/consumer/publications/fiduciaryduties.asp (last visited July 24, 2017) (providing more information on the subject).

Q4. How frequently should a board of directors review financial information to meet its fiduciary responsibilities?

A4. A board of directors should review financial information on a regular basis, commonly either monthly, bimonthly, or quarterly. An organization undergoing a change in financial circumstances (e.g., a budget reduction, a building project, expansion of program activities, etc.) may require more frequent review than a stable organization, as may an organization in financial difficulty. Certain events may also inspire a need for financial review. If the board procures an independent audit, the board should review the auditor's findings. For example, if the organization prepares an IRS Form 990 information return, the board should review and approve that filing as well.

Q5. What are financial policies and procedures?

A5. Financial policies and procedures are written rules adopted by an organization, often in the form of a specific document, describing what steps an organization will take to ensure that it accomplishes its mission in an effective and efficient manner.[3]

Q6. Does a nonprofit organization need a set of financial policies and procedures?

A6. An explicit financial policy will generally describe where in an organization the authority and responsibility lies for the range of financial decisions an organization needs to make and the reporting it needs to do. Such a policy can clarify a board member's task of making financial decisions and help to eliminate confusion about an organization's financial goals. When applying for loans or grants, a financial policy can also help build the confidence of a prospective lender or grantor in the quality of the organization's management.

Q7. What is segregation of financial duties and is it required?

A7. Segregation of financial duties consists of assigning multiple people to different steps of each financial transaction so that no one person is in control of all stages. Segregation of financial duties is not required by law, but it does help an organization prevent inaccurate record-keeping and possible misappropriation of funds (weaknesses an auditor might find to materially impact an organization's financial statements). Embezzlement is a danger for all organizations, whether volunteer or staffed.

Q8. What financial records does a nonprofit organization need to maintain?

A8. A tax-exempt organization needs to maintain its filings with the IRS, including its IRS Form 1023 Application for Tax Exempt Status or Form 1023-EZ and all attachments thereto, its annual IRS Form 990/990-EZ/990-N information returns (more on this later) and all schedules thereto, and its IRS form 990-T (reporting taxable income) if one is required to be filed by the organization. In addition to these tax-exempt-specific filings, an organization must also maintain the records of a business corporation: a summary of business transactions, as well as all supporting documents (invoices, paid bills, canceled

---

3 Minnesota Council of Nonprofits, *Financial Management Resources*, www.minnesotanonprofits.org/nonprofit-resources/financial-management/financial-managment-resources-overview (last visited July 24, 2017) (providing a sample set of financial policies and procedures).

checks, etc.). It must maintain employee/independent contractor tax records if it has employees or independent contractors, property tax records if it owns property, etc. Finally, the organization should maintain the documents relating to its governance, e.g., its Articles of Incorporation, Bylaws, board-level policies and the minutes from its board meetings and committees of the board having board-delegated authority.

The Minnesota Attorney General also has requirements on charities' financial records. For more information, see Chapter Four: Charitable Solicitation Registration and *A Guide to Minnesota's Charities Laws* at www.ag.state.mn.us/Consumer/Publications/GuideCharityLaws.asp.

Q9. How long should a nonprofit organization keep its financial records?

A9. A Minnesota nonprofit is required by state law to maintain "correct and complete" copies of its Bylaws and Articles of Incorporation, accounting records, and voting agreements, as well as the minutes from any board, member or committee meeting in the last six years.[4] The organization must maintain these records for internal use, so that they may be accessed by the members and directors of the organization, and by their agents or attorneys if necessary.

Federal law, on the other hand, requires nonprofit organizations to maintain the records, financial and otherwise, that support annual IRS tax and information returns. After a return has been filed, there is a period of time in which either the filing organization or the IRS can amend it, known as the statute of limitations. The statute of limitations on a nonprofit's annual return is generally three years.[5] However, if an organization has made a substantial omission (more than 25 percent) from its statement of gross income or of items subject to excise tax, the statute of limitations will be extended to six years.[6] The burden of proof is on the IRS to show that an organization has made a substantial omission.

Federal law also requires an organization to maintain its IRS Form 1023 Application for Tax-Exempt Status in perpetuity for the benefit of the public, as well as its Form 990 information returns and form 990-T (if applicable) for the last three years. Additionally, federal law (the Sarbanes-Oxley Act) prohibits the destruction of documents to prevent them from being used in official proceedings. For more information on a nonprofit's public disclosure requirements and the Sarbanes-Oxley Act consult Questions 49 and 71, respectively.

Federal and state requirements aside, retaining financial documents can help an organization analyze its financial performance. Comparing old financial records with current records can help an organization track its growth over time, for example, or analyze trends in its funding patterns. Some financial records, such as the records needed to support IRS tax and information returns, will gradually become obsolete and should be purged once the burden of maintaining them outweighs the benefit to the organization of doing so (many standard records retention policies suggest seven years). Other records never become obsolete and should be maintained in perpetuity. These records include an organization's Articles of Incorporation and the minutes of its board meetings; accounting records such as a general ledger, year-end financial statements and audited financial reports; current contracts and the deeds and titles to currently owned property.

4 Minn. Stat. § 317A.461 (2016).
5 *See* I.R.C. § 6501(a) (2015).
6 *See* I.R.C. § 6501(e)(1)(A) (2015).

Q10. Can a nonprofit organization seek a credit check of prospective employees whose duties include working with money?

A10. Yes, with the prospective employee's written consent. Once consent has been obtained and the credit check carried out, the federal Fair Credit Reporting Act ("FCRA") requires an employer to notify the prospective employee if the results of the credit check might motivate a decision not to hire the individual. The organization must provide the prospective employee with a copy of the credit report and a written statement of his or her rights under the FCRA. Then, if the organization does ultimately choose not to employ the individual, it must provide him or her with written notice of the name, address and phone number of the Credit Reporting Agency ("CRA") that supplied the report and of his or her right to dispute the accuracy and completeness of the information, which the CRA furnished.[7]

Q11. Can a nonprofit organization authorize multiple staff and/or board members to sign bank checks? If so, how is this done?

A11. Yes, an organization can authorize multiple parties to sign bank checks. The procedure for doing so will vary between financial institutions, so an organization should consult with its own bank to see what is necessary. Most banks require a corporate bank resolution for this authorization, and some require a bank signature card for each authorized signer.

Q12. What is a bank resolution and how is it updated?

A12. A bank resolution is a document an organization provides to a bank to authorize specified officers to access the corporate accounts (e.g., sign checks and make transfers). In order to obtain this authorization, the board of directors must pass the resolution, a designated officer must verify it, and a copy must be provided to the bank. The list of approved signers can be updated by repeating the procedure with a subsequent resolution.

Q13. What information does the Patriot Act require for signers on nonprofit bank accounts?

A13. The Patriot Act requires the Treasury Department and federal banking agencies to establish minimum customer identification standards for setting up new accounts. If an organization opens a new bank account or adds a new signer to an existing bank account, each authorized signer must provide their bank with their name, physical address, birth date and Social Security number. This information will be kept on file by the bank until five years after the account is closed or the authorized signer is removed from the account.

Q14. Does every staff and board member who has the authority to sign bank checks or handle cash need to be bonded and insured?

A14. A nonprofit organization can choose to bond and insure employees who work with money, but it is not legally required to do so. Acquiring a fidelity bond on an employee will indemnify an organization for losses sustained through that employee's theft or embezzlement. Though each organization should decide

7 Federal Trade Commission, *Using Consumer Reports: What Employers Need to Know*, www.ftc.gov/tips-advice/business-center/guidance/using-consumer-reports-what-employers-need-know (last visited July 24, 2017) (providing more information about the FCRA and how it affects the hiring process).

for itself whether or not to insure itself against employee dishonesty, many employers consider it a good business practice to do so. Also, some grants or contracts may include a bonding requirement.

Q15. Can a nonprofit organization borrow funds from a financial institution, like a bank or credit union?

A15. Yes. Authority to borrow may be spelled out in the organization's Bylaws. A Board of Directors has the authority to borrow funds for the benefit of the organization, and may authorize employees to do so.

Q16. Can a nonprofit organization issue tax-exempt bonds?

A16. A private nonprofit organization may not issue tax-exempt bonds, though state and local governments may agree to issue tax-exempt bonds on an organization's behalf. For this reason, tax-exempt bonds benefiting nonprofit organizations are sometimes called conduit bonds.

Available to 501(c)(3) charitable organizations, tax-exempt or conduit bonds benefit an organization by allowing it to borrow at a lower interest rate than is commercially available. These bonds may be issued in a public offering or a private placement with a fixed or variable interest rate. Organizations interested in borrowing via a conduit bond should consult with a legal or investment professional before making inquiries with an appropriate issuing agency (e.g., city, state, school district, port authority, etc.).

Q17. Can a nonprofit organization issue stock?

A17. A nonprofit organization cannot issue stock in the sense the term is commonly used, i.e., an ownership share in a corporation that entitles the holder to a proportional share of its profits. No part of the earnings of a nonprofit organization may inure to the benefit of a private individual, so a nonprofit may not issue stock and pay dividends to its shareholders, nor may it issue stock that its shareholders may buy and sell to realize capital gain.

This is not to say, however, that a nonprofit organization cannot assign memberships (i.e., a percentage share of voting rights). Minnesota law allows a nonprofit organization to set forth the terms of one or more classes of members in its articles or Bylaws.[8] Any person can be admitted to an organization as a member, and an organization may assign memberships to donors in recognition of financial gifts. The key difference between stock and memberships is that members may not benefit financially from owning a membership, as do stockholders.

Q18. Can a nonprofit organization borrow funds from board members?

A18. A nonprofit organization should be extremely careful about borrowing funds from board members or officers. Before accepting the loan, however, the board should be sure that the loan does not violate the organization's Conflict of Interest policy and that the loan is truly in the organization's best interest—e.g., the terms of the loan are acceptable (fair market value or better for the organization), the funds will be used to support necessary services, etc. It should also carefully document its decision with the insider providing the loan absent from discussion and voting. If the IRS judges that the loan was not in the organization's best interest, but instead provided an improper benefit to the insider (e.g., an officer, director, major donor

8 Minn. Stat. § 317A.401 (2016).

or key employee), the IRS could negate the transfer and levy a fine on the borrower personally and upon those directors who approved the loan. For more detail on improper transactions and their legal remedy, see Section I: Private Inurement and Intermediate Sanctions.

Q19. Can a board member get a loan from his or her organization?

A19. A nonprofit organization should have a policy against making loans to insiders. Minnesota law only allows a nonprofit organization to make a loan to a director, officer or employee (or family member of any of these persons) when the loan is approved by the board and can reasonably be expected, in the board's judgment, to benefit the organization.[9] If an organization makes a loan to an insider in violation of these conditions, the directors and officers who approved the loan will join the borrower in being liable for its repayment.

Some loans from an organization to an individual might carry a low risk of disapproval by the Attorney General. A nonprofit that provides occasional paycheck advances to its low-income employees, for example, might argue that these advances are in the regular course of business as an employer and benefit the nonprofit organization by building employee goodwill. If the same nonprofit offered a loan to its chief executive officer, however, these arguments would have much less force and the consequences to the board that approved the loan could be severe.

Additionally, loans from an organization to an individual bear the same risk of private inurement as do the loans from an individual to an organization mentioned in the previous question. Again, for more detail on improper transactions between an organization and one of its managers and directors and their IRS consequences, see Section I: Private Inurement and Intermediate Sanctions.

Q20. Is a written lease required by law?

A20. Not necessarily. Minnesota law does not require leases to appear in writing, while the federal Statute of Frauds, which requires certain agreements to appear in writing, only applies to leases for a period of longer than a year. Thus, any lease lasting a year or less can be oral rather than written and still be legally binding.

A written lease is nonetheless a good idea. It helps both parties to the lease understand and remember the precise terms of their agreement, especially when new parties succeed to the agreement (e.g., the landlord dies and someone else inherits the leased property, the nonprofit director who negotiated the lease is replaced by a new director, etc.).

Q21. Do leases require approval by a board of directors?

A21. The president of a nonprofit organization has the right to sign and deliver leases in the name of the organization, unless the articles, Bylaws or a board resolution prevents the president from doing so.[10] An organization can enter into a lease without the board's explicit approval if the board had previously authorized an organization executive to obligate the organization in this way. Some property owners, however, require an organization to provide an explicit board resolution approving the lease. An organization

9 Minn. Stat. § 317A.501 (2016).
10 Minn. Stat. § 317A.305, subd. 2 (2016).

should consult with the other party in a lease to see what that party requires.

Q22. Do contracts require approval by the board of directors?

A22. The board determines which contracts require approval of the board. A board of directors can approve a contract in a variety of ways. The board could provide an organization executive with unrestricted prior authorization to enter into certain kinds of contracts (e.g., employment contracts for temporary workers, etc.) or prior authorization to enter into contracts subject to board ratification (e.g., contracts less than $25,000 that need immediate approval). Most organizations, however, choose to have the board approve contracts that exceed a certain financial threshold on a case-by-case basis by means of board resolutions, unless the contact is clearly contemplated by the organization's budget for the year.

C. Limitations on the Expenditure of Restricted Funds

Q23. What are temporarily and permanently restricted funds?

A23. The law allows donors to attach restrictions to their gifts. Temporarily restricted funds are those ear marked for a particular purpose and/or within a particular window of time, e.g., $10,000 to defray the heating bills of low-income families or $10,000 to be used in fiscal year 2017. These restrictions will lapse when the conditions are met by the funds being used for the designated purpose.

Permanently restricted funds are funds in which the restrictions do not lapse. These funds generally take the form of donor-designated endowments, or investments the organization is not free to liquidate and spend but which generate investment returns or interest income for the organization. This income can also be either restricted or unrestricted. One common example of a permanently restricted gift that generates temporarily restricted gifts is an endowment supporting scholarships with its interest income.

Donor restrictions can also apply to gifts other than funds. A work of art that must be displayed in a museum for a certain length of time would be a temporarily restricted gift, and a tract of land that must be used for a particular purpose in perpetuity is an example of a permanently restricted gift. Assigning a value to these types of gifts requires special expertise, in some cases even professional appraisal.

Q24. Is a nonprofit organization legally required to separate its restricted funds from its unrestricted funds?

A24. An organization must be able to separately account for its use of restricted funds. This does not mean that an organization must establish a separate cash account in its financial statement for each restricted gift, only that the organization must be able to document that restricted funds are going to their designated purpose. If the organization's accounting system will support detailed records, a less cumbersome way to account for restricted funds would be to record the restricted gift as an addition to the main cash account and attach a category to it, e.g., "low-income heating assistance." When funds are used for this purpose, they should be recorded as expenses in this category. Looking at the category will then give an organization the balance of the restricted gift as yet unspent on its designated purpose without having to maintain a separate cash account for this gift. Whatever method is used, the accounting system must maintain detailed records of the receipt and use of restricted gifts and grants.

Minnesota law provides that the assets of a charity or trust may not be diverted from the uses and purposes for which they were originally received and held; it does not require a particular accounting method for these assets.[11]

Q25. *What are the legal ramifications of improperly spending restricted funds?*

A25. In Minnesota, the Attorney General's Office has standing to enforce charitable intent and protect charitable assets. The Attorney General can petition a court to order a nonprofit organization to properly spend restricted funds, and to require it to replace the restricted funds out of general funds if they have already been improperly spent. Additionally, the Attorney General can sue for monetary damages, request the removal of a trustee, or ask the court to appoint a receiver to take over the financial and other operations of the organization. The Attorney General also has authority to seize charitable assets to prevent their waste or loss.

As a matter of long-standing common law, the donor of a restricted gift generally does not have standing in court to enforce those restrictions. Once the gift has been given, the reasoning goes, it ceases to be the property of the donor and becomes the property of the organization. The donor generally has no more right to sue than does a non-donor. Organizations should be mindful that courts in different states may or may not allow a donor to have standing to bring suit to enforce a restriction on a charitable gift, and there is no overarching Supreme Court guidance.[12]

Improperly spending restricted funds also risks serious consequences short of legal action. Accepting a donor's restricted gift and then refusing to abide by the restriction is likely to alienate that donor. Moreover, if the misappropriation becomes public, it could hurt public confidence in an organization and discourage contributions to it.

Q26. *Is it unlawful to spend endowment and capital funds for program costs?*

A26. It is only unlawful to spend endowment or capital funds for program costs if donor-imposed restrictions apply to these funds that would restrict their use to some purpose other than program costs. If, on the other hand, the organization was under no legal requirement to invest these funds (e.g., if the money came from general revenue), the organization has discretion over how to use them within the constraints of the organization's mission and purposes.

Furthermore, an organization is only required to abide by donor restrictions for that part of the fund the donor provided. For example, if an organization accepted $200,000 from a donor in order to endow a scholarship fund and it later decided to add another $300,000 to the endowment from general revenues, the restriction would apply only to the donor's $200,000 rather than the combined $500,000.

Q27. *Can income from one program of the organization be used to support another program?*

A27. Yes. So long as an organization did not represent to the public that the income, whether earned or

11 Minn. Stat. § 317A.671 (2016); see also Minn. Stat. § 501B.31 (2016).

12 For example, in case *L.B. Research & Ed. Found. v. UCLA Found.*, 130 Cal. App. 4th 171 (2005), donor of a restricted gift had standing to enforce the terms of the restriction. However, in a later case Hardt v. Vitae Found., Inc., 302 S.W.3d 133 (Mo. Ct. App. 2009), donors did not have standing to enforce gift restrictions under common law.

donated, would go to a particular program, it is free to allocate the funds as it wishes. To give an example, if an organization held a youth literacy event at which it sold children's books, it would be free to use the proceeds for another program, say adult literacy. But if the organization had advertised that all proceeds were to benefit youth literacy specifically or had used the event to solicit donations specifically for youth literacy, the organization would have an obligation to use the proceeds for that specific purpose.

Q28. Can a nonprofit organization use restricted funds in a way contrary to donor restrictions? If so, in what circumstances does a nonprofit organization need to get government approval?

A28. If an organization seeks to use an asset in a way other than the donor specified, the organization must, in general, petition a court for permission to divert the assets to another purpose, and in so doing must give notice to the Minnesota Attorney General.[13] UPMIFA, which became law in Minnesota in 2008, would allow an organization to modify the uses and purposes for which a donor-restricted fund is held if the donor restricted fund is more than 20 years old and holds less than $50,000. For example, if a person donated a house to a non-profit hospital with the stipulation that it go to housing to visiting nurses, and donor consent to change the use was not available; the hospital would have to get the approval of a court to sell the house or use it for another purpose.

For a court to approve an organization's request to depart from the terms of a restricted gift, the organization must first show that the original terms are impossible, impractical or illegal.[14] The terms of the above restriction, for example, would be arguably impossible if the hospital canceled its visiting nurse program, impractical if the federal or state government already provided subsidized housing to visiting nurses, and impermissible if the conditions of the restriction were illegal (e.g., only for the use of female nurses, or Christian nurses or nurses younger than forty).

If a court does approve the organization's request to depart from the current terms of a restricted gift, this does not mean that gift becomes unrestricted. Instead, the court will seek to substitute an acceptable new restriction that follows as near as possible the original intent of the restricted gift. If the court determined that the intent behind the gift was to help attract skilled staff to the hospital, for example, the restriction might be changed from housing visiting nurses to housing visiting doctors, or the house liquidated and the funds devoted to providing more attractive employee compensation packages. This commitment to donor intent is known as the *cy pres* doctrine (French for "as near as possible").

D. Payroll Taxes

Q29. What payroll taxes must a nonprofit organization pay on behalf of its employees?

A29. Like any U.S. employer, a nonprofit organization is responsible for withholding applicable federal and state employment taxes. On a federal level, these taxes include: federal income tax, which an employer withholds from its employees' wages; and Social Security and Medicare taxes, which an employer withholds from its employees' wages and matches from its own funds. A Minnesota employer is also

13 *See generally*, Minn. Stat. §501B (the Supervision of Charitable Trusts and Trustees Act) for more information on the Attorney General's oversight of charitable trusts.

14 Generally speaking, the government cannot legally enforce private agreements that deny persons equal rights or the due process of law. Other constitutional rights, such as the freedom of speech, may be legally abridged by private contract. For example, workplace confidentiality agreements can abridge an employee's freedom of speech and still be legally permissible.

responsible for Minnesota income tax, which it withholds from its employees' wages; and state unemployment tax, which it pays from its own funds.

Q30. Who is legally responsible for making payroll tax payments? How often?

A30. An employer is legally required to deposit the taxes it withholds from its employees and its matching share of FICA taxes to the IRS on a regular basis along with Form 941. In the first year of business, an employer is considered a monthly schedule depositor (with some special exceptions) and should deposit each month's payroll taxes by the fifteenth of the next month. After this first year, employers who have paid more than $50,000 in payroll taxes during the past year (the lookback period) are considered semiweekly schedule depositors and should deposit payroll taxes every Wednesday (for wages paid Saturday through Tuesday) and every Friday (for wages paid Wednesday through Friday).

Q31. What happens if a nonprofit organization fails to withhold taxes from an employee's compensation?

A31. Failure to withhold payroll taxes and remit them to the government will result in monetary fines that will continue to accrue for each additional day taxes are not withheld. The IRS can levy funds directly from an organization's bank accounts, and if the organization does not satisfy the obligation, board members are individually liable for the amount owed.

Q32. Who is legally responsible for maintaining payroll tax records?

A32. The employer.

Q33. If a nonprofit organization contracts with a payroll service provider, who is responsible for making sure that taxes are properly withheld and remitted?

Q33. Generally speaking, when a nonprofit organization contracts with a payroll service provider, the provider agrees to calculate the proper amount of payroll tax, withhold it from the wages of organization employees and submit it to the appropriate federal and state agencies. The nonprofit organization nonetheless bears the ultimate responsibility for these taxes. If its payroll service provider fails to make a payment, the IRS will assess penalties and interest on the organization.

The IRS will contact the organization by mail if issues arise with its tax account, and prompt response by the organization may help to mitigate the penalties and interest imposed. Alternately, an organization whose provider is enrolled in EFTPS (the Electronic Federal Tax Payment System) can verify via phone or the internet that tax payments are being made. Finally, if an organization's payroll service provider has a fiduciary bond in place, the provider's insurance may reimburse the organization for the penalties and interest.

E. Fiscal Agency or Sponsorship

Q34. What does it mean to be a "fiscal sponsor" or "fiscal agent"?

A34. In certain circumstances, a nonprofit organization can accept tax-deductible donations on behalf of a project or organization that is not itself tax-exempt. This is called acting as a "fiscal sponsor," but is more appropriately described as accepting expenditure responsibility.

Fiscal sponsorships usually are created when individuals or groups would like to serve a charitable purpose without first securing tax-exempt status for themselves. They could be unwilling to do so (because their goal is limited enough that they do not think it is worth the time and effort of establishing a new tax-exempt charity) or perhaps unable (because the window of opportunity for their charitable purpose is too short for them get tax-exempt status in time). In either case, this non-tax-exempt group, also called the project, can find a fiscal sponsor under whose umbrella they can operate, receiving tax-deductible donations, applying for grants, and reporting to funding sources. So long as the sponsorship agreement lasts, the sponsor agrees to accept and manage funds on the project's behalf and to satisfy its reporting and record-keeping requirements. The project is considered to be part of the operations and financial activity of the fiscal sponsor.

A tax-exempt organization can only sponsor a project when the sponsor and project share a charitable purpose. For example, while a tax-exempt organization founded to protect Minnesota wildlife could sponsor a project to prevent development of a wetlands area, it could not sponsor a project to provide mathematics tutoring to inner-city children.

Q35. What are the legal responsibilities of a fiscal sponsor or agent?

A35. A fiscal sponsor has a legal duty to ensure that the project properly expends its funds for appropriate exempt purposes, and that the project receives the full benefit of the funds the sponsor manages on its behalf. A sponsor would also be well advised to take precautions against improper action by the project, for which it would bear legal responsibility. The best precaution is proper oversight.

Q36. Is a contract necessary in fiscal sponsorship? What should it contain?

A36. A contract is not required by law, but it is a good idea. By accepting an organization's sponsorship, a project is giving up a good deal of control over its own activities. On the other hand, improper action by the project could put the sponsor's tax exemption at risk. A contract should thus contain a procedure by which to terminate the relationship if either side becomes uncomfortable.

A good contract is tailored to the parties signing it; it should cover every issue important to both parties. For a fiscal sponsorship agreement, these issues may include the conditions for the use of funds, the services the sponsor will provide, and the policies the project will follow (e.g., financial and employment policies, etc.). Sample fiscal sponsorship agreements provide a good starting point for contract negotiations,[15] but should not be used verbatim. A contract is legally enforceable; it should be tailored to the needs of the contracting parties and reviewed by an attorney if possible.

---

15 The Colorado Trust, *Sample Fiscal Sponsorship Agreement*, www.coloradotrust.org/sites/default/files/Fiscal_Sponsorship_Agreement_Sample.pdf (last visited July 24, 2017).

F. Audit Requirements

Q37. Are all nonprofit organizations required by law to procure an audit each year?

A37. Minnesota law requires those charitable organizations that solicit funds from the public and have annual revenue in excess of $750,000 to procure an annual audit that complies with Generally Accepted Accounting Principles ("GAAP") and has been examined by an independent certified public accountant.[16] Charitable organizations that solicit funds from the public in excess of $25,000 in a year are required to submit an annual financial report to the Minnesota Attorney General, as are soliciting organizations that maintain any paid staff or retain professional fundraisers.[17]

Additionally, federal law requires organizations receiving federal funds to undergo an annual single audit. For more information on this single audit, see Question 44.

Q38. Do in-kind contributions contribute to the audit threshold of $750,000?

A38. Gifts of property (e.g., stocks and bonds, real estate, food and clothing, motor vehicles, etc.) are the only type of in-kind contributions that contributes to the audit threshold. Other kinds of contributions (e.g., gifts of services, free or reduced rent) do not. Though gifts of services and of free or reduced rent have monetary value to an organization, they are not deductible financial contributions as defined by the Internal Revenue Code and do not count in determining an organization's revenue for purposes of the $750,000 audit threshold.

Q39. Are there legally acceptable alternatives to an audit?

A39. If an organization is required to procure an audit under Minnesota Statutes Chapter 309, it has no legally acceptable alternatives. Some other kinds of annual reporting requirements may be satisfied by a more limited financial review. For example, Minnesota Statutes § 297E.06 (2016) provides that an organization with revenues from lawful gambling in excess of $750,000 per year must procure an annual audit, while an organization with yearly gambling revenues of $750,000 or less may instead procure a certified inventory and cash count. During a limited financial review, a CPA will make a limited examination of an organization's financial statements and make inquiries to the management. It is less comprehensive than an audit and thus may be less costly and time consuming.

Q40. For nonprofit organizations that are required to procure an audit, what are the legal consequences of not complying?

A40. A nonprofit organization that receives federal funds and fails to procure an audit can suffer a reduction in the amount of federal funds awarded, while a Minnesota charitable organization that solicits funds from the public and fails to procure a required audit can have a court action brought against it by the Attorney General. In addition, an organization's right to solicit contributions in Minnesota may be revoked until the audit requirement is met.

16 Minn. Stat. § 309.53, subd. 3 (2016) ("For purposes of calculating the $750,000 total revenue threshold provided by this subdivision, the value of donated food to a nonprofit food shelf may not be included if the food is donated for subsequent distribution at no charge, and not for resale.").

17 Minn. Stat. § 309.52 (2016).

Q41. If a particular nonprofit is not legally required to procure an audit, are there other reasons an audit should still be procured?

A41. An audit is a professionally trained outsider's diagnostic of the quality of financial information available to an organization. It may assist the board of directors in assessing the organization's financial health and suggest ways in which an organization's internal controls may be enhanced. Also, many grantors and funders may require an organization to undergo an audit as a condition of their gifts.

Q42. What internal financial controls are assessed during an audit?

A42. An audit assesses the adequacy of an organization's internal controls. It neither requires nor forbids any specific methods of internal controls; it merely evaluates whether the system of controls effectively mitigates against fraud and embezzlement and whether the system of controls is sufficient to allow for adequate accounting. If not, the auditor may suggest changes or enhancements in the current policies and procedures.

Q43. What is an opinion without qualifications?

A43. An opinion without qualifications, also called an "unqualified opinion" is the highest assurance an auditor can give an organization. This opinion is an auditor's statement that the organization's financial statements fairly represent the condition of the organization.

Q44. When are nonprofit organizations required to do a "single audit"?

A44. Nonprofit organizations receiving federal grant money are required to undergo a single audit of the program receiving federal funds. The audit is called a single audit not because it is a one-time event (an organization must procure one each year in which it receives the grant money), but because it combines both a financial and a compliance function within one audit.

The financial function of a single audit analyzes an organization's book of accounts and financial statements for compliance with Generally Accepted Accounting Principles ("GAAP") and the organization's federal assistance for the more rigorous Generally Accepted Government Accounting Standards ("GAGAS").

The compliance function of a single audit evaluates whether an organization's finances are efficiently managed and whether the organization is complying with Office of Management and Budget ("OMB") procedures for organizations receiving federal funds. For more information on a single audit, also called an A-133 audit, consult OMB Circular A-133, available at the OMB website obamawhitehouse.archives.gov/omb/circulars/a133_compliance_supplement_2016.

G. IRS Information Return (Form 990) Requirements

Q45. Does a nonprofit organization need to file Form 990 with the IRS each year?

A45. Most tax-exempt organizations are required to file an annual Form 990 (or Form 990-EZ) information return with the IRS. Organizations with less than $50,000 in financial activity and certain religious organizations are instead required to file a Form 990-N, and organizations with private foundation status must file an annual Form 990-PF return. A revised Form 990 series return was effective for 2008 tax years (returns filed beginning in 2009). To allow organizations time to adjust to the new forms, the IRS allowed for the filing of the new returns during a three-year transition period. From tax year 2010 and later, the chart below indicates the general exempt organization filing requirements.

2010 Tax Year and later (Filed in 2011 and later)	**Form to File**
Gross receipts normally ≤$50,000	990-N (e-postcard)
Gross receipts > $50,000 and < $200,000, and Total assets < $500,000	990-EZ or 990
Gross receipts ≥ $200,000, or Total assets ≥ $500,000	990
Private foundation - regardless of financial status	990-PF

Q46. What are the legal consequences if a nonprofit organization fails to file a complete an accurate Form 990?

A46. Failure to file a complete and accurate Form 990 in a timely manner can result in monetary fines to the organization. In addition, responsible persons within the organization may also have penalties assessed against them personally if the errors and/or omissions are not corrected in the IRS-specified time frame. Under Internal Revenue Code § 6652(c)(1)(A), an organization can be fined $20 a day for each day the errors and/or omissions continue (not to exceed $10,000 or 5 percent of the organization's gross income, whichever is smaller), and under I.R.C. § 6652(c)(1)(B)(ii) an individual can be fined $10 a day (not to exceed $5,000). Organizations with annual gross receipts exceeding $1 million are subject to a penalty of $100 a day for each day the errors and/or omission continue (with a maximum penalty for any one return of $50,000.) Willful misrepresentation in a Form 990 can result in additional monetary fines and possible jail time (under I.R.C. §§ 7203, 7206 and 7207). The failure to file a Form 990 series return for three consecutive years will result in an organization losing its tax-exempt status.

Q47. Once they are assessed, can penalties arising from a nonprofit organization's failure to file Form 990 be removed?

A47. Yes. The IRS may waive the monetary penalties for late filing of the Form 990 if the organization can demonstrate that it had a reasonable cause for filing late, or filed late because of relying upon the incorrect advice of an IRS employee. The IRS may also waive accruing interest that results from an IRS delay in processing the Form 990. Fines already levied may be refunded for these same reasons. However, the abatement (or waiving) of these penalties is not guaranteed.

Q48. When is Form 990 due? Are filing extensions available?

A48. The IRS Form 990 is due the fifteenth day of the fifth month following the end of the organization's fiscal year (tax year). The organization can acquire an automatic three-month extension by filing a Form 8688, after which it can acquire a subsequent (non-automatic) additional three-month extension by filing another Form 8688 and showing good cause. An organization required to file a Form 990-T may request an automatic six-month extension by also filing a Form 8868 and checking the appropriate box to indicate the filing of the Form 990-T. It is very important to remember the extension of time to file does not extend the time to pay any tax, which may be due with the return.

Q49. Besides the IRS, who can see a nonprofit organization's Form 990?

A49. Everyone. Any nonprofit organization required to provide a Form 990 information return to the IRS (generally, Section 501(c) tax-exempt organizations, but also Section 527 political organizations) is required to make the contents of that return available to the public. The organization is required by federal law to make its annual returns for the previous three years available for public inspection during normal business hours (either in physical form at the office or in electronic form on the organization's website). It is also required to provide free copies of its returns to members of the public upon request, though it may charge requestors for postage and photocopying costs.

Alternately, the public can request any organization's Form 990 information return from the IRS by filing a Form 4506-A, or find the Form 990 of most 501(c)(3) charitable organizations at www.guidestar.org. (It is important to note Schedule B, which includes the names and addresses of donors, is not required to be included in the public inspection copy of the Form 990 for 501(c)(3) public charities.)

Q50. Why is it important to report program expenses separately from administrative and fundraising expenses on the Form 990?

A50. The Form 990 return serves as a primary source of information about an organization to the public. By reporting program expenses separately from administrative and fundraising expenses, the Form 990 helps show the public how much of an organization's resources go directly to program activities and how much is used to support the organization's management and infrastructure.

Q51. What is required on the Form 990 regarding reporting amounts of compensation paid to directors, officers, key employees and other employees?

A51. Form 990 requires full disclosure of compensation from the organization and related organizations, average hours per week each person works for the organization, and position(s). For Part VII, Column (D) of the Form 990, compensation includes box 5 of Form W-2 and box 7 of Form 1099 MISC or "fees for services paid pursuant to a contractual agreement or statutory entitlement" for institutional trustees. Individuals that require disclosure include:

- Current officers, directors, and trustees;

- Current key employees (over $150,000);
- Five highest compensated employees (over $100,000);
- Former officers, key employees, and 5 highest compensated employees (over $100,000);
- Former directors and trustees (over $10,000).

Form 990, Part VI requires detailed disclosure of the business and family relationships between these persons. Schedule J of Form 990 has additional compensation reporting requirements.

Q52. Can the Form 990 be amended after it is filed with the IRS? If so, how is this done?

A52. Yes, it can be amended. To amend its Form 990 return, an organization must submit a new Form 990 to the IRS, making sure to check the Amended Return box in the heading of the form. It is not sufficient to only submit the new or amended information; the entire form must be completed again.

H. Unrelated Business Income Tax (UBIT)

Q53. What is UBIT (Unrelated Business Income Tax)?

A53. UBIT is a tax levied on the taxable income a tax-exempt organization realizes from activities that are not substantially related to its charitable mission.

The IRS considers an activity to be unrelated when all three of the following components of the unrelated business income test are met:

- The activity constitutes a "trade or business," i.e., the sale of a good or service. When an organization conducts workshops, provides counseling or sells goods for a fee, for example, it may be engaged in a trade or business. However, a fundraising event or when the organization rewards donations with coffee mugs and tote bags, it is not engaged in a trade or business.
- The nonprofit organization conducts the activity as would a similarly situated for-profit (the activity is "regularly carried on"). In general, an organization that engages in an activity year-round is considered to be regularly carrying on that activity, as is an organization that engages in an activity intermittently, but in the same time manner as would for-profit competitors (e.g., publishing a quarterly magazine/journal but regularly soliciting advertising to be placed in the magazine/journal).
- The activity is "not substantially related" to the organization's exempt purpose, except to fund that purpose. An activity bears substantial relation to an organization's exempt purpose when it "contributes importantly" to that purpose (according to Treasury Regulation § 1.513-1 (d)(2)). For example, a nonprofit hospital's gift shop, which is open to patients and their visitors, makes an important contribution to the hospital's exempt purpose by raising the spirits of its patients.

Organizations with specific UBIT concerns can consult IRS Publication 598, which is available on the IRS website. There is also a set of Revenue Rulings that describe how the IRS has dealt with specific UBIT situations in the past. For example, the previously mentioned nonprofit hospital gift shop was first mentioned in Revenue Ruling 69-267, 1969-1 C.B. 160.

Q54. What level of unrelated business activity will jeopardize an organization's tax exemption?

A54. Treasury Regulation § 1.501(c)(3)-1(e)(1) holds that a tax-exempt charity must not be "organized or operated for the primary purpose of carrying on an unrelated trade or business." Though the "size and extent of the trade or business and the size and extent of the activities . . . in furtherance of one or more exempt purposes" must be taken into account, the regulation fails to provide a formula for deciding "the existence or non-existence of such a primary purpose." Instead, the regulation leaves this for the IRS to decide on a case-by-case basis.

This lack of a bright-line rule makes it hard for an organization to predict what level of unrelated business activity will result in the IRS revoking an organization's tax exemption. Depending on the facts and circumstances of each organization, the IRS may revoke the tax exemption of an organization whose unrelated business activity generates 15 percent of its net income and preserve the tax exemption of an organization with 25 percent of net income from unrelated business. In addition, the threshold is not merely defined as "net income."

One way to reduce the chances of the IRS revoking an organization's tax exemption would be to form a taxable subsidiary to conduct the activity, or enter into a joint venture to conduct the activity with a separate taxable corporation. These topics are covered in more detail in Chapter 12: Relationships with Other Entities. An organization may reduce the chances of an IRS finding of excessive unrelated business activity by ensuring that all business activities conducted are appropriately characterized as "related" income, is accurately described to the IRS as related income on the IRS Form 1023 and annual IRS Form 990 information returns.[18]

Q55. How does a nonprofit organization report UBIT to the IRS?

A55. When a nonprofit organization receives unrelated business income, this is reported on its IRS Form 990 information return. When the gross receipts from unrelated activities is $1,000 or more, the organization is required to also complete an IRS Form 990-T to calculate the unrelated business taxable income and determine how much tax is owed. Though the majority of an organization's sources of earned income (e.g., tuition, clinic fees, theatre fees, etc.) may be considered related business activities, common sources of unrelated business income includes rental and advertising income.

I. Private Inurement and Intermediate Sanctions

Q56. What is private inurement?

A56. Private inurement occurs when the assets of a charitable organization are diverted for the private use of an organization insider, i.e., when an organization insider receives a greater compensation for his or her services than is reasonable. Because IRS recognition of a charitable organization is conditioned on the organization serving the public rather than benefiting private individuals, private inurement poses a severe threat to an organization's 501(c)(3) status.

---

18 These two suggestions were first mentioned in an article in the *William Mitchell Law Review*. The full citation for the article is as follows: Plunkett, J. Patrick & Christianson, Heidi Neff, *The Quest for Cash: Exempt Organizations, Joint Ventures, Taxable Subsidiaries, and Unrelated Business Income, 31* Wm. Mitchell L. Rev. 1 (2004).

Q57. How does a nonprofit organization avoid paying or otherwise providing private inurement?

A57. Contracts between an organization and an officer, director or family member of an officer or director can result in private inurement if what the organization receives in return is less than the fair market value of what is paid to the insider or the insider's family. Excessive compensation is the most common private inurement concern for a 501(c)(3) organization, though private inurement can also result when an organization and its executives conduct business together as separate entities (e.g., a board member makes a loan to his or her organization, an organization contracts with a company owned in whole or in part by an organization insider). As such, one way to avoid private inurement is to adopt a comprehensive conflict of interest policy.

Q58. How can board members disclose their conflicts of interest and the board of directors follow up on that disclosure in such a way that will avoid accusations of private inurement?

A58. A successful conflict of interest policy will be tailored to the needs of a specific organization. However, Minnesota Statutes Section 317A.255 (2016) provides that majority approval of a contract will prevent it from being void or voidable due to conflict of interest if a conflicted party makes a "full disclosure of all material facts" and absents himself or herself for voting. The majority can be a two-thirds majority of voting members, a unanimous affirmative from all voting and non-voting members or a simple majority of board or committee members (depending on how the specific organization is structured). Alternately, if the conflicted party fails to make a full disclosure or to absent himself or herself from the voting and the contract is later contested, the conflicted party has the burden of proving that the contract was reasonable to the organization.

Q59. Who are disqualified persons? Are these the parties to whom private inurement must not be provided?

A59. Disqualified persons are those persons in a position to exercise substantial influence over an organization's decisions, e.g., the executives of an organization, its founders, substantial contributors, their families and those corporate entities in which they have a significant ownership interest (at least 35 percent). Though charitable assets may not lawfully be diverted to the use of private persons, this diversion only qualifies as private inurement when it is disqualified persons who are benefiting. When organization outsiders are benefiting, the diversion of charitable assets is known as private benefit.

Q60. What are intermediate sanctions?

A60. Intermediate sanctions (so called because they stop short of the ultimate sanction, the revocation of an organization's tax-exempt status) are monetary fines, actually excise taxes, designed to deter the private inurement of disqualified persons.

Before imposing intermediate sanctions, the IRS will first examine a transaction between a disqualified person and a 501(c)(3) or (c)(4) organization to see whether or not the price paid to a disqualified person for a good or service exceeds its fair market value. Fair market value is defined as the price at which a willing buyer and willing seller would make an exchange if both were in possession of all relevant facts. One way to establish the fair market value of a good or service provided by a disqualified person would be to see what price the person's competitors ask for similar goods and services. If most lenders in an area would make a loan to an organization at 8 percent interest, for example, then 8 percent is likely to be the fair market value of that loan, and a disqualified person who makes the loan at 10 percent has probably received greater than fair market value.

If a disqualified person receives greater than fair market value for a good or service he or she provided to a charitable organization, the IRS considers that person to have made an "excess benefit" from the exchange, and considers the transaction to be an "excess benefit transaction." The amount of the excess benefit is equal to the difference between what the disqualified person received for a good or service and the fair market value of that good or service.

Q61. What are the actual penalties that may be assessed if sanctions apply?

A61. If the IRS finds that a disqualified person participated in an excess benefit transaction with a 501(c)(3) or (c)(4) organization, the IRS will levy monetary fines against the disqualified person in the amount of 25 percent[19] of the excess benefit. Additionally, if the disqualified person does not reverse the transaction within a certain time, the IRS will increase the fine to 200 percent[20] of the excess benefit.

The IRS will also fine organization managers (board members) who authorized the transaction if it finds that the managers acted knowingly, willfully and without reasonable cause. The amount of the monetary fine on the organization manager is 10 percent[21] of the excess benefit, but not to exceed $20,000[22].

Q62. What is the safe harbor provision?

A62. Treasury Regulation § 53.4958-6 provides that (under certain circumstances) organization managers and disqualified persons are entitled to a rebuttable presumption that a transaction was reasonable. Given these circumstances, a court will presume that private inurement has not taken place unless the IRS can prove otherwise. For an organization to benefit from this presumption, the following must be true:

- Interested parties must have absented themselves from the voting on the contract or transaction.
- Before deciding to enter into the contract, the voting body must have accumulated data showing that the transaction was reasonable (e.g., bids from similarly situated competitors, compensation surveys compiled by independent firms, etc.).
- The voting body concurrently documented the terms of the contract and the date it was approved, as well as the parties who debated the contract and voted on it, the comparability data the parties relied on and any actions taken with respect to conflicts of interest.

The IRS can rebut a properly established presumption only by demonstrating that the comparability data was incorrect or inconclusive (e.g., that it was too limited to establish what the true fair market value of a good or service was).

---

19 *See* I.R.C. § 4958(a)(1) (2010).
20 *See* I.R.C. § 4958(b) (2010).
21 *See* I.R.C. § 4958(a)(2) (2010).
22 *See* I.R.C. § 4958(d)(2) (2010).

J. Other Issues

Q63. Can funders disguise their identity by passing a contribution to one organization through another organization?

A63. A donor can attempt to maintain anonymity by passing a contribution through an intermediate nonprofit organization, but this process has its complications and is not strictly necessary. If the donor wishes to make a tax-deductible donation, the intermediate nonprofit must have tax-exempt status under Section 501(c)(3) of the Internal Revenue Code. Moreover, the intermediate organization must be able to legitimately transfer the money to the final organization. A community foundation could properly donate to a nonprofit employment training organization in its area, for example, but a nonprofit wilderness preservation organization could not make this same transfer (because the transfer would not support its charitable mission).

Most private nonprofit organizations are under no obligation to disclose the identity of individual contributors, so the donor could usually more easily donate to the final recipient organization directly and request not to be listed in the organization's publications or website.

Q64. Are reimbursements to be reported as income or do they reduce the expense amount shown on the operating statement?

A64. Reducing the expense amount more properly reflects reimbursements to an organization. When an organization makes a purchase on behalf of another person (e.g., an employee) and is reimbursed for it, it is as if the person made the purchase directly. The person has paid the purchase price and received the benefit of the goods or services rendered, whereas the organization has neither a net benefit nor a net expense. Moreover, reporting reimbursements as income may improperly inflate the apparent financial size of an organization. An organization which grosses $100,000 a year in revenue and makes and is reimbursed for $10,000 worth of purchases on behalf of its employees would appear on the books to make $110,000 a year in gross if reimbursements were reported as income.

Q65. Does a nonprofit organization need to collect sales taxes?

A65. A nonprofit organization that provides goods and services to others in Minnesota for a fee may need to collect and remit Minnesota sales tax. A full list of the activities that may obligate an organization to pay state sales tax can be found on the Sales & Use Tax section of the Minnesota Department of Revenue website (www.revenue.state.mn.us/tax_prof/Pages/all_factsheets.aspx) in the form of a set of fact sheets. Among others, taxable activities include providing financial services (Fact Sheet #138: Financial Institutions) and health care services (Fact Sheet #172: Health Care Facilities). Organizations in specific regions in Minnesota may also be subject to special sales taxes. Consult Fact Sheet #164: Local Sales and Use Taxes and Fact Sheet #164S: Special Local Taxes; Minneapolis, Rochester, St. Cloud and St. Paul.

Q66. Does a nonprofit organization need to pay sales taxes?

A66. A nonprofit organization that can receive tax-deductible donations may be eligible for exemption from Minnesota sales tax on most items that it purchases from others. Not all 501(c)(3) organizations have their ST-16 application approved. To apply for state sales tax exemption, go to the Minnesota Department of Revenue website (www.taxes.state.mn.us) and download a Form ST-16 at www.revenue.state.mn.us/Forms_and_Instructions/st16.pdf.

Q67. When must an organization file Form 1099?

A67. An organization should file a Form 1099 when it undertakes certain financial transactions. The most common of these transactions is making payments to an independent contractor, reported on Form 1099-MISC[23]. Other transactions include acquiring or abandoning secured property (Form 1099-A[24]) and receiving payments from qualified education programs (Form 1099-Q[25]). For a full list of transactions that require a Form 1099 information return, consult the IRS publication "Instructions for Forms 1099, 1098, 5498, and W-2G."

Q68. Regarding fundraising events, can a nonprofit organization report just the net proceeds, or does it need to record gross receipts and all expenses?

A68. A nonprofit organization must record gross receipts and all expenses for fundraising events. Financial reports for each event may summarize this information with a "net revenue" reported, but an organization must nonetheless keep detailed records so that it can accurately complete its annual Form 990 return and so its donors can get the appropriate tax deduction for their donations.

The Form 990 information return requires a list of expenses both itemized by category (salaries, legal fees, supplies, etc.) and function (program services, management and fundraising expenses). The expenses of the fundraising event must be itemized both ways.

Q69. What is donor substantiation? What does it require?

A69. The IRS requires that when substantiating a donation (thanking a donor and acknowledging the donation for tax deduction purposes) an organization deduct the fair market value of the goods and services it provides to a donor from the amount of the donation made (unless the value is insubstantial). For example, if a donor makes a $100 donation to an organization and receives in exchange a chicken dinner worth $20 and attendance at a concert worth $30, the organization should give the donor written confirmation of a $50 tax-deductible contribution and describe the $50 worth of goods and services provided to the donor.

Q70. If a nonprofit organization does not spend all of its money by the end of its fiscal year, is it obligated to return its surplus to its funders?

A70. A nonprofit organization has no obligation to return unused funds to its donors. Its duty is to use the funds to further its mission, and in the unlikely case that the funds are restricted in such a way that the organization has no possible way to make use of them, its obligation would be to obtain court approval to pass them to an organization whose mission is as near as possible to their own. Nonprofit organizations frequently have a reasonable surplus of income over expenses in any given year. These surpluses can be used by the organization to build financial reserves, start new programs or enhance organization infrastructure.

23 *See* I.R.S., Form 1099-MISC (2017), www.irs.gov/pub/irs-pdf/f1099msc.pdf.
24 *See* I.R.S., Form 1099-A (2017), www.irs.gov/pub/irs-pdf/f1099a.pdf.
25 *See* I.R.S., Form 1099-Q (2017), www.irs.gov/pub/irs-pdf/f1099q.pdf.

Q71. How does the Sarbanes-Oxley Act apply to nonprofit organizations?

A71. Though most of the provisions of the Sarbanes-Oxley Act apply only to publicly traded corporations, two of them also apply to nonprofit organizations—the whistleblower protection and document destruction provisions. Sarbanes-Oxley makes it illegal for any organization to retaliate against an employee who reports suspected illegal activity by the organization (a whistleblower). The Act also makes it illegal to destroy or alter documents so that they cannot be used in official proceedings (e.g., criminal trials or bankruptcy proceedings).

K. Related Resources

Websites:

CompassPoint
www.compasspoint.org/
This site answers a series of frequently asked questions relating to nonprofit organization finances.

Financial Accounting Standards Board for accounting standard updates
www.fasb.org/jsp/FASB/Page/BridgePage&cid=1351027226246#section_4

Free Management Library
www.managementhelp.org
This site provides a categorized set of articles designed to help nonprofit and for-profit executives manage their organizations, including articles on the taxation and nonprofit finance.

GuideStar
www.guidestar.org
This site provides information for nonprofit donors and potential donors, including a list of the Form 990 information returns for many tax-exempt organizations.

Minnesota Department of Revenue sales and use tax fact sheets
www.revenue.state.mn.us/businesses/sut/Pages/Fact-Sheets.aspx

The Office of Minnesota Attorney General, Charities Division
www.ag.state.mn.us/charities
This site provides information about the role of the Minnesota Attorney General in regulating state nonprofits, as well as the forms an organization must file to satisfy state reporting requirements.

Propel Nonprofits
www.propelnonprofits.org
This site provides a set of articles and publications relating to nonprofit financial management.

TechSoup
www.techsoup.org/support/articles-and-how-tos/quickbooks-and-accounting-resources

Organizations:

IRS Exempt Organization
www.irs.gov/charities-non-profits

Nonprofit Risk Management Center
www.nonprofitrisk.org/resource-library

CHAPTER 9

HUMAN RESOURCES

Topics

A. Overview

A qualified and motivated workforce is central to the success of any nonprofit organization. Unfortunately, employment issues also present some of the most difficult challenges a nonprofit organization will face. Employer organizations must meet their organizational needs while respecting the rights of their employees. These rights change depending upon the size of the organization and nature of the business. Additional conflicts result from the different requirements imposed on employer organizations at the federal and state level.

This chapter addresses some of the most common employment law issues that a Minnesota nonprofit employer may experience. It analyses the distinction between exempt and nonexempt employees, and between employees and independent contractors. This chapter discusses appropriate practices when hiring and firing individuals, including what questions can and cannot be asked and what steps should be taken when terminating an employee. In addition, many of the most common employee benefit considerations and questions are introduced. Key federal and state employment laws are discussed. Finally, this chapter addresses some issues affecting management of volunteers.

Some of the topics discussed in this chapter are relatively straightforward; others are significantly more complex and will likely require additional research into the resources provided at the end of this chapter. This chapter cannot replace the service of a qualified employment law attorney, and does not constitute specific legal advice, but it should provide most employer organizations an introduction to some of the most common legal issues impacting their employees and employment practices.

B. Distinctions between Employees and Independent Contractors

Q1. How do I know if one of my workers should be classified as an employee or an independent contractor?

A1. The distinction between employee and independent contractor depends on the amount of control an employer organization has over the individual. The more control an employer organization has, the more likely the individual should be classified as an employee rather than an independent contractor.

Different agencies of both state and the federal governments apply their own tests to determine whether or not an individual should be classified as an employee or an independent contractor. The tests may vary to some degree, but a number of factors overlap.

For example, the IRS examines the following to determine whether a worker is an employee or independent contractor: the degree of behavioral control, financial control and relationship of the parties.[1]

Important factors to determine behavioral control are: 1) *instructions* – is the worker directed as to when, where and how to accomplish the work; 2) *training* – is the worker required to follow specific procedures or methods to complete the work.[2]

To determine financial control, the IRS looks at these factors: 1) *significant investment* – does the worker own standard tools and equipment, bear their own expenses and have a separate office; 2) *unreimbursed expenses;* 3) *services available to others*; 4) *method of payment* – is it flat fee or per-job, or is the worker

1 *See*, e.g., Independent Contractor (Self-Employed) or Employee?, www.irs.gov/Businesses/Small-Businesses-&-Self-Employed/Independent-Contractor-Self-Employed-or-Employee (last visited July 24, 2017).

2 *See*, e.g., Behavioral Control, www.irs.gov/Businesses/Small-Businesses-&-Self-Employed/Behavioral-Control (last visited July 24, 2017).

paid on an hourly or weekly basis; 5) *opportunity for profit or loss.*[3]

To determine relationship of the parties, the IRS looks at: 1) *the intent of the parties/written contracts* – contract language is important, but the IRS looks at the actual substance of the relationship as well; 2) *employee benefits* – providing a worker with benefits is generally evidence of employee status; 3) *discharge/termination* – can the firm terminate or discharge the worker before the task is completed without liability to the worker; 4) *regular business activity* – are the services performed a key aspect of the regular business of the firm.[4]

On a state level, Minnesota specifies several factors in addition to control that are significant to determine whether a worker is to be classified as an employee or an independent contractor:[5]

- **Right to discharge -** The right to discharge exists if the individual may be terminated with little notice, without cause, or for failure to follow specified rules or methods. There is no right to discharge if an independent worker produces an end result, which measures up to contract specifications. Contracts, which provide for termination upon notice or for specified acts of nonperformance or default, are not solely determinative of the right to discharge. Restrictions on the right to discharge because of a contract with a labor union or with other entities are not relevant for purposes of this factor.
- **Availability to public -** If an individual makes services available to the general public on a continuing basis, independent contractor status is indicated. An individual's services are offered to the public by, among other things: having an office and assistants; displaying a sign in front of a place of business; holding a business license; having a listing in a business directory or a business listing in a telephone directory; or advertising in a newspaper, trade journal, or magazine.
- **Compensation on job basis.** Independent contractor status is indicated by payment on a job basis rather than payment by the hour, week, or month. Payment on a job basis is customary where the worker is independent. Payment by the job may include a predetermined lump sum which is computed by the number of hours required to do the job at a fixed rate per hour or periodic partial payments based upon a percent of the total job price or the amount of the total job completed. The granting of a drawing account at stated intervals with no requirement for repayment of the excess drawn over commissions earned or the guarantee of a minimum salary indicates an employment relationship.
- **Realization of profit or loss.** Independent contractor status is indicated where an individual is in a position to realize a profit or suffer a loss as a result of their services. Opportunity for higher earnings from piecework or commissions does not indicate an opportunity for profit or loss. An opportunity for profit or loss is indicated by the following factors, among others: hire, direct, and pay assistants; provide own office, equipment, materials, or other facilities for doing the work; continuing and recurring financial liabilities or obligations, relating to the work; profit or loss in the work depends upon the relationship of receipts to expenditures; expenses incurred in connection with the work are paid by the individual; specific jobs are performed for prices agreed upon in advance; and performance of the services affects the individual's business reputation, and not the business reputation of those who purchase the services.
- **Termination.** The worker's right to terminate the working relationship with the purported employer at will and without incurring liability for non-completion indicates employment. A requirement to provide notice of termination for some period in advance of the termination is not relevant for

3 *See,* e.g., Financial Control, www.irs.gov/Businesses/Small-Businesses-&-Self-Employed/Financial-Control (last visited July 24, 2017).
4 *See*, e.g., Type of Relationship, www.irs.gov/Businesses/Small-Businesses-&-Self-Employed/Type-of-Relationship (last visited July 24, 2017).
5 Minn. R. 5224.0340 (2008).

purposes of this factor. Independent contractor status is indicated where the individual agrees to complete a specific job, is responsible for its satisfactory completion, and is liable for failure to complete the job.

- **Substantial investment.** A substantial investment by a person in facilities used in performing services for another indicates an independent contractor status. The furnishing of all necessary facilities by the employer indicates the absence of an independent contractor status. Facilities include equipment or premises necessary for the work, but not tools, instruments, clothing, and similar items that are provided by individuals working in employment as a common practice in their particular trade. Substantial investment means a monetary investment representing something of considerable worth, in relation to the overall requirements of the person's chosen profession, trade, occupation, or vocation. A substantial expenditure of time or money for an individual's education is not indicative of an independent contractor status.
- **Responsibility.** If an employing unit is responsible for the negligence, personal behavior, and work actions of an individual in contacts with customers and the general public during times that services are performed for the employing unit, an employment relationship is indicated.
- **Services fundamental to business.** Employment is indicated where the services provided are necessary to the fundamental business purpose for which the organization exists.

The following agencies will help employers correctly classify workers as independent contractors or employees. Call the following numbers for more information.

Internal Revenue Service 1-800-829-1040
Minnesota Unemployment Insurance Program 651-296-6141
Minnesota Department of Revenue 651-282-9999
Minnesota Department of Labor and Industry....................... 651-284-5005 or 1-800-342-5354

Q2. What are the consequences and implications of claiming that a worker is an independent contractor instead of an employee?

A2. The consequences an employer organization faces for misclassification of an individual can be severe. Employers may be required to pay all withholding tax amounts that should have been withheld from the employee's wages, along with the corresponding employer portion of withholding tax, along with penalties and interest accrued due to late payment of these taxes. (On a separate note, employers may also be required to calculate and pay applicable overtime payments if the worker is determined to be "nonexempt" under the federal or Minnesota Fair Labor Standards Act; see Question 4). The U.S. Department of Labor and the Internal Revenue Services have increased enforcement efforts in the area of independent contractor classifications, as well as in the area of exempt/nonexempt workers.[6]

Q3. Can a current employee sub-contract for a different job within the same organization? That is, can they be both an employee and an independent contractor?

A3. It is unlikely that a situation would arise in which an individual would properly be paid both as an employee and as an independent contractor by the same organization. Regulators will apply the appropriate tests to determine whether or not the individual is an employee or independent contractor in each context, and if an employer organization inappropriately classifies an individual, the employer organization will be

6 Cf. Employee Misclassification as Independent Contractors - Wage and Hour Division (WHD) - U.S. Department of Labor, www.dol.gov/whd/workers/misclassification/ (last visited July 24, 2017).

liable for the consequences.

Note that many organizations have adopted conflict of interest policies that may restrict current employees (especially key staff members), their family members and organizations with which they are connected financially from contracting with the organization for sales of goods or services. These policies may prevent a situation in which an individual would be paid both as an employee and as an independent contractor.

C. Distinctions between Exempt and Nonexempt Employees

Q4. What does it mean to be an "exempt" employee?

A4. The federal Fair Labor Standards Act (FLSA)[7] was enacted by Congress in 1938 to regulate minimum standards for hours and wages of employees who are covered by the Act, i.e., "nonexempt" from the Act. Those to whom the minimum wage and overtime provisions of the Act do not apply are "exempt" from the Act. To be "exempt" from the FLSA, typically a worker must be paid on a salary basis without deductions for quality or quantity of work performed; must be paid no less than $455 per week;[8] and must have job duties that qualify as "exempt" under the FLSA (see Question 5). **Being paid on a salary basis, by itself, does not determine whether or not an employee is "exempt."** (See Question 6).

The federal Fair Labor Standards Act may apply to either an "enterprise" or to individual "employees," as these terms are defined in the Act.

The federal Act covers an "enterprise," which is generally defined as an entity with a common business purpose, engaged in commerce or in the production of goods, or which has employees handling, selling or otherwise working on goods or materials, as long as the enterprise has annual gross sales of $500,000.

Other "enterprises" are covered regardless of their dollar volume of business: hospitals; institutions primarily engaged in the care of the sick, aged, mentally ill or disabled who reside on the premises; schools for children who are mentally or physically disabled or gifted; preschools, elementary and secondary schools, and institutions of higher education; and federal, state and local government agencies.

Even if a worker is employed by an employer that does not meet the definition of "enterprise," the worker may be covered individually as an "employee." The Act defines an "employee" as one who is individually engaged in interstate commerce, the production of goods for interstate commerce, or an activity that is closely related and directly essential to the production of such goods. The U.S. Department of Labor indicates that such employees include those who: work in communications or transportation; regularly use the mails, telephones, or telegraph for interstate communication, or keep records of interstate transactions; handle, ship or receive goods moving in interstate commerce; regularly cross state lines in the course of employment; or work for independent employers who contract to do clerical, custodial, maintenance or other work for firms engaged in interstate commerce or in the production of goods for interstate commerce.

7 Cf. Compliance Assistance - Wages and the Fair Labor Standards Act (FLSA) - Wage and Hour Division (WHD) - U.S. Department of Labor, www.dol.gov/whd/flsa/ (last visited July 24, 2017).

8 *Fact Sheet #17A: Exemption for Executive, Administrative, Professional,Computer & Outside Sales Employees Under the Fair Labor Standards Act (FLSA)*, www.dol.gov/whd/overtime/fs17a_overview.pdf (last visited September 22, 2017).

If the federal Fair Labor Standards Act does not apply, it is possible that the Minnesota Fair Labor Standards Act applies instead. That Act covers Minnesota employers generally.

Unless employees are exempted from coverage of the federal and/or state Fair Labor Standards Acts, by falling into a statutory category of "exempt" workers, employees are covered by the provisions of these laws, i.e., they are "non-exempt" from coverage. See more on nonexempt employees at Question 7.

This area of employment law has increasingly become the source of litigation, and it is important for employers to ensure that their employees are properly classified. See www.dol.gov for more information on the federal Act, for helpful and practical fact sheets on topics related to the FLSA and for information on other labor laws under the jurisdiction of the Department of Labor. See Minnesota Statutes Chapter 177 for information relating to the Minnesota Fair Labor Standards Act. Consult an employment law attorney if you have questions about the application of the federal or Minnesota law in this area to your organization.

Q5. How do I know if my employees qualify as "bona fide executive, administrative and professional" exempt employees under the federal Fair Labor Standards Act?

A5. FLSA provides for an exemption from minimum wage and overtime pay provisions for employees who meet all of the following tests:

- Salary level – for most exempt employees, the minimum salary level required for exemption is $455 per week.[9]
- Salary basis – the employee must regularly receive a predetermined amount of compensation on each pay period, which must be weekly or less frequently. The compensation may not be adjusted on account of the quality or quantity of work performed.
- Job duties – the employee must meet the duties tests identified in one of the exempt categories contained in the Act. The most common exemptions for nonprofit organizations are executive, administrative and professional. The regulations also recognize that highly compensated employees performing office or non-manual work and paid total annual compensation of $100,000 or more, which must include at least $455 per week paid on a salary or fee basis, are exempt if they customarily and regularly perform at least one of the exempt duties or responsibilities of an exempt executive, administrative or professional employee identified in the standard tests for exemption.[10]

Each of the categories of "executive," "administrative" and "professional" is defined in the FLSA or its regulations, and is not necessarily the same as the common-sense definition.

1. "Executive," refers to employees who earn a salary of at least $455 per week (exclusive of board, lodging or other facilities) whose primary duty is management of an enterprise in which the employee is employed, or of a customarily recognized department; who customarily and regularly directs the work of two or more other employees; and who has the authority to hire or fire other

9 *Id.* www.dol.gov/whd/overtime/final2016/overtime-factsheet.htm (last visited July 25, 2017).

10 *See*, e.g., *Fact Sheet #17D: Exemption for Professional Employees Under the Fair Labor Standards Act* (FLSA), US Dept. Labor, www.dol.gov/whd/overtime/fs17d_professional.pdf (last visited Jul. 24,2017).

employees or whose suggestions and recommendations as to hiring, firing or other similar matters are given particular weight.[11]

"Management" tasks can include:

- Interviewing, selecting and training employees;
- Setting and adjusting pay and work hours;
- Maintaining production or sales records;
- Appraising employee productivity and efficiency;
- Handling employee complaints and grievances;
- Disciplining employees;
- Planning and apportioning work among employees;
- Determining the techniques to be used; the type of materials, supplies, machinery, equipment or tools to be used; or the merchandise to be bought, stocked and sold;
- Providing for the safety and security of employees or property;
- Planning and controlling the budget;
- Monitoring or implementing legal compliance measures.[12]

2. "Administrative," means an employee who earns at least $455 per week (exclusive of board, lodging or other facilities) whose primary duty is the performance of office or non-manual work directly related to the management or general business operations of the employer or its customers; and whose primary duty includes the exercise of discretion and independent judgment with respect to matters of significance.[13]

   "Management or general business operations of the employer" means work that is directly related to assisting with the running or servicing of the business, and does not include delivering service. Examples are:

   - Tax
   - Finance
   - Accounting
   - Budgeting
   - Auditing
   - Insurance
   - Quality control
   - Purchasing
   - Procurement
   - Advertising
   - Marketing
   - Research
   - Safety and health
   - Human resources
   - Employee benefits
   - Labor relations
   - Public and government relations
   - Legal and regulatory compliance

11 *See* 29 C.F.R. § 541.100 (2016).
12 *See* 29 C.F.R. § 541.102 (2016).
13 *See* 29 C.F.R. § 541.200 (2016).

- Computer network, Internet and database administration[14]

"Discretion and independent judgment" means:

- Whether the employee has authority to formulate, put into effect, interpret, or implement management policies or operating practices
- Whether the employee carries out major assignments in conducting the operations of the organization
- Whether the employee performs work that affects business operations to a substantial degree, even if the employee's assignments are related to operation of a particular segment of the business
- Whether the employee has authority to commit the employer in matters that have significant financial impact
- Whether the employee has authority to waive or deviate from established policies and procedures without prior approval
- Whether the employee has authority to negotiate and bind the company on significant matters
- Whether the employee provides consultation or expert advice to management[15]

3. "Professional," includes employees earning not less than $455 per week (exclusive of board, lodging or other facilities) whose primary duty is the performance of work: (i) requiring knowledge of an advanced type in a field of science or learning customarily acquired by a prolonged course of specialized intellectual instruction; or (ii) requiring invention, imagination, originality or talent in a recognized field of artistic or creative endeavor.[16]

Although not as common for nonprofit organizations, there are two other "exempt" categories to consider for employees. "Computer employees," constitute a subset of "professional" exempt employees. The computer employee must be compensated either on a salary or fee basis at a rate not less than $455 per week or, if compensated on an hourly basis, at a rate not less than $27.63 an hour;[17] and the employee must be employed as a computer system analyst, computer programmer, software engineer or other similarly skilled worker in the computer field performing duties specified in the regulations.[18]

"Outside Sales" employees, must have as their primary duty making sales or obtaining orders or contracts for services or for the use of facilities for which a consideration will be paid by the client or customer; and must be customarily and regularly engaged away from the employer's place or places of business.[19]

Q6. If all of my employees are salaried, does that mean they are all exempt and I can make them work as many hours as I want?

A6. No. See Question 5. Paying an employee on a salary basis alone is **not** sufficient to create an "exempt" position. Salaried status is a factor in determining whether or not an employee is exempt, but it is not the only factor; an employee must meet all the requirements of "exempt" under the Fair Labor Standards Act

14 *See generally* 29 C.F.R. § 541.203 (2016)
15 *See* 29 C.F.R. § 541.202 (2016).
16 *See* 29 C.F.R. § 541.300 (2016).
17 *See* 5 C.F.R. § 551.210 (2007).
18 *See* 29 C.F.R. § 541.400 (2016).
19 *See* 29 C.F.R. § 541.500 (2016).

(being paid the minimum required salary at least weekly, which salary must not be subject to deductions for the quality or quantity of work performed AND meeting one of the job duties tests for "exempt" workers)[20] Any deductions made from pay of exempt employees may be made in no less than full day increments for time off, including vacation, sick leave and disciplinary deductions.

Q7. What does it mean to be a nonexempt employee?

A7. See Question 5 for a fuller description of the differences between exempt and nonexempt workers. In short, a nonexempt employee is an employee who is covered by the minimum wage and overtime provisions of the federal and/or Minnesota Fair Labor Standards Act ("FLSA"). FLSA requires that workers be paid at least minimum wage for "hours worked." For each hour worked over 40 hours per week, employers subject to the federal Act must pay their employees 1½ times their "regular rate of pay." The regular hourly rate of pay is determined by dividing an employee's total remuneration in any workweek by the total number of hours worked.

The Minnesota FLSA requires that overtime pay be paid to employees who work over 48 hours per week,unless the employee is specifically exempt under the Minnesota Statutes Section 177.23, subdivision 7.

The **federal** minimum wage rate is $7.25 per hour. Minimum wage provisions apply to part-time as well as full-time employees. Employees under 20 years of age may be paid $4.25 per hour during their first 90 consecutive calendar days of employment.[21]

In **Minnesota**, the minimum wage requirement is as follows: For large employers (any enterprise whose annual gross volume of sales made or business done is not less than $500,000), employees must be paid a minimum of $9.50 per hour beginning August 1, 2016.[22] For small employers (any enterprise whose annual gross volume of sales made or business done is less than $500,000), employees must be paid a minimum of $7.75 per hour beginning August 1, 2016.[23] An employer may pay $7.75 an hour (beginning August 1, 2016) to employees who are younger than age 20 during their first 90 consecutive days of employment. New employees covered by the training wage may not displace permanent or current employees.

Under Minnesota Statutes Section 177.24, subdivision 1(f), beginning in 2017 and no later than August 31 of each year, the Minnesota Department of Labor and Industry commissioner shall determine the percentage increase in the rate of inflation, as measured by the implicit price deflator, national data for personal consumption expenditures as determined by the United States Department of Commerce, Bureau of Economic Analysis during the 12-month period immediately preceding that August or, if that data is unavailable, during the most recent 12-month period for which data is available. The rate established under this law begins January 1, 2018.[24]

Employees must be paid the higher of the state or federal minimum wages if the federal FLSA applies.

20 *See* 29 CFR § 541.602 (2016).

21 U.S. Department of Labor Wage and Hour Division, *Fact Sheet #32: Youth Minimum Wage - Fair Labor Standards Act* (2008), www.dol.gov/whd/regs/compliance/whdfs32.pdf.

22 Minn. Stat. § 177.24, subd.1 (2016).

23 *Id.*

24 *Id.*

Deductions are permitted for "reasonable cost" or "fair value" of "board, lodging or other facilities." Deductions for cash shortages are considered illegal to the extent that they reduce the wages of employees below the required minimum or reduce the overtime compensation due under FLSA; however, if criminal action has been determined in court, such deductions do not violate FLSA.

Q8. Do I need to post any notices about the Act in my workplace?

A8. Covered employers must display an official poster outlining the provisions of the federal Fair Labor Standards Act, available at no cost from local offices of the Wage and Hour Division and toll-free, by calling 1-866-4USWage (1-866-487-9243). This poster is also available electronically for downloading and printing at www.dol.gov/osbp/sbrefa/poster/main.htm. Minnesota law requires any covered employer to post the provisions of the Minnesota Fair Labor Standards Act: download posters at www.dli.mn.gov/LS/Posters.asp.

Q9. What records do I need to keep in order to comply with the Fair Labor Standards Act? How long do I have to keep them?

A9. Every covered employer must keep certain records for each non-exempt worker. The federal Act requires no particular form for the records, but does require that the records include certain identifying information about the employee and data about the hours worked and the wages earned. The law requires this information to be accurate. The following is a listing of the basic records[25] that an employer must maintain:

1. Employee's full name and social security number;
2. Address, including zip code;
3. Birth date, if younger than 19;
4. Sex and occupation;
5. Time and day of week when employee's workweek begins;
6. Hours worked each day;
7. Total hours worked each workweek;
8. Basis on which employee's wages are paid (e.g., "$x an hour," "$y a week," "piecework");
9. Regular hourly pay rate;
10. Total daily or weekly straight-time earnings;
11. Total overtime earnings for the workweek;
12. All additions to or deductions from the employee's wages;
13. Total wages paid each pay period;
14. Date of payment and the pay period covered by the payment.

Each employer must preserve for at least three years payroll records, collective bargaining agreements, sales and purchase records. Records on which wage computations are based should be retained for two years, e.g., time cards and piece work tickets, wage rate tables, work and time schedules, and records of additions to or deductions from wages. These records must be open for inspection if the employer is audited regarding its compliance with the Fair Labor Standards Act. The records may be kept at the place of employment or in a central records office.

25 *Fact Sheet #21: Recordkeeping Requirements under the Fair Labor Standards Act (FLSA)*, US Dept. Labor, www.dol.gov/whd/regs/compliance/whdfs21.htm (last visited July 25, 2017); see also 29 C.F.R. pt. 516 (2017).

Q10. How do I decide if a particular job should be classified as exempt or non-exempt?

A10. See Question 5. To qualify for exemption, an employee must meet three tests: salary level, salary basis and job duties. To be classified as "exempt," a job **as it is performed** (not as described in the job description) must require that an employee's "primary duty" is the performance of exempt work. Employees who spend more than 50 percent of their time performing exempt work will generally satisfy the primary duty requirement, but time alone is not the sole test. Determination of an employee's primary duty is based on a review of the employee's job as a whole. Factors considered include: the relative importance of the exempt duties as compared with other types of duties; the amount of time spent performing exempt work; the employee's relative freedom from direct supervision; and the relationship between the employee's salary and the wages paid to other employees for the kind of nonexempt work performed by the employee.[26]

Q11. Are the exempt categories of "bona fide executive, administrative and professional" defined the same under Minnesota's Fair Labor Standards Act as under the federal Act?

A11. No. Here are the tests for these categories, as set out in Minnesota Rules:

- **Executives**:
  - An executive is exempt if they receive at least $250 a week in salary, manage the enterprise by which the person is employed or a recognized department or subdivision thereof, and customarily directs the work of two or more employees.[27]
  - An executive is exempt if they receive at least $155 a week in salary; supervise a department of at least two other full-time people; has authority to hire, fire or suggest changes in employees' status; regularly exercises discretionary powers; and either
    - devotes less than 20 percent of time worked (40 percent in retail or service establishments) to nonexempt work; or
    - owns 20 percent or more of the business; or
    - has sole charge of an independent or branch establishment.[28]

- **Administrators**:
  - An administrator is exempt if the administrator receives at least $250 per week in salary or fee, performs office or non-manual work directly related to management policies or general business operations; performs functions in the administration of a school system or subdivision thereof, in work directly related to academic instruction; and regularly exercises discretion or independent judgment.[29]
  - An administrator is exempt if the administrator receives at least $155 per week in salary or fee; performs office or non-manual work directly related to business operations or management policies, or administers an educational system or subdivision thereof in work relating to academic instruction; regularly exercises discretion and independent judgment and makes important decisions; and either:
    - directly assists owner or bona fide executive or administrative employee;
    - performs supervised works only along lines requiring special training or experience; or

26 *See* 29 C.F.R. § 541.700 (2014).
27 Minn. R. 5200.0190, subp. 1 (2017).
28 Minn. R. 5200.0190, subp. 2 (2017).
29 Minn. R. 5200.0200, subp. 1 (2017).

        - executes special assignments; and
        - devotes less than 20 percent of time worked (or 40 percent in retail or service establishments) to nonexempt work.[30]

- **Professionals**:
    - A professional is exempt if the professional receives at least $250 per week in salary or fee, consistently exercises discretion and judgment, and either:
        - performs work requiring advanced knowledge in a field of science or learning;
        - performs work as a teacher in the activity of imparting knowledge;
        - performs work requiring invention, imagination or talent in a recognized field of artistic endeavor;[31]
    - A professional is exempt if the professional receives at least $170 per week in salary or fee, consistently exercises judgment and discretion, performs predominantly intellectual work so varied that the output cannot be standardized by time necessary for accomplishment, devotes less than 20 percent of the hours worked to activities not essential to the person's professional work, and either:
        - performs work requiring advanced knowledge in a field of learning customarily acquired by prolonged specialized intellectual study, not general academic education, an apprenticeship or training in routine mental or physical processes;
        - performs original work dependent on the person's own creativeness in a recognized field of artistic endeavor; or
        - is a certified teacher working as such or recognized as such in the school system where the person works.[32]

- **Outside Sales:**
    - An outside salesperson is an individual hired for the express purpose of performing sales duties away from the employer's place of business and conducts no more than 20 percent of sales on those premises.[33]

Q12. Do I need to provide compensatory time to exempt employees in the private sector who work more than 40 hours per week?

A12. No. Compensation of "exempt" workers, by definition, is not based on the numbers of hours worked per pay period. Exempt employees are paid on a salary basis, in no less than weekly increments. There is a risk that the Department of Labor may view an employer keeping track of hours worked by its exempt employees and compensating them hour-for-hour for hours worked over 40 hours per week is treating its employees as nonexempt workers, who do not meet the salary test for exemption from the Fair Labor Standards Act.

Some private sector employers, however, strive to provide some time off for exempt employees who have worked an excessive amount of time during a busy period. Time off under these circumstances should be coordinated between employer and employee so as to ensure sufficient coverage for the employer's work. Note that there are different rules for public sector employers, which are not covered here.

30 Minn. R. 5200.0200, subp. 2 (2017).
31 Minn. R. 5200.0210, subp. 1 (2017).
32 Minn. R. 5200.0210, subp. 2 (2017).
33 Minn. R. 5200.0220, subp. 1 (2017).

Q13. Do I need to provide compensatory time to non-exempt employees who work more than 40 hours per week?

A13. No. With limited exceptions, non-exempt employees may not waive the requirement that they be paid overtime pay, and may not agree to receive compensatory time off in lieu of overtime pay. Organizations that provide "comp time" to employees in lieu of overtime are, in most cases, is a violation of law.

Q14. Do I have to pay exempt employees for accumulated compensatory time when they leave employment?

A14. See Question 12. Generally, nonprofit employer organizations should not allow exempt employees to maintain a "bank" of, or pay, compensatory time when exempt employees leave employment. Note that there is a different rule for public employers.

D. Hiring and Firing Employees

Q15. Is an employer organization required to advertise job openings?

A15. Generally, unless an employer organization has an internal policy or agreement with employees that requires that job openings be posted or advertised, or is party to a collective bargaining agreement or a party to an agreement with a unit of government that requires posting or advertising openings (such as an affirmative action plan that requires specified outreach strategies to attract a diverse pool of job applicants), an organization is not required to advertise job openings. If the employer organization does choose to advertise, it must take care to ensure that the advertisement does not violate the Equal Employment Opportunity Commission guidelines and the Minnesota Human Rights Act.

The employer organization must make sure that the job posting does not discriminate against applicants on the basis of race, color, creed, religion, national origin, sex, marital status, familial status, status with regard to public assistance, membership or activity in a local commission, disability, sexual orientation, genetic information or age.

Q16. Is an employer organization required to treat internal job candidates differently than external job candidates?

A16. Employer organizations are not legally required to treat internal job candidates differently than external ones, unless the organization has established policies that, for example, prefer internal candidates as applicants for open positions.

Q17. What can and can't be asked in a job interview?

A17. Employer organizations should only ask questions related to the essential functions of the job and its performance. Employers are precluded from asking questions, which may violate the Human Rights Act or indicate any sort of discriminatory bias.

Employer organizations should avoid questions that might overlap with any of the protected areas indicated in Question 15. Examples include "Are you and your husband planning to start a family soon? When did you graduate from high school? Were you born in the United States? Have you ever been arrested? What is your religious affiliation? Have you ever made a workers' compensation claim in a previous job?" Interviewers should understand the essential functions of the job for which they are interviewing, and should focus their questions to elicit information that will help them determine which candidate is best suited to perform those essential functions.[34]

Q18. Can an employer organization do a background check on a potential employee? How about a driving record check?

A18. Employer organizations may be required to perform background checks in certain contexts (e.g., schools and youth service providers, residential building managers, home care providers). Generally, an employer organization must exercise reasonable care in hiring individuals who may pose a threat of injury to members of the public. Employer organizations may also want to perform background checks on potential employees in other positions, such as those involving responsibility with finances of the organization.

Minnesota prohibits an employer from inquiring about an applicant's criminal history or conducting a criminal background check until AFTER the applicant has been selected for an interview or AFTER a conditional job offer has been extended. An employer may inform candidates of categories of criminal convictions that will bar them from employment for particular positions with the employer.

Employer organizations should obtain a waiver from candidates granting permission to perform a background check, and the organization should only obtain information relevant to the essential functions of the position for which the candidate was interviewed. Employers should develop criteria to apply if a criminal background check returns information showing a candidate's criminal history, to ensure that an employer's rejection of a candidate on the basis of criminal background is based on a uniform policy, equally applied, and that the criteria are consistent with business necessity.

Similarly, an employer organization may conduct a motor vehicle check on a potential employee if the employee will be engaged in transporting school children or delivering meals to senior citizens, but probably not if an individual will be, for example, a grant writer or office manager.

Q19. Can an employer organization conduct medical or psychological tests prior to hiring an employee?

A19. Employers can require that prospective employees take job-related medical and/or psychological tests prior to employment. However, in order not to violate the Americans with Disabilities Act, employers must conduct these tests ONLY AFTER a conditional job offer has been extended to the prospective employee(s). Also, employers may not conduct genetic tests or require disclosure of protected genetic information (i.e., information about genetic tests of the prospective employee or blood relatives) as a condition of employment.

34 *See*, e.g., Michigan Technological University, *What You Can Ask and What You Can't- Legal/Illegal Interview Questions*, (May 15, 2013) www.mtu.edu/equity/pdfs/whatyoucanandcantasklongversion8-12-04.pdf (providing an example of questions that can and cannot be asked, there are many other resource examples online).

Q20. Can an employer organization hire someone under the age of 18?

A20. The answer depends upon the exact age of the individual and the type of work the individual will be performing.[35]

State and Federal law overlap in the area of child labor. Employer organizations are required to follow both when possible, but to follow the stricter of the two when different standards are provided for the same situation. All Minnesota employer organizations are required to follow the state guidelines, but only employer organizations engaged in interstate commerce are required to follow the federal guidelines.

Organizations should not employ individuals under the age of 14, except hiring the minor:

- as a newspaper carrier (at least 11 years of age);
- in agriculture (at least 12 years of age and with parental/guardian consent);
- as an actor, actress or model; or
- as a youth athletic program referee (at least 11 years of age and with parental/guardian consent).[36]

Minors under the age of 16 cannot work for more than 40 hours per week and 8 hours per 24-hour period (except in agriculture). Minors under the age of 16 may not work before 7 a.m. or after 9 p.m. (with the exception of a newspaper carrier). Additionally, minors younger than 16 years old may not work on school days during school hours, without an employment certificate issued by the school district superintendent. Minors under the age of 16 are restricted to 3 hours per day, 18 hours per week and may work no later than 7 p.m. during the school year under federal law.

By Minnesota state law, 16- and 17-year-old high school students may not work after 11 p.m. on evenings before school days or before 5 a.m. on school days. With written permission from a parent or guardian, these hours may be expanded to 11:30 p.m. and 4:30 a.m.[37]

Minors are prohibited from performing a number of tasks classified as hazardous or detrimental to the well-being of a minor. The vast majority of these restrictions are beyond the scope of nonprofit employment, but employer organizations should check with the Minnesota Department of Labor and Industry at www.dli.mn.gov/LS/ChildLabor.asp or the U.S. Department of Labor at www.dol.gov/dol/topic/youthlabor/hazardousjobs.htm if they believe the position may be hazardous. Hazardous activities include operating heavy machinery, welding, mining and working with toxic chemicals.

While minors employed in a business solely owned and operated by their parents are exempt from most restrictions, Minnesota nonprofit organizations are not "owned" in a similar sense and therefore cannot benefit from these exemptions.

Q21. Does an employer organization have to give verbal and written warnings to an employee before they are fired?

A21. Minnesota is generally an "at will" employment state. This means that either the employer or the employee may generally terminate the employment relationship at any time for any legal reason, with or without

35 *See* Labor Standards—Age restrictions, MN Dept. Labor & Industry, www.dli.mn.gov/ls/minage.asp (last visited July 25, 2017).
36 *Id.*
37 *See* Labor Standards—Age restrictions, MN Dept. Labor & Industry, www.dli.mn.gov/ls/minage.asp (last visited July 25, 2017).

warning.[38] However, if the employee has been hired pursuant to an employment contract or a collective bargaining agreement that specifies progressive disciplinary steps prior to termination, then the terms of the contract modify the "at-will" nature of employment and termination must occur according to the conditions provided in the contract.

The Minnesota Supreme Court determined in 1983 that handbooks or company practices may constitute a type of employment contract, unless the policies express state that they do not modify the "at-will" nature of employment. Employers should review their personnel policies and/or employee handbook carefully and ensure that they do not create a contractual relationship with employees. However, in order to be consistent with the employer's own policies, if the handbook includes progressive disciplinary steps, the employer should follow these steps prior to terminating the employment of an employee.

While prior notice via verbal and written warnings may not be legally required, however, good management practices suggest that an employee typically be given notice of the need for performance improvement prior to terminating employment. Regular performance evaluations function to alert employees to problems before they become so critical that an employer views termination of employment as the only viable solution. As discussed more fully in Question 22, a clearly documented record of the employer's efforts to improve performance of an employee may help to protect an employer from charges by the discharged employee that the termination was undertaken for an unlawful reason rather than for poor performance.

Q22. What should an employer organization do to prepare for a meeting in which they are going to fire an employee? Are there certain things that should be said or should not be said? Should the employee be given a written statement of the reasons for termination?

A22. Prior to meeting with the employee, the employer organization should analyze its reasons for seeking termination. While Minnesota is generally an "at-will" employment state, as defined in Question 21, employers may not terminate employment of employees for an unlawful reason. Employers may want to consult with legal counsel prior to terminating an employee's employment to evaluate the risks involved in the particular case.

If the termination involves multiple employees, additional preparation may be required. For example, the federal Worker Adjustment and Retraining Notification Act (WARN Act) requires an employer of 100 or more employees to give 60 days' notice if an employment site (or one or more facilities or operating units within an employment site) will be shut down, and the shutdown will result in an employment loss (as defined later) for 50 or more employees during any 30-day period; or a "mass layoff" for (i) at least 33 percent of the active employees, excluding part-time employees and (ii) at least 500 employees, excluding part-time employees.[39]

In an economic downturn, legitimate budgetary constraints may justify reducing staff costs. Employers can maximize their organizational strength and minimize employee claims if cuts proceed only after the employer develops a clear written plan. The plan should review the employer's priorities in its existing strategic plan, in light of expected financial reductions. If existing priorities need to be retooled or eliminated, the plan can identify corresponding staff positions that will be affected. The employer can more

38 *See* generally Labor Standards-Termination, MN Dept. Labor & Industry, www.dli.mn.gov/ls/Termination.asp (last visited July 25, 2017).

39 The Worker Adjustment and Retraining Notification Act, Dept. Labor Emp't & Training Admin., www.doleta.gov/programs/factsht/warn.htm (last visited July 25, 2017).

clearly communicate its situation in the financial downturn to stakeholders, including employees, if it has developed a clear written strategy that supplements its current strategic plan.

Before laying off or terminating the employment of multiple employees, employers should consider the impact on employees in protected classes (see Section H: Complying with Other Federal and State Employment Laws). This review allows the organization to identify and avoid bias or adverse impact, thus minimizing legal risk. A similar risk management review should occur before terminating the employment of any employee. Consider such questions as these: Could the termination appear to be in retaliation for recent protected activities taken by the employee (e.g., whistleblowing or vesting in an ERISA benefit plan)? Is the proposed termination based on verifiable performance or conduct issues, or is there a question whether prohibited discrimination or harassment of the employee has occurred? Is there a company policy for reprimanding employees short of termination? Has this policy been followed? Could the employee argue that they are being treated in a manner inconsistent with other employees in similar situations?

Employer organizations should treat the employee whose employment is being terminated with dignity and respect. For example, it's generally best to conduct termination meetings when few coworkers are present. Employee reactions will vary drastically depending upon the personality of the individual being terminated and the circumstances of the termination. Employer organizations should try to determine how the employee will respond and conduct the termination in a manner intended to minimize conflict.

It is generally best to have at least one management- or board-level witness present who will be able to verify the facts of the situation. Get to the point quickly when terminating an individual's employment. Explain how the individual's final payment will be addressed, and provide information about when and how the individual may retrieve any personal belongings in the workplace.

No written statement is required to be provided to an employee at the time of termination, but the terminated employee may request a written statement within 15 days of termination of the truthful reason for termination.[40] Upon receipt of this request, the employer must provide the employee with the written statement containing the truthful reason(s) within 10 days.[41] No statement provided by the organization via this method can be used against the organization for libel, slander or defamation by the employee.

Employer organizations should be careful with what they tell other employees and in providing future references for the terminated employee. Criticism about the terminated employee's conduct voiced to individuals inside the organization may have a negative impact upon morale. Additionally, negative remarks and references risk a claim of defamation. See Question 25 for more information on providing references.

Q23. If someone quits or is fired, is that employee eligible for unemployment benefits?

A23. Generally, individuals are eligible for unemployment benefits in Minnesota if they have not voluntarily resigned their employment or been terminated from employment for misconduct.

Certain situations may arise where an individual may voluntarily quit and still be eligible for unemployment benefits, such as harassment and gross misconduct by the employer organization.

40 *See* Labor Standards-Termination, MN Dept. Labor & Industry, http://www.dli.mn.gov/ls/Termination.asp (last visited July 25, 2017).
41 *See* Labor Standards-Termination, MN Dept. Labor & Industry, http://www.dli.mn.gov/ls/Termination.asp (last visited July 25, 2017).

The unemployment applicant or the employer has the opportunity to appeal the unemployment determination within 30 days of when the determination has been made. All relevant parties (typically the terminated employee and their former employer) will have the opportunity to present further evidence to help prove their case. Such evidence typically consists of employee handbook policies, timesheets, records, etc. Both parties will make their arguments before the unemployment law judge, who will then issue a ruling either agreeing with the previous determination or overruling it. For further information on unemployment hearings, visit the Minnesota Unemployment Insurance at www.uimn.org/uimn/employers/publications/emp-hbook/appeal.jsp or obtain an employer handbook with information about the unemployment insurance program at http://www.uimn.org/uimn/employers/publications/emp-hbook/index.jsp.

Q24. Should an employer organization offer a terminated employee a severance package?

A24. Severance packages are not required when terminating an employee, unless the employer has a policy or practice of providing them. Some employer organizations offer such packages in exchange for a release of legal claims from the terminated employee.

Typically, such releases state that the employee waives all claims they may have against the employer organization that arise out of their employment and termination or separation from employment. Some civil rights legislation require specified time periods for employees to review prospective releases before signing, or require that employees have a specified period to rescind their agreement after signing. For example, employees covered by the federal Age Discrimination in Employment Act must be given 21 days to review the severance package and waiver of legal claims prior to signing, and the Minnesota Human Rights Act requires that employees have 15 days after signing the release of legal claims under that Act to rescind the agreement.

Because a legal release of claims and/or severance agreement typically creates legal obligations for employers and employees, it is strongly recommended that both employer organizations and employees seek legal counsel to advise them on preparation of such agreements.

Q25. What can someone say about a former employee when they are asked to serve as a reference?

A25. The following information may be provided by a former employer organization without written authorization by the former employee and without risk of incurring liability unless (1) the information is false and defamatory, and (2) the employer organization knew or should have known that the information was false and acted with malicious intent to injure the employee:

- Dates of employment;
- Compensation and wage history;
- Job description and duties;
- Training and education provided by employer;
- Acts of violence, theft, harassment or illegal conduct documented in the personnel record that resulted in disciplinary action or resignation and the employee's written response, if any, contained in the employee's personnel record.
    - Such disclosure must be in writing with a copy sent to the employee's last known address.

The following information may be provided without risk of incurring liability with the written authorization of the employee:

- Written evaluations of the employee and the employee's written response if contained in the employee's personnel record;
- Written disciplinary warnings and actions in the five years before the date of authorization and the employee's written response, if contained in the employee's personnel record;
- Written reasons for separation from employment.
    - The employer must provide both copies of this information and to whom it was disclosed to by mailing the information to the employee's last known address.

The employer organization is not required to provide references for current or former employees, but the employer organization should take care to ensure information related to evaluations and disciplinary warnings are not provided without the written consent of the employee.

E. Employee Benefits

Q26. When and what benefits does an employer organization need to provide to its employees?

A26. Certain "benefits," such as social security and unemployment insurance must be provided immediately upon commencement of employment. Others, such as required leaves of absence, must be provided when the employee has satisfied the federal or state eligibility requirements. There are also benefits that the employer can, to some extent, design for its group of employees and establish eligibility and participation criteria within a range of acceptable time frames under the labor and tax laws that apply to such benefits. Finally, there are benefits in which an employer plays a very limited role – such as individual coverage that an employee can choose and pay for solely by themselves. Sometimes an employer will facilitate this kind of benefit by taking payroll deductions and forwarding premium amounts on behalf of employees.

FICA and FUTA. For example, most employer organizations are required to contribute to federal and state programs that provide social security and unemployment insurance benefits to qualifying employees and are required to obtain workers' compensation insurance to provide benefits to workers who suffer a work-related injury (see Questions 51 and 52).

Employer organizations that are exempt from federal income taxation under Section 501(c)(3) of the Internal Revenue Code because they are organized and operated exclusively for religious, charitable, scientific, literary or educational purposes are exempt from paying federal unemployment tax. Additional exceptions are available to organizations that exclusively operate to prevent cruelty to animals or children, or that foster amateur sports competitions. Such employer organizations may be exempt from federal unemployment tax but are still required to pay state unemployment tax.

Required Leaves of Absence. The federal Family and Medical Leave Act[42] requires that employers that employ more than 50 employees provide eligible employees up to 12 weeks of unpaid family and medical leave in any 12 months. An eligible employee is one who has worked for the employer for 12 months and has completed 1,250 hours of employment in the 12 months preceding the start of the leave. An eligible

42 Cf. Family and Medical Leave Act: Overview, US Dept. Labor, www.dol.gov/whd/fmla/ (last visited July 25, 2017) (providing an overview of the act and links to may helpful resources).

employee also work at a location where at least 50 employees are employed at the location or within 75 miles of the location.[43] There are options to performing the 12-month calculation to determine whether a new 12-week leave is available. The leave is available for certain serious health conditions of the employee or a family member, child care for a newborn or adopted child, and certain military leave situations. Generally, health benefits must be permitted to be continued as if the employee was actively at work during FMLA leave. In addition, certain job-related status and rights to return to the same or an equivalent position generally applies to such leave.

Minnesota employers must provide time off to employees under certain circumstances. See Question 56.

Additional benefits are generally not required, though organizations may find it difficult to obtain and retain well qualified employees without offering some sort of comprehensive benefits package.

"Required" Benefits. Effective July 1, 2009, Minnesota employers with 11 or more full-time equivalent workers that do not offer health insurance plans must establish a cafeteria plan or affirmatively opt out of this requirement.[44] Employers that sponsor health insurance plans are not subject to this new law.

Other Benefit "Requirements." While employers are not required to provide other benefits to employees, once they establish such benefits, the benefit plans become subject to certain requirements under federal law. The Employee Retirement Income and Security Act of 1974 ("ERISA") and the Internal Revenue Code ("IRC") impose requirements on benefit plans to prove that the benefits provided do not discriminate in favor of highly paid employees in order for an employer to provide and its employees to receive those benefits on a tax-preferred ("non-tax") basis. ERISA generally provides requirements for employers to maintain and provide certain records and documents related to benefits in order to avoid penalties under the law. The IRC generally provides the nondiscrimination and benefit structure required for benefits to be provided on a tax-preferred basis. In addition, several IRC sections provide sanctions and penalties to employers and plans that do not comply with these rules. The IRC provides that employer and employee contributions used toward certain benefits, such as retirement and health care, can be contributed on a tax-preferred basis, as long as the specific requirements for the type of benefit are satisfied. Other benefits, such as life insurance and disability insurance, can be a combination of tax preferred and after tax, depending on how the benefit is structured.

Common Benefits

Retirement. Most employers provide some kind of retirement benefit. IRC Sections 401(k) and 403(b) provide the framework for nonprofit employers to establish retirement plans for employees to set aside some of their own income on a tax-preferred basis, invest those deferrals, and sometimes provide some employer contributions as well.

Health Care. Employers also commonly provide health care benefits, through either an insurance policy with an insurer or by "self-insuring" the health care benefits by hiring a third party administrator to administer the health care claims while retaining the liability for the cost of the benefits. Employers sponsoring self-insured medical plans obtain "stop loss" insurance to protect the financial status of the organization against unanticipated, large claims. In addition, group health plans are now being designed to use High Deductible Health Care Plans with Health Spending Accounts or Health Reimbursement Accounts. Special rules apply to these types of benefits and their coordination with other benefits that an employer may provide. In addition, Wellness Programs, either as part of a health care plan or as a standalone benefit, are becoming very popular and have a number of regulations to follow for compliance.

43 *See* The Family and Medical Leave Act - Wage and Hour Division - U.S. Department of Labor, www.dol.gov/whd/regs/compliance/1421.htm

44 *See* Section 125 plans - Minnesota Dept. of Health, www.health.state.mn.us/healthreform/sec125plan.html (last visited July 25, 2017).

Cafeteria or Flexible Spending Account Plans. Employers often establish cafeteria or flexible spending account plans to permit employees to contribute their portion of the cost of coverage for medical benefits on a tax-preferred basis. Such plans also often include dependent care spending accounts for employees to set aside tax-preferred money to be used to reimburse day care expenses for eligible dependents, and health care spending accounts to be used to reimburse certain medical expenses for the employee and their eligible dependents.

Insurances. Common group insurance plans that many employers provide include Life Insurance, Short-Term Disability and Long-Term Disability. Some employers also obtain group policies to provide dependent coverage for these benefits. In Minnesota, group life insurance coverage is eligible for an employee to continue upon termination of employment.

Concierge Benefits. Some employers provide their employees with the opportunity to obtain other insurance coverage, group legal assistance, long-term care assistance, discount programs and education assistance programs.

Q27. Must my organization provide the same benefits to all employees?

A27. ERISA and the IRC place certain limits upon employers for establishing one set eligibility criteria for certain employees and a different eligibility standard for others. These restrictions are placed upon group benefit plans to reduce the disparity between benefits provided to key and Highly Compensated Employees ("HCEs") and Non Highly Compensated Employees ("NHCEs"). While the common theme is that more-highly paid employees cannot receive more or significantly more benefits than those who are not highly paid, these nondiscrimination rules apply differently to retirement (pension) benefits and welfare (group health care, etc.) benefits.

Retirement:

- ERISA establishes certain age and service requirements employer organizations may use to limit participation in pension plans. Employers need not have any eligibility requirements, but they can require employees to be older than 21 or complete more than one year of service.
- The Internal Revenue Code (IRC) allows employers to set additional standards for participation in pension plans based on job classifications, but these additional standards cannot be used to exclude all part-time workers from the plan.
- NONDISCRIMINATION
    - The IRC requires that a plan not discriminate in favor of HCEs. An HCE is an employee who is a 5 percent owner in the organization or who earned at least $80,000 in a year[45].
    - Also, the IRC requires that the plan not provide disproportionate benefits to HCEs.
    - If a plan does not include all employees, then organizations are required to demonstrate that enough NHCEs are participating in the plan to offset the number of HCEs receiving benefits. Organizations can generally demonstrate this by using one of three different tests. Each test begins by determining which employees are "excludable" from the testing, which must be counted, and whether employees are HCEs or NHCEs. The easiest is usually the "70 percent" minimum coverage test. Under this test, at least 70 percent of all the employer's non-excludable NCEs must benefit under the plan. For the purpose of this test, to "benefit" means to be eligible to make deferrals. The second test is the "ratio-percentage" test, where the ratio of NHCEs receiving benefits is compared to the ration of

45 *See* I.R.C. § 414(q) (2015).

HCEs receiving benefits, and the ratio of NHCEs benefiting under the plan compared to the ration of HCEs benefiting under the plan must be at least 70 percent. To satisfy the third test, the "average benefit percentage test," an organization must show that the average benefit received by NHCEs is at least 70 percent of the average benefit received by HCEs. This test is the most complicated to perform, as actual deferrals and contributions must be compared against compensation for each participant in order to determine the percentages to be compared.

Welfare:

- The IRC applies non-discrimination rules only to an employer's self-insured group health plan. As described above, these are plans where an employer provides the benefits through its general funds and hires a third party administrator to process the claims. The presence of stop loss insurance does not make an otherwise self-insured plan become considered an insured group health plan. If health benefits are provided under a group insurance policy, no non-discrimination rules apply; however, most insurers impose requirements on the employers when they make risk determinations through the underwriting process. It is common for an insurer to require an employer contribution toward the health care coverage or for an employer to make sure that a certain percentage of the employees eligible for coverage actually elect and pay for that coverage.
- Additional non-discrimination rules apply to tax-preferred benefits such as dependent care, health care, pre-tax payment of premiums and certain educational assistance programs. A health care reimbursement program is subject to both the non-discrimination rules for pre-tax benefits as well as the nondiscrimination rules for a self-insured health plan.
- While employers are not required to provide health care benefits, if they do, certain other requirements also apply. For example, the Paul Wellstone and Pete Domenici Mental Health Parity and Addiction Equity Act of 2008[46] requires that employers offering mental health and substance abuse benefits must provide equivalent coverage for those conditions as for other medical conditions covered under the employer's health insurance plan. This Act does not require that employers offer mental health or substance abuse coverage, however. In addition, health care plans are subject to continuation rules through the Consolidated Omnibus Budget and Reconciliation Act of 1985 ("COBRA") and sometimes, state continuation requirements. Minnesota has continuation requirements that generally mirror those of COBRA, but the Minnesota requirements are more generous in certain situations.

Some situations permit employers to make distinctions between employees for purposes of providing or determining the employee cost of the benefit. Minnesota employers may offer health or life insurance plans that make distinctions between employees for the type of coverage or cost of coverage based upon the employee's use of "lawful consumable products" (defined to include food, alcoholic or nonalcoholic beverages, and tobacco), as long as different premium rates charged to employees reflect the actual differential cost to the employer.[47]

46 Mental Health Parity and Addiction Equity Act (MHPAEA), Center for Consumer Info. & Insurance Oversight, www.cms.gov/CCIIO/Programs-and-Initiatives/Other-Insurance-Protections/MHPAEA.html (last visited July 25, 2017) (providing information on the act).

47 Minn. Stat. § 181.938 (2016).

Q28. An organization has only a few employees and does not have a group health plan. It encourages employees to get individual plans and then helps them pay for the premiums. Should it directly reimburse the employee for their premiums or should it pay the insurance provider?

A28. This situation is becoming more and more common as the cost of health care rises. The amount of the employee premiums can only be provided by the employer on a tax-preferred basis if the employer pays the insurance provider directly, or if the employee provides certain substantiation information to the employer before the reimbursement is made. The employee must show that the coverage is in effect and that the amount was paid to the insurer for the coverage. If that information is not provided, the reimbursement would need to be on an after-tax basis.

This practice raises several other issues. Some Internal Revenue Service ("IRS") personnel have informally indicated that the IRS would consider the individual policies, together, to constitute an employer group health plan. If the IRS took this position, the "group health plan" would be required to comply with the requirements of COBRA and the Health Insurance Portability and Accountability Act ("HIPAA") of 1996, among others. One of the HIPAA requirements is that a group health plan cannot discriminate on the basis of a health condition. Individual policies are underwritten on the basis of an individual's health status, and each policy is likely to provide different benefits at different costs depending on that status. This practice would not be considered to comply with the HIPAA nondiscrimination rules.

Some employers, in an effort to avoid the possibility of having group health requirements apply to them by virtue of their reimbursement of individual premiums, have decided to give all employees an additional monthly amount of taxable pay, for individual employees to use themselves for purchasing coverage.

F. Personnel Policies and Job Descriptions

Q29. Should my organization have an employee (or personnel) handbook?

A29. Employee handbooks or personnel policies serve a number of important functions in an organization, such as protecting the organization from liability by ensuring employees are informed of vital rules and regulations, and providing employees a useful reference when faced with certain scenarios. Most organizations are not required to have an employee handbook; however, some nonprofit organizations, including Minnesota charter schools, are required to have personnel policies and to distribute them to their employees.

Employer organizations should be careful when choosing the language included in an employee handbook, as the Minnesota Supreme Court has held that language contained in employee handbooks may constitute an employment contract. These modifications have restricted an organization's ability to terminate employment according to the usual "at-will" procedures.

Generally the benefits of an employee handbook outweigh the drawbacks. Organizations who want to obtain more information about handbooks can download "An Employer's Guide to Employment Law Issues in Minnesota," a free publication distributed by the Minnesota Department of Employment and Economic Development.[48]

48 *See* Minnesota Department of Employment and Economic Development, *An Employer's Guide to Employment Law Issues in Minnesota* (2016), mn.gov/deed/assets/an-employers-guide-to-employment-law-issues-in-minnesota-13th-ed-2016_tcm1045-133700.pdf.

Q30. What issues should my employer organization consider if it decides to develop an employee handbook?

A30. Helpful issues to consider include:

- What are the key policies of the organization that the employer wants to communicate to employees?
- Who will be responsible for maintaining and updating the handbook in the future? Will there be a set revision schedule or committee?
- Will our organization follow the handbook's policies at all times? Failure to follow policies established and distributed in an employee handbook may result in legal liability.

Q31. What topics should be included in an employee handbook?

A31. Typical topics that are included in an employee handbook are:

- Notice that the handbook is not a contract with employees and can be changed in the employer's discretion at any time;
- Employee Acknowledgment: a page to be signed by each employee, indicating that the employee has read and understands the policies included in the handbook, and that the employee understands that the provisions in the handbook do not amount to a contract, and an equal opportunity statement and an affirmative action statement, if applicable;
- Holiday, vacation and various absentee and leave policies;
- "Safe harbor" policy for Fair Labor Standards Act purposes;
- Harassment prohibition policy;
- Acceptable Internet use policy;
- Firearm possession policy;
- Termination and layoff policy;
- Drug/alcohol testing policy, if applicable (note that state law mandates that this policy follow specific legal requirements, which must be communicated to employees).

Q32. What topics should not be included in an employee handbook?

A32. Employers should consider excluding policies that may change relatively quickly, so that policies in the handbook do not become outdated, leaving the employer vulnerable to an argument that the employer is not following its stated policies. For example, an employer may not want to include a policy in its handbook stating that the employer pays the full cost of all benefit programs made available to employees, if its cost of health insurance premiums has increased dramatically in recent years. Employers should also be wary of specifying precise, time-limited procedures for certain employer actions, unless the employer is certain to follow them, e.g., promises for annual performance reviews, time periods for grieving, disciplinary procedures, etc.

Q33. Can my employer organization's handbook include policies about what employees can and cannot do on their own time?

A33. Employer organizations can only restrict their employee's behavior if that behavior relates to employment activities or responsibilities, or if the employee's behavior may create a conflict of interest or the appearance of a conflict of interest. Minnesota Statute Section 181.938 greatly restricts an employer's power to restrict their employee's legal off-work activities.

Employer organizations can restrict their employee's use of "lawful consumable products" (see Question 27) when the use of such product: 1) relates to a bona fide occupational requirement and is reasonably related to employment responsibilities; 2) is necessary to avoid a conflict of interest or perceived conflict of interest with the employee's responsibilities; 3) would violate a chemical dependency or aftercare treatment program.

Q34. Should an attorney review my employer organization's handbook?

A34. While not necessary, it is advisable, in order to ensure that the handbook does not modify existing employment offers or create additional liability for the employer organization.

Q35. What should be covered in an Acceptable Internet Use Policy?

A35. Acceptable Internet Use Policies should make clear that the employee's computer, software, email and Internet access should be used only for organizational business. Employees should be told clearly to not use the electronic equipment to obtain, view, or reach any pornographic material, or to use the electronic equipment to illegally obtain copyrighted files. The policy may also contain clauses related to the use of bandwidth, social media, and downloading of software or applications.

The policy should state clearly that emails should be used for company business only, and that the employer organization owns any electronic communication sent through their equipment. Therefore the employer organization has the right to access any material in email or stored on any computer at any time.

Note that the National Labor Relations Board issued a 2012 memorandum[49] that found employer policies unlawful that attempted to restrict employees from using social media to try to improve their pay and working conditions or fix job-related problems, even if they aren't in a union. Be sure that any Internet Use Policies are narrowly focused to prevent employee use or dissemination of unlawful information, but not so broad as to inhibit employees from discussing working conditions and job-related problems.

Q36. What posters should an employer organization display according to state and federal law?

A36. The Minnesota Department of Labor and Industry and several federal agencies require that employers post notices to employees that contain information on employee rights. These notices are required to be displayed in conspicuous work locations. These posters are available in multiple languages, and are typically placed in the employee break room.

Visit the Minnesota Department of Labor and Industry at www.dli.mn.gov/main.asp, the Equal Employment Opportunity Commission at www.eeoc.gov, and the U.S. Department of Labor at www.dol.gov/osbp/sbrefa/poster/main.htm for more information about ordering your required posters.

---

49 *See* Anne Purcell, *Report of the Acting General Counsel Concerning Social Media Cases* (May 30, 2012), www.michiganemploymentlawadvisor.com/wp-content/uploads/sites/341/2012/09/NLRB-Report-Concerning-Social-Media-Cases.III_.pdf.

If a Minnesota employer wants to limit the carrying of firearms on its property, a statement to that effect must be posted at each entrance.

Q37. Are employer organizations required to have job descriptions?

A37. Job descriptions are not required by law. However, periodic analysis and revision of jobs in the workplace enables employers to properly identify essential job functions of each job. Accurate identification of essential job functions enables employers to prepare focused and appropriate job interview questions; to provide clear and helpful criteria for employee evaluations; and to establish standards for performance that will justify disciplinary action.

Q38. What should be included in job descriptions?

A38. Good job descriptions include:

- Organization information: title, department title, supervisors, full time/part time and exempt/non-exempt designation;
- Job summary;
- Essential job functions;
- Working conditions;
- Specifications: requirements for education, experience, knowledge and other requisite skills;
- Salary range.

G. Personnel Records

Q39. What documents do employer organizations need to keep in an employee's personnel file? Are there any documents that should not be kept?

A39. Minnesota employers who have 20 or more employees (other than the state, political subdivisions, advisory boards, commissions, agencies, etc. that are separately governed by the Minnesota Governmental Data Practices Act, Minnesota Statutes Chapter 13) must maintain certain documents related to employees in a personnel file, and employees must have access to their personnel files under certain conditions.[50] Employers with even one employee must allow employees to review their personnel files under the conditions outlined in the statute if they maintain personnel files.

Under Minnesota Statute §181.960, the following documents should be kept in an employee's personnel file:[51]

- Applications for employment
- Wage or salary history
- Notices of commendation, warning, discipline or termination
- Authorization for a deduction or withholding of pay
- Fringe benefit information

50 Minn. Stat. § 181.960 (2016).
51 *Id.*

- Leave records
- Employment history documents:
  - Salary and compensation history
  - Job titles
  - Dates of promotions
  - Transfers
  - Attendance records
  - Performance evaluations
  - Retirement records

The following documents should *not* be kept in the employee's file:

- Written references respecting the employee, including letters of reference supplied to an employer by another person;
- Information relating to the investigation of a violation of a criminal or civil statute by an employee or an investigation of employee conduct for which the employer may be liable, unless and until:
  - The investigation is completed and, in cases of an alleged criminal violation, the employer has received notice from the prosecutor that no action will be taken or all criminal proceedings and appeals have been exhausted; and
  - The employer takes adverse personnel action based on the information contained in the investigation records;
- Education records, pursuant to section 513(a) of title 5 of the Family Educational Rights and Privacy Act of 1974,[52] that are maintained by an educational institution and directly related to a student;
- Results of employer testing, except that the employee may see a cumulative total test score for a section of the test or for the entire test;
- Information relating to the employer's salary system and staff planning, including comments, judgments, recommendations or ratings concerning expansion, downsizing, reorganization, job restructuring, future compensation plans, promotion plans and job assignments;
- Written comments or data of a personal nature about a person other than the employee, if disclosure of the information would constitute an intrusion upon the other person's privacy;
- Written comments or data kept by the employee's supervisor or an executive, administrative or professional employee, provided the written comments or data are kept in the sole possession of the author of the record;
- Privileged information or information that is not discoverable in a workers' compensation, grievance arbitration, administrative, judicial or quasi-judicial proceeding;
- Any portion of a written or transcribed statement by a coworker of the employee that concerns the job performance or job-related misconduct of the employee that discloses the identity of the coworker by name, inference or otherwise; and
- Medical reports and records, including reports and records that are available to the employee from a health care services provider.

52 *See* 20 U.S.C. §1232(g) (2013).

Q40. Can employer organizations keep notes on performance and other issues related to particular employees? Can these notes be kept separate from the employee's personnel file?

A40. A supervisor can keep notes on a particular employee they supervise out of the personnel file so long as they are kept in the sole possession of the author of the notes. Typically, these notes would be used by the supervisor to prepare periodic performance evaluations, disciplinary memos, etc. However, information properly belonging in an employee's personnel record that was omitted from the record provided by the employer to an employee for review may not be used by the employer in a legal proceeding, unless the employer did not intentionally omit the information, and the employee is given a reasonable opportunity to review the omitted information prior to its use.[53]

Q41. How long should employer organizations retain records on former employees or job applicants?

A41. If possible, keep all records related to former employees indefinitely and hiring records for one year. If permanent retention is impossible, organizations should retain employee personnel files for seven years past termination unless there is litigation pending.

H. Complying with Other Federal and State Employment Laws

Q42. Can I deduct money from an employee's paycheck for things other than employment tax payments?

A42. Certain scenarios exist in which employer organization can deduct amounts from their employee's checks.

Deductions for purposes other than the employer's, such as union dues, charitable contributions and insurance premiums, if authorized by the employee, may be deducted.

Other deductions, such as costs for lodging at the worksite, board, work uniforms and costs for cleaning uniforms can be deducted from employee's paychecks, but such deductions cannot cause the employee's wages to fall below the state or federal minimum wage.

The employer organization may be required to garnish the employee's wage if the organization receives a wage garnishment notice from the appropriate governmental agency. Rules limiting the amount of money that can be garnished from an employee's paycheck are discussed in Minnesota Statutes Section 571.922. An organization is forbidden from retaliating against an individual because of a garnishment order.

Finally, there can be no deductions from an employee's final paycheck without prior approval of the employee or a court order.

Q43. What is the Equal Employment Opportunity Act and how does my organization comply with it?

A43. The Equal Employment Opportunity Act expanded the scope of Title VII of the Civil Rights Act of 1964, broadening who must adhere to Title VII's requirements. As amended, Title VII now applies to:

- All employers with 15 or more employees;

53 Minn. Stat. § 181.963 (2016).

- All educational institutions;
- All state and local governments;
- Labor unions with 15 or more members.

The Equal Employment Opportunity Act ("EEO") is enforced by the Equal Employment Opportunity Commission, and it is one of several laws used by the Commission to ensure equity in employment. Other laws include:

- Title VII of the Civil Rights Act of 1964, prohibiting employment discrimination based on race, color, religion, sex or national origin.
- The Equal Pay Act of 1963, which protects men and women who perform substantially equal work in the same establishment from sex-based wage discrimination.
- The Age Discrimination in Employment Act of 1967 ("ADEA"), which protects individuals who are 40 years of age or older.
- Title I and Title V of the Americans with Disabilities Act of 1990 ("ADA"), which prohibit employment discrimination against qualified individuals with disabilities in the private sector, and in state and local governments.
- Sections 501 and 505 of the Rehabilitation Act of 1973, which prohibit discrimination against qualified individuals with disabilities who work in the federal government.
- The Civil Rights Act of 1991, which provides monetary damages in cases of intentional employment discrimination.

Compliance with EEO requires organizations to avoid discrimination and make reasonable accommodations whenever possible.

Employer organizations must not discriminate in:

- Hiring and firing;
- Compensation, assignment or classification of employees;
- Transfer, promotion, layoff or recall;
- Job advertisements;
- Recruitment;
- Testing;
- Use of company facilities;
- Training and apprenticeship programs;
- Fringe benefits;
- Pay, retirement plans and disability leave;
- Other terms and conditions of employment.

Employer organizations may not:

- Harass on the basis of race, color, religion, gender, national origin, disability, or age;
- Retaliate against individuals for filing a charge of discrimination, participating in an investigation or opposing discriminatory practices;
- Make employment decisions based on stereotypes or assumptions about the abilities, traits or performance of individuals of a certain gender, race, age, religion, ethnic group or disability;
- Deny employment opportunities to a person because of marriage to, or association with, an individual of a particular race, religion, national origin or disability, or for participation in a school or place of worship associated with a particular racial, ethnic or religious group.

Employer organizations must post notices to all employees advising them of their rights under the laws the Equal Employment Opportunity Commission ("EEOC") enforces and their right to be free from retaliation.[54] Such notices must be accessible as needed to persons with visual or other disabilities that affect reading.

Employer organizations may not intentionally discriminate, nor can they permit practices that have the effect of discriminating against individuals because of their race, color, national origin, religion or gender. Discrimination on the basis of gender has been interpreted to cover pregnancy, childbirth and, in Minnesota, gender identity.

Employer organizations must not discriminate because of birthplace, ancestry, culture or linguistic characteristics common to a specific ethnic group. While employer organizations are required to ensure that employees are legally authorized to work in the United States, an employer organization who requests employment verification only for individuals of a particular national origin may violate Title VII.

An employer organization must reasonably accommodate the religious beliefs of employees or prospective employees, unless such accommodation would impose an undue burden or hardship.

Age discrimination is prohibited. Employer organizations cannot:

- State or specify in job notices or advertisements an age preference or limitation. Age limits may only be specified in the rare circumstance where age has been proven to be a bona fide occupational qualification.
- Discriminate on the basis of age by apprenticeship programs, including joint labor-management apprenticeship programs.
- Deny benefits to older employees. Employers are only permitted to reduce benefits based on age only if the cost of providing the reduced benefits to older workers is the same as the cost of providing benefits to younger workers.

Employer organizations may not discriminate on the basis of sex in the payment of wages or benefits where men and women perform work of similar skill, effort and responsibility for the same employer in similar working conditions.

Employer organizations cannot discriminate on the basis of disability in employment practices.

Employer organizations cannot discriminate against employees or applicants because of genetic information. Title II of the Genetic Information Nondiscrimination Act ("GINA") prohibits the use of genetic information in making employment decisions, restricts employers and other entities covered by Title II (employment agencies, labor organizations and joint labor-management training and apprenticeship programs—referred to as "covered entities") from requesting, requiring or purchasing genetic information, and strictly limits the disclosure of genetic information.

Q44. Does my organization need to adopt an equal opportunity policy?

A44. Equal opportunity policies are commonly adopted by Minnesota organizations. Typically, they recite the requirements of the Minnesota Human Rights Act, which prohibits discrimination because of race, color,

54 *See* EEO is the Law Poster, US Equal Emp't Opportunity Comm'n, www1.eeoc.gov/employers/poster.cfm (last visited July 27, 2017).

creed, religion, national origin, sex, marital status, status with regard to public assistance, membership or activity in a local commission, disability, sexual orientation, genetic information or age. Organizations engaged in interstate commerce and that employ 15 or more individuals are covered by the federal Civil Rights Act of 1964, which also prohibits discrimination because of race, color, religion, gender or national origin.

Organizations that hold government contracts or subcontracts are required to adopt and abide by an equal opportunity policy.

Q45. What is the Americans with Disabilities Act and how does my organization comply with it?

A45. The Americans with Disabilities Act ("ADA")[55] is an act prohibiting discrimination against qualified individuals with disabilities on account of their disability. Additionally, the Act requires that reasonable efforts be made by an employer to accommodate qualified individuals with disabilities, unless such accommodations would create an undue burden or hardship to the organization.

An individual with a disability is a person who: 1) has a physical or mental impairment that substantially limits one or more major life activity; 2) has a record of such an impairment; or 3) is regarded as having such an impairment.

In 2009, Congress expanded the definitions of some of the terms describing an "individual with a disability" in the Americans with Disabilities Amendment Act ("ADAAA"). The Act:

- Directs the EEOC to clarify through regulations what is meant by "substantially limits"; expands the definition of "major life activities";
- States that mitigating measures other than "ordinary eyeglasses or contact lenses" shall not be considered in assessing whether an individual has a disability;
- Clarifies that an impairment that is episodic or in remission is a disability if it would substantially limit a major life activity when active;
- Changes the definition of "regarded as" so that an applicant or employee is "regarded as" disabled if the applicant is subject to an action prohibited by the ADA (e.g., failure to hire or termination) based on an impairment that is not transitory and minor;
- Provides that individuals covered only under the "regarded as" prong are not entitled to reasonable accommodation.

An individual is considered to be a "qualified individual with a disability" if the individual meets the requirements of a position they seek and can perform the essential functions of the position with or without reasonable accommodation.

The reasonable accommodation provision can be divided into three areas: changes to the job application process, changes in how a task is performed or in the work environment, and changes that assist an employee with a disability to enjoy equal benefits and privileges of employment. Employees must inform the employer organization when they require reasonable accommodations and employers then have a legal duty to communicate with the employee to arrive at a mutually acceptable accommodation, within the limits discussed below.

55 *Cf.* ADA.gov homepage, www.ada.gov/ (last visited July 27, 2017).

Reasonable accommodations include modifying work schedules, acquiring or modifying equipment, providing readers or interpreters, modifying work sites and facilities, and reassignment of an individual seeking a reasonable accommodation to a vacant position for which the individual is qualified.

The employer organization is not required to make accommodations for disabilities that are not known, and the employer organization does not need to make accommodations that would impose an undue hardship upon the organization. Undue hardship is defined as any action that would require significant difficulty or expense. Factors such as organization size, type of organization and budget are all taken into consideration when considering if an accommodation would create an undue burden.

The ADA applies to organizations with 15 or more employees. However, the Minnesota Human Rights Act applies to all Minnesota employers, and also prohibits discrimination on the basis of disability. Small employer organizations may be eligible for tax credits to aid in compliance with the ADA.

Q46. What is the Family Medical Leave Act and how does my employer organization comply with it?

A46. The Family Medical Leave Act requires "covered employers" to provide "eligible employees" up to 12 work weeks of unpaid leave during any 12-month period:[56]

- For the birth or care of a newborn child of the employee;
- For the adoption of a child or foster care placement;
- To care for an immediate family member (spouse, child or parent) with a serious health condition;
- To take medical leave when the employee is unable to work due to a serious health condition.

A **covered employer**[57] is a:

- Private-sector employer, with 50 or more employees in 20 or more workweeks in the current or preceding calendar year, including a joint employer or successor in interest to a covered employer;[58]
- Public agency, including a local, state, or Federal government agency, regardless of the number of employees it employs; or
- Public or private elementary or secondary school, regardless of the number of employees it employs.

An **eligible employee** is one who:

- Works for a covered employer;
- Has worked for the employer for at least 12 months;
- Has at least 1,250 hours of service for the employer during the 12 month period immediately preceding the leave; and
- Works at a location where the employer has at least 50 employees within 75 miles.

Note that sometimes an employee may have a health condition that qualifies as a disability and/or that

56 *See* Family and Medical Leave Act - Wage and Hour Division - U.S. Department of Labor, www.dol.gov/whd/fmla/ (last visited July 27, 2017).
57 *See* 29 C.F.R. § 825.104 (2017).
58 *See* U.S. Department of Labor, *Fact Sheet #28: The Family and Medical Leave Act* (2012), www.dol.gov/whd/regs/compliance/whdfs28.pdf.

was prompted by an injury on the job. As a result, an employer's response to an employee's request for time off may be affected by the requirements of the Americans with Disabilities Act, workers' compensation law and/or Family Medical Leave Act. In these situations, it is best to consult with legal counsel to ensure compliance and thereby minimize legal risk.

Q47. What is the Minnesota Human Rights Act and how does my organization comply with it?

A47. The Minnesota Human Rights Act forbids employer organizations from discriminating on the grounds of race, color, creed, religion, national origin, gender, marital status, familial status, status with regard to public assistance, membership or activity in a local commission, disability, sexual orientation, genetic information or age. It also forbids retaliation against an employee who has complained of discrimination or participated in an investigation of discrimination in the workplace.

In order to comply with the Minnesota Human Rights Act, employer organizations should avoid discriminating against an applicant or employee on the basis of a protected class characteristic. Decisions regarding hiring, terminating employment, promotion, etc. should be made based on capacity for or performance of essential job functions. Employers should be scrupulous in protecting those who bring forward complaints of harassment or discrimination in the workplace from retaliation.

Q48. What is Title VII and how does my organization comply with it?

A48. Title VII of the Civil Rights Act of 1964 prohibits discrimination in employment on the basis of race, sex, national origin or religion. Title VII prohibits employer organizations from retaliating against employees for filing discrimination charges under Title VII, or for testifying, assisting or participating in investigations proceedings under Title VII.

Employer organizations comply with Title VII by adhering to non-discrimination policies and avoiding retaliation against employees who report discrimination or participate in investigations.

Title VII generally applies to employers with 15 or more employees, including federal, state, and local governments. Title VII also applies to private and public colleges and universities, employment agencies, and labor organizations.[59]

Q49. What is HIPAA and how does my organization comply with it?

A49. HIPAA, the Health Insurance Portability and Accountability Act of 1996, was passed to increase portability and continuity in health insurance, promote efficiency throughout the health care industry and protect the privacy of health care information. Title I of HIPAA deals with health care access, portability, and renewability, while Title II addresses health care fraud and abuse, focusing mainly on protecting privacy.

HIPAA's Title I restricts group health plans' power to deny coverage to individuals with preexisting conditions by instituting limits of 12-18 months, and requiring plans to provide credit to individuals for previous continuous health care coverage.

59 *See* Know Your Rights: Title VII of the Civil Rights Act of 1964, www.aauw.org/what-we-do/legal-resources/know-your-rights-at-work/title-vii/

Title II provides detailed standards for protecting the privacy of participating individuals. The privacy rule allows patients to access their protected health information (PHI), request corrections, and restrict who can access the information and how it can be released. Additionally, the privacy rule restricts the amount of information that can be released by a covered entity to the minimum needed for treatment purposes. Title II also provides various administrative requirements to aid in the protection of PHI.

The majority of HIPAA's requirements apply only to covered entities such as health care providers, health plans and health care clearinghouses. Organizations that provide their own organization-funded health care may be required to follow HIPAA's privacy rules, but only if they have 50 or more participants. If you are unsure whether or not your organization is a covered entity, visit the "Am I a Covered Entity" tool on the Department of Health and Human Services website at www.hhs.gov/ocr/hipaa.

The penalties for violating HIPAA's requirements can be very severe. Organizations that provide organization-funded health care should seek legal counsel to ensure they have met the appropriate requirements.

Q50. Are there any OSHA or other health and safety requirements with which employers need to comply?

A50. All Minnesota employers must adhere to the Federal and Minnesota versions of the Occupational Safety Health Act ("OSHA").

Employer organizations must provide employees conditions and places of employment free from hazards that are likely to cause death or serious injury. Additionally, organizations must provide training for any harmful agents, physical hazards or infectious agents that employees may encounter while working.

Employer organizations must establish written workplace accident- and injury-reduction policies that detail how their training programs will be implemented and maintained, how hazards will be identified and controlled, how the plan will be communicated to employees, how accidents will be investigated and dealt with, and how safe work practice rules will be enforced.

Q51. What should an employer organization do when an employee is injured at work?

A51. Employer organizations should first assist their employee in receiving the appropriate level of medical care.

Employer organizations must report the injury to their workers' compensation insurance carrier using a First Report of Injury form. The form should be completed by the employee or someone who has observed the details and circumstances surrounding the injury. This form must be submitted to the employer organization's insurance carrier within 14 days. If death or serious injury occurs, the employer organization must notify both their insurance carrier and the Department of Labor and Industry within 48 hours.[60]

If an employee dies or three or more employees are hospitalized, the employer organization must report the incident to OSHA within eight hours. Employer organizations can find contact information for their OSHA office at www.dli.mn.gov/main.asp.

Additionally, employer organizations are required to keep track of all workplace accidents on their OSHA Form 300, available at www.dli.mn.gov/OSHA/PDF/form300.pdf.

60 *See* Workers' Compensation- General Information, MN Dept. Labor & Industry, www.dli.mn.gov/wc/GeneralFR.asp (last visited July 28, 2017).

Q52. What is workers' compensation and how do I comply with the related regulations?

A52. Workers' compensation insurance is a required insurance coverage system by which employers fund care for injuries experienced by employees that arise during the course of employment.

The term "employer" includes any person who hires another to perform a service, including corporations, partnerships, LLCs, associations, groups of persons, the state, counties, towns, cities, school districts and governmental subdivisions. Employers are required to carry workers' compensation insurance or become self-insured.

Workers' compensation payments are used to pay for medical care, wage-loss benefits for lost income, benefits for permanent damage or loss of functionality of a body part, and benefits to surviving family members in case of death and job retraining, if applicable.

Employer organizations who fail to carry workers' compensation insurance may be fined as much as $1000 per week for every uninsured employee, and employer organizations without workers' compensation insurance will typically suffer severe penalties and civil liabilities in the case of employee injury.

Workers' compensation insurance can be obtained through an insurance agent or company. Additional possibilities may exist for organizations unable to obtain insurance through an agent or company. Contact the Minnesota Workers' Compensation Insurers' Association for more information.

Q53. When do employer organizations need to submit I-9 forms to the U.S. Citizenship and Immigration Service ("USCIS")?

A53. An Employment Eligibility Verification Form, or Form I-9, must be completed and retained by the employer for every individual an organization employs after November 6, 1986. The Form I-9 is required for both citizen and non-citizen employees, and is completed by both the employer and employee. The employee must complete Section I of the Form I-9 as of the first date of employment. The employer must review the employee's documentation and verify the employee's eligibility to work by completing Section II of the Form I-9 within three business days thereafter. The Form I-9 requires the employee to provide the employer with original documentation (consistent with a "List of Acceptable Documents" listed on the I-9 form) to establish identity and eligibility for employment. Employers are not required to obtain I-9 forms for independent contractors.

Organizations must keep an employee's I-9 on file for three years after the date of hire or one year after termination, whichever is longer. I-9 forms do not have to be submitted to USCIS. Form I-9s should not be kept with personnel files. Employers must establish a "tickler" system to track work authorization expirations for employees who are not citizens, and must re-verify employment following reauthorization to work. A new Form I-9 is not required to be completed following promotion or transfer of an employee within the same employer organization.

For questions about the I-9 form or requirements for verification, employers can refer to *Handbook for Employers: Instructions for Completing Form I-9* (Publ. M-274), which can be downloaded for free at www.uscis.gov/i-9-central/handbook-employers-m-274.

It is unlawful for employers to treat any group of employees differently when completing the Form I-9 because the employer believes them to be non-citizens. Employer organizations must provide an employee's

I-9 to authorized government officials upon request.

USCIS requires certain federal contractors and subcontractors to use a free federal system called E-Verify to verify their employees' eligibility to work in the United States. E-Verify compares information from the Form I-9 against federal government databases to verify workers' employment eligibility. The system is intended to facilitate compliance with federal immigration laws, to deter unauthorized individuals from attempting to work and to help employers avoid employing unauthorized aliens. See www.uscis.gov-/e-verify for more information about E-Verify.

Q54. Do employer organizations need to give workers lunch or other breaks?

A54. Employers must give workers who are working for eight or more consecutive hours sufficient time to eat a meal. Many employers provide a 30 minute lunch break, but the law does not specifically require 30 minutes.

Employers must also allow employees adequate time every four hours to use the nearest restroom.[61]

Q55. Do lunch and other breaks need to be paid time?

A55. Lunch breaks need to be paid if the nonexempt employee is not fully relieved of their duties. If the employee is not fully relieved of duty or required to eat the meal at a workstation or desk, then this time is not free from duty and must be paid. If the employee voluntarily continues to work during a lunch or other break, the employer is also obligated to pay a nonexempt employee for the "hours worked," according to the Fair Labor Standards Act.

Other rest periods of less than 20 minutes should be paid.[62]

Q56. Are employer organizations legally required to provide time off to employees for things like funerals, jury duty, voting, birth or adoption of a child, or other reasons?

A56. **Funerals or Compassionate Leave**– Not required, but typically granted for a certain number of days

Jury Duty – Specific pay is not required, but Minnesota employers cannot threaten to fire or fire an employee on account of their reporting for jury duty or service as a juror.

Voting - Employees have the right to be absent from work for the purpose of voting, during the morning of the day of the election, without penalty or deduction from salary or wages because of the absence. "Election" means a regularly scheduled state primary or general election, election for U.S. Senator, U.S. Representative, state senator or state representative.

Parental Leave or Birth or Adoption of Child – If a Minnesota employer has 21 or more employees, it is required to provide an unpaid leave of absence of up to twelve weeks to an employee who is a birth or adoptive parent, in conjunction with the birth or adoption of the child. "Employee" is defined as a person who has worked for the employer at least half-time for at least 12 consecutive months immediately

61 *Cf.* Breaks and Meal Periods, US Dept. Labor, www.dol.gov/general/topic/workhours/breaks (last visited July 28, 2017).
62 *Id.*

preceding the request.[63] If the employer has 50 or more employees working within a 75-mile radius, then the employer must provide time off according to the federal Family Medical Leave Act (see Question 46). Some employers offer paid family leave for a certain period of time (six or twelve weeks, for example) that extends to all parents in the event of a birth or adoption of a child.

Other Medical Leave - Minnesota employers must grant paid leaves to employees who wish to undergo a medical procedure to donate bone marrow[64]. The leave may not exceed 40 work hours, unless the employer agrees to a longer leave. Similarly, Minnesota employees are able to obtain paid leave of up to 40 working hours for each organ (or partial organ) donation made to another person.[65]

Military Family Leave –Minnesota employers are required to grant up to ten working days' leave without pay to an employee whose immediate family member, as a member of the U.S. armed forces, has been injured or killed while engaged in active service.[66] Minnesota employers are also required to grant unpaid leaves to employees whose immediate family member has been ordered into active service with the U.S. armed forces in support of a war or other national emergency, unless granting the leave would unduly disrupt the operations of the employer.[67] The length of the leave may be limited by the employer to the actual time necessary for the employee to attend a send-off or homecoming ceremony, not to exceed one day in any calendar year.

Military Leave - In accordance with the federal Uniformed Services Employment and Reemployment Act of 1994 ("USERRA") employees called to active duty in the military, or to reserve training, are permitted to be on military leave of absence. In addition, Minnesota Statutes § 192.26 provides that employees who are members of the National Guard, or a reserve component of the military or naval forces of the United States, be granted a leave of absence without any loss of pay or benefits for up to a total of 15 days in a calendar year for purposes of training or active service.[68] Upon being informed of a military obligation, the employee must make every effort to contact their supervisor immediately, and apply on the specified form for military leave. Special conditions and rights may apply regarding the continuation of certain benefits while employees are on military leave serving in one of the uniformed services.

School Conference and Activities Leave - A Minnesota employer must grant an employee leave of up to 16 hours per 12-month period to attend school conferences or activities related to the employee's child, if the conferences or activities cannot be scheduled during non-work hours.[69] An "employee" is one who has worked for the employer at least half-time for at least 12 consecutive months immediately preceding the request.

Sick Leave – Employers are not required to provide sick leave benefits to employees. However, employers must allow "eligible employees" to use any available paid sick leave for absences to care for a sick or injured child, adult child, spouse, sibling, parent, step-parent or grandparent on the same terms that the employee is able to use paid sick leave benefits for their own illness or injury. An employee's available sick time may be used for relatives (not including to care for a sick or injured child) up to a maximum of 160 hours per year.

63 Minn. Stat. § 181.941 (2016).
64 Minn. Stat. § 181.945 (2016).
65 Minn. Stat. § 181.9456 (2016).
66 Minn. Stat. § 181.947 (2016).
67 Minn. Stat. § 181.947 (2016).
68 Minn. Stat. § 192.26 (2016).
69 Minn. Stat. § 181.9412 (2016).

An "eligible employee" is one who has been employed for (a) the previous 12 consecutive months and (b) at least one-half the full-time equivalent position in the employee's job classification during those 12 months.

POLICY UPDATE

The City of Minneapolis and City of St Paul both adopted slightly different Sick and Safe Time Ordinances that went into effect on July 1, 2017. The ordinances create access to time off work for employees across the two cities. Full and part-time staff, temporary employees and paid interns are included. Sick and safe time is flexible, extendscoverage to more employees while preserving many employer controls. See more details at sicktimeinfo.minneapolismn.gov and https://www.stpaul.gov/departments/human-rights-equal-economic-opportunity/contract-compliance-business-development/earned.

Other cities in Minnesota are preparing to update the similar policies soon.

Q57. Does my employer organization need a harassment policy? Should the policy apply to both staff members and volunteers?

A57. Yes, every employer organization needs to draft, distribute and enforce a harassment policy, in order to minimize risk of legal liability. Such policies should provide protection of employees from harassment from board members, volunteers, other employees, vendors and anyone else that may come into contact with the organization.

The harassment policy should cover all forms of harassment on the basis of protected class characteristics (see Question 15).

An employer organization may be liable whenever it can be shown that the employer organization knew or should have known about inappropriate conduct and failed to take immediate and appropriate corrective action. Employer organizations must therefore not only have a harassment policy in place, but also regularly inform employees of its existence, train managers on its implementation and enforce it diligently.

The law prohibiting harassment on the basis of protected class characteristics does not specifically apply to volunteers. However, many organizations also draft harassment policies that provide avenues by which volunteers can report incidents of harassment, and procedures for the organization to follow up on any reports it receives.

I. Volunteer Personnel

Q58. What can and can't be asked when interviewing a potential volunteer?

A58. Typically, most questions should be focused on the particular volunteer opportunity. Employer organizations should avoid questions that focus on protected class characteristics (see Question 15).

Q59. Can an employer organization ask its potential volunteers for a list of references?

A59. Yes.

Q60. What can and can't be asked when talking to a potential volunteer's references?

A60. Typically, the organization should restrict their questions to issues closely related to the volunteer and volunteer opportunity.

Q61. When do employer organizations need to do a background check on potential and current volunteers?

A61. Organizations are required by statute to conduct background checks in certain situations, such as employment/volunteering in schools and school districts, when working with children and/or vulnerable adults. Additionally, employer organizations are expected to use reasonable care in accepting volunteers. Organizations that fail to use reasonable care may be found liable for injuries to members of the public.

Q62. What types of background checks does an employer organization need to do on its volunteers?

A62. Reference checks are typically advised. Additional checks, such as criminal background checks, should be conducted when required by law. Driving record checks should be done for volunteers who will be driving organization vehicles or transporting organization employees or clients in a personal vehicle. As with employees, it is good practice to request a waiver from the prospective volunteer before a background check is conducted.

Q63. Who pays for background checks – the volunteer or the organization?

A63. Employees or volunteers may be required to pay for the cost of a background check, but typically, the organization covers the cost of the background check.

Q64. Are there any legal issues involved when a volunteer is terminated by the employer organization?

A64. Organizations are advised to adopt and enforce clear policies regarding volunteer expectations, reviews and termination. Terminating a volunteer's work with the organization should be a last resort typically, as it may have a detrimental impact upon clients and other volunteers. Still, organizations should retain the right to end their volunteer relationship if discussions, training and reassignments fail.

Q65. What are a volunteer's responsibilities for reporting abuse?

A65 A volunteer's responsibilities for reporting abuse vary depending upon the type of organization and the individual volunteer's role within that organization. While anyone is encouraged to voluntarily report abuse as soon as possible, only certain individuals are considered "mandatory reporters" who must report child or vulnerable adult abuse under Minnesota law or face legal consequences. See also Chapter 13: Other Regulatory Issues, Question 14.

Q66. Can a person both work for and volunteer for the same organization?

A66. An individual may work and volunteer for the same organization if the following criteria are met:

1. The volunteered services or duties are performed outside the employee's regular assignments such that the employee is not performing the same or similar type of services as during regular working hours;
2. The services are entirely voluntary, with no coercion by the employer, no promise of advancement and no penalty for not volunteering;
3. The activities are predominantly for the employee's own benefit;
4. The employee does not replace another employee or impair the employment opportunities of others by performing work that would otherwise be performed by regular employees;
5. The employee serves without contemplation of pay or other benefit;
6. The activity does not take place during the employee's regular working hours or scheduled overtime hours; and
7. The volunteer time is insubstantial in relation to the employee's regular hours.

Q67. Do child labor laws apply to minors who perform volunteer work?

A67. According to the Minnesota Department of Labor and Industry, the hazardous occupation restrictions for minors are designed to protect the well-being of children. It is unlikely that the department would permit a minor to volunteer to perform a task that they would be forbidden from performing if they were being paid.

It is not clear whether the department has interpreted the maximum hours of work restrictions placed on minors in the context of volunteer work, and therefore it is unclear if an organization could allow a minor to volunteer for more than the maximum number of hours the minor could work as an employee. According to the department, organizations that wish to allow a minor volunteer to serve more than the maximum number of hours provided by law should apply for an exemption permit and work directly with the department in order to avoid a legal challenge in the future. In Minnesota, there is work that is prohibited for minors under the age of 18, as well as work that is prohibited for minors under the age of 16.[70] Detailed lists can be found in Minnesota Rules 5200.0910 and 5200.0920.

Q68. What risks are associated with utilizing volunteers?

A68. Employer organizations should be conscious of the possibilities that volunteers may be injured while volunteering and also that the volunteers may injure others inside or outside the organization while volunteering. Appropriate insurance should be obtained to manage the risks in these areas. See Chapter 10: Insurance for Nonprofit Organizations for a larger discussion of risk management and the types of insurance available to nonprofits.

Other risks that are inherent in working with volunteers are similar to those that occur in working with employees. Deficits in volunteers' experience, training or capacity may create risk to the organization. It is important for organizations that work with volunteers to carefully screen prospective volunteers, train them thoroughly, set up clear expectations and rules for volunteer service and supervise them to be sure that standards are being met.

70 *See* Labor Standards – Child labor: Prohibited Work for Minors, www.dli.mn.gov/ls/ProhibWork.asp (last visited July 28, 2017).

Q69. What is AmeriCorps, and what must my organization know if we are getting an AmeriCorps member?

A69. The AmeriCorps program is administered by the Corporation for National and Community Service. Employer organizations wishing to learn more or apply for an AmeriCorps participant should visit www.americorps.gov. There are several types of AmeriCorps programs:

AmeriCorps State and National: AmeriCorps State and National supports a broad range of local service programs that engage thousands of Americans in intensive service to meet critical community needs.

AmeriCorps VISTA: AmeriCorps VISTA provides full-time members to community organizations and public agencies to create and expand programs that build capacity and ultimately bring low-income individuals and communities out of poverty.

AmeriCorps NCCC: The AmeriCorps National Civilian Community Corps is a full-time residential program for men and women, ages 18-24, which strengthens communities while developing leaders through direct, team-based national and community service.

AmeriCorps members typically enroll for year-long terms, and in return receive a modest living stipend and an end-of-service educational award or cash lump-sum payment.

Individuals serving through the AmeriCorps program are classified as "participants," and as such are distinct from employees or volunteers. Employer organizations should treat participants as employees for most tax purposes. AmeriCorps participants are not covered by Fair Labor Standards Act or state labor employee laws, but the structure of the AmeriCorps program limits the participant's actions in similar ways.

Employer organizations are required to provide AmeriCorps participants with health care, and this policy must meet certain service and cost benchmarks. Organizations are prohibited from using AmeriCorps members in certain ways; for instance, AmeriCorps participants are prohibited from engaging in political activity, assisting or deterring union activity, or aiding or impairing partisan political groups. Participants are required to avoid these activities while working for their organization or community, but they are permitted to engage in these activities on their own personal time.

J. Related Resources

Organizations:

AmeriCorps
1201 New York Ave., NW
Washington, DC 20525
www.americorps.gov

Department of Health and Human Services
The U.S. Department of Health and Human Services
200 Independence Ave., SW
Washington, DC 20201
www.hhs.gov/

Department of Labor
U.S. Department of Labor
Frances Perkins Building
200 Constitution Ave. NW
Washington, DC 20210
www.dol.gov

EEOC Headquarters
U.S. Equal Employment Opportunity Commission
131 M Street, NE
Washington, DC 20507
Phone: 202-663-4900 / (TTY) 202-663-4494
www.eeoc.gov/
Find Nearest EEOC Offices: www.eeoc.gov/field/index.cfm

Internal Revenue Service
10th St & Pennsylvania Ave, NW
Washington, DC 20004
www.irs.gov

IRS Local Offices in Minnesota
www.irs.gov/localcontacts/article/0,,id=98289,00.html

Minnesota Department of Employment and Economic Development
1st National Bank Building
332 Minnesota St., Suite E200
St. Paul, MN 55101-1351
www.positivelyminnesota.com/

Minnesota Department of Human Services
Child Protection Services
444 Lafayette Rd. N
St. Paul, MN 55155
Minnesota Department of Labor and Industry
443 Lafayette Rd. N.
St. Paul, MN 55155
www.dli.mn.gov/main.asp

Minnesota Department of Labor and Industry
Minnesota OSHA Compliance
443 Lafayette Road N.
St. Paul, MN 55155
www.dli.mn.gov/MnOsha.asp
Phone: (651) 284-5050
Toll-free: 1-877-470-6742
Fax: (651) 284-5741
Email: osha.compliance@state.mn.us

Nonprofit Risk Management Center
204 South King Street
Leesburg, VA 20175
Phone: (703) 777-3504
Email: info@nonprofitrisk.org
www.nonprofitrisk.org

Occupational Safety & Health Administration (OSHA)
200 Constitution Ave. NW
Washington, DC 20210
www.osha.gov

U.S. Department of Justice
950 Pennsylvania Ave, NW
Civil Rights Division
Disability Rights Section – NYAV
Washington, D.C. 20530
www.ada.gov

Publications:

An Employer's Guide to Employment Law Issues in Minnesota (2016), Minnesota Department of Employment and Economic Development, mn.gov/deed/assets/an-employers-guide-to-employment-law-issues-in-minnesota-13th-ed-2016_tcm1045-133700.pdf.

Resource Guide for Mandated Reporters of Child Maltreatment Concerns (2016), Minnesota Department of Human Services, edocs.dhs.state.mn.us/lfserver/Public/DHS-2917-ENG

Statutes:

Minnesota Statutes
www.revisor.mn.gov/statutes

Occupational Safety and Health Administration Regulations
www.osha.gov/pls/oshaweb/owasrch.search_form?p_doc_type=standards&p_toc_level=0

U.S. Code: Title 29 – Labor
www.law.cornell.edu/uscode/text/29

Websites:

FAQs about Employees and Employee Benefits
www.law.georgetown.edu/workplaceflexibility2010/law/general/faqEmployees_perun.pdf

The Health Insurance Portability and Accountability Act (HIPAA)
www.dol.gov/ebsa/newsroom/fshipaa.html

HIPAA FAQs for Professionals
www.hhs.gov/hipaa/for-professionals/faq

Minnesota Law and Legal Resources
www.revisor.mn.gov

Minnesota Unemployment Insurance Program
www.uimn.org

Youth & Labor Regulations and Rules
www.dol.gov/dol/topic/youthlabor/index.htm
www.youthrules.dol.gov/
www.youth.eeoc.gov/

CHAPTER 10

INSURANCE FOR NONPROFIT ORGANIZATIONS

Topics

A. Overview

A nonprofit organization is responsible for the consequences of its actions, and bears considerable risk merely by operating. Anything it owns, it stands to lose. An organization's office building, for example, could be lost to earthquake; its furnishings lost to fire or flood; and its supplies and equipment lost to employee theft. Aside from property risk, an organization must also deal with the threat of legal liability—a court judgment that an organization is responsible for causing damage to a person or entity and must therefore pay compensation.

An organization can manage its risks internally (by changing its policies and activities to better avoid risk) and externally (by arranging to share its risks with another party, such as an insurance company). Many organizations form committees to identify and safeguard against potential risks; these committees are known sometimes as risk control or risk management committees and other times as safety committees. Alternately, an organization can shift the liability for potential accidents to other parties via contract. One example of this is an indemnification agreement, a contract whereby one party promises to make good the losses suffered by another person.

Another way an organization can share its risks is by buying insurance, available in a variety of policies, each with its own scope of coverage and conditions. An insurance broker or agent can help an organization identify the policies best suited to its specific exposures. Agents or brokers with experience advising other nonprofits generally best serve nonprofit organizations.

The remainder of this chapter identifies and discusses the kinds of insurance policies of interest to a nonprofit organization, as well as the coverage exceptions that commonly appear in these policies. It also describes methods of risk management and explains where an organization's volunteer's liability begins and ends.

B. Risk Management

Q1. For a nonprofit organization, what is at risk?

A1. Risk is "a measure of the possibility that the future may be surprisingly different from what we expect."[1] A nonprofit organization bears the risk of losing its assets, either directly, to a natural disaster or another party's adverse action (e.g., arson or embezzlement), or indirectly, as property is seized to settle legal claims against the organization.

An organization can be subject to claims when the organization or its agent causes harm to an outside party or employee, fails to meet its contractual obligations, or fails to comply with regulatory or legal requirements. If the court finds in a claimant's favor, the nonprofit may be required to pay monetary damages or perform some act (e.g., return a donation or other property or restore a volunteer to his or her prior position) to remedy the alleged harm.

Thus, the tangible assets of an organization are at risk on many sides. If an organization owns its office building, for example, the building could be damaged by an earthquake or by an intentionally set fire, or it could be liquidated in order to settle a personal injury suit against the organization.

Another asset at risk is intangible. A nonprofit organization's reputation in the community allows it to attract contributions and volunteers and a good reputation is essential to its continuing success. Care needs

1 Melanie Lockwood Herman, *Ready…or Not: A Risk Management Guide for Nonprofit Executives* (Nonprofit Risk Mgmt. Ctr. 2nd ed., 2011)

to be taken to preserve this reputation, which is at risk from allegations of financial mismanagement, employee misconduct, etc.

An organization also creates risks for the people with whom it interacts, including those who work or volunteer for it (board members and employees) and those for whom it works (service recipients). Failure to maintain a safe work environment may cause employee injury, while failure to conduct thorough background screenings of employees and volunteers could expose service recipients to harm.

Q2. What policies and procedures should a nonprofit organization put in place to manage its risk?

A2. Though specific procedures will vary from organization to organization, the task of identifying, minimizing and protecting against potential harms generally requires ongoing review of activities that could harm the organization or result in legal claims against the organization. The board of directors is ultimately responsible for managing the risks of a nonprofit. However, in many organizations, the day-to-day task of risk identification and strategy design is delegated to a risk management committee, the professional management staff of the organization, or may fall under the purview of a board committee.

After selecting the priority risks on which it seeks to focus, the risk management committee or board should consider how to treat those risks. In some cases avoiding an exposure altogether may be warranted. In most cases, however, making modifications to the program, activity or operation offers the most appropriate response. For example, a wilderness preservation organization that leads nature hikes over uneven ground could reduce the risk of client injury by grading hills and installing guardrails. Alternatively, the organization could insure itself against personal injury lawsuits (shifting the financial component of the risk to the insurance company) or require hikers to sign a waiver before permitting their participation (requiring the clients of the nonprofit to bear responsibility for the risk of harm).

Insurance is often an appropriate part of an overall risk management program, however, nonprofits often find they cannot afford all of the coverage their insurable exposures call for. Insurance also can help provide peace of mind for nonprofit managers and board members.

Q3. What types of insurance should a nonprofit organization consider?

A3. A nonprofit organization can purchase a variety of different insurance policies to address its insurable exposures.

- **General liability.** Insurance addresses third-party claims alleging bodily injury or property damage.
- **Workers' compensation.** Insurance covers injuries to employees.
- **Directors and officers (D&O).** Insurance for nonprofit organizations covers the errors and omissions of the organization and its board of directors, staff and other volunteers. An example of this is MCN's cost saving partner Monitor Liability Managers D&O policy.
- **Professional liability.** Insurance covers against allegations of errors or omissions in the delivery of professional services, such as educational services, social services, legal services and more.
- **Property.** Insurance compensates an organization for the damage or destruction of buildings and personal property.
- **Automobile.** Insurance compensates for damage and injuries resulting from motor vehicle accidents.

- **Special event** insurance can compensate for accidents or injuries arising at special events.

There are many other policies available to nonprofit organizations and the above summary is a starting point.

Some insurance protections are legally required such as workers compensation insurance if a nonprofit has employees or automobile insurance if a nonprofit owns vehicles. Insurance may also be required by contracts with landlords, funding sources, lessors of equipment, or others. Other forms of insurance such as directors' and officers' liability may not be legally required and may be provided at an organization's discretion.

Q4. What should a nonprofit organization do to avoid a lawsuit?

A4. There is no single list of steps or strategies that will guard against legal claims and there is nothing a nonprofit can do to completely insulate the organization from legal claims. One step an organization can take to avoid lawsuits is to develop an internal procedure for dealing with employee complaints. Employment disputes are a major source of litigation for nonprofit organizations, and having an internal procedure to deal with these disputes can help prevent them from escalating into legal action. Though resolution procedures can take many forms (including an internal grievance procedure, binding and non-binding arbitration, referral to an ombudsman, an open door policy, etc.), effective resolution generally requires a full hearing of each employee complaint by an impartial party and a prompt, positive response by the management without retaliation.

Q5. When can a nonprofit organization legally deny providing services to a particular individual or organization?

A5. Generally, a nonprofit organization can legally deny services to individuals or organizations. Nonprofits that may face scarce resources or limited capacity are not required to assist all those who request services or admission to programs. Unlike government agencies and departments, nonprofits may not be faced with strict "denial of services" rules. However, if an organization receives government grants to administer public services, it should review the accompanying contract for legal restrictions and anti-discrimination clauses with which it must comply as a condition of funding. Additionally, under the Minnesota Human Rights Act, it is:

> "An unfair discriminatory practice for a person engaged in a trade or business or in the provision of a service...to intentionally refuse to do business with, to refuse to contract with, or to discriminate in the basic terms, conditions, or performance of the contract because of a person's race, national origin, color, sex, sexual orientation, or disability, unless the alleged refusal or discrimination is because of a legitimate business purpose."[2]

> A "business" is defined, among other entities as any corporation or association and would include organizations incorporated under Minnesota Statute chapter 317A as nonprofit corporations.[3] In light of the Minnesota Human Rights Act, nonprofits should consider establishing policies and procedures to determine eligibility for services, document eligibility administration and perhaps even document nondiscriminatory reasons for denials of services.

2 Minn. Stat. § 363A.17(3) (2016).
3 Minn. Stat. § 363A.03, subd. 4 (2016).

Q6. What laws and types of insurance protect a nonprofit organization's board members in the case of a lawsuit?

A6. The personal obligations of a board of directors differ from the corporate obligations of their nonprofit organization. While the organization itself has a duty to pay its debts and fulfill its obligations (contractual or otherwise), board members are responsible for the fiduciary duties of their office (the duties of care, loyalty and obedience). See Chapter 6: Board of Directors, Section C: Board Duties and Responsibilities for more information. Thus, board members can be sued for breaching these duties. For example a director can be sued for a violation of the duty of care if he/she is negligent in carrying out his/her management duties as a board member.[4] A director may be in violation of the duty of loyalty for the violation of a conflict of interest policy, for intentionally not acting in the organization's best interest, or for improper material benefit (private inurement).[5] Failure to abide by the organization's founding documents and donor-imposed spending restrictions on restricted funds may be a violation of the duty of obedience to the organization, and criminal activity is probably a violation of the duty of obedience to the law.[6] Lawsuits arising under other causes of action should be brought against the organization itself rather than its board members.

Additionally, the Volunteer Protection Act of 1997 ("VPA")[7] may offer board members a defense to claims against them, while directors and officers ("D&O") insurance may provide indemnity for claims arising from a board member's service to a nonprofit. More information on the fiduciary duties of a nonprofit's board of directors can be found in Chapter 6: Boards of Directors and Chapter 8: Financial Accountability. For more information about D&O insurance and the VPA, see Questions 18 and 36.

Q7. What services should a nonprofit organization expect from its insurance professional (agent or broker)?

A7. At a minimum, an agent or broker should take time to familiarize himself or herself with the organization and its exposures. A nonprofit daycare organization, for example, will have different risks and insurance needs than a nonprofit anti-pollution organization that handles hazardous waste. Insurance agents are professionals licensed by the state of Minnesota. They are required to pass a licensure exam and can be subject to lawsuits alleging errors and omissions in the delivery of professional services.

Once an insurance agent has assessed an organization's insurance needs, he or she will market the organization's account with one or more insurance companies. An insurance agent is legally an agent of the insurance companies from whom he or she has received appointments, while an insurance broker is an agent of the insured (the nonprofit organization). It is considered best practice for brokers to disclose their fees/payments as part of the premiums that a nonprofit may pay. An underwriter is a professional who works at an insurance company and determines whether the company will offer coverage, and if so, at what terms and conditions and price.

Should a nonprofit face a claim, it should promptly report the claim and work closely with its insurance agent or broker throughout the process, particularly if questions arise about the applicability of the policy to the claim.

4 Office of the Minnesota Attorney General, *Fiduciary Duties of Directors of Charitable Organizations*, 3 (2009) www.ag.state.mn.us/Brochures/pubFiduciaryDutiesofDirectors.pdf.

5 *Id.* at 5.

6 *Id.* at 7.

7 The Volunteer Protection Act, 42 U.S.C. §§ 14501-14505 (1997).

Additionally, many insurance agents also offer risk management assistance as an inducement for organizations to retain them. This assistance generally includes loss control services (e.g., help determining the frequency and severity of accidents and the best way to manage them), though it may include other risk management services as well. One service sometimes offered by insurance agents marketing D&O policies is advice on minimizing employment-based lawsuits, for example.

Q8. What are the characteristics of a good insurance agent or broker?

A8. A good insurance agent is familiar with both the client (the nonprofit organization) and the specific insurance companies that serve organizations in the client's line of work (the nonprofit sector). Because policy renewal windows are often narrow, a good agent is well organized. A good agent is assertive in advocating client interests and responsive to client needs.

C. Common Coverage Exceptions

Q9. How standard are insurance policies?

A9. State governments regulate insurance.[8] The specific terms and conditions of an insurance policy can vary depending on the state, the insurance company and the nonprofit organization. Generally, each kind of policy will have a standard range of coverage subject to exclusions that can differ among insurers. For example, a general liability policy will typically cover an organization against claims alleging bodily injury or property damage and may contain a molestation and abuse exclusion, which would exclude allegations of molestation or abuse. For more information on the abuse exclusion, see Question 12.

Q10. What is the intentional misconduct exclusion? When does it commonly apply?

A10. Under directors & officers liability insurance, the intentional misconduct exclusion excludes from coverage claims based upon intentionally dishonest or fraudulent acts or willful violations of laws by an agent of the insured organization.[9] An example of such a violation includes a situation where a director intentionally embezzles funds from an organization in violation of the law.[10] Typically, this exclusion applies to loss other than defense costs, and the exclusion does not apply unless a court establishes that the intentional misconduct was actually committed.

General professional and automobile liability policies have similar exclusions barring coverage for intentionally caused harm.

Q11. What distinction can an insurer make between reimbursement and direct cost recovery?

A11. Some liability insurance policies will directly cover an organization's legal costs (cover each cost as it is incurred), while other policies will only reimburse an organization for incurred expenses after legal action has ceased. A reimbursement policy may require that an insured organization pay all legal costs on its

8 Minn.Stat. ch. 59A-79A (2016).

9 *B.M.B. v. State Farm Fire & Cas. Co.*, 664 N.W.2d 817, 819 (Minn. 2003).

10 For more information see, Stephen M. Foxman, "Directors and Officers Liability Insurance for Nonprofits: Is Your Client Adequately Protected?" (July/Aug. 2009), www.abanet.org/buslaw/blt/2009-07-08/foxman.shtml.

own for the duration of the legal action (some drag on for years), and the policy may not provide reimbursement until after the matter has ended. Thus, an insured organization whose liability insurance policy contains a reimbursement clause may have to mount its legal defense to lawsuits as if it were not insured. If purchasing this type of reimbursement policy, an organization should ensure that it has sufficient cash reserves to mount an effective legal defense for the duration of potential lawsuits. The upside of insurance policies with reimbursement clauses is that they tend to cost less in premiums than those with direct recovery clauses.

Q12. What is the molestation and abuse exclusion? When does it apply?

A12. The molestation and abuse exclusion excludes from liability coverage any allegations of molestation or abuse by an agent of the insured organization (e.g., an employee, volunteer, contractor, etc.). It is commonly found in general liability policies. Whereas the intentional misconduct exclusion applies only when a court determines that intentional misconduct was committed, the molestation and abuse exception generally applies to mere allegations of molestation and abuse. While allegations of molestation and abuse are excluded from most general liability policies, this type of coverage may be purchased separately or may be added to a policy.

Q13. What is the insured vs. insured exclusion? When does it apply?

A13. The "insured vs. insured exclusion" excludes from coverage of claims against an organization, director or officer brought by another member from the same organization, such as a manager, director or employee. This type of coverage denial is most likely in situations where one insured party sues another insured party both of whom are insured under the same policy. This situation commonly occurs with professional liability and directors' and officers' liability policies.[11]

D. General Liability Insurance

Q14. What does commercial general liability insurance typically cover?

A14. Commercial general liability insurance typically protects an organization against claims alleging bodily injury, property damage, personal injury (injury to a person's reputation, e.g., through false arrest, malicious prosecution, libel or slander), or advertising injury (e.g., the use of another's advertising idea in your advertisement). Common commercial general liability policy exclusions include workers' compensation, intellectual property and pollution. In addition, commercial general liability insurance will not reimburse an organization for damage done to its own property; such damage would typically be covered by a property insurance policy.

11 Stephen M. Foxman, "Directors and Officers Liability Insurance for Nonprofits: Is Your Client Adequately Protected?" (July/Aug. 2009) www.abanet.org/buslaw/blt/2009-07-08/foxman.shtml (To get around the insured vs. insured exclusion, "insureds may negotiate endorsement carve-backs to provide coverage for derivative claims, employee practices claims, and claims by a bankruptcy trustee, or a receiver or liquidator.").

Q15. Are volunteer workers insured under a commercial general liability policy?

A15. Most general liability policies extend insured status to volunteer workers. An organization should examine the specific terms of a prospective commercial general liability policy, most likely the "Who is an Insured" section, to confirm it extends insured status to volunteer workers. Keep in mind that if volunteer workers are insured under your commercial general liability policy, typically they are only insured while performing duties related to the conduct of the nonprofit organization's business. In addition, volunteer workers may themselves have some liability protection under their homeowners or renters insurance.

Q16. Should a nonprofit organization purchase commercial general liability insurance?

A16. Each nonprofit organization should consider purchasing commercial general liability insurance. Lawsuits against an organization can be devastating and even put it out of business. The financial drain from paying thousands of dollars in legal defense fees to paying an out of court settlement or a court awarded judgment for damages can have a lasting negative impact on the organization. Insurance coverage is extremely important to help offset this financial impact to the organization. Keep in mind that even the most scrupulous organization cannot guarantee it will never be sued. It is likely prudent to pay a comparatively small annual premium for liability insurance rather than risk being bankrupted by a lawsuit.

Q17. Does commercial general liability insurance cover data security breaches?

A17. Increasingly organizations electronically store donor information and other confidential data, and also increasingly organizations are exposed to the risk associated with the breach of that secure data. Coverage for data security breaches *may* be available under a nonprofit's commercial general liability policy. Some organizations purchase a separate liability policy designed to specifically cover this exposure.[12] These policies are often known as "cyber risk" or "privacy and security liability" policies.

E. Directors and Officers Liability (D&O) Insurance

Q18. What does directors and officers (D&O) liability insurance typically cover?

A18. A D&O insurance policy generally protects the organization and its officers, directors, staff and other volunteers from claims for wrongful acts or acts in violation of fiduciary duties. Common claims may include employment-related issues such as discrimination, harassment and wrongful termination, failure to provide services, and the mismanagement of assets.

Q19. Should a nonprofit organization purchase D&O insurance?

A19. An organization's need for D&O insurance depends upon how often it expects to face lawsuits. Employment disputes are a primary source of the litigation an organization faces, so an organization with a large staff may wish to purchase a D&O insurance policy that includes coverage (within the base policy or by

12 John Iole, *Data Security, Third Party Privacy Claims, And Insurance Coverage Under CGL 'Personal And Advertising Injury' Coverage* (Feb. 2010), www.jonesday.com/data_security/ (last visited July 28, 2017).

endorsement) for claims based upon employment-related wrongful acts. Breach of fiduciary duty (duty of care, duty of loyalty or duty of obedience) can also be a source of litigation, so operations with large operating budgets may also wish to purchase this insurance. Finally, D&O insurance can help an organization recruit a skilled board of directors, see Chapter 6: Board of Directors, Section C: Board of Directors Responsibilities. Ultimately, however, each organization needs to assess its own situation to decide whether or not D&O insurance is appropriate.

Q20. How does D&O insurance protect a nonprofit organization from legal costs?

A20. Often the greatest expense to an organization from D&O claims is the cost of its directors' and officers' legal defense. A D&O insurance policy can either protect an organization from legal costs by covering each cost as it is incurred or by reimbursing the organization for the total cost after a lawsuit is completed, whether won, lost or settled.

Q21. Are there differences between particular board members regarding their fiduciary duties and the liability they may incur if they do not fulfill these duties?

A21. Generally, each board member has the same fiduciary duties and the same liability exposure for breaching these duties. From a practical standpoint, however, it is worth mentioning that an organization's president or chair and treasurer are more likely to be named as defendants in a lawsuit than other members of the board. The chair is an attractive legal target by virtue of his or her status as the presiding officer of an organization, as is the treasurer by virtue of his or her oversight of the organization's finances.

F. Professional Liability Insurance

Q22. What does professional liability insurance typically cover?

A22. Professional liability insurance typically covers injury or damage that arises out of the rendering of or failure to render professional services, including the services of a doctor, lawyer, psychologist, social worker, accountant, architect, surveyor or engineer, to name a few. It is important to note that coverage for liability that arises out of professional services is typically excluded from commercial general liability policies.

Q23. Should a nonprofit organization purchase professional liability insurance?

A23. A nonprofit organization should consider purchasing professional liability insurance if it provides professional services, because the injury or damage that can arise out of the providing of such professional services can be very significant. For example, a nonprofit hospital or dental clinic that provides medical services is liable to its patients for errors that cause bodily injury. Medical malpractice claims can have a devastating financial impact on an organization. Nonprofit organizations would be well-served in purchasing professional liability insurance for professional services provided by its doctors, dentists and other medical professionals, as well as for the other professional services it offers.

G. Automobile Insurance

Q24. Does a nonprofit organization need to have automobile insurance?

A24. A nonprofit organization that owns vehicles is required by law to purchase insurance or self-insure those vehicles for the minimum state required limits of liability. Even if an organization were not required to have insurance, it would be a good idea to do so because the organization may be exposed to liability for the use of a non-owned vehicle (such as an employee transporting volunteers in the employee's personal vehicle). Motor vehicle accidents can expose an organization to liability for a number of costs, including vehicle damage, expensive hospital costs and personal injury claims, among others. Because there is no way for an organization to accurately predict when these costs will occur and how much they will be, automobile liability insurance is a good investment for an organization to make.

Q25. Should a nonprofit organization purchase insurance to cover the exposure created by employees who use their own cars for employment-related travel?

A25. If an organization has employees who use their own cars for employment-related travel, it should consider obtaining automobile insurance to cover its potential liability for that risk (often known as a "non-owned" automobile policy). An employee's insurance will generally be the first to respond to an accident involving his or her vehicle. There is no guarantee, however, that his or her insurance will be sufficient to cover claims arising from the accident. The amount of the claims, for example, may exceed the amount of the employee's personal coverage, potentially rendering the organization liable for the remainder, or the claim may be of a nature that the employee's own policy does not cover.

Q26. What can a nonprofit organization require of their employees or volunteers who are driving for purposes related to their duties to the organization?

A26. An organization can require employees or volunteers who are driving for the organization to possess a valid driver's license. It can require them to obey traffic laws (e.g., speed limits) and to stay on certain routes while engaging in employment-related travel. In this way, an organization may decrease its chances of being liable for driving-related injuries.

Q27. Can a nonprofit organization check the driving record of employees or volunteers who need to drive for purposes related to their duties to the organization?

A27. A nonprofit organization can check a driving record with the employee's or volunteer's written consent. The federal Fair Credit Reporting Act (FCRA)[13] requires an employer to take specific actions when requesting certain records, including driving records. For more information about the FCRA, consult "Using Consumer Reports, What Employers Have to Know," a publication of the Federal Trade Commission's Bureau of Consumer Protection, which is available at www.ftc.gov/tips-advice/business-center/guidance/using-consumer-reports-what-employers-need-know.

13 The Fair Credit Reporting Act, 15 U.S.C. § 1681 (1970).

H. Insurance for Special Events

Q28. Should a nonprofit organization purchase insurance for its special events?

A28. General liability policies often automatically cover most special events. An organization should consult with its insurance agent to determine to what extent its existing insurance policies provide coverage for a particular event.

Q29. How can a nonprofit organization reduce the risk of being found legally responsible for an injury or loss during a special event?

A29. An organization can reduce its liability risk for injury or loss by drafting and implementing a comprehensive safety plan. Implementing the safety plan will reduce the risk of injury or loss, while documenting the safety plan can provide evidence in court that the organization did not negligently create a risk of injury and thus should not be found liable for it. Checklists of potential risks are available to aid this process.

Q30. Who is held liable for an incident that happens during a co-sponsored event?

A30. When two or more parties jointly sponsor an event, they should prepare a written agreement detailing their respective responsibilities. One of those responsibilities is responsibility for harm that results from the activity.

A court could find both parties jointly liable (each liable for the full amount of the injury), both parties severally liable (each liable for a fractional share of the injury, which could be equal, e.g. 50%-50%, or unequal, e.g. 70%-30%), both parties jointly and severally liable, or one party individually liable and the other not liable, depending on the facts of the situation. If one organization made all decisions relating to catering, for example, and an event attendee sues for food poisoning, that organization may be found individually liable. Alternately, if representatives from both parties made a joint decision relating to tent rental and a defective tent causes an injury, both parties might be found liable for fractional shares of the injury. Litigation is complex, expensive and uncertain. Some of the uncertainty can be averted by means of a prior written agreement.

I. Property Insurance

Q31. What does property insurance typically cover?

A31. Property insurance covers damage to an organization's property, both real property (land and buildings) and personal property (office furnishings, equipment, etc.).

Q32. Should a nonprofit organization purchase property insurance?

A32. Each organization should evaluate its exposure to loss and ability to afford coverage when deciding whether or not to purchase property insurance. When deciding whether or not to acquire property insurance, an organization may wish to compare the annual cost of property insurance with the potential cost for replacing stolen or damaged property in the event of a large loss. If the organization can financially survive a large loss it may feel less of a need to acquire property insurance.

An organization that rents office space would also be advised to read the terms of its property lease. Some landlords require their tenants to acquire property insurance as part of their rental agreements.

J. Workers' Compensation Insurance

Q33. What does workers' compensation insurance cover?

A33. Workers' compensation insurance provides coverage for medical claims that result from illnesses or injuries caused or aggravated by work or the workplace. Workers' compensation insurance also provides employees with wage loss benefits for a portion of their income loss. It also provides payment for reasonable and necessary medical and rehabilitative expenses, as well as death benefits for surviving spouses and dependents if employees die on the job.

Workers' compensation medical benefits can be extended to volunteers, however, most nonprofits find it cost prohibitive to include volunteers in their workers' compensation coverage. Volunteers are not eligible for wage loss benefits.

Q34. Are nonprofit organizations required to purchase workers' compensation insurance?

A34. Minnesota employers are legally required to purchase workers' compensation insurance or become self-insured. For more information on the statutory minimum requirements for workers' compensation coverage, consult the Minnesota Department of Labor and Industry (www.dli.mn.gov/main.asp) and Minnesota Statutes Chapter 176, the Workers' Compensation Act.[14]

K. Volunteer Liability and Immunity

Q35. What can a nonprofit organization do to reduce its risk of liability due to the actions of its volunteers?

A35. There are a number of steps a nonprofit can take to reduce its exposure to liability. The specific steps that are appropriate in a given instance depend upon the nature of the nonprofit and the work that volunteers will perform for the organization. For example, nonprofits that engage volunteers as "mentors" who will work one-on-one with children should institute a number of measures to ensure that anyone selected to be a mentor is suitable for the role and does not have a background that poses an undue risk to the nonprofit's clients. A nonprofit that deploys volunteers on a crisis hotline should make certain that volunteers

14 Minn. Stat. ch. 176 (2016).

have appropriate training before they are permitted to answer calls from clients in crisis.

A Minnesota nonprofit can conduct background checks through a variety of sources. An organization can request a copy of an individual's record of state criminal convictions from the Minnesota Bureau of Criminal Apprehension (BCA).

To receive a written record of state convictions, an organization should mail a notarized informed consent signed by the subject of the record, including the individual's full name, other names used and date of birth, along with a stamped, self-addressed envelope and a check for $15.00 to the BCA at: Minnesota Bureau of Criminal Apprehension, Attn. MNJIS Criminal History Access Unit, 1430 Maryland Ave. E., St. Paul, MN 55106. The fee for charitable nonprofits, with appropriate documentation, is $8.00 when proof of status is provided in the form of a 501(c)(3). A sample informed consent form can be found at the BCA Forms website, dps.mn.gov/divisions/bca/pages/background-checks.aspx.

Alternately, the organization can go to the office of the Bureau of Criminal Apprehension (at the same address) and view criminal records on file there. An organization can also view an individual's public criminal history record via the internet, at www.cch.state.mn.us.

To receive an individual's federal criminal record from the FBI, an organization should relay a request through the Minnesota Bureau of Criminal Apprehension, taking care to include with this request the individual's written consent, a copy of his or her fingerprints, and a check for $25 (of which $7 goes to the BCA and $18 goes to the FBI).

Alternately, the organization can use an online background checking service to obtain an individual's federal and state criminal record. Prices for this service vary by company.

Q36. Can volunteers be sued?

A36. No laws preclude lawsuits against volunteers. However, Congress passed the Volunteer Protection Act of 1997 (VPA)[15] to limit the liability of volunteers while acting within the scope of their responsibilities for nonprofit organizations. Similar laws exist in all states. For more information on the various conditions, requirements and exceptions to the laws, see *State Liability Laws for Charitable Organizations and Volunteers*, published by the Nonprofit Risk Management Center and available for download at www.nonprofitrisk.org. The VPA does not apply when a volunteer causes the claimant harm in the operation of a motor vehicle or while under the influence of alcohol, or when the volunteer's misconduct constitutes a crime, sexual offense or civil rights violation.

Q37. Can a nonprofit organization insure its volunteers?

A. 37 Volunteers are usually automatically included as insureds under general liability and automobile liability policies. A nonprofit should check with its insurance agent to verify that its liability policies provide coverage for volunteers. Claims against the volunteers may also be covered under the volunteers renters' or homeowners' insurance policies, if they have them. Individual volunteers should check their policies to determine whether or not they are covered.

15 The Volunteer Protection Act, 42 U.S.C. §§ 14501-14505 (1997).

A nonprofit should also consider whether it will provide coverage (e.g., through a volunteer accident policy) for accidental injuries a volunteer suffers while serving the organization. Some organizations take the position that volunteers should be solely responsible for any injuries they suffer while serving the nonprofit and require volunteers to execute waivers to that effect. Others look for cost effective ways to provide a safety net in the event a volunteer does not have personal medical coverage that will cover the cost of injuries suffered while volunteering.

Q38. Is a nonprofit organization required to provide training to its volunteers if they are working with vulnerable adults and children?

A38. Unfortunately, several cases of abuse by volunteers have occurred in organizations that serve children and vulnerable adults. Though an organization is not legally required to train its volunteers who work with vulnerable persons, it is sound risk management to do so. The common sense of well-intentioned volunteers is rarely adequate to prevent claims and losses stemming from volunteer service. A record of training provided to volunteers who work with vulnerable clients could also help an organization defend allegations of inappropriate conduct and may enable a nonprofit to demonstrate that the organization met the required standard of care.

Q39. Can an organization be liable for injuries caused by a volunteer who uses his or her own vehicle while performing duties for the organization? If so, should the organization obtain insurance to cover this liability?

A39. An organization may be liable for injuries caused by a volunteer while acting within in the scope of their duties for the organization. The volunteer's liability insurance will generally be the first to respond in cases of accident or injury. If the amount of the claim, however, is greater than the amount of the volunteer's coverage, or the claim is of a nature not covered by the volunteer's policy, the organization could potentially be liable for the portion of the claim not covered by the volunteer's insurance. For this reason, an organization should consider purchasing non-owned auto liability insurance to cover the exposure created by volunteers using their vehicles for organization business. See Section G: Automobile Insurance.

L. Related Resources

Publications:

Enlightened Risk Taking: A Guide to Strategic Risk Management for Nonprofits, Nonprofit Risk Management Center, www.nonprofitrisk.org/products/enlightened-risk-taking-a-guide-to-strategic-risk-management-for-nonprofits.

Financial Risk Management: A Guide for Nonprofit Executives, Nonprofit Risk Management Center, www.nonprofitrisk.org/products/financial-risk-management-a-guide-for-nonprofit-executives.

Managing Special Event Risks: Ten Steps to Safety – 2nd Edition, Nonprofit Risk Management Center, www.nonprofitrisk.org/products/managing-special-event-risks-ten-steps-to-safety-2nd-edition.

Managing Facility Risks, 10 Steps to Safety, Nonprofit Risk Management Center, Nonprofit Risk Management Center, www.nonprofitrisk.org/products/managing-facility-risks-10-steps-to-safety.

No Surprises: Harmonizing Risk and Reward in Volunteer Management, Nonprofit Risk Management Center, www.nonprofitrisk.org/products/no-surprises-harmonizing-risk-and-reward-in-volunteer-management.

Pillars of Accountability: A Risk Management Guide for Nonprofit Boards, Nonprofit Risk Management Center, www.nonprofitrisk.org/products/pillars-of-accountability-a-risk-management-guide-for-nonprofit-boards.

Ready in Defense: A Liability, Litigation and Legal Guide for Nonprofits, Melanie L. Herman, Nonprofit Risk Management Center (2003).

Organizations:

Nonprofits' Insurance Alliance Group
www.niac.org
This insurance company is a source for many helpful insurance and liability booklets. They deal with, among other things, volunteers, special events, collaboration and vehicle safety.

Nonprofit Risk Management Center
www.nonprofitrisk.org
The Nonprofit Risk Management Center is a nonprofit organization that advises other nonprofits on a wide range of risk management and insurance matters. The Center's website contains numerous free resources as well as access to affordable online tools, books and educational resources.

CHAPTER 11

DISCLOSURE AND PRIVACY REQUIREMENTS

Topics

A. Overview

The Internal Revenue Service (IRS) and the State of Minnesota require nonprofit organizations to publicly disclose a variety of information. Congress and the state Legislature enacted specific public disclosure requirements to increase the accountability of organizations that are exempt from corporate income tax liability. These requirements include submitting reports to the Office of the Minnesota Attorney General, allowing for public inspection or copying of certain IRS Forms and supporting documents, and providing access to or a summary of other information to donors or members of the organization.

IRS Guidelines. To comply with guidelines of the IRS, a tax-exempt organization must allow the public to inspect required documents, including: its exemption application (IRS Form 1023/1023-EZ); annual information returns (Form 990s); and its election to use the 501(h) expenditure test to evaluate its lobbying activity (Form 5768). Also, annual information Form 990 returns must be available for inspection for three years from the date they are required to be filed (including any extensions) or from the date they are actually filed, whichever is later. Amended returns must be available for three years from the date they are actually filed with the Internal Revenue Service.

A nonprofit organization has a separate obligation to provide hard/paper copies of these same documents upon request from members of the public. An organization may charge a fee for copies up to the current per-page rate designated by the Freedom of Information Act, as well as the actual cost of postage. A nonprofit organization is not required to comply with a request for copies of a required document if the organization has made the requested document widely available (such as by posting it on the internet) and has met a specific set of requirements regarding reproduction and accessibility, explained further in Question 1. Even if required documents are widely available the nonprofit organization must have the document available for public inspection. Most Form 990's of public charities and private foundations are available online at www.guidestar.org.

Although nonprofits must provide the IRS with detailed donor information for all types of contributions made totaling $5,000 or more for the year, this information may be omitted from the copy of the Form 990 that the public may inspect.[1]

Minnesota Guidelines. The Minnesota Charitable Solicitation Act requires nonprofit organizations that receive or expect to receive total charitable contributions in excess of $25,000 to register with the Office of the Minnesota Attorney General and file annual reports with that office.[2] The information required on the registration and reporting forms becomes part of the public record. The summary is accessible to the public on the website of the Office of the Minnesota Attorney General at www.ag.state.mn.us/.

As part of the requirement to file annual reports under the Minnesota Charitable Solicitation Act, organizations must retain detailed books and records to substantiate the information submitted in their annual reports. These records must be open to inspection by the Attorney General at all reasonable times, and should be retained for a period of three years from the date the corresponding report was filed.

In Minnesota, nonprofits must allow members or directors to inspect certain documents, including the organization's Articles of Incorporation and Bylaws, financial statements, and minutes of meetings for the last seven years. An organization must, prior to a meeting of members with voting rights, make a complete list of members with voting rights available to all members with voting rights.

1 *See* I.R.S., *Schedule B (Form 990, 990-EZ, or 990-PF), Schedule of Contributors* (2016), www.irs.gov/pub/irs-pdf/f990ezb.pdf.

2 *A Guide to Minnesota's Charities Laws*, Minnesota Attorney General, www.ag.state.mn.us/consumer/publications/GuideCharityLaws.asp (last visited Aug. 1, 2017).

Prior to soliciting any contribution, organizations should be prepared to provide prospective donors with certain information, including:

- The name and location (city and state) of the organization.
- The tax deductibility of the contribution.
- A description of the charitable program to which the requested donation will be applied. If the donation is solicited for the organization's general use and not for a specific program, a description of the programs and activities of the organization is required.

If the organization plans to sell or exchange donor information, the Minnesota Charitable Solicitation Act requires the express consent of the donor prior to the exchange. If the organization plans to publish a list of donors in a periodic report to its members, it is good practice to give donors an opportunity to opt out of such a list at the time of the solicitation, although donor consent is not required.

For contributions greater than $75 where the donor receives something of value in exchange for their contribution (quid pro quo), the IRS requires the organization to issue a disclosure statement to the donor.[3] The statement must (1) inform the donor that the amount of the contribution that is tax deductible is limited to that portion of the donation that exceeds the fair market value of the goods or services provided by the charity; and (2) provide the donor with a good faith estimate of the fair market value of the goods or services that the donor received.[4] For example, if a donor makes a $100 contribution and receives two tickets to the opera valued at $60 from the organization, the organization would in a disclosure statement indicate that $40 of the gift is tax deductible and that the fair market value of the tickets is $60.[5] For more information, see Chapter 5: Charitable Donation Regulations, Section C: Donor Substantiation Requirements.

In addition, the IRS will not allow a donor to deduct a charitable contribution of $250 or more unless the donor has a written acknowledgment from the organization to which the contribution was made.[6] The donor is responsible for requesting and obtaining the written acknowledgment, but it is good practice for a nonprofit organization to have regular procedures in place to issue these written acknowledgments as donations are received.

B. Public Inspection Requirements for IRS Filings

Q1. Is a nonprofit organization required to provide a paper copy of its Form 990 to the public or can Form 990 simply be made available for inspection?

A1. A nonprofit organization must allow the public to inspect required documents, including its Form 990. In addition, an organization must provide a paper copy of required documents upon request or make the document widely available.

Widely Available. Over the last several years in the electronic and digital age, many nonprofits have started to make founding documents, financial statements and Form 990s available online, mostly through

---

3 *I.R.S., Charitable Contributions - Quid Pro Quo Contributions*, www.irs.gov/charities-non-profits/charitable-organizations/charitable-contributions-quid-pro-quo-contributions (last updated Apr. 13, 2017).

4 *Id.*

5 *Id.*

6 *I.R.S., Substantiating Charitable Contributions*, www.irs.gov/charities-non-profits/substantiating-charitable-contributions (last updated Jan. 31, 2017).

organizational websites. Guidestar.org also allows users to search for a particular organization and view its Form 990. Organizations can opt to upload additional documents and organizational information to the Guidestar website at www.guidestar.org. An organization may make its application for federal tax-exempt status (Form 1023 or Form 1023-EZ) and annual information return (Form 990) widely available by posting the documents to an internet page.[7] The document is then considered "widely available" if it is an exact copy or reproduction of the image as it was originally filed with the IRS.[8]

If a nonprofit organization has made its required documents widely available, it must notify any individual requesting a copy where the documents are available, including the web address. Notification must be made immediately if the request for copies is made in person, or within seven days of receiving the request if it is submitted in writing. See Question 9 for more information about the requirements for wide availability.

Public Inspection. While it may seem that the old rules related to hard copy access are obsolete, they are still legally recognized. If an organization does not post Form 990s or its Form 1023 online, a nonprofit organization must allow the public to view its annual information return and its exemption application during regular business hours at its principal, regional and district offices at no charge.[9] The organization may have an employee present in the room during an inspection, but it must allow the individual conducting the inspection to take notes and, if the individual provides their own photocopying equipment at the inspection site, the organization must allow the individual to photocopy the document at no charge.[10]

A site is considered a regional or district office if (1) the site's paid employees work more than 120 hours a week in aggregate, or (2) the site serves as an office for management staff, other than those involved solely in managing the exempt function activities on site.[11] For example, an organization headquartered in St. Paul may also operate in Greater Minnesota, and have one paid employee located in Duluth. That site would be considered a regional office **only if** that one paid employee worked more than 120 hours a week or the organization employed three full-time employees working a total of 120 hours per week. In contrast, if the organization has one or more paid employees who share an office with other nonprofit organizations in Duluth, where the employees do not work more than 120 hours a week and are not management staff, then the site would probably not be considered a regional or district office.

Requests for copies made in person at an organization's principal, regional or district office during regular business hours should be provided on the day the request is made, unless unusual circumstances exist and such a request places an unreasonable burden on the organization. Unusual circumstances include a large number of requests that exceed the organization's daily capacity to make copies; requests received shortly before the end of regular business hours that require an extensive amount of copying; or requests received on a day when the organization's managerial staff capable of fulfilling the request is conducting special duties rather than their regular administrative duties.[12]

Requests for copies made in writing must be honored if they (1) are addressed to the exempt organization and delivered by mail, electronic mail, facsimile or a private delivery service to a principal, regional or district office of the organization, and (2) provide the address to which the copy of the document(s)

7 *See* I.R.S. Pub. 557, *Tax-Exempt Status for Your Organization*, 21 (2017), www.irs.gov/pub/irs-pdf/p557.pdf.
8 *See* I.R.C. § 301.6104(d)-2(b)(2)(B) (2000).
9 *See* I.R.S. Pub. 557, *Tax-Exempt Status for Your Organization*, 19 (2017), www.irs.gov/pub/irs-pdf/p557.pdf.
10 *Id.* at 18.
11 *Id.*
12 If unusual circumstances exist, the organization must provide the copies no later than the next business day following the final day the unusual circumstances exist, or the fifth business day after the date of the request, whichever occurs first. See I.R.C. § 301.6104(d)-1(d)(1)(ii) (2003).

should be sent.[13] Copies must be provided within 30 days from the date the request is received by the organization, or if the organization requires prepayment of copy and postage fees, within 30 days from the date it receives payment.[14]

Q2. Does a nonprofit organization have to provide its exemption application (IRS Form 1023 or IRS Form 1024) and tax-exempt letter to the public?

A2. Yes, along with its annual information return (Form 990), a nonprofit organization must make its exemption application available for public inspection. For purposes of public disclosure requirements, the exemption application includes the tax-exempt letter issued by the IRS. For a complete list of the documents that must be publicly disclosed as part of the exemption application, see Question 5.

An organization must provide copies of the application upon request. If the organization makes the exemption application widely available, it is not required to provide copies upon request. See Question 1 for more information on "wide availability" and "public inspection requirements."

Q3. My organization does not maintain a permanent business office. Do we still have to allow public inspection of our required documents?

A3. Organizations that do not maintain permanent offices must permit public inspection at a reasonable time of day within a reasonable time after receiving a request, normally not longer than two weeks, at a reasonable location of its choice.[15] This location may be a public library, local coffee shop or another nonprofit. Organizations without permanent offices have the option of mailing, within two weeks of receiving the request, a copy of requested documents in lieu of allowing an inspection. The organization may charge the requester for copying and postage only if the requester consents to the charges. An organization that maintains a permanent office but has no office hours or very limited office hours during certain times of the year must make its documents available for public inspection during those times of the year as though it were an organization without a permanent office.[16]

Q4. Can a nonprofit organization block out the name and social security number of the person filing the annual IRS Form 990 return on the copy it provides for public inspection?

A4. The public inspection copy of the IRS Form 990 must be an "exact copy of the return" and cannot omit any information submitted to the IRS, except that a nonprofit organization may omit the names and addresses of contributors listed in Schedule B.[17]

When filling out the IRS Form 990, no person from the filing organization needs to report their social security number. In the "Paid Preparer's Use Only" section, it indicates that the preparer report their "PTIN" or Preparer Tax Identification Number. This is the identification number for the paid organization or person filling out the form. If an accountancy or other firm prepares the form, the preparer will use the firm's Employer Identification Number (EIN). If it is an independent accountant without an organizational

13 *See* I.R.S. Pub. 557, *Tax-Exempt Status for Your Organization*, 18 (2017), www.irs.gov/pub/irs-pdf/p557.pdf.
14 *Id.*
15 *Id.*
16 *Id.* at 19.
17 *Id.*

EIN, they will use their personal social security number. An employee of the filing organization cannot be a paid preparer. See the instructions for the Form 990, at www.irs.gov/pub/irs-pdf/i990.pdf, page 10 and 11, Part II "Signature Block" for more information.

Q5. What documents must be included with the annual information return, IRS Form 990 when providing a copy or allowing for public inspection?

A5. For purposes of public disclosure requirements, the annual information return includes:

- An exact copy of any return filed by a tax-exempt organization;
- Any amended return the organization files with the Internal Revenue Service after the date the original return is filed; and
- All schedules, attachments and supporting documents.[18]

Tax-exempt organizations other than private foundations may omit the name and address of any contributor to the organization, listed on Schedule B of Form 990, when providing copies or allowing inspection of their annual information returns.

Q6. How long must a nonprofit's Form 990s be available?

A6. Annual information returns must be available for three years from the date they are required to be filed (including any extensions) or from the date they are actually filed, whichever is later. Amended returns must be available for three years from the date they are actually filed with the Internal Revenue Service.[19]

Q7. What documents must be included with the exemption application (IRS Form 1023) when providing a copy or allowing for public inspection?

A7. For purposes of public disclosure requirements, the application for exemption includes:

- Any prescribed application form, such as Form 1023 or 1024 (exemption applications filed prior to July 15, 1987, are exempt from these requirements);
- All documents and statements the Internal Revenue Service requires an applicant to file with the form;
- Any statement or other supporting document submitted by an organization in support of its application; and
- Any letter or other document issued by the Internal Revenue Service concerning the application.[20]

The application for exemption does NOT include:

- Any application filed by an organization that the Internal Revenue Service has not yet recognized as exempt from taxation;
- Any application for tax exemption (IRS Form 1023 or 1024) filed before July 15, 1987 if the organization did not have a copy of the application on July 15, 1987;

18 *See* I.R.S. Pub. 557, *Tax-Exempt Status for Your Organization*, 17 (2017), www.irs.gov/pub/irs-pdf/p557.pdf.
19 *Id.*
20 *Id.* at 18.

- The name and address of any contributor to the organization; or
- Any material required to be withheld, for example, trade secrets.[21]

Q8. Can a nonprofit charge for the related copying and postage costs when providing a copy of its Form 990 to a member of the public? How much can it charge?

A8. A nonprofit organization may charge a reasonable fee for providing copies to the public. The copying fee must not exceed the per page copying charge prescribed by the Freedom of Information Act (FOIA) fee schedule, except that nonprofits are not required to copy a minimum number of initial pages free of charge. The FOIA fee schedule is accessible online at www.irs.gov/pub/irs-utl/irs_foia_guide.pdf. As of August 2017, the copying charges price for commercial requesters is $.20 per page. For media requesters, the copying charges price is free for first 100 pages, $.20 per page thereafter. The nonprofit may also charge for the actual postage costs incurred by the organization to send the copies.[22]

Q9. What does it mean if an organization makes its documents "widely available?" What steps must an organization take to make its documents "widely available?"

A9. A nonprofit organization is not required to comply with a request for copies of its documents if the organization has made the requested document widely available. Making required documents widely available does not, however, exempt the nonprofit organization from the requirement to make hard copies of the document available for public inspection.[23] See Question 1 for more information.

A nonprofit can make its required documents widely available by posting them on an internet page that the tax-exempt organization establishes and maintains or by having the document posted as part of a database of similar documents or tax-exempt organizations on web page maintained by another entity, such as www.guidestar.org.

To be considered widely available, the following requirements must be met:

- The web page through which the document is available clearly informs readers that the document is available, and provides instructions for downloading it.
- The document is posted in a format that, when accessed, downloaded, viewed and printed, exactly reproduces the image of the original document, except for any information permitted to be withheld.
- Any individual with access to the internet can access, download, view and print the document without special computer hardware or software, other than software that is readily available to members of the public at no charge, and without payment of a fee to the nonprofit or to the entity maintaining the website.

The organization or entity maintaining the web page must have procedures for ensuring the accuracy and reliability of the document and must correct or replace the document if it is altered, destroyed or lost.[24]

If a nonprofit organization has made its required documents widely available, it must notify any

21 *See* I.R.S. Pub. 557, *Tax-Exempt Status for Your Organization*, 18 (2017), www.irs.gov/pub/irs-pdf/p557.pdf.
22 *Id.* See also I.R.C.§ 301.6104(d)-1(a) (2003).
23 *See* I.R.S. Pub. 557, *Tax-Exempt Status for Your Organization*, 17 (2017), www.irs.gov/pub/irs-pdf/p557.pdf.
24 *See* I.R.C. § 301.6104(d)-2(b)(2) (2000).

individual requesting a copy where the documents are available, including the web address. Notification must be made immediately if the request for copies is made in person, or within seven days of receiving the request if it is submitted in writing.[25]

Q10. If a nonprofit organization does put their Form 990 on the internet, does that it meet all public disclosure requirements?

A10. Posting the Form 990 on the internet does not fulfill all public disclosure requirements. If the organization posts their Form 990 on the internet and meets the requirements to make it "widely available" (see Question 9 for a definition of "widely available"), it is not required to provide copies of the Form 990 to the public on request. (See Question 9 for a list of the requirements that must be satisfied for a document to be considered widely available.) The nonprofit is still required to make hard copies of the Form 990 available for public inspection. The nonprofit must also provide hard copies of or make widely available its exemption application, and make the exemption application available for public inspection.[26]

Q11. My organization's Form 990 is available on the websites of other organizations (like guidestar.org). Does this meet the IRS's "widely available" requirement?

A11. IRS regulations state that an organization may make its documents widely available on a third-party's site, as long as the other requirements for wide availability are met (see Question 9 for "widely available" requirements). However, as of August 2017, the IRS has not recognized any third-party sites as in satisfaction of the "widely available" requirements. Organizations are advised to post their required documents on their own websites to ensure that they are considered widely available.[27]

Q12. What are the penalties for not disclosing an organization's IRS Form 990, Form 1023 or Form 1024, and tax-exempt letter to the public?

A12. The IRS will fine an organization that fails to meet public disclosure requirements. The IRS imposes a fine of $20 per day for each day an organization fails to allow public inspection of an annual return, with a maximum penalty of $10,000 for each return. Failure to allow public inspection of an exemption application is also fined at a rate of $20 per day, with no maximum penalty limit. Organizations that willfully fail to allow public inspection or provide copies of an annual return or exemption application are fined $5,000 for each return or application.

Q13. How can members of the public request 990 information from the IRS?

A13. IRS Form 4506-A, Request for Public Inspection or Copy of Exempt or Political Organization, can be used to request a copy of a 990 Form for a tax-exempt or political organizations. Form 4506-A can be found online at www.irs.gov/pub/irs-pdf/f4506a.pdf.

25 *See* I.R.S. Pub. 557, *Tax-Exempt Status for Your Organization,* 19 (2017), www.irs.gov/pub/irs-pdf/p557.pdf.
26 *See* I.R.S. Pub. 557, *Tax-Exempt Status for Your Organization*, 18 (2017), www.irs.gov/pub/irs-pdf/p557.pdf.
27 *See* I.R.S., *Instructions for Form 1023* (2006), www.irs.gov/pub/irs-pdf/i1023.pdf. *See also* I.R.S., *Instructions for Form 1023-EZ* (2017), www.irs.gov/pub/irs-pdf/i1023ez.pdf.

C. Sharing other Information with Members with Voting Rights, Donors and the General Public

Q14. What types of information must a nonprofit organization disclose to its members with voting rights?

A14. The Minnesota Nonprofit Corporations Act (Minnesota Statutes Chapter 317A) requires an organization to allow a member or director to inspect certain documents at its office for a proper purpose.[28]

Under that Act, a member of an organization is a person with membership rights as defined in the organization's Articles of Incorporation or Bylaws. Similarly, a director is any member of the board vested with the general management of the internal affairs of the corporation.

These documents include the organization's articles and Bylaws, accounting records, voting agreements, and minutes of meetings for the last six years.[29] Members and directors may also inspect an organization's financial statement showing the result of all operations and transactions affecting income and surplus during the last annual accounting period, as well as a balance sheet showing a summary of the organization's assets and liabilities.[30] (Note that financial records are statements and compilations, not a list of all transactions.)

Q15. What types of information must a nonprofit organization disclose to donors?

A15. In addition to the information that must be disclosed to the general public (see Section B: Public Inspection Requirements for IRS Filings), organizations must provide their contributors with certain additional information based upon IRS rules.

- The IRS will not allow a donor to deduct a charitable contribution of $250 or more unless the donor has a written acknowledgment from the organization to which the contribution was made.[31]
- The donor is responsible for requesting and obtaining the written acknowledgment from the donee, but it is good practice for a nonprofit organization to have regular procedures in place to issue these written acknowledgments as donations are received. For more information see Chapter 5: Charitable Donation Regulations, Section C: Donor Substantiation Requirements.
- For contributions greater than $75 where the donor receives something of value (*quid pro quo*), the IRS requires a nonprofit organization to issue a disclosure statement to the donor (1) informing the donor that the amount of the contribution that is tax deductible is limited to that portion of the donation that exceeds the fair market value of the goods or services provided by the charity, and (2) providing the donor with a good faith estimate of the fair market value of the goods or services that the donor received. Even if the deductible part of a payment is less than $75, a disclosure statement must be filed if the donor's total payment is more than $75. A nonprofit that fails to issue the required disclosure statement is assessed a penalty of $10 per contribution, up to a maximum of $5,000 per fund-raising event or mailing.[32]

28 Minn. Stat.§ 317A.461, subd. 2 (2016).
29 Minn. Stat §§ 317A.461, subd. 1, 3 (2016).
30 Minn. Stat § 317A.461 (2016).
31 *See* I.R.S. Pub. 1771, *Charitable Contributions - Substantiation and Disclosure Requirements* (2016), www.irs.gov/pub/irs-pdf/p1771.pdf.
32 *See* I.R.S. Pub. 557, *Tax-Exempt Status for Your Organization*, 15-16 (2017), www.irs.gov/pub/irs-pdf/p557.pdf.

Minnesota state law also requires that charitable organizations and professional fundraisers make the following disclosures prior to an oral request and together with a written request for a contribution:

- The name, city and state of the charitable organization;
- The tax deductibility of the contribution; and
- A description of the charitable program to which the solicited contribution would be applied and a description of the programs and activities of the organization generally.[33]

Q16. What types of information must a nonprofit organization disclose to the general public?

A16. In addition to its exemption application and annual information return that a nonprofit must make available for public inspection (see Question 1 for more information), the IRS also requires retention and public disclosure of Form 5768, Election/Revocation of Election by an Eligible Section 501(c)(3) Organization to Make Expenditures to Influence Legislation.[34] For more information about the effect of filing Form 5768, see Chapter 3: Tax Exemptions.

In Minnesota, the Minnesota Charitable Solicitation Act (Minnesota Statutes Chapter 309) requires organizations that receive or expect to receive charitable contributions in excess of $25,000 from Minnesota residents to register with the Office of the Minnesota Attorney General. [35] For information on registering with the Attorney General's Office, see Chapter 4: Charitable Solicitation Registration. The information provided on the registration becomes part of the public record and the Attorney General's Office maintains a searchable online database of the information. Some organizations are exempt from registration requirements, such as religious organizations that are exempt from filing IRS Form 990, certain educational institutions and organizations that limit their solicitations to their own members with voting rights. For a complete list of organizations exempt from registration, see A Guide to Minnesota's Charities Laws, published by the Office of the Minnesota Attorney General, available at www.ag.state.mn.us/Brochures/pubGuidetoCharitiesLaws.pdf.

Organizations required to register under the Minnesota Charitable Solicitation Act are also required to file annual reports with the Office of the Minnesota Attorney General. These annual reports include a financial statement covering the preceding 12-month period of operation and a copy of all withholding tax forms and information returns (990 and 990-EZ), including all schedules and amendments (except that any schedules of contributors may be withheld).[36] The information provided on the registration becomes part of the public record and the Attorney General's Office maintains a searchable online database of the information.

Q17. Must a nonprofit organization disclose information about its finances to members with voting rights?

A17. The Minnesota Nonprofit Corporations Act requires an organization to allow a member or director to inspect certain documents at its office for a proper purpose (see Question 14 for more information). These documents include the organization's accounting records as well as a financial statement showing the result of all operations and transactions affecting income and surplus during the last annual accounting

33 *A Guide to Minnesota's Charities Laws*, Minnesota Attorney General, www.ag.state.mn.us/consumer/publications/GuideCharityLaws.asp (last visited Aug. 1, 2017).
34 John Roman Faron & David Flavin, *Publicity and Disclosure of Form 990* (1997), www.irs.gov/pub/irs-tege/eotopicb97.pdf.
35 Minn. Stat. § 309.515 (2016).
36 Minn. Stat. § 309.53 (2016).

period and a balance sheet showing a summary of the organization's assets and liabilities.[37] (Note that financial records are statements and compilations that reflect, but not merely list, all transactions.)

Under the Act, a member of an organization is a person with membership rights as defined in the organization's articles or Bylaws. Similarly, a director is any member of the board vested with the general management of the internal affairs of the corporation.

Q18. Must a nonprofit organization disclose information about its finances to donors?

A18. Nonprofit organizations are not required to disclose information about their finances to donors beyond what is contained in IRS Form 990 or is provided for in an agreement with the donor, for example, a foundation grant agreement. Donors may also, as members of the general public, use the website of the Office of the Minnesota Attorney General to view the information organizations required to register with that office and report on an annual basis, such as a copy of the organization's audit. The State of Minnesota does require organizations to make certain non-financial disclosures when soliciting contributions (see Question 15 for more information), and the IRS requires very specific information be included on a disclosure statement for quid pro quo contributions of more than $75 (see Question 15 for more information).[38]

Q19. Must a nonprofit organization disclose information about its finances to the general public?

A19. A nonprofit organization is required to make certain financial disclosures to the general public. See Question 16 for details on the documents and information required by the IRS and the State of Minnesota.

Q20. Are nonprofit organizations required to follow the Minnesota Open Meeting and Data Practices Act?

A20. Only nonprofit organizations created by the government are required to follow the Minnesota Open Meeting Law, which requires that notice of meetings be given, meetings be open to the public and relevant meeting materials be made available. Exceptions to the law are made for attorney client privilege, employee evaluations and labor negotiations.

Q21. Are nonprofit organizations required to follow the Minnesota Government Data Practices Act?

A21. Nonprofit organizations under contract with a government entity are required to follow the Minnesota Government Data Practices Act, which carries the presumption that government data is available to the public. If the data sought by an individual is "public," the organization has an obligation to allow public inspection or provide copies of the data. If government data is not "public," it may be classified in one of four ways:

1. Private – Minnesota Government Data on an individual, which is available to the subject. May be disclosed with the subject's consent, or 10 years after the death of the subject or 30 years after the creation of the data, whichever is later.[39]

---

37 Minn. Stat. § 317A.461 (2016).

38 *See* I.R.S. Pub. 557, *Tax-Exempt Status for Your Organization*, 16-17 (2017), www.irs.gov/pub/irs-pdf/p557.pdf.

39 Minn. Stat. § 13.10 (2016).

2. Confidential – Minnesota Government Data on an individual, which is not available to the subject of the data or to anyone else outside the government agency holding the data. May be disclosed only with that subject's consent, or 10 years after the death of the subject or 30 years after the creation of the data, whichever is later.[40]
3. Nonpublic – Minnesota Government Data on an organization or other entity (not an individual), which is available to the subject of the data. May be disclosed only with that entity's consent or 10 years after the creation or receipt of the information, unless the government agency determines disclosure is not in the public interest.[41]
4. Protected nonpublic – Minnesota Government Data on an organization or other entity, which is not available to the subject of the data or to anyone else outside the government agency holding the data. May be disclosed only with the consent of the data subject or 10 years after the creation or receipt of the information, unless the government agency determines disclosure is not in the public interest.[42]

If the requester is allowed to access the information, they may be charged the actual cost of retrieving and copying the requested information.[43] Someone who is harmed by a violation of the Data Practices Act, or anyone merely seeking to require a government agency to follow the Data Practices Act may have recourse through civil and administrative remedies.[44]

D. Sharing Information about Donors

Q22. What information about donors does a nonprofit organization need to provide to the IRS?

A22. The general rule is that a nonprofit organization must provide the IRS with the name, address, zip code, total contribution amount and type of contribution made by each donor who has given money, securities or another type of property totaling $5,000 or more for the year. This information is reported on Schedule B of the organization's Form 990 or 990-EZ. IRS also has special rules for different types of nonprofit organizations. See Schedule B (attached to Form 990, 990-EZ, or 990-PF), at www.irs.gov/pub/irs-pdf/f990ezb.pdf for more information.

Q23. What information about donors does a nonprofit organization need to provide to the general public?

A23. A nonprofit organization is not required to provide information about its donors to the general public. Although a member of the general public may inspect or request a copy of a nonprofit organization's Form 990, the names and addresses of contributors, listed on Schedule B, are not open to public inspection. All other information on the Form 990 will be open to public inspection unless it clearly identifies the contributor.

40 Minn. Stat. § 13.10 (2016).
41 Minn. Stat. § 13.03, subd. 8 (2016).
42 Minn. Stat. § 13.03, subd. 8 (2016).
43 Deborah A. Dyson, Minnesota House of Representatives Research Department, *Minnesota Open Meeting Law,* 1 (2014), www.house.leg.state.mn.us/hrd/pubs/openmtg.pdf; see also Matt Gehring, Minnesota House of Representatives Research Department, *Minnesota Government Data Practices Act An Overview*, 1, 3 (2010), www.house.leg.state.mn.us/hrd/pubs/dataprac.pdf.
44 Minn. Stat. §§ 13.08-085 (2016). See also Matt Gehring, Minnesota House of Representatives Research Department, *Minnesota Government Data Practices Act An Overview*, 1, 3 (2010), www.house.leg.state.mn.us/hrd/pubs/dataprac.pdf.

Nonprofit organizations are allowed to publish a list of donor names in a periodic report issued to its members, but they are not required to do so. If the nonprofit organization plans to publish a list of donors in such a publication, it is good practice to give donors an opportunity to opt out of such a list at the time of the solicitation.[45]

Q24. What information about donors are nonprofit organizations prohibited from sharing?

A24. An organization is prohibited from selling a donor list without the consent of the donor.[46] Some nonprofit organizations expand their donor base by exchanging lists of contributors with other organizations. Nonprofit organizations may also generate income by selling or renting their donor lists. The sale or exchange of donor lists is prohibited in Minnesota unless the donor has consented to the transaction.[47] In effect, this requires nonprofit organizations to maintain an "opt in" donor list. That is, if a nonprofit plans to sell or exchange its donor list, it must inform donors of its intentions at the time of solicitation and ask if they want their information to be included in this exchange. In addition, if the nonprofit initially told donors that their information would not be sold or exchanged and then changes its policy, the organization must contact donors to get their permission prior to using it in any exchange.

The names and addresses of donors, although reported on Schedule B of IRS Form 990 or Form 990-EZ, may be omitted from copies made widely available, produced for public inspection or copied for members of the general public.

Q25. Is a nonprofit organization required to have an "opt in" or an "opt out" donor list for donor privacy? What precautions must a nonprofit organization take to ensure that it meets a donor's request for anonymity?

A25. In Minnesota, nonprofit organizations are prohibited from selling or exchanging lists of contributors without the express consent of the contributors.[48] In effect, this requires nonprofit organizations to maintain an "opt in" donor list. That is, if a nonprofit plans to sell or exchange its donor list, it must inform donors of its intentions at the time of solicitation and ask if they want their information to be included in this exchange. The nonprofit must use clear and unambiguous language when describing its intentions and give donors an opportunity to "opt in" to the exchange of their information, or the nonprofit risks prosecution for fraud.[49]

Nonprofit organizations that do not exchange or sell their donor lists and therefore do not include an "opt in" provision at the time of solicitation should nevertheless be prepared to receive and track "opt out" statements from their donors. "Opt out" letters are statements that positively request that personal information not be sold or exchanged. The Minnesota Attorney General's website provides a sample "opt out" letter for use by consumers who wish to restrict the exchange of their information, available at www.ag.state.mn.us/Consumer/Handbooks/GuardingYPrivacy/OptOutSample.pdf.

Nonprofit organizations are allowed to publish a list of donor names in a periodic report issued to its members, but they are not required to do so. If the nonprofit organization plans to publish a list of donors

45 Minn. Stat. § 309.55, subd. 1 (2016).
46 Minn. Stat. § 309.55, subd. 6 (2016).
47 Minn. Stat. § 309.55, subd. 6 (2016).
48 Minn. Stat. § 309.55, subd. 6 (2016).
49 Minn. Stat. § 309.55, subd. 5 (2016).

in such a publication, it is good practice to give donors an opportunity to opt out of such a list at the time of the solicitation.[50]

E. Sharing Information about Members

Q26. What information about its members do nonprofit organizations need to provide to others?

A26. A nonprofit organization is not required to provide information about its members to the government[51] or to the general public, but it must under certain circumstances make information available to its own members with voting rights. Two business days after the notice of a meeting of members with voting rights is given, an alphabetical list of the names of members with voting rights must be made available to all members with voting rights, either at the corporation's office or at a reasonable place identified in the meeting notice in the city where the meeting will be held. The list must include the members' addresses and the number of votes each member is entitled to cast. A member, or a member's agent or attorney, is entitled to inspect and to copy the list at a reasonable time and at the member's expense.[52]

A member of an organization is a person with membership rights as defined in the organization's articles or Bylaws. Members with voting rights are that subclass of members who have, in addition to their membership rights, the right to vote on some issues before the organization. Organizations may have either members with voting rights or without voting rights, or only one type of member; this is typically defined in organizational Bylaws.

Q27. What information about members is a nonprofit organization prohibited from sharing?

A27. Unless restricted by its own Bylaws, an organization is not prohibited from sharing information about its members with other individuals or organizations. Additionally, if an organization has a privacy policy to which members are a party, it must abide by restrictions found in the policy.

Q28. Does a nonprofit organization need to inform its members before it shares information about them with others?

A28. If a nonprofit organization has provided its members with a privacy policy stating that it will not share their information with other individuals or organizations and later changes this policy, it should contact its members to inform them of the policy change. If the organization has not previously provided its members with a privacy statement, it is under no obligation to give them notice prior to sharing their information.

---

50 Minn. Stat. § 309.55, subd. 1 (2016).
51 *NAACP v. Ala. ex rel. Patterson*, 357 U.S. 449, 78 S. Ct. 1163 (1958).
52 Minn. Stat. § 317A.439 (2016).

F. Sharing Information about Clients

Q29. What information about its clients do nonprofit organizations need to provide to others?

A29. A nonprofit organization is not required to provide information about its clients to other individuals or organizations, unless it falls under the Minnesota Government Data Practices Act That is, unless it receives funding from a government entity. For more on the Data Practices Act, see Question 21. If a nonprofit plans to provide information about its clients to other individuals or organizations, it should inform the clients of its intention and give them an opportunity to withhold their information. If a nonprofit organization collects sensitive information about their clients, such as financial or medical data, it should consider structuring their methods of data collection and storage such that identifying information, such as name or address, is not stored with other data, such as employment status, criminal record or medical history.

Also, the Health Insurance Portability and Accountability Act of 1996 ("HIPAA") applies to client medical information. Additionally, specific contracts may require a report for eligibility, such as reimbursement for client stays, etc.

Q30. What information about clients are nonprofits prohibited from sharing?

A30. A nonprofit organization is required to adhere to the HIPAA and may not be otherwise prohibited from providing any information about its clients to other individuals or organizations. If a nonprofit plans to provide information about its clients to other individuals or organizations, it should inform the clients of its intention and give them an opportunity to withhold their information. If a nonprofit organization collects sensitive information about their clients, such as financial or medical data, it should consider structuring their methods of data collection and storage such that identifying information, such as name or address, is not stored with other data, such as employment status, criminal record or medical history.

G. Other Disclosure and Privacy Issues

Q31. What are the essential legal documents nonprofit organizations are obligated by law to retain?

A31. Nonprofits are required to retain their exemption application and their IRS Form 990s. Exact copies of these documents should be retained, but organizations must also have copies suitable for public disclosure. In other words, organizations should have copies that have been amended to withhold name and address information of donors, trade secrets or any other information required or permitted by law to be withheld.

For purposes of public disclosure, the exemption application includes not only the actual application form, but also any statement or document offered in support of the application and any letter or document issued by the IRS concerning the application. By federal statute, exemption applications filed prior to July 15, 1987, are exempt from these requirements. The annual information returns, or Form 990s, include an exact copy of the actual return; any amended return; and all schedules, attachments, and supporting documents. Publicly disclosed annual information returns should not include the name and address of contributors to the organization. These returns must be available for three years from the date they are required to be filed, including extensions, or from the date they are actually filed, whichever is later. Amended returns must be available for three years from the date they are actually filed with the IRS.53

The IRS also requires retention and public disclosure of Form 5768, Election/Revocation of Election by an Eligible Section 501(c)(3) Organization to Make Expenditures to Influence Legislation.[54] For more information on election and lobbying activities, see Chapter 7: Lobbying, Election-related Activity and Voter Education.

As part of the requirement to file annual reports under the Minnesota Charitable Solicitation Act, organizations must retain detailed books and records to substantiate the information submitted in their annual reports, including records of all donations of money or other property collected from Minnesota residents, and the disbursement of such money or property. These records must be open to inspection by the Attorney General at all reasonable times, and should be retained for a period of three years from the date the corresponding report was filed.[55]

Although it is not required by law, an organization may consider adopting a Document Retention Policy as a way to retain, track and appropriately destroy documents. The following are only intended to serve as examples and are not intended to be an exhaustive list of categories of records or files and documents goodly retained:

- Corporate records, including:
  - Foundational documents such as Articles of Incorporation and Bylaws.
  - Governance and Board policies including corporate resolutions, board agendas and minutes and conflict-of-interest disclosure forms, among others.
- Finance and Administration files, including:
  - Financial statements, payroll records, bank deposits and statements, invoices, and sales records.
  - Equipment files and maintenance records, contracts, general administrative and legal correspondence, donor records, and grant applications.
- Insurance Records, including:
  - Policies and claims made on policies, accident reports, Occupational Safety and Health Administration ("OSHA") safety reports and group disability records.
- Real Property records, including:
  - Real property deeds, leases (current and expired), mortgages and security agreements.
- Tax documents, including:
  - 501(c)(3) application – Form 1023, IRS Form 990s, charitable organization registration statements and exemption application.
- Human Resources documents, including:
  - Employee personnel files, retirement benefit plans, employee handbooks and training materials, and employment applications.
  - IRS Form I-9, tax withholding statements and payroll tax returns.
- Technology
  - Software licenses and support agreements.
- Other
  - Press releases and publicly filed documents.[56]

53 I.R.S. Pub. 557, *Tax-Exempt Status for Your Organization*, 17-18 (2017), www.irs.gov/pub/irs-pdf/p557.pdf.
54 I.R.S., *Instructions for Form 1023* (2006), www.irs.gov/pub/irs-pdf/i1023.pdf.
55 Minn. Stat. § 309.54 (2016).
56 Minnesota Council of Nonprofits, Document Retention Policy Template. (This document can be downloaded at www.minnesotanonprofits.org)

Q32. Must nonprofit organizations publicize their annual meeting? If so, to whom?

A32. The Minnesota Nonprofit Corporations Act requires an organization to give members with voting rights notice of its annual meeting. At least five days before the date of the meeting, or a shorter time provided in the organization's articles or Bylaws, but not more than 60 days before the meeting, notice of the time, date and place of the annual meeting must be given to every voting member.[57]

The Act also requires an organization to allow a member or director to inspect the minutes of annual meetings for the last six years at its office.[58] There is no requirement to publish or otherwise make the minutes of the annual meeting available to the general public.

Q33. Are nonprofit organizations required to have a privacy policy? Are they required to inform members, donors or clients of the particulars of their privacy policy?

A33. Nonprofit organizations are not required to develop a privacy policy. However, if an organization collects data from clients, donors or members, it may consider adopting a privacy policy that can be distributed to let these individuals know whether the organization will share any of their information with others. If an organization changes its policy on distribution of collected data, it may consider informing the affected parties to give them an opportunity to opt out of the sale or trade of their information. This is particularly true for information collected via internet transactions, including use of email addresses.

Q34. Are there other laws governing collection and distribution of information, solicitation of donations, or advertisement of services of which nonprofit organizations need to be aware?

A34. Some nonprofit organizations may be subject to the Children's Online Privacy Protection Act, www.law.cornell.edu/uscode/uscode15/usc_sup_01_15_10_91.html. If an organization operates an online service directed to children under the age of 13 that collects personal information from children, or operates a general audience website and knows that it is collecting personal information from children under 13, the organization must comply with this Act. The Act requires the organization to post a link to its privacy policy on the homepage and on every page that collects information from children. In addition, prior to collecting, using or disclosing personal information from a child, the organization must obtain consent from the child's parent. Specific information regarding the details of the privacy policy and the method of seeking parental consent may be found on the Federal Trade Commission's website at www.ftc.gov/tips-advice/business-center/guidance/complying-coppa-frequently-asked-questions .

All nonprofit organizations are subject to the Controlling the Assault of Non-Solicited Pornography and Marketing Act of 2003 (CAN-SPAM), www.law.cornell.edu/uscode/15/usc_sup_01_15_10_103.html. The Act requires organizations sending "commercial" emails to obtain the explicit permission of the recipient prior to sending the email. Commercial emails must also contain an electronic link to opt-out of future messages, a valid postal address for the organization and a notice at the beginning of the message that the email is commercial in nature.

To determine if an email is "commercial" in nature, organizations must evaluate their email correspondence according to a two-part test:

57 Minn. Stat. § 317A.435 (2016).
58 Minn. Stat. § 317A.461 (2016).

- If the e-mail's content exclusively advertises or promotes a product or service, it is commercial.
- If the email contains transactional or relationship—as well as commercial—content, then the primary purpose of the email must be examined. The primary purpose shall be deemed "commercial" if:
    - o A recipient interpreting the subject line of the email would reasonably conclude that the message contains the advertisement or promotion of a commercial product or service; or
    - o The e-mail's transactional or relationship content does not appear, in whole or in substantial part, at the beginning of the body of the message.

To avoid sanction under CAN-SPAM, organizations sending electronic mail messages to members, clients or donors must not refer to a commercial advertisement or promote a commercial product or service in the subject line of the email and they must place at least the majority of the transactional or relationship content at the beginning of the body of the message.[59]

H. Related Resources

Publications:

CAN-SPAM Act: A Compliance Guide for Business
Published by the Federal Trade Commission
www.ftc.gov/tips-advice/business-center/guidance/can-spam-act-compliance-guide-business

Give me your 990! Public Disclosure Requirements for Tax-Exempt Organizations, by Liz Towne
Published by Alliance for Justice
bolderadvocacy.org/wp-content/uploads/2012/01/AFJ_990_Final_web.pdf

A Guide to Minnesota's Charities Laws
Published by the Office of the Minnesota Attorney General
www.ag.state.mn.us/Brochures/pubGuidetoCharitiesLaws.pdf

How to Comply with the Children's Online Privacy Protection Rule
Published by the Federal Trade Commission
www.ftc.gov/tips-advice/business-center/guidance/complying-coppa-frequently-asked-questions

Information Brief of the Minnesota Government Data Practices Act
Published by the Minnesota House of Representatives Research Department
www.house.leg.state.mn.us/hrd/pubs/dataprac.pdf

Information Brief of the Minnesota Open Meeting Law
Published by the Minnesota House of Representatives Research Department
www.house.leg.state.mn.us/hrd/pubs/openmtg.pdf

Tax-Exempt Status for Your Organization
I.R.S. Publication 557
www.irs.gov/pub/irs-pdf/p557.pdf

59 *CAN-SPAM Act: A Compliance Guide for Business*, Federal Trade Commission, www.ftc.gov/tips-advice/business-center/guidance/can-spam-act-compliance-guide-business (last visited Aug. 02, 2017).

Websites:

Office of the Minnesota Attorney General
www.ag.state.mn.us/Default.asp

Statutes:

Minnesota Statutes, Chapter 309 Social and Charitable Organizations
www.revisor.leg.state.mn.us/stats/309/

Minnesota Statutes, Chapter 317A Nonprofit Corporations
www.revisor.leg.state.mn.us/stats/317A/

CHAPTER 12

RELATIONSHIPS WITH OTHER ENTITIES

Topics

A. Overview

This chapter addresses common relationships a nonprofit might form with other entities, both tax-exempt and taxable. It provides some insight into legal responsibilities and issues associated with the formation and participation in each type of relationship.

This chapter covers basic information on mergers between organizations and working in coalitions. It outlines merger procedure under Minnesota law and presents some legal issues and considerations related to mergers. The chapter also covers the various types of subsidiaries or separate organizations a tax-exempt organization may form and the considerations for formation of each. In its exploration of for-profit subsidiaries and LLCs, the chapter provides analysis of how a nonprofit organization might maintain tax exemption or form a new exempt organization. It covers questions that arise in relation to partnerships with different levels of government and the implications and obligations of receiving grants from or contracting with the federal or state government. It explores the mechanics of chartered organizations and analyzes legal relationships between chartered organizations.

B. Collaborative Ventures

Q1. Do all collaborative ventures need to be formalized legally? What are the considerations when deciding to legally formalize a collaborative venture?

A1. Nonprofit organizations are not required to legally formalize their collaborative ventures, but nonprofit organizations may wish to do so to avoid confusion and resolve conflicts if questions arise. Legal formality can be achieved simply by having a written agreement among collaborating organizations. A collaboration by written agreement is the "domestic partner" of the relationship; there is not an established legal framework, so the participants are free to—and must—create their own. If a collaboration will involve significant financial or legal risk, or will continue over many years, a new organization may be appropriate, as discussed in Question 4.

Any written document detailing the circumstances of the collaborative venture will typically be viewed as a contract, and therefore organizations should ensure that the written agreement is clear and accurate before they legally bind their organization.

Q2. When is a written agreement necessary or recommended in a collaborative venture? What should this document contain?

A2. Written agreements for collaborative ventures or other coalition work are typically recommended, but are not required. Written documents become important as the nature of the collaborative venture becomes more complex. A written agreement can assist all the participating organizations obtain clarity regarding their roles and responsibilities, the purpose of the collaboration, as well as addressing legal considerations.

Written documents should contain the specific responsibilities and duties of each party participating in the collaboration. It should delineate a proper procedure for when conflicts arise, to help mitigate difficult control issues. Additional items such as timelines, revenue and expense allocations among participants, use of each other's names, and acceptable conditions for early termination may also be helpful. A written agreement should make it clear that no participant is authorized to bind another, that they are not agents of each other, and that they are each independently responsible for their own conduct. Any written document detailing the circumstances of the collaborative venture will typically be viewed as a contract, and therefore organizations should ensure that the written agreement is clear and accurate before they legally bind their organization.

The written agreement should also address any legal or funding-related compliance obligations that are applicable to the project, such as licensure or insurance requirements.

Q3. Who is legally responsible in a collaborative venture between multiple organizations?

A3. Without a written agreement, there may be confusion as to which organization is responsible for the collaborative venture, and there is a risk that any organization participating in the collaboration could be legally responsible for any injuries, damages or violations that may occur from actions of the other collaborating organizations.

Carefully worded written agreements stating each organization's roles and responsibilities, and stating that no organization is responsible for the acts of the others, can alleviate some risk of liability for organizations. However, such agreements do not protect an organization from incidents caused by its own volunteers or staff members. An organization's general casualty and liability policy would typically cover these actions.

Q4. Can multiple organizations create a new organization for a specific venture? How and when would they want to do so?

A4. Yes, multiple organizations can create a new organization for a specific venture. Typically, these organizations will choose to create a new organization because the collaboration involves a significant initial investment, material financial or legal risk, will be ongoing over many years or is somehow outside of the normal mission of the existing organizations. Depending on its purpose, such a new organization could be a 501(c)(3) charitable nonprofit organization, a 501(c)(4) social welfare organization, a limited liability for-profit company or a for-profit corporation.

Organizations wishing to create a new organization for a specific venture will create the new organization in the same manner as any other nonprofit or business corporation: choosing the mission, Bylaws and board of directors, and filing the appropriate documents. This type of entity and its tax status must be determined based on an analysis of the new organization's planned activities, operations, legal and financial risks, and other legal and tax considerations.

Nonprofit organizations can also create a new organization for a specific venture with a for-profit business, but doing so raises important legal and tax considerations that should be addressed with legal counsel before proceeding. Generally, such a joint venture must be structured to ensure the nonprofit gets a fair return on its investment of assets and effort, and that the for-profit does not unduly benefit from the venture. In addition, some income from such a joint venture may be taxable as unrelated business income. This may be permissible but it must be evaluated and, if permitted, taken into account in the business planning. For more information see Chapter 8: Financial Accountability, Section II: Unrelated Business Income Tax (UBIT).

Q5. *Are there limits on what activities can be conducted through a collaborative venture?*

A5. A nonprofit can only conduct activities through a collaboration that it is permitted to do on its own, as it relates to its mission (unless the collaboration is established as a separate legal entity).

A collaboration to share resources may raise tax issues as well. For example, if one organization provides the services of its accounting staff to another unrelated nonprofit for a fee to cover costs, the net income over expenses would likely be considered unrelated business income and be subject to unrelated business income tax (UBIT). The net income may be zero if the fee is at cost, but it should be reported appropriately. In addition, conducting the "unrelated" activity may raise compliance issues with bond financing covenants, and it must in any event be insubstantial. Also see Chapter 8: Financial Accountability, Section H: Unrelated Business Income Tax (UBIT).

Q6. What are the legal ramifications of entering into a cause-marketing relationship with a for-profit entity?

A6. A cause-marketing relationship is one in which a nonprofit organization licenses its name and/or logo to use in connection with a commercial product or service. In exchange for use of a nonprofit's name, logo and reputation in a commercial enterprise, a for-profit or corporate entity may offer a flat fee or a percentage of the proceeds from the sale of a commercial product. Cause-marketing relationships with for-profit entities can be very rewarding for both the for-profit and nonprofit entities, but nonprofit organizations must beware of the potential pitfalls and requirements that such relationships produce.

Nonprofit organizations must ensure that they are appropriately involved in the cause-marketing venture. The organization must ensure the venture is consistent with its mission, principles and reputation. The organization may face legal liability if it allows its name or logo to be used for advertising that violates federal or state advertising law or charitable solicitation rules. However, if the organization takes a very active role in the cause-marketing relationship, the income from it may be subject to unrelated business income tax (UBIT). Having some unrelated business income may be permissible if it is insubstantial, but it is important to evaluate at the front end to determine whether it is permissible for the organization, and if the income will be taxed, to take that into account in business planning.

In addition to UBIT considerations, most states regulate solicitation of charitable contributions, which can include some cause-related marketing ventures. Minnesota, for example regulates "professional fundraisers," which can include a business corporation's cause-related marketing campaign. Wisconsin specifically regulates cause-related marketing and commercial co-ventures. If the advertising or promotion will reach consumers in multiple states, each state's rules must be evaluated. In addition, organizations should also be aware of the Federal Trade Commission Act[1] and Minnesota consumer protection laws.[2] Messaging and advertising must be accurate, truthful and not misleading to the public.[3]

1 15 U.S.C.A. 41 (West, Westlaw currently through Pub. L., 115-43).

2 Minnesota Unlawful Trade Practices Act, Minn. Stat. §§ 325D.09-16 (2016).

3 For step-by-step guidance on cause-marketing considerations, see Jenny Gillon, "Cause-Related Marketing Campaigns May Contain Pitfalls for the Unwary." This article is available to be downloaded at www.harmoncurran.com.

C. Mergers

Q7. What is a merger?

A7. A merger is the joining of two or more organizations into a single entity, going from multiple boards, Internal Revenue Service ("IRS") returns and audits, to one. Organizations engage in mergers for numerous reasons, but mergers are frequently spurred by financial or efficiency goals. Additional causes may be to reduce competition between organizations or expand their capacity. A merger is the organizational equivalent of a marriage: two individual organizations become one by operation of law. Thus, all their assets and liabilities are automatically brought into the merger. A merger may be most effective when there is a cultural synergy and the partnership meets a strategic goal to extend the reach of the nonprofits, share expertise and gain efficiencies.[4]

Q8. What are the different types of mergers?

A8. There are several basic types of mergers.

- **Horizontal Mergers** occur between two or more organizations that provide the same sorts of services or products. An example would be two organizations that provide free meals to the elderly joining together.
- **Vertical Mergers** occur between two or more organizations that provide different services that are compatible. An example of this would be a merger between organizations providing shelter for people experiencing homelessness with one that provides free health care services to indigent individuals.
- **Merger of Subsidiary** occurs when a wholly owned single-member limited liability company subsidiary merges into a parent that is a nonprofit corporation organized under the Minnesota Statutes Chapter 317A.[5]
- **Other Mergers** occur when two organizations engaged in disparate activities decide to merge together.[6]

To learn more about realignment options and find out if merger is the right option for a nonprofit organization, visit Propel Nonprofits' Strategic Alignment (Realignment) Resources at www.propelnonprofits.org. See also a publication from Propel Nonprofits—*Merge Minnesota: Nonprofit Merger as an Opportunity for Survival and Growth.*

Q9. What are the procedural requirements for doing a merger?

A9. Because a merger customarily brings each organization's assets and liabilities to the merged organization, a thorough understanding of each organization's activities, operations, finances, debt obligations, contracts, known liabilities and possible unknown liabilities is crucial. To the extent liabilities can be resolved before the merger, they should be. An alternative to a merger is an asset transfer, which is a more legally complex transaction but which can better protect the rescuing organization (the organization that survives the asset transfer) from the liabilities of its predecessors.

4 For more information on organizational considerations, see David La Piana, Collaboration and Strategic Restructuring, www.lapiana.org/solutions-for-nonprofits/solutions/collaboration-and-strategic-restructuring (last visited Aug. 4, 2017).

5 *See* Minn. Stat. § 317A.621 (2017).

6 *5 Types of Company Mergers*, www.mbda.gov/news/blog/2012/04/5-types-company-mergers (last visited Aug. 4, 2017).

Additionally, each organization considering a merger should be sure the merger is consistent with its tax-exempt status. A merger among two 501(c)(3) organizations with similar charitable programs probably would raise few tax-exemption issues, while a merger between a 501(c)(3) and 501(c)(4) would only be permissible in very limited circumstances.

Finally, each organization considering a merger should evaluate whether it is subject to any restrictions or notice requirements related to a merger, such as from its licensing, bond financing, covenants, and payment grant or program contracts. For example, the Financial Accounting Standards Board (FASB) released Statement No. 164 in 2009, which requires the application of the carryover method of accounting for an appropriately determined nonprofit merger.[7] Generally, this method requires the new entity to combine the assets and liabilities in its initial financial statements at the merger date.[8]

Nonprofit organizations incorporated in Minnesota undergoing a merger must abide by the procedural requirements of Minnesota Statute Chapter 317A.[9] Organizations must first have a plan of merger or consolidation, which must list the names of the corporations proposing to merge, the name of the surviving corporation, the terms and conditions of the merger, the manner of converting the membership of the constituent corporations into memberships of the surviving corporation and any other conditions that are considered necessary or desirable.[10]

The plan must be approved and adopted by each constituent corporation.[11] When a constituent corporation has members with voting rights, the board of directors of the corporation should adopt a resolution by the affirmative vote of a majority of all directors approving a proposed plan of merger or consolidation and directing that the plan be submitted to a vote at a meeting of the members with voting rights.[12] When a constituent corporation does not have members with voting rights, and unless the articles or bylaws require a greater vote, a plan of merger or consolidation is adopted at a meeting of the board of directors of the corporation upon receiving the affirmative votes of a majority of all directors.[13]

A nonprofit that is exempt under Code Section 501(c)(3) or which otherwise holds assets for charitable purposes must also notify the Attorney General of its intent to transfer or convey assets as part of a dissolution, merger or consolidation until 45 days after it has given notice to the Attorney General, unless the Minnesota Attorney General waives all or part of the waiting period.[14] The Attorney General may extend this time period with notice to the organization.[15]

After all of the organizations have approved the merger, an article of merger must be filed; this document should contain the plan of merger, a statement that the plan has been approved by each corporation and that notice of the merger has been provided to the Minnesota Attorney General and the waiting period has elapsed.[16] The papers must be signed on behalf of each corporation, and the merger is effective when these papers are filed with the Secretary of State or at a later date, if specified by the plan.[17] See Minnesota Statutes Section 317A.641 for more information about the effective dates of mergers. A copy of the

7 FASB Issues Statement No. 164, Not-For-Profit Entities: Mergers And Acquisitions (2009), www.fasb.org (last visited Aug. 4, 2017).

8 Trenton Fast, New FASB Update Challenges Nonprofits to Improve Financial Reporting (Aug. 18, 2016), www.claconnect.com/resources/articles/new-fasb-update-challenges-nonprofits-to-improve-financial-reporting.

9 Minn. Stat. §§ 317A.601, 611-651 (2016).

10 Minn. Stat. § 317A.611 (2009).

11 Minn. Stat. § 317A.613, subd. 1 (2016).

12 Minn. Stat. § 317A.613, subd. 2 (2016).

13 Minn. Stat. § 317A.613, subd. 3 (2016).

14 Minn. Stat. § 317A.811 (2016).

15 *Id.*

16 Minn. Stat. § 317A.615 (2016).

17 Minn. Stat. § 317A.641 (2016).

certificate of merger must be provided to the Attorney General and filed with each organization's IRS Form 990. Organizations should also identify any consent or notice requirements arising from their licensing, bond financing covenants, funders and major contracts.

Q10. How can members of a board of directors ensure they are carrying out their fiduciary duties when considering a merger?

A10. Members of nonprofits' boards of directors are obligated to carry out their duties of care, loyalty and obedience as provided by Minnesota Statutes Chapter 317A. As always, this requires board members to ensure they are getting adequate information and asking appropriate questions to ensure they are making thoughtful, well-informed decisions. The liability legal and organizational issues discussed in the preceding questions should be part of the board's consideration of a merger and its determination whether the proposed merger is in the best interest of the organization and its mission.

Board members must at all times act in the best interest of the nonprofit, and should use such care as an ordinary person in their position would use. The board should ensure it receives or obtains sufficient information to make an informed decision. It should ensure that neither actual nor potential conflicts of interests exist. If a conflict arises at any time, the board member should immediately disclose the information to the full board and then remove him or herself from the action.

It is often useful for the board to consult with appropriate constituents, external consultants and legal counsel when beginning merger negotiations to ensure the board and organization understand the risks, benefits and consequences of the proposed merger.

D. Forming Related Exempt Organizations: 501(c)(3)s, 501(c)(4)s and PACs

Q11. When and why would a 501(c)(3) charitable nonprofit organization form a 501(c)(4) nonprofit organization?

A11. 501(c)(3) organizations that are public charities are limited in their lobbying activities;[18] they are permitted to engage in unlimited amount of general issue advocacy, but they cannot have a substantial part of their activities involve attempting to influence legislation either through grassroots efforts or by directly contacting legislators.[19]

501(c)(4) organizations are allowed greater flexibility in lobbying and political activities. Such organizations are allowed to engage in unlimited lobbying and may make partisan endorsements and communications about candidates, consistent with applicable campaign finance laws. Additionally, such election-related activity must not be a "primary purpose".

Organizations that wish to engage in a greater degree of lobbying than is permitted by their 501(c)(3) status may look to forming a 501(c)(4) to conduct their lobbying activity. Before forming a 501(c)(4),

18 "Although private foundations do incur a prohibitive tax on any lobbying expenditure, private foundations may participate in many forms of advocacy activities and may fund advocacy." Bolder Advocacy, Private Foundations May Advocate (2012), bolderadvocacy.org/wp-content/uploads/2012/05/Private_Foundations_May_Advocate.pdf.

19 *See* I.R.C. § 501(c)(3).

organizations should be aware that the new lobbying organization is a separate entity and must be governed accordingly. This means that the new organization must have its own bank account, board of directors, books and records, and file its own Form 990. The 501(c)(4) must pay for its own expenses, such as use of staff, space, equipment, mailing lists, logos and so on. Donations to 501(c)(4)s are not tax deductible, and solicitation materials must include a disclaimer to this effect. See Chapter 7: Lobbying, Election-related Activity and Voter Education, Section G: Differences between Restrictions on 501(c)(3) and 501(c)(4) Tax Exempt Organizations.

Q12. When and why would a 501(c)(3) charitable nonprofit organization form another 501(c)(3) organization?

A12. A separate 501(c)(3) can be useful in many circumstances. For example, it may be useful for conducting a new activity that may carry unique legal or financial risks, when having a separate board or membership is desirable, or to address specific licensure or regulatory requirements. Organizations often create a separate 501(c)(3) to operate a fundraising foundation or manage an endowment. The new organization is a separate legal entity and must be governed accordingly. Legal separation for liability purposes is generally only respected if the organizations also respect the separateness of the two. Thus, the new organization should have its own board of directors, books and records. It must apply for its own 501(c)(3) status and file its own Form 990.

Q13. When and why would a non-501(c)(3) nonprofit organization form a 501(c)(3) nonprofit organization to support its charitable activities?

A13. Non-501(c)(3) organizations may wish to retain their non-501(c)(3) status while taking advantage of the tax-deductible benefits associated with 501(c)(3) organizations. Organizations such as 501(c)(4)s and 501(c)(6)s may form 501(c)(3)s, but the 501(c)(3)s may only engage in activities that are charitable, educational, religious or scientific. The 501(c)(3) is a separate legal entity and must be governed accordingly. It must have its own board of directors, books and records, and file its own Form 990. Donations to 501(c)(3)s are generally tax deductible for donors as charitable contributions. In addition, 501(c)(3)s are generally eligible to receive grants from private foundations. A 501(c)(3) must only pay for charitable and educational activities . It cannot just funnel funding or otherwise subsidize the lobbying or political activities of its affiliated 501(c)(4) or 501(c)(6).

501(c)(3)s formed in such a way can accept tax-deductible donations from donors and engage in charitable and educational activities while allowing the parent 501(c)(4) or (6) to engage in activities otherwise unavailable to 501(c)(3) organizations.

Q14. When and why would a nonprofit organization initiate a Political Action Committee (PAC) fund to support its political activity?

A14. A PAC is a fund established by different entities, such as corporations, labor unions, 501(c)(4)s and trade associations, to support political election-related activity. PACs collect contributions and use this money to make contributions and expenditures to influence federal[20] or state elections.[21] 501(c)(3)s cannot initiate

20 *See* 11 C.F.R. § 100.6 (2014).
21 *See* Minn. Stat. § 10A.12 (2016).

a PAC to support partisan, electoral political activity. However, 501(c)(4)s affiliated with 501(c)(3)s can form PACs, as can independent 501(c)(4)s.

PACs formed in connection with a 501(c)(4) benefit from their relationship in that the 501(c)(4) can pay all the overhead costs associated with the PAC. Depending on whether the PAC is state or federal, there may be limits on which individuals it may accept contributions from.

Individuals may choose to form a PAC when they decide that restrictions placed on 501(c)(3) and 501(c)(4) election activities are too strict. PACs are typically created for the sole purpose of influencing electoral activities, and they have considerably more freedom to directly support or oppose candidates.

Federal PACs are required to register with the Federal Election Commission (FEC) and report to the FEC either monthly or quarterly as required by the FEC. For more information and "Registration Toolkits" for forming a federal PAC, visit the FEC's website www.fec.gov/ans/answers_pac.shtml. In Minnesota, state level PACs are required to register with the Minnesota Campaign Finance and Public Disclosure Board (Board) within 14 days of receiving or expending $750 or more.[22] Minnesota PACs must also annually report to the Board on or before January 31. For more information on Minnesota PACs (referred to as political committees or political funds), see the Board's "Political Committee and Political Fund Handbook" at www.cfboard.state.mn.us/handbook/pcf_handbook.pdf.

Although certain types of PACS are permitted by campaign finance laws to accept contributions from corporations and nonprofits, 501(c)(3) organizations are still prohibited by tax-exemption laws from making contributions to or otherwise supporting any PAC.

E. For-profit Subsidiaries

Q15. Can a tax-exempt nonprofit organization "own" a for-profit business?

A15. Yes. If the for-profit business activity is conducted by the organization itself and is not directly related to the organization's mission (other than the need for funding), the for-profit business activities must be insubstantial in relation to the nonprofit's exempt activities. Income from the venture would be subject to unrelated business income tax (UBIT). It may be permissible to have some unrelated business income. If permitted, it must be insubstantial and should be taken into account in business planning. If the nonexempt activities are substantial, then the nonprofit risks losing its exempt status unless the business activity is conducted through a subsidiary.

As for when an unrelated business activity may be considered "substantial" and jeopardize the organization's tax-exempt status, there is not a bright-line rule. As a rule of thumb, practitioners generally consider unrelated activities constituting 15% or less of the organization's total activities to be safely insubstantial. If the activities exceed this amount, the organization should evaluate it carefully and consider moving the activity into a subsidiary, as discussed below.

A for-profit subsidiary formed as a business or nonprofit corporation and taxed as a "C-Corporation" can conduct unlimited for-profit activities without jeopardizing the nonprofit's tax-exempt status. The for-profit pays state and federal corporate income tax, and then may distribute any remaining profits to its nonprofit shareholder as dividends, which are tax-free to the nonprofit.

22 Minn. Stat. § 10A.14, subd. 1 (2016).

The for-profit subsidiary is a separate legal entity and must be governed accordingly. It must have its own board of directors, books and records, and file its own tax returns. It must pay for all of its own expenses.

If the for-profit subsidiary will use any assets of its parent nonprofit—such as staff, space, equipment, mailing lists, logos and so on—it must pay fair market value for them, and the income to the nonprofit will generally be taxed as unrelated business income. A written agreement is recommended.

Although the nonprofit may transfer funds or other assets to its nonprofit subsidiary, it must generally receive a fair return on the transfer. The transfer can be a capital investment in the subsidiary, a loan or a sale with fair market payment. A nonprofit should not just give away charitable assets to its for-profit subsidiary.

Properly formed and operated, a for-profit subsidiary enables a nonprofit organization to protect its tax-exempt status while controlling the subsidiary as the sole shareholder and maximizing the revenue from the for-profit business.

F. Limited Liability Companies (LLCs)

Q16. What is a limited liability company or LLC?

A16. An LLC is a type of legal entity that offers the liability shield of a corporation but the tax advantages of a partnership or disregarded entity. In particular, properly formed and operated, an LLC is a separate entity for liability purposes. But if owned entirely by a nonprofit tax-exempt organization and operated for charitable purposes, the LLC is treated for tax-exemption purposes as if it did not exist. Thus, it is automatically tax-exempt and its activities and finances are treated, for tax purposes, as those of the nonprofit.

First, a single-member LLC is useful for conducting an activity or owning an asset in furtherance of the nonprofit's tax-exempt purposes where liability issues are present. For example, an organization may use a single-member LLC to own a piece of real estate or operate a new program that carries operation risks.

Second, an LLC can also be used as a vehicle for a joint venture which, if structured properly, could include equity ownership with a for-profit partner. The activities of the LLC are attributed to each member/owner in proportion to their ownership, so a careful analysis must be made of the joint venture's activity relative to the nonprofit's tax-exempt status. Consultation with legal counsel is recommended before entering into such a joint venture.

Generally, LLCs offer business flexibility and some protection against liability and taxation. For more information about LLCs, visit the IRS website or the Minnesota Secretary of State's website.

Q17. Can a Minnesota LLC be tax-exempt?

A17. Yes, a Minnesota LLC may be tax-exempt, but only if it meets certain criteria.

As with all LLCs, Minnesota LLCs have two options when it comes to tax-exempt treatment. First, the LLC may wish to be viewed as a disregarded entity. A business entity with only one owner is classified as a corporation or is disregarded; if the entity is disregarded, its activities are treated in the same manner as a sole proprietorship, branch, or division of the owner.[23] An LLC with one owner that is tax-exempt is treated as a disregarded entity unless it elects otherwise.[24] If it is a disregarded entity, then the parent organization treats the LLC as its own for tax and information reporting purposes. This is true for state sales tax and property tax purposes as well.[25] The second option is to elect taxation as a corporation and apply to the IRS for recognition as a 501(c)(3). This is an unusual use of an LLC and, generally, formation as a nonprofit corporation in this situation would be preferable.

Q18. What is a nonprofit LLC?

A18. In 2008, the Minnesota Limited Liability Company Act was amended to permit an LLC to be formed for "any lawful purpose" rather than being limited to any "business purpose" as was the case before the 2008 amendments. This opened the possibility for nonprofit organizations to form LLCs that would conduct charitable or other non-business activities, as discussed above. In addition to making this change, the Legislature also added the notion of a "nonprofit LLC," which includes limitations on monetary gain and distributions to members for nonprofit LLCs, similar to the restrictions required under the Minnesota Statutes Chapter 317A and section 501(c)(3) for federal tax-exempt status.[26] It also requires nonprofit LLCs to abide by the Minnesota Statutes Chapter 317A and empowers the Attorney General to the same enforcement authority under Chapter 317A.[27] Use of a "nonprofit LLC" is not required, but may be of interest because it incorporates familiar nonprofit-type limitations into the entity form. It is advisable to consult legal counsel when deciding entity structure and formation.

One thing to note regarding treatment of LLC's: the LLC statute 322B has been replaced with 322C, which became effective as of August 1, 2015 for newly established LLCs. Thus any new LLC must be established using the requirements of 322C. However, LLCs formed prior to August 1, 2015 can continue using 322B until August 1, 2018 at which point they will automatically switch to being governed by 322C or they can elect prior to that time to be governed by the new statute.

Q19. Who can be a member of a nonprofit LLC?

A19. A "natural person" cannot be a member of a nonprofit LLC, nor own any financial or governance rights in a nonprofit LLC.[28] Thus, nonprofit LLCs are comprised of other entity members.

The most common form of a nonprofit LLC is a single member LLC. This type of LLC is usually formed when an existing tax-exempt organization creates a subsidiary that is organized as an LLC. This structure allows tax-exempt organizations to develop new facilities that are separate entities with liability protection. Additionally, if the single member is tax-exempt, the LLC will be disregarded for federal tax purposes.[29]

---

23 Treas. Reg. 301.7701-2(a) (2016). See Treas. Reg. 301.7701-2(c)(2)(iii)- (vi) (2016) for special rules that apply to an eligible entity that is otherwise disregarded as an entity separate from its owner.

24 Treas. Reg. 301.7701-3(b)(ii) (2006).

25 "For purposes of the exemptions granted by subdivisions 1 to 33, property owned or operated by a limited liability company consisting of a sole member shall be treated as if owned or operated by that member." Minn. Stat. § 272.02, subd. 35 (2016). See also Minn. Stat. § 297A.70, subd. 4(d) (2016) for taxation information on sales to nonprofit groups.

26 Minn. Stat. § 322B.975, subd 2 (2016).

27 Minn. Stat. § 322B.975, subd. 5-6 (2016).

28 Minn. Stat. § 322B.975, subd. 3 (2016).

29 *See* I.R.S. Announcement 99-102, 1999-43 I.R.B. 545 (available at www.irs.gov/pub/irs-irbs/irb99-43.pdf).

A multi-member nonprofit LLC may facilitate a joint venture or collaboration amongst several tax-exempt organizations. Similar to the single member structure, the multi-member LLC provides limited liability protection and other efficiencies. The tax-exempt members should consider the activities of the LLC and how those activities relate to the members' exempt purposes.[30] Unrelated LLC activities may lead to revenue that may be considered unrelated business income or may jeopardize tax-exempt status.

Q20. What is an "L3C"?

A20. A low-profit limited liability company (L3C) has been introduced and adopted by some states as hybrid for-profit and nonprofit entities.[31] Although Minnesota has not adopted legislation that recognized L3C entities, Minnesota organizations may incorporate an L3C in a state that does recognize them and conduct business in Minnesota. An L3C is basically a type of LLC but is required by law to have a primary charitable goal and secondary profit concern. The same result can be achieved using a regular LLC and incorporating these principles into its organizational documents. While this structure may attract attention, L3Cs are not exempt from federal or state corporate income taxes. For more information and links to legislation enacting L3Cs in other states, visit the "Nonprofit Law Blog" entry "L3C – Developments and Resources" at www.nonprofitlawblog.com/home/2009/03/l3c-developments-resources.html#more. For a more critical analysis of the L3C model, see Daniel Kleinberger and J. William Callison, "When the law is understood – L3C No" at www.papers.ssrn.com/sol3/papers.cfm?abstract_id=1568373##.

F. Government Contracting

Q21. What are the legal ramifications of accepting federal grant or contract dollars?

A21. In accepting a federal grant or contract, a nonprofit organization agrees to abide by the terms and obligations associated with the grant or contract. These obligations vary with each grant, but they typically include strict standards regarding costs and audit procedures. These audits must typically be performed by independent certified public accountants.

Information regarding the consequences of accepting federal grants and contracts are discussed in the Office of Management and Budget ("OMB") circulars available at www.whitehouse.gov/omb/information-for-agencies/circulars. Circulars A-110, A-122 and A-133 provide the general requirements for nonprofits. Circular A-110 establishes uniform administrative requirements for federal grants and agreements awarded to institutions of higher education, hospitals and other nonprofit organizations. Circular A-122 establishes principles for determining costs of grants, contracts and other agreements with non-profit organizations. Circular A-133 sets forth standards for obtaining consistency and uniformity among federal agencies for the audit of states, local governments, and non-profit organizations expending federal awards. Many state and local government contracts incorporate these federal standards as well.

Consequences for improper use of federal, state or local government money range from the loss of the contract or grant to imprisonment for misuse of public funds.

30 Jennifer Reedstrom-Bishop, Address at the 2010 Nonprofit Law Conference: Nonprofit LLCs and L3Cs (Mar. 9, 2010).
31 *See* Americans for Community Development FAQs, americansforcommunitydevelopment.org/frequently-asked-questions.

Q22. What are the legal ramifications of accepting state grant or contract dollars?

A22. When accepting state grant or contract dollars, nonprofit organizations are also accepting the requirements and conditions placed upon those dollars.

Typically, such grants or contracts come associated with strict reporting requirements. Most state grants require a minimum annual reporting that includes a financial statement noting the status of the funds allocated to the organization, along with some sort of narrative explaining the organization's experience and uses of the funds. Additional requirements may include curriculum review for organizations involved in education, member participant demographics for some service grants and training progress reports for organizations involved in employment training.

In the State of Minnesota's recent Drive to Excellence initiative, the state developed a new Grants Management office to streamline and administer the grant process. Visit the Office of Grants Management website at www.grants.state.mn.us/public. Service contracts are generally by each state agency.

Q23. What accounting procedures are required for government grants and contracts?

A23. OMB Circulars provide the general default rules related to accounting procedures for government grants and contracts, but each governmental agency is typically allowed to enact their own unique rules or requirements. Organizations should look to the exact language in their grant to determine which rules apply to them, or contact their granting agency.

OMB Circular A-110 provides administrative requirements for organizations receiving government funding. Organizations governed by Circular A-110 are required to use a financial management system to relate financial data to performance data when practical.[32] This system should identify the source and application of all funds, and should safeguard all assets and ensure they are only used for authorized purposes.[33]

Recipients are required to monitor their projects, programs, sub-awards, etc. and ensure all groups have met the audit requirements provided in OMB Circular A-133.[34] Performance reports will be required at least annually, but no more than quarterly. These performance reports shall contain a comparison with the actual accomplishments of the project versus the goals and objectives; why the goals were not met, if appropriate; and any other pertinent information.[35] Recipients must contact the agency providing their grant immediately if circumstances develop that will significantly impact the organization's activities.

Each organization must provide some sort of financial status report: either SF-269, SF -269A, SF-270 or SF-272. The awarding agency will determine which form is appropriate.

Organizations generally must retain records for three years beyond the end of the grant.

32 Office of Management and Budget, *Uniform Administrative Requirements for Grants and Other Agreements with Institutions of Higher Education, Hospitals and Other Non-Profit Organizations*, Circular A-110 (Sept. 1999), www.whitehouse.gov/omb/circulars_a110.

33 Id.

34 Office of Management and Budget, *Uniform Administrative Requirements for Grants and Other Agreements with Institutions of Higher Education, Hospitals and Other Non-Profit Organizations*, Circular A-110.51(a) (Sept. 1999), www.whitehouse.gov/omb/circulars_a110.

35 Office of Management and Budget, *Uniform Administrative Requirements for Grants and Other Agreements with Institutions of Higher Education, Hospitals and Other Non-Profit Organizations*, Circular A-110.51(d) (Sept. 1999), www.whitehouse.gov/omb/circulars_a110.

OMB A-133 lays out the appropriate auditing requirements for nonprofit organizations receiving federal and many state grants. Generally, organizations expending more than $500,000 from federal sources must perform an audit. Organizations expending less than $500,000 are exempt from this requirement, unless they are required to perform an audit by the organization providing their funding.[36] Audits should generally be run annually, and organizations may risk losing their award if they fail to perform their audit in a timely manner.

Prior to the audit, the organization being audited must identify the source and destination of all federal funds, prepare all applicable federal statements and ensure that the audit will be performed when due. Auditees are expected to follow OMB Circular A-102 when employing an auditor, and are encouraged to employ small business, minority owned firms and women's business enterprises.[37]

The auditee must follow up with all audit findings and take corrective actions when appropriate. A reporting package must be submitted to the agency providing the grant and include:

- Financial statements and schedule of expenditure awards
- Summary schedule of prior audit findings
- Auditor's report
- Corrective action plan

G. Chartered National, State or Local Organizations

Q24. What does the term "chartered organization" mean?

A24. While the Articles of Incorporation filed by a nonprofit are occasionally called articles of charter, this does not mean that every nonprofit is a chartered organization. The term "chartered organization" is typically applied only to organizations specifically chartered by Congress (I.R.C. § 501(c)(1) organizations), a state legislature, or chartered by certain national or regional groups. For purposes of this chapter, the term "chartered organization" is used to refer to organizations chartered by a national or regional group rather than by Congress or a state legislature.

Though there is nothing to stop a nonprofit organization from calling itself a chartered organization merely because of their filed Articles of Incorporation, such a practice is imprecise and may lead to confusion in the future.

Q25. If an organization is the state or local branch of a national or regional organization, does it have the same tax-exempt status as the chartering organization?

A25. State or local branches typically fall under the same category of tax-exempt status as their national or regional group (i.e., 501(c)(3), 501(c)(4), or 501(c)(6)), but such status may not be automatic. Depending on how the chartering organization is structured, the state or local branch may be covered by a group exemption, discussed below, or may be required to obtain its own tax-exempt status. A state or local branch organization should consult with its national or regional organization to confirm its tax-exempt status.

36 Office of Management and Budget, *Audits of States, Local Governments and Non-Profit Organizations*, Circular A-133(b).200(a)-(d) (June 2007), www.whitehouse.gov/sites/whitehouse.gov/files/omb/circulars/A133/a133_revised_2007.pdf.

37 Office of Management and Budget, *Audits of States, Local Governments and Non-Profit Organizations*, Circular A-133.305 (a) (June 2007), www.whitehouse.gov/sites/whitehouse.gov/files/omb/circulars/A133/a133_revised_2007.pdf.

Q26. What legal links should be maintained between state and local organization and their national or regional entities?

A26. Each chartered organization's relationship with their larger national or regional entity is different, and therefore organizations should turn to their articles of charter or charter contract for precise information, or contact the national or regional entity directly. There is very little law regarding the relationship between state and local organizations and their national or regional entities. Therefore, the agreement between the two entities is decisive.

Most national or regional organizations require some sort of annual dues from member organizations. In return, member organizations may receive resources, funding, equipment, advice, training, advocacy or some other compensation. Additionally, organizations may receive benefits from the national or regional organizations tax exemption status.

Each chartered relationship is different; nonprofits should consult with their national or regional organization or their articles or contract of charter to determine what steps the nonprofit must take to maintain their charter.

Q27. Who controls the use of the organization's name in a chartered relationship?

A27. Most chartered organizations, once recognized, are permitted to use the organization's name and logo to promote their activities. The parent organization typically retains the right to modify this arrangement, and most chartered organizations are limited in the ways a name or logo can be used.

These agreements generally require that the chartered organization refrain from using the name, logo or trademark in any way that might diminish its value.

Chartered organizations should consult their charter contract or agreement for more information about the appropriate use of an organization's name or logo, or contact their parent organization.

Q28. Does a Minnesota nonprofit corporation need to submit changes in its Articles of Incorporation or Bylaws to the organization it is related to by charter?

A28. Probably. The answer depends upon the language of the nonprofit corporation's articles or contract of charter with the nonprofit branch. Most charter documents require organizations to submit changes to their parent organization for approval and many restrict what amendments are permitted.

Nonprofit organizations should look to their charter documents or contact their parent organization to determine which changes must be submitted.

H. Other Issues

Q29. What is a group exemption?

A29. A group exemption is a tax-exempt status that is conferred upon an organization solely because of the organization's relationship with a greater central organization.[38] This central organization is typically a statewide or national group.

Because of the group exemption, the local organization is not required to apply for its own tax-exempt status. The central organization is required to apply for a group exemption letter and maintain its status annually.

The central organization is then responsible for determining whether its subordinates are covered by the group exemption and maintaining records of its subordinates. In order for a subordinate organization to qualify for a group exemption, the parent organization must be able to demonstrate that the subordinate is:

- affiliated with it;
- subject to its general supervision or control;
- exempt under the same paragraph of IRC 501(c) as all other subordinates (but in some instances not necessarily the same paragraph of IRC 501(c) under which the parent is exempt);
- not a private foundation or a foreign organization; and
- on the same accounting period as the parent.

Organizations covered by a group exemption can choose to file a group return, Form 990, or file their 990s' separately. More information on group exemptions can be found on the IRS web site.[39]

Q30. Can related nonprofit organizations share a taxpayer identification number?

A30. No. Each nonprofit corporation must have its own taxpayer identification number (EIN), which is used to submit employee tax withholding and on IRS Form 990.[40]

Q31. Must related nonprofits share financial information?

A31. It depends on the nature of their relationship. If one is a parent of the other, it has the right to access certain records of the subsidiary.

Accounting standards may require that the finances of related organizations be consolidated for financial reporting purposes. Even if audited financial statements are consolidated, however, nonprofit organizations must generally file separate IRS 990 Forms.

38 I.R.S. Pub. 557, Tax-Exempt Status for Your Organization (Jan. 2017), www.irs.gov/pub/irs-pdf/p557.pdf.
39 I.R.S. Group Exemptions, www.irs.gov/Charities-&-Non-Profits/Group-Exemption-Resources (last updated Feb. 7, 2017).
40 I.R.S. Form SS-4 (Jan. 2010), www.irs.gov/pub/irs-pdf/fss4.pdf.

I. Related Resources

Publications:

Guide for the Voluntary Dissolution of Minnesota Nonprofit Corporations, LegalCORPS
legalcorps.org/wp-content/uploads/2012/03/LegalCorps-Nonprofit-Dissolution-Guidelines.pdf

Tax Information for Charities and Nonprofits, Internal Revenue Service
www.irs.gov/charities-non-profits

Organizations:

Alliance for Justice
11 Dupont Circle, NW
Washington, DC 20036
www.afj.org

GuideStar
4801 Courthouse St., Suite 220
Williamsburg, VA 23188
www.guidestar.org

Minnesota Attorney General's Office
445 Minnesota Street, Suite 1400
St. Paul, MN 55101
www.ag.state.mn.us

Minnesota Secretary of State
Elections Counter:
180 State Office Building
St. Paul, MN 55155
Business Counter:
60 Empire Dr.
St. Paul, MN 55103
www.sos.state.mn.us/home/index.asp

Nonprofit Risk Management Center
204 South King Street
Leesburg, VA 20175
www.nonprofitrisk.org

Office of Management and Budget
725 17th St., NW
Washington, DC 20503
www.whitehouse.gov/omb/

Statutes:

Minnesota Statutes
www.leg.state.mn.us/leg/statutes.asp

United States Code
www.law.cornell.edu/uscode/

CHAPTER 13

OTHER REGULATORY ISSUES

Topics

A. Overview

In addition to being subject to regulation and scrutiny by the Internal Revenue Service ("IRS"), the Attorney General and the Secretary of State, nonprofit organizations may encounter several other regulatory agencies in the course of their work. These regulatory agencies can add complexity and time-consuming paperwork to the life of a nonprofit. That time spent must be balanced with the rewards that can come from satisfying the requirements of a law, such as lawful charitable gambling in Minnesota.

This chapter deals with several of the regulatory issues that a nonprofit may encounter over the course of its existence. Some of them, such as lawful gambling, may require significant ongoing compliance. Others, such as parade regulations, may only arise occasionally, if at all. The chapter begins with lawful gambling, a highly regulated and taxed process that requires a significant commitment from any organization that undertakes it. Next, the chapter explores the issues dealing with nonprofit postal rates, a simple way for mail-dependent nonprofits to cut costs. Third, the chapter addresses the issue of parades which, while regulated, enjoy considerable First Amendment protection.

Several of these topics, lawful gambling for example, are complex beyond the scope of this publication. The purpose of the chapter, more so than elsewhere in this handbook, is to raise awareness of these topics and point the reader to additional resources where appropriate.

Each organization should familiarize themselves with the particular regulatory and compliance requirements that are relevant to the programs or products of their organization. This could include and is certainly not limited to: commercial food preparation standards and commercial kitchen standards for organizations that prepare food as part of the services they provide; childcare license and space requirements; and health care licenses and facility requirements for organizations that have clinic space.

B. Minnesota Lawful (or Charitable) Gambling

Q1. What types of activities are considered lawful (or charitable) gambling?

A1. In Minnesota, lawful gambling is the operation, conduct or sale of bingo, raffles, paddlewheels, tipboards and pull-tabs.[1]

Q2. How do nonprofit organizations set up a lawful (or charitable) gambling program?

A2. There are four types of nonprofit organizations that are eligible to conduct lawful gambling: fraternal, religious, veteran, and other nonprofit.[2]

Beyond the exempted or excluded activities detailed below, the process for establishing a lawful gambling program requires providing rigorous detail about the organization, its personnel, internal controls, and the type of gambling the organization intends. The best place to begin is the Minnesota Gambling Control Board's website at mn.gov/gcb, which has the forms necessary for the application. In addition, the Gambling Control Board has created a Lawful Gambling Manual available for download at mn.gov/gcb/lawful-gambling-manual.html.

1 Minn. Stat. § 349.12, subd. 24 (2016).
2 Minnesota Gambling Control Board, Nonprofit Requirements, mn.gov/gcb/ (last visited Aug. 9, 2017).

First, an organization must provide proof of its nonprofit status to the Gambling Control Board by submitting documents issued by the IRS or the Secretary of State.[3] Nonprofit organizations must provide proof of nonprofit status by ONE of the following:[4]

1. Certificate of Good Standing for current calendar year. If you don't have a copy, contact the Secretary of State at 651-296-2803.
2. IRS income tax exemption 501(c) letter in your organization's name. If you don't have a copy, contact the IRS at 877-829-5500.
3. IRS - Affiliate of national, statewide, or international parent nonprofit organization (charter).

If your organization falls under a parent organization provide BOTH:[5]

1. An IRS letter showing parent organization is a nonprofit 501(c) with group ruling; and
2. A charter or letter from parent organization recognizing your organization as a subordinate.

Next, the organization must elect or hire someone to be its gambling manager. The gambling manager must complete an application that requires, among other things, a $10,000 dishonesty bond, a background check, and a signed and notarized affidavit stating his or her fitness of character for the position. The gambling manager and the executive director of the organization must also attend a training on lawful gambling held by the Gambling Control Board. The gambling manager will be required to pass an exam before a license for lawful gambling can be acquired.[6]

Due to past problems of theft, missing funds, and complaints of unfair administration that benefits insiders, a heavy layer of reporting, recording and personal liability is required of gambling sponsors. The executive director and treasurer of the organization must sign affidavits indicating their fitness of character related to gambling operations. The organization must detail the internal controls established to prevent fraud, including a flow chart of the organization and the list of signatories on the gambling account. The treasurer of the organization may not be a signatory on the gambling account, even if the treasurer and the executive director are the same person. The compensation of all paid employees connected to the gambling operation must be submitted. All gambling operation employees must wear a name badge that includes their picture. If the organization has members, it must submit a list of at least 15 active members; however, 501(c)(3) organizations are exempt from this requirement.

Once a gambling license has been issued, the organization is responsible for notifying the Gambling Control Board in writing of any changes regarding the license or the employees involved in the gambling operation. Situations that require notification include new hires, compensation changes, bank changes and address changes, among others.

Q3. Do raffles count as lawful (or charitable) gambling?

A3. Gambling is defined by the state of Minnesota as an activity that involves consideration or payment for a chance in being selected as a winner of an awarded prize.[7] A raffle is defined as a "game in which a participant buys a ticket in an event where the prize determination is based on a method of random selection

3 Minnesota Gambling Control Board, *Lawful Gambling Manual*, Chapter 1 Organization License (2017), mn.gov/gcb/assets/ch-1-org-license-2017.pdf.
4 Minnesota Gambling Control Board, Nonprofit Requirements, mn.gov/gcb/ (last visited Aug. 9, 2017).
5 Minnesota Gambling Control Board, Nonprofit Requirements, mn.gov/gcb/ (last visited Aug. 9, 2017).
6 Minn. Stat. § 349.167 (2016).
7 Minnesota Gambling Control Board, *Lawful Gambling Manual*, Chapter 7 Raffles (2017), mn.gov/gcb/assets/ch-7-raffles-2017.pdf.

and all entries have an equal chance of selection."[8] As a payment is exchanged for a change of winning a prize, raffles count as lawful gambling. Regulations of raffles depend on the value of prizes awarded in a year. If an organization awards less than $1,500 in raffle prizes in a calendar year, or, if the organization is a 501(c)(3) organization and the value of all raffle prizes awarded by the organization at one event in a calendar year does not exceed $5,000, raffles may be conducted by an organization without registering with the board.[9] If an organization awards more than $1,500 and less than $50,000 in prizes per year, it is exempt from the ongoing registration requirements, but it does need to apply for an exempt permit for each raffle conducted.[10]

Q4. Do raffles need to be registered with the Minnesota Gambling Control Board?

A4. Organizations may conduct raffles without a license from the Minnesota Gambling Control Board if the total prize award amount does not exceed $1,500 in a calendar year.[11] If the total prize amount, including donated prizes, are less than $50,000 in a calendar year and raffles are conducted on five or fewer days during the year, then the organization can file the Application for Exempt Permit.[12] If the organization wants to award more than $50,000 a year in prizes or have raffles on five or more dates, it will have to follow the process to be licensed as an ongoing lawful gambling sponsor.

Q5. What steps does a nonprofit organization need to take to legally set up a raffle as a fundraiser?

A5. Depending on the value of prizes an organization plans to raffle, it may fall into one of three categories of regulation by the Minnesota Gambling Control Board. The first category is for those organizations that do not award more than $1,500 in prizes in one calendar year. Organizations in this category are excluded from Gambling Control Board oversight, and registration is not required.[13]

The second category of regulation is for organizations that do not award more than $50,000 in prizes in lawful gambling in a calendar year and who also conduct lawful gambling on five or fewer days in a calendar year. Organizations in this category must complete the Application for Exempt Permit each time they wish to conduct a raffle. The form must be submitted 30 days before the proposed raffle date along with an application fee of $100 ($150 if less than 30 days before the raffle date).[14] While the requirements for the exempt permit are significantly less than the requirements for ongoing compliance of a full lawful gambling license, the application for an exempt permit still requires proof of nonprofit status with either the state or federal government, and the Gambling Control Board and the local unit of government (city and/or county) must approve the application before the raffles can be held.

The third category of regulation is for organizations that award prizes greater than $50,000 or conduct lawful gambling on five or more days in a calendar year. Organizations in this category must apply for a lawful gambling license as discussed in Question 2.

If an organization is conducting an excluded or exempt raffle (category one or two) and is only selling the tickets at the event where the drawing is held, then it is permissible to use raffle tickets with just a sequen-

---

8 *Id.*
9 Minn. Stat. § 349.166, subd. 1(c) (2016).
10 Minn. Stat. § 349.166, subd. 2(a) (2016).
11 Minn. Stat. § 349.166, subd. 1(c) (2016).
12 Minn. Stat. § 349.166, subd. 2(a)(3) (2016); see also Minnesota Lawful Gambling, LG220 Application for Exempt Permit, mn.gov/gcb/assets/lg220-exempt-permit-application.pdf.
13 Minn. Stat. § 349.166, subd. 1(c) (2016).
14 Minn. Stat. § 349.166, subd. 2(a)(3) (2016).

tial number and no other information. The prize list and other drawing information must be available to the purchasers of raffle tickets upon request. However, if the organization plans to sell tickets in advance of the event, the format of the tickets must include the following information:

- Organization name and Minnesota Gambling Control Board permit number;
- Drawing details, including time, date and location;
- Sequential numbering, starting at 1;
- Price of the ticket – note that multiple purchase discounts are not permitted;
- A listing of at least the top three prizes, along with a statement indicating that a complete list of all prizes is available; and
- A detachable stub with corresponding sequential numbers to be filled in with the purchaser's name, address, and phone number.[15]

The conduct of the raffle must be fair to all purchasers. As a result, the following conditions are also imposed on organizations conducting raffles:

- Purchasers cannot be expected to buy anything other than the raffle ticket, except that a certificate of participation may be a button with a nominal value of less than $5;
- Each ticket must have an equal chance to win;
- Method of selection must be conducted in a public forum;
- The method of selection cannot be manipulated or based on the outcome of an event not under the control of the organization;
- All sold and unsold tickets must be accounted for; and
- Winners do not need to be present to win.[16]

Finally, for each raffle, the organization must keep extensive records in a logbook. The logbook is required to include:

- Name of the organization and date of the raffle;
- Total number of tickets printed and the price of each ticket;
- Name and phone numbers of all persons to whom tickets were given to sell;
- Number and sequential range of tickets given to each person to be sold; and
- Number of tickets sold and unsold as well as actual gross reported proceeds, cash received, and cash differential of each ticket seller.[17]

Q6. Does a nonprofit organization need to be incorporated in order to conduct a raffle?

A6. Yes, all organizations must be incorporated or granted tax-exempt status under the internal revenue code section 501(c) in order to conduct a raffle. This includes organizations that are exempt and excluded from gambling registration requirements (those in categories 1 and 2 as explained in Question 5). In fact, not only must the organization be incorporated, but the organization must have been in existence for the three and a half years preceding the application for a gambling license.[18]

15 Minnesota Gambling Control Board, *Lawful Gambling Manual* Chapter 7 Raffles (2017), mn.gov/gcb/assets/ch-7-raffles-2017.pdf.

16 Minn. Stat. § 349.173 (2016); see also Minnesota Gambling Control Board, *Lawful Gambling Manual* Chapter 7 Raffles (2017), mn.gov/gcb/assets/ch-7-raffles-2017.pdf (providing more details on additional requirements, for example, persons under 18 may sell raffle tickets but not purchase or win).

17 Minnesota Gambling Control Board, *Lawful Gambling Manual,* Chapter 7 Raffles (2017), mn.gov/gcb/assets/ch-7-raffles-2017.pdf.

18 *See* Minn. Stat. § 349.166, subd. 2(b) (2016).

Q7. Is the cost of a raffle ticket deductible to the purchaser as a charitable contribution?

A7. No. The Internal Revenue Service does not regard gambling as a charitable activity, even if funds raised through the ticket sale support a charitable organization. As a result, the purchase of a raffle ticket does not constitute a charitable contribution and cannot be used to reduce personal income tax liabilities for the purchaser.[19]

C. Nonprofit Postal Rates

Q8. How does a nonprofit organization apply for a nonprofit bulk mail permit with the U.S. Postal Service?

A8. Nonprofit bulk mailing rates (now known as "standard") can save qualified organizations a considerable percentage off the cost of regular standard rate for mailings larger than 200 pieces sorted by zip code and labeled in a manner set by the postal service. A nonprofit organization that wants to take advantage of nonprofit standard mail rates must complete Postal Service Form 3624, available from the U.S. Postal Service at about.usps.com/forms/ps3624.pdf. In addition to basic contact information, the form requires some detailed information about the organization in order to make a determination about eligibility. The organization must identify which eligible category best describes its work. Examples of eligible nonprofits include religious, educational, scientific, philanthropic (charitable), and fraternal organizations. Examples of ineligible organizations include business leagues, chambers of commerce, and automobile clubs.[20]

The application also requires document attachments that provide additional evidence of nonprofit status, organization, and financial operations. Examples of such documentation include the articles of incorporation, the IRS 501(c)(3) determination letter, an independent audit, program brochures, meeting minutes, and newsletters. These documents help the USPS Business Mail Unit make a determination of eligibility for nonprofit standard mail rates.[21]

You take the completed PS Form 3624 and supporting documents to the Post Office where your organization intends to mail. You should request a copy of the application that has been date-stamped by postal personnel.[22]

Applications take approximately two weeks to process. During that period, an organization may send mail at the standard rate and request a refund of the difference in cost between the two rates after the nonprofit mailing eligibility is approved.[23] Once approved, a nonprofit maintains its eligibility by doing at least one mailing during a two-year period.

Q9. What types of information are not eligible for inclusion in nonprofit rate mailings?

A9. In order for a particular mailing to be eligible for the nonprofit standard mailing rate, the content of the mailing must meet certain eligibility requirements. If a mailing piece fails to meet these content

19 *See* I.R.S. Pub. 526, Charitable Contributions, 6 (Jan. 19, 2017), www.irs.gov/pub/irs-pdf/p526.pdf.
20 See United States Postal Service, Nonprofit USPS Marketing Mail Eligibility: Nonprofit and Transmittal Letter Other Qualified Organizations 2-2.1 (Jan. 2017), pe.usps.com/cpim/ftp/pubs/pub417/pub417.pdf.
21 United States Postal Service, Application to Mail at Nonprofit Standard Mail Prices (Jan. 2017), about.usps.com/forms/ps3624.pdf.
22 United States Postal Service, Nonprofit USPS Marketing Mail Eligibility: Nonprofit and Transmittal Letter Other Qualified Organizations 3-1.6.1 (Jan. 2017), pe.usps.com/cpim/ftp/pubs/pub417/pub417.pdf.
23 *Id.* at 3-1.6.3.

requirements, the mailing can proceed at the standard rate, not discounted nonprofit mailing rate. First, the mailing must be free of references to travel services, insurance, or financial instruments (these restrictions are in response to past complaints of unfair competition from taxable businesses).[24]

Second, advertising in the mailing must be "substantially related" to the organization's tax-exempt purpose. However, this requirement does not apply to advertisements for travel arrangements, insurance policies, and financial instruments, or periodicals; to be considered a periodical, a mailing must: 1) have a title, 2) be formed from printed sheets, 3) contain an identification statement on one of the first five pages, and 4) consist of at least 25 percent material that is not advertising.[25]

The third and final content requirement for nonprofit mailing rates applies to cooperative mailings where more than one organization shares the cost, risk or benefit of the mailing. These sorts of mailings are only eligible for nonprofit standard mailing rates if each of the cooperating organizations is individually qualified to mail at those rates. However, a limited exception has been adopted to this policy to assist nonprofits in obtaining funding needing to support their programs. [26] The cooperative mail rule does not apply if the mailing is soliciting monetary donations for the authorized nonprofit mailer, it does not promote or facilitate the sale or lease of goods or services and the authorized nonprofit mailer is given a list of each donor, contact information for each donor, the amount of the donation or waives in writing receipt of this information.[27]

To verify compliance with these regulations, the Post Office examines individual mailings and is authorized to bill organizations for the difference in postage rates if it discovers that a mailing does not meet the nonprofit rate requirements.

D. Parades

Q10. What legally constitutes a parade?

A10. Both state and local government regulate parades and therefore have differing definitions of parade. However, most units of government use similar definitions of what constitutes a parade. For example, the Minneapolis Municipal Code § 447.10 defines a parade as "any parade, march, or procession in or upon any street except the sidewalks thereof, or in or upon any alley of the city." It may be helpful to call or visit the website of the municipality where the parade will take place to discern its definition of parade.

Q11. When does an organization need to secure a permit for a parade?

A11. An organization should look into the parade regulations for each state and local government jurisdiction that the proposed parade route will cross. These regulations will usually require a parade application to be submitted to a unit of government such as the police department or the public works department. These applications often request details about the size and composition of the parade as well as a detailed route proposal. They may also include a processing fee, and the organization may also be responsible for paying for police and safety protection during the parade.

24 *Id.* at 6-3.4.2-3.
25 *Id.* at 6-3.6.1.
26 *See generally id.* at 5.2.
27 *Id.* at 5-2.1.

Q12. Can local governments deny a parade permit for a protest march?

A12. As long as they are nonviolent, the First Amendment to the U.S. Constitution protects parades and protest marches as free speech. Because the free speech takes the form of conduct, the Constitution does permit some reasonable regulation by government. A permit-issuing body, such as a city council, may balance the rights of a group to freely express their views with the safety and welfare of the rest of its citizenry. It is permissible for state or local government to impose reasonable restrictions on groups seeking to conduct parades or protest marches. However, such regulations must not impose unfair restrictions that could be used to regulate the content of the speech. Favoring one group over another or creating an excessively burdensome application process is unconstitutional.[28] Many restrictions could also be considered unfair and burdensome. As a result, civil liberties groups often negotiate with state and local government to consider the rights of the marchers and, when unsuccessful, sometimes litigate these matters in court.

Q13. How do parades compare to assemblies (protest or otherwise) on public land?

A13. Parades and public assemblies are treated similarly. The First Amendment to the U.S. Constitution states that, among other things, "Congress shall make no law . . . abridging . . . the right of the people peaceably to assemble, and to petition the Government for a redress of grievances." Therefore, a nonprofit can organize a public assembly but must follow proper procedures and any appropriate time, place and manner restrictions. For example, in order to publicly assemble in the Minnesota State Capitol rotunda, an organization must submit a written application to the State of Minnesota's Plant Management Division for a permit to hold a "public rally" on the Capitol Complex.[29] In addition to the necessary permits, the organization must comply with certain public safety rules and other restrictions, depending on the type of public venue used.

Q14. Do nonprofit organizations have a right to distribute leaflets or solicit at shopping malls or city streets?

A14. The right to distribute leaflets is protected under freedom of speech in the First Amendment to the U.S. Constitution.[30] However, it is not an absolute right but rather one that may be reasonably restricted based on the government's compelling interest. In general, handing out leaflets in a traditionally public space (such as a sidewalk, street or park) is permissible. Unless the dissemination of leaflets causes a traffic or safety concern, a permit is probably not required. As leafleting is most likely a non-disruptive activity, there are probably not any local ordinances that regulate this activity. Soliciting donations in a public space, however, may be regulated to prevent fraud. Organizations that plan to solicit donations in a public space should check with the Minnesota Attorney General's Office and local law enforcement authorities before beginning such activities. In Minnesota, shopping malls are considered private property and the property owners reserve the right to control activity in the common areas of the shopping mall.[31]

---

28 *See generally Edwards v. South Carolina*, 372 U.S. 229 (1963).
29 Public Events, MN Dept. of Administration, www.mn.gov/admin/government/public-events/index.jsp (last visited Aug. 10, 2017).
30 *See generally Lovell v. City of Griffin*, 303 U.S. 444 (1938).
31 *See generally State v. Wicklund*, 589 NW.2d 793 (1999).

E. Other Regulatory Issues

Q15. What regulations do nonprofit organizations need to follow when they provide food at an event, either for free or for a charge?

A15. It is the nature of the event and not the cost of the food that raises food safety issues. Generally, any organization that is "engaged in the business of conducting a food and beverage service establishment", is required to obtain an annual license. Nonprofit organizations operating a special event food stand with multiple locations at an annual one-day event will be issued only one license.[32] With a few exceptions, nonprofit organizations with 501(c)(3) status are exempt from obtaining a license for events held in the building or on the grounds of the organization and at which home-prepared food (potluck or bake sale) is donated by organization members for sale at the events.[33]

Depending on the size of the community in which the event will be held, licenses are obtained from the city, the county, or the Minnesota Department of Health. Licensing requirements for a special event food stand from the Minnesota Department of Health include providing information about the food; the sources of the food; a list of equipment involved in food preparation; a description of the hand washing, dish-washing and waste-disposal facilities; and the time and location of the operation. A fact sheet detailing these requirements is available at www.health.state.mn.us/divs/eh/food/license/specevent.pdf.

Q16. What are the mandatory reporting requirements regarding the abuse of a child or vulnerable adult?

A16. Individuals are subject to mandatory reporting requirements regarding the abuse of a child or a vulnerable adult if they are engaged in health care, education, law enforcement, correctional supervision, childcare, social services, hospital administration, or psychological or psychiatric treatment. Members of the clergy are also required to report such abuses, with some limited exceptions. These individuals who know or have reason to believe a child is being neglected or physically or sexually abused, or have been within the preceding three years, must immediately report this information.[34] The report can be made to a local public welfare agency or other agency responsible for investigating child protection or to the local police department. A report must be made within 24 hours of becoming aware of the abuse.

For vulnerable adults, mandated reporters are people engaged in social services, law enforcement, education, direct care, licensed heath and human service professionals, those employed in a licensed facility, and medical examiners or coroners.[35]

If there is immediate danger to a vulnerable adult, call 911. Otherwise, contact a county "Common Entry Point," which receives all reports of known or suspected maltreatment of vulnerable adults and works with the appropriate authorities.[36] Reports of suspected maltreatment of a vulnerable adult are made 24/7/365 to the MN Adult Abuse Reporting Center at 844-880-1574. The Minnesota County Common Entry Point (CEP) Phone List is available at www.dhs.state.mn.us.

If the report is made in good faith, the individual reporting is immune from civil liabilities for any lawsuits brought as a result of the report. If, on the other hand, a person in one the above described roles

---

32 Minn. Stat. § 157.16 (2016).
33 Minn. Stat. § 157.22(7) (2016).
34 Minn. Stat. § 626.556 subd. 3(a) (2016).
35 Minn. Stat. § 626.557 (2016).
36 Common Entry Point, registrations.dhs.state.mn.us/WebManRpt/Who_CEP4.html (last visited Aug. 10, 2017).

knows of abuse and does not make a report, the individual can be subject to criminal penalties ranging from a misdemeanor to a felony.[37]

Q17. Is a nonprofit organization required to provide free or reduced-cost services to people who cannot afford its fees or charges?

A17. There is no general legal requirement for nonprofits to provide reduced-cost services to the poor. Doing so is not required for incorporation as a nonprofit corporation in the state of Minnesota, nor is it required to obtain or maintain income tax-exempt 501(c)(3) status with the IRS. However, to be eligible for the Minnesota charitable property and sales tax exemption, one consideration is whether or not an organization provides reduced-cost services to its clients or beneficiaries. For more information see Chapter 3: Tax Exemption, Section E: Property Tax Exemption. As organizations vary in mission, scope of work, and organizational structure, it may not be reasonable for every organization to provide reduced-cost services to all beneficiaries, or even to anyone.

F. Related Resources

Publications:

Minnesota Department of Human Services, *An Interactive Informational Guide for Mandated Reporting*, www.dhs.state.mn.us (last visited Aug. 10, 2017).

Minnesota Department of Human Services, *Child Protection in Minnesota: Keeping Children Safe* (Apr. 2017), edocs.dhs.state.mn.us/lfserver/Public/DHS-4735-ENG.

Minnesota Department of Human Services, *Resource Guide for Mandated Reporters of Child Maltreatment Concerns* (Apr. 2017), edocs.dhs.state.mn.us/lfserver/Public/DHS-2917-ENG.

Organizations:

American Civil Liberties Union of Minnesota
2300 Myrtle Ave, Suite 180
Saint Paul, MN 55114
Phone: 651-645-4097
Email: support@aclu-mn.org
www.aclu-mn.org

Minnesota Adult Abuse Reporting Center
Toll-free Number: 844-880-1574
The general public can call to report suspected maltreatment of vulnerable adults.
mn.gov/dhs/people-we-serve/seniors/services/adult-protection

37 Minn. Stat. § 626.556 subd. 4 (2016); see also Minn. Stat. § 626.557 subd. 5 (2016).

Minnesota Crime Victim Support Line
Call: 866-385-2699
Text: 612-399-9977
dayoneservices.org

Minnesota Day One Crisis Hotline
Call: 866-223-1111
Text: 621-399-9995
dayoneservices.org

Minnesota Department of Health
Environmental Health Division
Freeman Building
625 Robert St. N
PO Box 64975, St. Paul, MN 55164
www.health.state.mn.us/foodsafety/index.html

Minnesota Department of Human Services
Children and Family Services, Assistant Commissioner's Office
PO Box 64244
St. Paul, MN 55164-0244
Phone: 651-431-3830
Fax: 651-431-7528
mn.gov/dhs/people-we-serve/children-and-families
Email: Dhs.Child.Safety-Permanency@state.mn.us
For concerns about the state's child protection system, not related to an individual concern, call the Minnesota Department of Human Services at 651-431-4661.

Minnesota Gambling Control Board
Suite 300 South
1711 West County Road B
Roseville, Minnesota 55113
Main office: 651-539-1900
Licensing fax: 651-639-4032
Compliance fax: 651-639-4043
www.gcb.state.mn.us
Regional offices are located in Fergus Falls, Hibbing and Saint Peter, addresses are available at mn.gov/gcb/main---regional-offices.html.

United States Postal Service - Business Mail Entry
PO Box 654015
Saint Paul MN 55164-5015
Phone: 651-681-2609
FAX: 651-681-2591
www.usps.com
District Business Mail Entry Locator
ribbs.usps.gov/locators/find-bme.cfm

CHAPTER 14

ONGOING COMPLIANCE

Topics

A. Overview

Nonprofit organizations are required to comply with numerous laws, regulations and ongoing compliance measures at the federal and state levels of government. These requirements include submitting annual informational returns to the Internal Revenue Service ("IRS") and annual reports of charitable solicitations to the Minnesota Attorney General's Office for the ability to solicit donations from the public. Many of these reporting requirements are technical, complex and may require professional accounting or legal assistance. Nonprofit organizations frequently use the services of legal counsel, certified public accountants and auditors to ensure compliance with ongoing requirements, and to promulgate efficient governance and transparent financial practices.

In addition to professional services, nonprofit organizations may benefit from ongoing compliance measures by adopting, implementing and enforcing their own organizational policies. Conflict of interest, whistleblower and document retention policies, among others, are considered best practices and are the subject of required disclosures on Part VI of IRS Form 990. Additionally, the IRS Form 990 requests disclosure of these policies and other mechanisms for good governance, transparency, accountability and compliance.

B. Use of Professional Legal Advisors

Q1. When should a nonprofit organization seek an attorney's advice?

A1. There is no set rule or standard for when an organization should seek the counsel of an attorney. An organization may consider seeking an attorney's advice when dealing with a complex and legally technical issue. Such situations may include a complicated incorporation and nuanced exemption application, when an organization is faced with an IRS audit, multi-million dollar contracts, merging with another organization, complicated employment law issues or purchasing real property. Please note this list is not exhaustive of when a nonprofit organization should seek the advice of an attorney. When organizations have casualty, liability or Directors and Officers liability insurance policies, the insurance company may be obligated to provide defense counsel if the organization is sued.

The 2004 Report of the Minnesota State Bar Association Task Force on Business Law Pro Bono lists the following as areas of law that represent ongoing concerns to established nonprofits according to a Minnesota Council of Nonprofits (MCN) survey:

- Human resources, including employment and benefits;
- Contracts related to leases, buying real estate, and signing state and county contracts;
- Constitutive documents such as Articles of Incorporation and Bylaws;
- Mergers and dissolutions;
- Intellectual property (particularly copyright and trademark);
- Special state and federal reporting requirements;
- Lobbying expenditures limits;
- Regulations directed at mitigating conflicts of interest and monitoring executive compensation;
- Tax-related issues concerning unrelated business income.[1]

1 MSBA, *Report of the Minnesota State Bar Association Task Force on Business Law Pro Bono*, 9 (2004), www.legalcorps.org/wp-content/uploads/2012/01/Task_Force_report.pdf.

Q2. How does a nonprofit organization find a competent attorney to meet its needs for advice?

A2. Minnesota has a thriving and competent nonprofit bar that is committed to serving the state's charitable sector. A nonprofit organization may find a competent attorney in several ways.

- **LegalCORPS.** LegalCORPS assists small nonprofit organizations by connecting them with free, high-quality legal services from volunteer lawyers. To find out more, visit www.legalcorps.org.
- **Referrals.** An organization may receive a referral from other nonprofit managers who have encountered similar issues for an area attorney who might specialize in a particular area of law and is familiar with nonprofit organizations.
- **Minnesota State Bar Association, Nonprofit Subcommittee.** The nonprofit subcommittee of the Business Law Section of the Minnesota State Bar Association (MSBA) may be a good resource to find competent attorneys who specialize in nonprofit issues.
- **The Nonprofit SpeciaLIST.** The Nonprofit SpeciaLIST is MCN's searchable database of vendors and consultants who work with nonprofit organizations and who submitted their listing for a fee. It may be found at www.nonprofitspecialist.org.
- **Propel Nonprofits** provides organizations with accounting and finance services, strategic services and governance-related services. Propel Nonprofits provides consulting and training in the following areas:

    - Contracts
    - Copyright and trademark issues
    - Articles of Incorporation and Bylaws
    - Liability and tax issues
    - Mediation
    - Merger/dissolution agreements
    - Risk management
    - Personnel issues

  To find out more about Propel Nonprofits' services visit www.propelnonprofits.org.

Q3. How does an organization engage an attorney?

A3. There are several options nonprofits may utilize to engage attorneys. Regardless of how an organization works with an attorney, the relationship should be defined clearly in writing. Options for engaging an attorney generally differ based on fee arrangements. Some attorneys may be open to negotiating hourly or flat fees, others may not. Regardless, attorneys are prohibited from collecting unreasonable fees. The Minnesota Rules of Professional Conduct provides eight factors to determine the reasonableness of a fee arrangement. These factors include:

- The time and labor required, the novelty and difficulty of the questions involved, and the skill requisite to perform the legal service properly;
- The likelihood, if apparent to the client, that the acceptance of the particular employment will preclude other conflicting employment by the lawyer;
- The fee customarily charged in the locality for similar legal services;
- The amount involved and the results obtained;
- The time limitations imposed by the client or by the circumstances;
- The nature and length of the professional relationship with the client;

- The experience, reputation and ability of the lawyer or lawyers performing the services; and
- Whether the fee is fixed or contingent.[2]

The following arrangements represent the wide spectrum of ways to engage attorneys for nonprofit organization purposes.

- ***Pro bono.*** Organizations may consider engaging an attorney *pro bono* (Latin, meaning "for the public good"). Pro bono attorneys take on clients without charge. Minnesota's LegalCORPS matches pro bono attorneys with small nonprofits in need of project-based legal services. Other ways to seek pro bono help may be through the Minnesota State Bar Association, by referral or perhaps through a board member of the organization who is also an attorney.
- **Project based.** If the reason an organization is seeking to engage an attorney is transactional or limited in some nature, it may consider hiring an attorney on a project basis. Fee arrangements for project-based legal work may be hourly or based on a standard or fixed fee.
- **Retainer.** Having an attorney on retainer may give an organization great peace of mind, but it may also come with a price tag. A retainer generally assumes that the attorney will be readily available to work or represent your organization related to a particular issue. In exchange for this availability, it is likely that the client will be billed at a higher rate for legal work.

Some retainers also function as a mechanism to ensure that an attorney is paid. Generally, the client pays a certain amount in advance, which is held in trusts. The legal fees are subtracted from the retainer as legal work is done until the retainer is depleted.

Q4. What are the limitations of the work an attorney can be expected to do for an organization?

A4. The cost of litigation and high attorney fees may limit the amount of work an attorney may do for an organization. If the cost of an attorney might inhibit an organization from seeking counsel, it may consider seeking pro bono representation, negotiating with the attorney or dedicating a staff person to work on the issue. For example, instead of hiring an attorney to draft a contract, perhaps a prudent alternative may be for a nonprofit staff person to draft the contract and then hire an attorney to review the contract. This type of arrangement would probably lower the hours billed and resulting fees.

C. Use of CPAs

Q5. When should a nonprofit organization seek the assistance of a certified public accountant (CPA)?

A5. CPAs may be valuable to nonprofits in many situations. CPAs perform a broad range of accounting, auditing, tax and consulting services for their clients. An organization may seek the assistance for many reasons including:

- to help prepare organizational financial statements;
- to complete and submit the IRS Form 990s;
- to aid when an organization is faced with a complicated financial issue;
- to help navigate new financial situations;

2 Minnesota Rules of Professional Conduct Rule 1.5(a) (2015).

- to design accounting and data-processing systems;
- to verify the effectiveness of an organization's internal controls and guard against mismanagement, waste or fraud;
- to consult on new fundraising opportunities and government grants that may trigger an audit; and
- to address board concerns regarding the presentation or preparation of its internal financials.

Q6. How does a nonprofit organization find a competent CPA to meet its needs for assistance?

A6. There are several ways an organization may find a competent CPA to meet its needs. In addition to inquiring with its own board members and volunteers, one way to find a CPA is by seeking a referral from other nonprofit managers who have encountered similar accounting issues. The Minnesota Society of CPAs also has a free referral service through www.mncpa.org/find-a-cpa/mn-cpa-referral.

Propel Nonprofits offers accounting and financial services for nonprofits through ongoing service and project based assistance. For more information visit www.propelnonprofits.org.

Additionally, the Nonprofit SpeciaLIST, MCN's searchable database of vendors, consultants, and services providers, is a resource to find CPAs that work with nonprofits. It may be found at www.nonprofitspecialist.org.

Q7. How does an organization engage a CPA?

A7. CPAs may be engaged through a bid, on a project basis or on an hourly basis. Nonprofit managers should meet with candidate CPAs to explain organizational expectations, inquire into experience and request references.

Q8. What are the limitations of the work a CPA may be expected to do for an organization?

A8. In addition to an organization's financial limitations to hire a CPA, an organization may also be limited by lack of experience with nonprofit-specific accounting practices.

Additionally, engaging or hiring a CPA does not necessarily ensure that all reporting and recording will be accurate. CPAs who are not involved in the day-to-day operations of an organization may review the books and still miss items. A CPA may be hesitant to sign off on financial statements for federal reporting if he/she is not intimately involved in their preparation.

D. Use of Auditors

Q9. What type of work do auditors perform?

A9. Internal auditors, who may be organizational accountants, verify the effectiveness of an organization's internal controls and evaluate for mismanagement, waste or fraud. Internal auditors may also review an organization's operations and evaluate efficiency, effectiveness and compliance with organizational policies and state and federal regulations.[3] An external auditor may be hired by an organization to act as an independent auditor for an audit of an their financial statements and to express an opinion on the statements to regulatory authorities as to whether or not the statements have been correctly prepared and reported.

Q10. When should a nonprofit organization engage a CPA for an audit of its financial statements?

A10. Minnesota's charitable organizations are required to submit to the Minnesota Attorney General's Office an audited financial statement performed in accordance with generally accepted accounting principles (GAAP) if the organization receives total revenue in excess of $750,000 for 12 months of operation covered by the statement.[4] Minnesota statutes require that an independent CPA must conduct the audit.[5] If an organization has an accountant on staff that manages day-to-day financial operations and internal auditing, that staff accountant would not be considered independent. An independent auditor is a CPA who is not affiliated with the organization and who may be engaged by the organization's board of directors' audit committee.

Additionally, if an organization expends more than $300,000 or more in federal awards in a fiscal year, there is an audit requirement under OMB Circular A-133.[6] In addition to state requirements, funders and lenders may also request full or single audits of organizational financial statements.

Additionally, external auditors may be engaged by an organization's board of directors for an independent review of financial statements, financial statement preparation, compilation, review of internal controls and recommendations for improvements. In single audits, auditors are required to issue an opinion on the financial statements and report on internal control over financial reporting and on compliance.[7]

Q11. How does a nonprofit organization find a competent auditor?

A11. In some situations, an organization may consider retaining a CPA firm for both IRS Form 990 preparation and auditing. An organization may find a competent auditor who is familiar with standards, regulations, laws and nonprofit operations through referrals from other nonprofit managers or through MCN's Nonprofit SpeciaLIST online directory. The SpeciaLIST is a searchable directory of vendors, consultants, and services providers, such as CPAs, that work with nonprofits. It may be found at www.nonprofitspecialist.org. For auditor referral resources, see Question 6.

Q12. How does an organization engage an auditor?

A12. External or independent auditors may be engaged through a Request for Proposal (RFP). An RFP is an invitation, through a bidding process, to submit a proposal on a service. Often organizations request a

3 *Occupational Outlook Handbook—Accountants and Auditors*, www.bls.gov/ooh/business-and-financial/accountants-and-auditors.htm (last visited Aug. 10, 2017).

4 Minn. Stat. § 309.53, subd. 3 (2016). *See also* Federal Law Audit Requirements, www.councilofnonprofits.org/nonprofit-audit-guide/federal-law-audit-requirements (last visited Aug. 10, 2017).

5 *Id.*

6 OMB Circular A-133 Audit Refresher—Major Programs, www.aicpa.org/interestareas/governmentalauditquality/resources/singleaudit/omb circulara133/ombcirculara-133auditrefresher-majorprograms/pages/default.aspx (last visited Aug. 10, 2017).

7 "If there is a glaring weakness in internal controls discovered during the audit, auditors would mention it in a management letter." Government Auditing Standards and Circular A-133, www.aicpa.org/Publications/AccountingAuditing/KeyTopics/Pages/GASCircularA133.aspx (last visited Aug. 10, 2017).

RFP for both IRS Form 990 and auditing services. Generally this type of RFP is for a three-year proposal and start at about $3,500, depending upon organizations' budget size and financial complexity.

Sample RFP letters may be found at:

- Propel Nonprofits (www.propelnonprofits.org, search for "*Audit Services RFP*")
- The American Institute of Certified Public Accountants (www.aicpa.org, search for "*AICPA Audit Committee Toolkits*")

An auditing firm will respond to the RFP with an "Engagement Letter" which, if the organization accepts, should be copied for organizational records, signed and returned.

Q13. What are the areas of work an organization should engage an auditor to do for an organization and at what cost?

A13. An organization may benefit from negotiating rates for audits, single audits, IRS Form 990 preparation, financial statement audit, forensic audit and agreed upon procedures with an auditor. For an excellent narrative on "Making the Most of Your Audit," see 187gerrard.com/2010/07/making-the-most-of-your-audit.

E. Organizational Policies and Procedures to Ensure Compliance

Q14. What policies and procedures should a nonprofit organization enact to ensure its compliance with relevant laws and regulations?

A14. The policies and procedures a nonprofit enacts to ensure, monitor and document compliance with laws and regulations are essential to good governance and organizational sustainability. An organization should consider the regulatory authorities to which it must report in adopting policies and procedures. In Minnesota, these authorities include the Minnesota Secretary of State's Office, the Minnesota Attorney General's Office, the Minnesota Department of Revenue and the Internal Revenue Service.

In addition to initial registrations and annual filings and reporting to the Secretary of State's office, the IRS Form 990 Part VI requires disclosure of organizational policies and procedures. While there is no legal requirement that organizations adopt these policies, they are viewed by the IRS to be indications of good governance and transparency. These policies and procedures include:

- Conflict of Interest Policy
- Document Retention Policy
- Executive Compensation Procedures
- Board approval of the Form 990
- Policy requiring annual disclosure of board, officer and employee relationships
- Contemporaneous documentation of meetings of the governing body and committees
- Public Documents Procedures
- Gift Acceptance Policy
- Joint Venture Policy
- Payment and Reimbursement Policy

- Whistleblower Policy

For more information and sample policies, search for "990-disclosures" at www.minnesotanonprofits.org.

F. Record Maintenance and Retention

Q15. What records should a nonprofit organization keep? How long should they be maintained? Who should maintain them?

A15. While the law does not require the adoption of a document retention policy, it is a recommended best practice. Most of the Sarbanes-Oxley Act (SOX) applies only to publicly traded companies. However, one key SOX document retention policy that does apply to nonprofits is that they may not destroy documents that are the subject of an investigation. In addition, the adoption of a document retention policy sets guidelines, facilitates directors' fulfillment of the duty of care, establishes transparency and ensures compliance.

A document retention policy generally sets out the length of time certain organizational physical and electronic documents must or should be retained (held in organizational files) and the manner of disposal of such documents. The adoption of this type of policy serves to provide notice to employees and board of the types of documents to be retained and for how long. It also helps guard against preemptive destruction or inappropriate disposal ahead of an investigation.

Generally, document retention policies contain a list of types of documents that an organization should retain and the length of time the organization should retain those documents. Policies specify who in the organization is responsible for retaining such documents, guidelines for electronic files and procedures for backup files, archiving documents and regular check-ups on system reliability.

This policy requires organizations to intentionally make several decisions surrounding which documents to include and the length of retention time. The documents and retention period identified below will vary for individual organizations.

Examples of Documents to Consider Retaining

Categories of records or files and documents commonly retained include.*

Corporate records, including:

- Foundational documents such as Articles of Incorporation and Bylaws
- Governance and Board policies, including corporate resolutions, board agendas and minutes and conflict-of-interest disclosure forms, among others

Finance and Administration files, including:

- Financial statements, payroll records, bank deposits and statements, invoices, and sales records
- Equipment files and maintenance records, contracts, general administrative and legal correspondence, donor records, and grant applications

Examples of Documents to Consider Retaining (continued)

Insurance records, including:
- Policies and claims made on policies, accident reports, OSHA safety reports, and group disability records

Real Property records, including:
- Real property deeds, leases (current and expired), mortgages and security agreements

Tax documents, including:
- 501(c)(3) application – Form 1023, IRS Form 990s, charitable organization registration statements and exemption application

Human Resources documents, including:
- Employee personnel files, retirement benefit plans, employee handbooks and training materials, and employment applications
- IRS Form I-9, tax withholding statements and payroll tax returns

Technology, including:
- Software licenses and support agreements

Other, including:
- Press releases and publicly filed documents

**The above mentioned list of documents to retain are only examples and should not be considered a complete list.*

Q16. How long does a nonprofit organization need to keep records of its board meetings, such as minutes?

A16. The retention period varies by type of document. Some documents, such as foundational documents, should be retained permanently; other documents, such as general correspondence, may be retained for a number of years. In determining retention periods, some considerations to keep in mind include:

- Federal or state legal requirement to retain certain documents
- Statutes of limitation for certain claims that may be brought against an organization by employees, third parties or the Minnesota Attorney General
- IRS audit cycles

Like foundational documents, board minutes should be retained permanently. For sample Document Retention policies, search "Document Retention Policy" at www.minnesotanonprofits.org or visit www.councilofnonprofits.org/tools-resources/document-retention-policies-nonprofits.

G. Related Resources

Organizations:

The American Institute of Certified Public Accountants (AICPA)
The AICPA is a national professional organization of Certified Public Accountants. It provides members with resources, information and leadership to enable them to provide valuable services to benefit the public.
www.aicpa.org

Charities Review Council
The Charities Review Council is an independent resource for nonprofits and donors. It helps nonprofits with management principles and accountability. It also helps donors make informed giving decisions.
smartgivers.org

LegalCORPS
LegalCORPS is a nonprofit organization that connects volunteer lawyers with small nonprofits in need of pro bono legal services.
www.legalcorps.org

Minnesota Council of Nonprofits
The Minnesota Council of Nonprofits is the largest state association of nonprofits in Minnesota. It provides educational and professional resources for nonprofit organizations.
www.minnesotanonprofits.org

Minnesota Council on Foundations
The Minnesota Council on Foundations is a community of grant makers provides programming and resources to strengthen and expand philanthropy.
www.mcf.org

Minnesota Society of Certified Public Accountants (MNCPA)
This nonprofit organization is a statewide association of CPAs. The website provides a searchable CPA database and referral service.
www.mncpa.org

Minnesota State Bar Association (MSBA)
The MSBA is the state association of Minnesota attorneys. The website provides more information on accessing legal services and public resources.
www.mnbar.org

The Nonprofit SpeciaLIST
The Nonprofit SpeciaLIST, a project of the Minnesota Council of Nonprofits (MCN), is a searchable database of vendors and consultants that work with nonprofit organizations.
www.nonprofitspecialist.org

Propel Nonprofits
Propel Nonprofits provides loans that help nonprofits realize their visions; financial management training; resources that promote sound financial practices; and guidance to nonprofit staff on strategic financial planning and management.
www.propelnonprofits.org

CHAPTER **15**

CONTRACTS

Topics

A. Overview

While contracts are involved, to one degree or another, in almost every business transaction, the presence of unfamiliar terms and unfortunate legalese in the "fine print" of contracts can make the documents more intimidating than they need to be. The goal of this chapter is to remove some of the ambiguity and mystique from the terms and mechanics of contracts, and help directors and officers of nonprofits feel more comfortable working with contracts that arise in the course of business for their nonprofit.

Section B: Basic Elements of a Contract, provides an overview of the basic elements of a contract—offer, acceptance, and consideration—as well as the means by which a contract may be created, and who may bind the nonprofit by contract. Section C: Boards and Contracts, specifically addresses and clarifies the directors' obligations regarding contracts that the nonprofit enters.

For many nonprofits, one of the greatest sources of uncertainty regarding contracts is what rights a nonprofit organization has when the other party to a contract fails to uphold its obligations under the agreement ("breaches the agreement"), and what conditions would create a right to terminate an agreement. Section D: Nonperformance, Breach and Escape, describes the rights that a party has upon the other party's breach of the agreement, the different ways that an agreement can be terminated, and the ways that a nonprofit can attempt to get out from under its own contractual obligations or obtain a release from a contract when it fails its original purpose.

Section E: Attorney Review identifies the types of contracts and contract terms a nonprofit would most benefit seeking the advice of an attorney. There are a number of terms that are found in the vast majority of contracts (e.g., term, price, description of goods or services to be provided). While these terms are critical to understanding the respective parties' rights and duties under the contract, the terms (commonly referred to as "boilerplate" language—i.e., the terms of an agreement that govern the contractual relationship itself, and which are usually ancillary to the business terms of the contract) can also have a significant effect on the parties, especially in the situation when a dispute arises. Section F: Contracts Checklist, provides descriptions of both material terms and boilerplate terms that are found in most contracts, as well as the ways that a nonprofit can use or avoid these terms to protect itself under a contract.

B. Basic Elements of a Contract

Q1. What are the basic elements of a contract that a nonprofit might enter?

A1. A contract is a promise or set of promises that the law recognizes as a legal duty. If the promise is broken, the law gives a remedy. The basic elements of a contract that a nonprofit might enter are the same as the elements of a contract that any individual or entity might enter. A contract is formed where there is an offer and acceptance supported by consideration.[1]

Offer.

An offer is simply an expression—a question, proposition, invitation or suggestion—that invites acceptance. The person or entity making the offer (the "offeror") needs to make the offer sufficiently specific, so that the person considering the offer (the "offeree") need only say "yes," in order to form an agreement. Otherwise, the expression is not an offer, but an invitation to the other party to make an offer.

1 *See, e.g.*, Contract, The Bus. Dictionary, www.businessdictionary.com/definition/contract.html (last visited Aug. 11, 2017).

Once the offeror has made an offer, a number of things can happen. For example, the offeror can revoke the offer. Unless its terms state otherwise, an offer is revocable at any time until acceptance. An offer can also lapse if the offeree takes too long in considering the offer. The offeree can also reject the offer, or the offeree can reject the offer by making a counter-offer.

For example, suppose a nonprofit needs customized envelopes for its upcoming fundraising campaign. One printer offers to make 500 printed envelopes for $25. If the nonprofit responded, "make 500 printed envelopes for $20," the statement would constitute both a rejection of the original offer and a counter-offer. This distinction is important because once the offeree rejects the initial offer, the printer is no longer bound to honor it. If the nonprofit does not receive a better offer, it cannot return to the printer and say "yes" to the original offer in order to form a contract. Instead, it must ask the printer to make 500 envelopes for $25, and the printer then has the power to accept or reject the new offer.

Acceptance.

An acceptance is an expression agreeing to the terms of the offer, communicated to the person or entity making the offer. The acceptance must be a "mirror image" of the offer. Again, suppose that one printer offers to make 500 printed envelopes for $25. The nonprofit could simply say "yes," and the offer would be accepted, or it could say, "We will pay $25 if you print 500 envelopes." The acceptance must match the offer in order to form a contract.

Consideration.

Consideration is required to transform an offer and an acceptance into a contract. Consideration exists when one party does something it is not required to do or refrains from doing something it has the right to do in exchange for the other party doing something it is not required to do or refraining from doing something it is allowed to do. In the envelope example, the printer agrees to make envelopes that it is not otherwise obligated to make and the nonprofit promises to give the printer money that it is not otherwise obligated to pay.

See Questions 15–18 for the elements that a nonprofit should include in its contracts.

Q2. Who has the authority to bind a nonprofit organization to a contract?

A2. The board of directors must manage or supervise the business and affairs of a nonprofit. The board can delegate authority to appropriate officers to negotiate and sign contracts on behalf of the organization, but the board still has oversight responsibilities.[2] An officer only has authority to the extent granted by the board. Bylaws, financial policies or motions memorialized in minutes from board meetings may all have such authorization language.

In order to give the executive director, or similar officer, the ability to manage the day-to-day affairs of the nonprofit, the board might grant him or her authority to:

- Make capital expenditures, investments or advances up to a certain dollar amount;
- Execute a contract that involves incurring operating expenses that are usual and customary up to a certain dollar amount and certain term of months or years;
- Execute a contract for a sale in the ordinary course of business for cash or its equivalent;
- Sell, transfer or retire an asset or write down an account if its book value does not exceed a certain dollar amount;

2 Minn. Stat. § 317A.237 (2016).

- Settle a claim if the settlement value does not exceed a certain amount; and
- Establish a banking account, make withdrawals of a certain amount, make withdrawals of a higher amount with the signature of the treasurer or vice president, and sign checks on behalf of the organization.

Third parties doing business with a nonprofit may request a "Secretary's Certificate," signed by the secretary of the nonprofit stating that the board passed a resolution authorizing an officer to sign on behalf of the nonprofit in the given circumstances. Such a certificate must include the date of the resolution.

To the extent the board authorizes other employees to enter into contracts, it should establish form contracts, require authorization (from the board or executive director) to deviate from the form, advise employees not to make verbal amendments to the contracts and establish some system to monitor compliance with the contracts.

Q3. Does accepting a gift or donation bind my organization to a contract?

A3. No contract is formed by accepting a gift or donation, but the organization may still be bound to use the donation for specific purposes. See Chapter 5: Charitable Donation Regulations, Section D: Responsibilities to Funding Sources for more information.

Q4. Does a contract need to be in writing?

A4. Generally, a written instrument is not required to form a contract between parties. Verbal discussions, and even actions alone, may form a contract and—in certain circumstances—can amend a written contract. For practical purposes, a nonprofit should put all of its agreements in writing. In Minnesota, certain types of contracts must be in writing to be enforced.[3] These contracts include:

- Agreements with performance that will not occur within one year of the effective date.
- Undertaking to be responsible for the debts or default of another person or entity (for example, co-signing or guaranteeing another's loan) or undertaking to pay a debt which has already been discharged by bankruptcy or insolvency proceedings.
- An agreement concerning the transfer of an interest in land, including leases and cohabitations agreements, and brokerage agreements.
- Grant or assignment of trust (where money or property is owned and managed on behalf of another).
- Credit agreement or an agreement to pay interest greater than the statutory amount of six percent.[4]
- Sale of goods in a transaction involving $500 or more or lease of goods with total payments of $1,000 or more.
- Security agreement (where a party offers collateral with a security interest to a lender or secured party), unless the secured party takes possession of the collateral.
- Any contract with the State of Minnesota.[5]

These contracts must specify five elements: (1) the identity of the parties; (2) the subject matter (if the contract is for an interest in real property, a description that identifies the real property with "reasonable

3 Minn. Stat. § 513.01 (2016).
4 Minn. Stat. § 334.01, subd 1 (2016).
5 While there is not a requirement for municipalities, it is strongly suggested.

certainty"); (3) the consideration; (4) the material terms; and (5) the signature of the parties who will perform under the contract.

See Questions 13-16 for other clauses that a nonprofit should consider including in its contracts.

C. Boards and Contracts

Q5. ***When does an organization's board of directors need to approve a contract? Is board approval required for an organization to sell assets or become party to a lease?***

A5. The board should review the terms of a contract for any significant transaction. Depending on the size of the organization, significant transactions may include the sale of assets or a lease.[6] It is common for third parties to request Secretary's Certificates in significant transactions to prove that the board authorized the signing party to enter into and execute the contract. The board should also review a contract that could contain a conflict of interest between the nonprofit and its directors or officers. Finally, the board should review employment contracts for the organization's highest paid officers.

Q6. ***When a nonprofit dissolves, is the board of directors liable for contract terms?***

A6. Generally, a board of directors is not liable for the contract terms once a nonprofit dissolves. An individual director may have individual liability if he or she (a) personally guaranteed an obligation of the nonprofit or (b) entered into a contract with the nonprofit that constitutes a conflict of interest transaction. See Question 17 for Internal Revenue Service ("IRS") penalties associated with conflict-of-interest transactions.

D. Nonperformance, Breach and Escape

Q7. ***What is a breach of contract, and what recourse does the non-breaching party have in the event of a breach?***

A7. A breach of contract occurs when one party fails to fulfill (or rejects altogether) one or more of its obligations under a contract, or when it interferes with another party's performance.[7] Breaches are classified as either material or immaterial. A breach is material when one party's rights under the agreement have been significantly harmed.[8] A material breach generally excuses the non-breaching party from further performance of its own obligations and provides the non-breaching party with the right to sue the breaching party for damages. Where a breach is merely a technical failure, however, and does not harm the interests of the non-breaching party expected under the contract, the breach is immaterial, and provides the non-breaching party with fewer rights.

Some contracts specifically define the consequences for certain breaches of the contract (e.g., failure to deliver goods in a timely manner) as well as the permitted response by the non-breaching party (e.g., withholding payment). In these cases, the terms of the agreement set out the non-breaching party's

6 *See, e.g.*, Minn. Stat. § 317A.613 (2016) (stating that the board of directors shall approve a merger, consolidation or transfer). Generally speaking, transactions outside the ordinary course of the business should be approved by the board.

7 *See, e.g.*, Breach of Contract, The Legal Dictionary, dictionary.law.com/Default.aspx?selected=93 (last visited Aug. 11, 2017).

8 Breach of Contract: Material Breach, NOLO, www.nolo.com/legal-encyclopedia/breach-of-contract-material-breach-32655.html (last visited Aug. 11, 2017).

recourse.[9] But for cases in which the contract does not provide a specific remedy, the non-breaching party's recourse can fall into a gray area.

When one party commits a material breach of the contract, the non-breaching party has two permissible courses of action: (1) suspend its own performance (and attempt to convince the other party to cure its breach); or (2) terminate the agreement and sue the breaching party for damages. The non-breaching party must respond carefully to a perceived breach, however, as a non-breaching party could find itself in breach of the agreement if it overreacts and takes unwarranted retaliatory actions against the breaching party (e.g., where a non-breaching party attempts to terminate an agreement upon an immaterial breach by the other party). If the breaching party refuses to cure a material breach and the non-breaching party wishes to take action against the breaching party, the non-breaching party should consult with an attorney before proceeding.

Q8. How can a contract be terminated?

A8. There are several ways in which a contract can be terminated.

- *Automatic Termination* – Where an agreement provides that it will be in force for a certain duration and does not automatically renew, the agreement will terminate without further action by either party at the end of the term.[10]
- *Termination by Agreement* – Parties may mutually agree to terminate an agreement, in which case the agreement will terminate as decided by the parties.
- *Termination for Breach* – If one party commits a material breach of the agreement, one option of the non-breaching party is to terminate the contract. After termination, a court will generally sort out any remaining issues or obligations.

Q9. How can an organization get out of or "escape" from a contract with minimal damage?

A9. Some agreements specifically provide that one party may easily terminate the agreement with little or no notice and no termination fees. In these cases, a party can usually exit the contractual relationship without incurring any additional costs or liabilities.

But where a party wishes to "escape" a contract under which it has agreed to take on significant liabilities (either now or in the future), it becomes more difficult for the liable party to terminate the contract "with minimal damage." Where a contract explicitly provides the means by which one party may terminate before completion of the contract's term (e.g., the exiting party must provide notice or pay an early termination fee), the party seeking to escape the contract has minimal leverage, and it will be difficult for that party to exit the agreement without complying with those terms. On the other hand, where an agreement does not specify the mechanics of a party's termination, that party's ability to terminate the agreement at minimal expense is primarily dependent on its ability to negotiate a favorable amendment to, or termination of, the agreement.

9 As a matter of practice, if a non-profit is entering into agreements it would be good practice to have this laid out in the contract to make expectations more clear. C.f. id. (stating that some parties provide guidance on what constitutes a breach rather than relying on a judge's discretion or interpretation of the law).

10 Some agreements provide for automatic renewal unless written notice of intent to terminate is given within a specific time period. Since nonprofit boards meet less regularly than other corporate executives, it would be wise to create a reminder system that reviews all upcoming contract renewal dates well in advance of the automatic renewal.

E. Attorney Review

Q10. What are some considerations in deciding when to involve an attorney in contract review?

A10. A nonprofit that executes similar contracts on a regular basis may feel comfortable reviewing those contracts on its own, without the aid of an attorney. There are, however, a number of circumstances in which a nonprofit could benefit substantially from involving an attorney in its contract review process, including where (a) the transaction underlying the agreement is novel, or the nature of the agreement is unfamiliar; (b) the agreement would restrict future actions of the nonprofit (e.g., contracts with non-compete clause, non-solicitation clause, or similar provisions); or (c) the contract involves more money than is usual for the nonprofit's contracts. In these circumstances, an overlooked or misunderstood term could create significant obligations or restrictions on the nonprofit that may be difficult to undo.

If a nonprofit chooses to involve an attorney in the review of a contract, it is important to bring him or her into the process as early as possible. When an attorney is involved at the beginning of an interaction, he or she can provide advice to guide the negotiations of the agreement and identify potential issues or risks, even if a nonprofit does not wish to use an attorney to review and negotiate an agreement in its entirety. The later in the process that an attorney is involved in such negotiations, the greater the risk that previously negotiated terms may need to be revisited, which makes it more difficult for the attorney to leave a small "footprint."

While smaller nonprofits may not feel that they have the resources to involve an attorney in their contract review process, there are a number of pro bono organizations that connect small nonprofit organizations with attorneys and whose services are available at no charge, including Minnesota LegalCORPS.[11] Attempting to prematurely end a contract is another time counsel could be extremely helpful to avoid a lawsuit for a breach of contract.

F. Contracts Checklist

Q11. What does "arbitration clause" mean?

A11. An arbitration clause (or alternative dispute resolution, or "ADR," clause) generally provides that the parties agree not to sue one another in court for any disputes related to the contract. Instead, the parties agree to resolve any contract-related disputes by submitting the dispute to a neutral arbitrator (or panel of arbitrators) in a process that is often similar to a lawsuit conducted in court and in which each side is represented by an attorney. Courts will almost always enforce this agreement between the parties and will often refuse to hear cases that arise from agreements that are subject to an arbitration clause. The decision of the arbitrator or panel is generally final and not subject to appeal or review in court. One benefit to this process is that it is generally considered less expensive and takes less time.[12]

11 *See* LegalCORPS, legalcorps.org (last visited Aug. 11, 2017).

12 *See generally* Arbitration Basics, NOLO, www.nolo.com/legal-encyclopedia/arbitration-basics-29947.html (last visited Aug. 11, 2017) (explaining in more detail the basics of arbitration and how the process works).

Q12. What does "indemnification clause" mean?

A12. An indemnification clause is an agreement by the parties that one party (the indemnifying party) will reimburse the other party (the indemnified party) for losses, or defend the indemnified party against claims, that arise from the indemnifying party's actions or failure to act.[13] For example, a contract between a county and a nonprofit service provider may require the organization to purchase insurance for a specified amount to indemnify the county against lawsuits that may be brought by a service recipient or other loss. The clause may be drafted to grant indemnification only as to claims by third parties against the indemnified party, or it may permit the indemnified party to seek reimbursement for losses it suffers directly because of the indemnifying party. The indemnifying party may be obligated to pay for damages or losses incurred by the indemnified party or to pay the legal expenses for any lawsuit or claim that is attributable to the indemnifying party's actions.

Q13. What are some common contract clauses?

A13. In addition to the contract terms described elsewhere in this chapter, other common contract terms include:

- *Recitals* – At the beginning of a negotiated agreement (recitals are seldom found in a form agreement), parties will often provide an overview, in plain business terms, of any understandings or rationale that may provide background to the agreement. These recitals may be helpful to future parties who attempt to interpret the agreement without the benefit of having been present during its negotiation.
- *Definitions* – These are used to make sure parties understand what is meant by the terms used in the body of the contract. For example, the term "temporary" might mean less than 30 days to one person, and up to one year to another person. Defining the word in advance makes certain there is a "meeting of the minds." If a problem arises, it also provides a method of interpretation so the court does not impose its own definition that may be contrary to what you understood when you entered into the contract.
- *Term* – The parties will specify the duration of the agreement, whether time-based or contingent upon the occurrence of an event. This clause will also usually provide the means by which the agreement will renew for an additional term — an agreement that provides for subsequent renewal periods is referred to as an "evergreen clause."
- *Termination* – One or both parties may be permitted to terminate the agreement before the end of the specified duration of the agreement. In these cases, the terminating party usually must provide a specified amount of advance notice, pay a termination fee or both.
- *Confidentiality* – In many cases, one or both parties will be exposed to the confidential or proprietary information of the other party. To protect the party whose information is exposed, the parties will often agree to either one-way or mutual confidentiality terms under the agreement that prohibit the receiving party from disclosing any confidential information to third parties. In some cases, confidentiality terms will prohibit disclosure of the terms of the agreement or even the existence of the agreement. If a nonprofit organization receives government funding, is bound to a government contract or is tied to the government, it may not be able to enforce a confidentiality clause because of the Data Practices Act.
- *Warranties and Representations* – Parties (1) provide explicit descriptions of any warranties or guarantees that apply to the goods, services or payment that they will provide under the agreement

13 *See, e.g.*, Indemnify, *The Legal Dictionary*, legal-dictionary.thefreedictionary.com/indemnify (last visited Aug. 11, 2017).

(warranties); or (2) make statements that they assert as true and for which they agree to be held liable if the statements are not true at the time of contract or within a specified period thereafter (representations). These terms clarify expectations between the parties at the time the contract is formed and provide clear standards to which the parties may hold one another during the term of the agreement. Violations of a warranty or representation may be treated as a breach of the agreement or may give rise to a specified remedy for the party who depended on the warranty or representation.

- *Limitation of Liability* – Parties will often disclaim certain warranties under an agreement, especially implied warranties (i.e., warranties that public policy has created and which create general expectations for contracting parties). These clauses often (a) limit the warranties to which the other party is entitled to those specifically stated under the agreement, and (b) confine the remedies of the parties to those specifically permitted under the agreement (as opposed to any and all remedies that might be available to a party under the law).
- *Assignment* – In most cases, the law permits a party to a contract to transfer or assign its rights to a third party, which is then obligated to fulfill the assigning party's duties under the agreement. Where one party wishes to ensure that it will not be contractually bound to a party not of its choosing, the contract can be drafted to prohibit the assignment or transfer of the agreement without the consent of the non-assigning party. It is a best practice for the agreement to not only prohibit assignments or transfers, but to also state that any assignment or transfer will be void if consent is not granted.
- *Delivery/Risk of Loss* – Where an agreement covers the sale or supply of goods, the parties can designate the point at which the delivering party is no longer liable for any damage to, or loss of, the goods; any loss or damage after this point is the responsibility of the buyer.
- *Insurance* – One party may wish to require that the other party maintain a certain amount of insurance in order to ensure that there is a guaranteed source of funds available to cover any losses that the other party is obligated to pay.
- *Choice of Law; Venue* – The parties agree that any interpretation of the contract or the parties' rights or duties will be enforced according to the law of a state of all parties' choosing. Generally, the parties choose to be governed by the laws of the state in which one or both parties are located, though in cases where the parties are located in different states, the law of the state of Delaware—which has a well-developed body of corporate and contract law that is familiar to most attorneys—may also be used. However, Delaware law often favors corporations. An alternative practice may be to use the law of the state where the contract is to be enforced. Similarly, the parties may also require that any lawsuits or other legal action arising from the agreement must be filed in a certain county (for state court actions) or federal district court.
- *Survival of Terms* – Parties may provide that certain terms of a contract (e.g., non-competition or non-solicitation periods) will survive the termination of the contract and will be enforceable even if the rest of the agreement has been properly terminated.
- *Force Majeure* – A *force majeure* clause excuses a party from liability for breach of the contract if the breach is due to an unforeseen event that is beyond the party's control. Events covered by a force majeure clause typically include natural disaster, war, terrorism, loss of power or other utilities, or "acts of God." While the party that is unable to perform because of the force majeure event is not liable for breach of the agreement, the other party is usually allowed to either seek the goods or services it needs from another party or to terminate the agreement altogether.
- *Waiver* – A contract will often provide that any failure of a party to exercise one or more of its rights under the agreement does not constitute a waiver of those rights in any future case. This clause provides clarity for any court that may, in the future, review the agreement and the parties' performance.

Q14. What clauses in a contract deserve particular attention? If I had a contracts checklist, what elements should be checked off?

A14. Depending on the type of contract, a nonprofit organization should make sure the contract is clear about the following terms:

- *Identify the parties* – Use the full legal name and address of the person or entity.
- *Subject matter* – Describe the goods or services clearly and fully.
- *Definitions* – Describe all significant terms.
- *Consideration* – Specify a one-time or installment payment for delivery (of goods) or for time (providing services).
- *Term* – State whether the contract will expire on a certain date or occurrence of an event, and if there is a renewal (evergreen) clause.
- *Termination* – Describe how the parties can terminate the agreement before the term expires and what happens if a party does so.
- *Intellectual property* – If there are any intellectual property rights for the material to be developed, clarify who will own it.
- *Confidentiality* – Before the nonprofit shares its confidential information, the other party should agree not to use the information and to keep it confidential.
- *Warranties and representations* – As negotiated between the parties.
- *Indemnification and insurance* – As negotiated between the parties.
- *Limitation of Liability* – As negotiated between the parties.
- *Signature* – The signature block should identify the nonprofit and the title of the officer authorized to sign on its behalf.
- Date of execution of contract.

Q15. What are things that should be avoided in a contract?

A15. Aside from price, a few clauses often require quite a bit of negotiation. These include indemnification, warranties and representations, non-competition clauses and ownership of intellectual property. A nonprofit should avoid indemnifying another party, to the extent possible, or should limit its liability. If the nonprofit does indemnify another party for legal expenses, it should retain some control of the legal strategy. A nonprofit should also limit, to the extent possible, the warranties and representations it makes about any goods and services it provides. As with indemnification, if the nonprofit does provide warranties and representations, it should attempt to limit its liability and narrow the survival clause. If a party the nonprofit is negotiating with is dead set on including a certain indemnity or representation and warrant, the nonprofit can use that as an opportunity to negotiate something beneficial to them in exchange. Depending on the nature of the contract, the other party may request a non-competition provision, but a nonprofit should avoid a non-competition clause that would interfere with its ability to conduct its work. Finally, a nonprofit should avoid giving up intellectual property rights to materials that it purchased and/or helped develop.

Q16. How does a nonprofit protect itself in a contract?

A16. The protective provisions that a nonprofit should use depend on the type of contract, but in many ways, the answer to this question is the opposite of Question 15. If the nonprofit is hiring another entity to provide services to a third party, the nonprofit should consider requiring the other party to carry insurance, asking the other party for indemnification and restricting the other party's limitations on liability. If the nonprofit is entering into a contract for goods, it should ask for warranties and representations from the supplier and restrict the other party's limitations on liability. If a contract results in any intellectual property rights, the nonprofit should attempt to retain ownership of the material, or alternatively, retain a royalty-free license to use the material.

Other provisions the nonprofit should use to protect itself include confidentiality, termination, survival, amendments and waiver (see Question 13 for details). To the extent that a nonprofit will reveal confidential or proprietary information, it should require the other party to keep the information confidential and not to use the information for its own purposes. The nonprofit should attempt to retain broad termination rights. Wherever there is a clause for confidentiality, indemnification and insurance, warranties and representations, or intellectual property, there should be a survival clause specifying that those obligations survive the termination of the agreement. Finally, particularly when the board authorizes officers to enter into contracts, it should specify in the contract that amendments must be in writing and that failure of the nonprofit to exercise its rights does not constitute waiver of those rights.

G. Other Issues

Q17. What taxes are associated with some contracts?

A17. Unless the Internal Revenue Service grants a nonprofit a tax exemption, which is obtained through filing the IRS Form 1023, the nonprofit must pay taxes on its net income. All tax-exempt organizations are subject to the Unrelated Business Income Tax (UBIT).[14] Tax-exempt public charities must be mindful of intermediate sanctions in transactions with people and entities related to the organization. Tax-exempt private foundations or private operating foundations are subject to private benefit excise tax and are also subject to lobbying excise taxes.

Unrelated Business Income Tax

The IRS charges tax-exempt entities UBIT tax on income from regular involvement in a business unrelated to their exempt purposes, known as the Unrelated Business Income Tax, or "UBIT." The UBIT rate is equal to regular corporate taxes. A contract may give rise to UBIT if the activity specified in the contract (1) constitutes a trade or business; (2) is carried out regularly; and (3) is unrelated to the organization's exempt purpose. A nonprofit should consult with a tax attorney if it confronts a transaction or business venture that may result in UBIT. Pay particular attention if the UBIT becomes a substantial portion of the nonprofit's overall income; an organization may lose its tax-exempt status if it has too much UBIT.[15]

Intermediate Sanctions

The IRS will impose excise taxes called "intermediate sanctions" where there is an "excess benefit transaction" between the organization and a "disqualified person." An excess benefit transaction is one in which the tax-exempt organization gives an economic benefit to a disqualified person, if the value of the economic benefit exceeds the value of the consideration. A disqualified person[16] is any person who was in a position to exercise substantial influence over the affairs of the applicable tax-exempt organization

14 *See, e.g.,* Unrelated Business Income Tax (UBIT), MN Council of Nonprofits, www.minnesotanonprofits.org (last visited Aug. 11, 2017)

15 *See id.*

16 *See, e.g.,* Disqualified Person - Intermediate Sanctions (Nov. 7, 2016), www.irs.gov/charities-non-profits/charitable-organizations/disqualified-person-intermediate-sanctions.

at any time during the lookback period.[17] It is not necessary that the person actually exercise substantial influence, only that the person be in a position to do so.[18] Family members of the disqualified person and entities controlled[19] by the disqualified person are also disqualified persons.[20]

There is a "rebuttable presumption of reasonableness" with respect to transactions where (1) the board (or committee) was composed entirely of individuals not related to the disqualified person (an "independent body"); (2) the independent body obtained and relied on appropriate data as to comparability; and (3) the independent body adequately documented the basis for its determination. Independence is determined as an absence of a conflict-of-interest. Appropriate data means sufficient information to determine whether the price reflects fair market value, including an evaluation of appraisals or a comparison of offers received through a bidding process.[21]

In contrast, the IRS considers certain transactions "automatic excess benefit transactions," even though the terms and conditions are reasonable.[22] For example, if a tax-exempt organization provides a disqualified person with use of a vehicle, access to charge accounts, use of a cell phone or use of a computer for personal purposes, the IRS can automatically find an excess benefit transaction. If the IRS finds an excess benefit transaction with a disqualified person, both the disqualified person and the managers and directors may be subject to the excise tax. Note that in some cases, the transaction (or series of transactions) is so egregious that the nonprofit can lose its exempt status.

Private Foundations and Private Operating Foundations
While public charities can engage in *reasonable* transactions with "disqualified persons," private foundations and private operating foundations (referred to below, collectively as "private foundations") are *prohibited* from entering into the following transactions with disqualified persons:

- Sale, exchange or lease of property;
- Lending money;
- Sale of goods, services or facilities;
- Compensation;
- Transfer of income or assets of the private foundation.

There are a limited number of exceptions, but a private foundation should consult a tax attorney before engaging in such a transaction. The disqualified person and the nonprofit's managers and directors are subject to the tax.

If a private foundation engages in certain lobbying activities, the organization is subject to a tax on the expenditure; a manager who authorized the expenditure, without reasonable cause, is also subject to tax.

17 The lookback period is the five-year period before the excess benefit transaction occurred. Lookback Period (Sep. 14, 2016), www.irs.gov/charities-non-profits/charitable-organizations/lookback-period.

18 *See, e.g.,* Disqualified Person - Intermediate Sanctions (Nov.7, 2016), www.irs.gov/Charities-&-Non-Profits/Charitable-Organizations/Intermediate-Sanctions.

19 "For this purpose, the term control is defined as owning more than 35 percent of the voting power of a corporation, more than 35 percent of the profits interest in a partnership, or more than 35 percent of the beneficial interest in a trust." Id.

20 *Id.*

21 *See, e.g.,* Rebuttable Presumption - Intermediate Sanctions (Feb. 16, 2017), www.irs.gov/Charities-&-Non-Profits/Charitable-Organizations/Rebuttable-Presumption-Intermediate-Sanctions.

22 *See, e.g.,* Lawrence M. Brauer & Leonard J. Henzke, "Automatic" Excess Benefit Transaction Under IRC 4958 (2004), www.irs.gov/pub/irs-tege/eotopicc04.pdf (detailing treatment of automatic excess benefit transactions).

Q18. How does a party to a contract know when contract terms are negotiable?

A18. Generally, *all* terms of a contract are negotiable, and a nonprofit should not enter into a contract if it is not comfortable with the terms. That said, it is more difficult to negotiate with certain entities. For example, units of government are often unwilling to change their form contracts. Banks may be unwilling to negotiate the terms of a loan. With large corporations, it may be difficult to reach a manager with the authority to change the terms of a supply or lease agreement.

When another party provides a nonprofit with a form contract to sign, the nonprofit should request a Microsoft Word® version of the document (or a version in whichever word processing software the organization uses). The organization can make the changes that it wishes to see in the contract and send it to the other party. For purposes of negotiation, it is helpful to describe the changes that were made in the document and the reasoning behind the changes.

H. Sample Contract

This sample is intended to serve only as an example and learning tool. It is for a fictional nonprofit and a fictional agreement. This sample should not be replicated for an actual contract.

Sample Contract[23]

Recitals
WHEREAS, the Neighborhood Partner will provide certain services described herein to assist the Nonprofit Center's Training and Program, as described in the attached Program Description, to find, assist and support nonprofits within the geographic boundaries of the Neighborhood Partner.

WHEREAS, the Nonprofit Center has agreed to compensate the Neighborhood Partner for said services as set forth in this Agreement

NOW THEREFORE, the parties hereto do mutually agree to the scope of services and the terms and conditions contained herein.

Agreement
THIS AGREEMENT, entered into as of this ____day of_________, 20 , by and between _______________________________ (hereafter referred to as the "Neighborhood Partner") and the Nonprofit Center a Minnesota non-profit corporation (hereafter referred to as "NC").

Definitions
As used in this paragraph, "Consultant" includes Consultant, Consultant's sub-consultants, and their respective partners, officers, directors, shareholders and employees.

Term
This Agreement shall remain in effect from ______ until _______ (the "Term"), unless terminated earlier by one or both of the parties as set forth herein.

23 Thank you to the Neighborhood Development Center for the inspiration and for permission to use some clauses of the "Neighborhood Partner Agreement" for this sample contract.

Termination
Either Party may terminate this Agreement upon 30-days written notice. Also, in the event of non-payment by NC, the Neighborhood Partner may terminate this Agreement upon 7 days written notice.

Assignment
This Agreement shall not be assigned by the Neighborhood Partner without the prior written consent of NC.

Venue
This Agreement shall be construed and governed by the laws of the State of Minnesota.

Arbitration
Any controversy, claim or dispute arising out of or relating to this Agreement, shall be settled solely and exclusively by binding arbitration in Hennepin County, Minnesota. Such arbitration shall be conducted in accordance with the then prevailing arbitration rules of Nonprofit Resolution Center. Nonprofit Resolution Center ("NRC"), with the following exceptions if in conflict: (a) one arbitrator shall be chosen by NRC; (b) each party to the arbitration will pay its pro rata share of the expenses and fees of the arbitrator, together with other expenses of the arbitration incurred or approved by the arbitrator; and (c) arbitration may proceed in the absence of any party if written notice (pursuant to the NRC rules and regulations) of the proceedings has been given to such party. Each party shall bear its own attorneys fees and expenses. The parties agree to abide by all decisions and awards rendered in such proceedings. Such decisions and awards rendered by the arbitrator shall be final and conclusive. All such controversies, claims or disputes shall be settled in this manner in lieu of any action at law or equity; provided however, that nothing in this subsection shall be construed as precluding the bringing an action for injunctive relief or other equitable relief. The arbitrator shall not have the right to award punitive damages or speculative damages to either party and shall not have the power to amend this Agreement. The arbitrator shall be required to follow applicable law. IF FOR ANY REASON THIS ARBITRATION CLAUSE BECOMES NOT APPLICABLE, THEN EACH PARTY, TO THE FULLEST EXTENT PERMITTED BY APPLICABLE LAW, HEREBY IRREVOCABLY WAIVES ALL RIGHT TO TRIAL BY JURY AS TO ANY ISSUE RELATING HERETO IN ANY ACTION, PROCEEDING, OR COUNTERCLAIM ARISING OUT OF OR RELATING TO THIS AGREEMENT OR ANY OTHER MATTER INVOLVING THE PARTIES HERETO.

Confidentiality
The Neighborhood Partner shall keep confidential all reports, information and data given to, prepared or assembled by the Neighborhood Partner pursuant to the Neighborhood Partner performance hereunder and NC designates as confidential. Such information shall not be made available to any person, firm, corporation, or entity without the prior written consent of NC first obtained.

NC and the Neighborhood Partner also shall keep confidential all information from and about every nonprofit involved in this program, including all former participants, and participants at every stage of this program.

Warranties and Representations
The Neighborhood Partner warrants that all labor, materials and taxes will be paid for, and there will be no potential lien claimants upon the completion of the work and final payment by the NC. All work will be performed in a commercially reasonable manner and will be performed to industry standards or better. The Neighborhood Partner will promptly return to the project and repair or replace, as necessary, any defect in workmanship at the Neighborhood Partner's sole expense. The Neighborhood Partner's warranty is for a period of 24 months from the date of this Agreement and thereafter expires. Any warranty claim of

the NC shall accrue only during this 24-month period.

Limitation of Liability
Warranty work performed by the Neighborhood Partner does not extend the warranty. The warranty is void if a person or firm other than this Neighborhood Partner performs or re-performs any work within the scope of this Agreement. The Neighborhood Partner is not responsible for consequential damages. This warranty is not transferable. This warranty is given in lieu of any express or implied warranty otherwise provided under the laws of Minnesota.

Indemnity
NC shall indemnify, save and hold harmless, the Neighborhood Partner from alleged damages or injuries arising directly or indirectly from NC or the Consultant's negligent acts or omissions while performing the work under the Consultant's Contract. The Neighborhood Partner shall indemnify, save and hold harmless, NC from alleged damages or injuries arising directly or indirectly from the Neighborhood Partner's negligent acts or omissions while performing the work under this Agreement.

Insurance
The Neighborhood Partner must provide a copy of an endorsement issued by its insurer to the NC at least two weeks prior to the first training, naming the NC as an additional insured, with the minimum requirements outlined below.

A. Commercial General Liability (Occurrence Form)	
General Aggregate (other than Prod/Comp Ops Liability	$2,000,000
Personal & Advertising Injury Liability	$1,000,000
Each Occurrence	$1,000,000
The Nonprofit Center is to be named an Additional Insured. Additional insured coverage shall apply as primary insurance with respect to the NC. The User shall obtain from its insurers a waiver of subrogation in favor of the NC.	
B. Workers Compensation and Employer's Liability	
Workers Compensation	State Statutory Limits
C. Automobile Liability	$1,000,000 each accident
D. Umbrella Liability	
Each Occurrence and Aggregate	$1,000,000
E. Liquor Liability	
If liquor is served, liquor liability of $1,000,000 is also required, either from the User or the vendor supplying the catering or service.	
The above coverage must be placed with an insurance company with an A.M. Best rating of A or better.	

Survival Terms
In the event that any part of this Agreement shall be declared unenforceable, the remaining parts shall continue to be valid and enforceable.

Force Majeure
A party is not liable for failure to perform the party's obligations if such failure is as a result of Acts of

God (including fire, flood, earthquake, storm, hurricane or other natural disaster), war, invasion, act of foreign enemies, hostilities (regardless of whether war is declared), civil war, rebellion, revolution, insurrection, military or usurped power or confiscation, terrorist activities, nationalization, government sanction, blockage, embargo, labor dispute, strike, lockout or interruption or failure of electricity or telephone service. No party is entitled to terminate this Agreement under the Termination Clause in such circumstances.

Waiver
Either party's waiver of, or failure to exercise, any right provided for herein shall not be deemed a waiver of any further or future right under this Agreement.

Other Agreements
This Agreement takes the place of and supersedes any earlier Agreement between these same two parties for the NC Training Program.

NOW, THEREFORE, the parties hereto have executed this Agreement as of the day and year first above written.

NONPROFIT CENTER

By________________________________
Date______________________________

____

By________________________________
Date______________________________

I. Related Resources

Organizations

American Society of Association Executives (ASAE)
www.asaecenter.org
The ASAE website has models and sample agreements and contracts.

LegalCORPS
www.legalcorps.org
LegalCORPS connects small businesses and nonprofits with volunteer attorneys who provide legal assistance for business matters at no charge.

Office of the Minnesota Attorney General
www.ag.state.mn.us/Charities
Provides links to laws regarding charitable organizations, filings and forms, sample policies and other information.

CHAPTER 16

INTELLECTUAL PROPERTY

Topics

A. Overview

Intellectual property is an overarching term for legal rights that are created by someone's intellectual creative efforts. Intellectual property law in the United States has its roots in the United States Constitution.[1] Historically, intellectual property has been a fundamental part of economic development fostered through public policy. Intellectual property law was developed, in part, to encourage economic development by creating a rich, diverse marketplace through the creation of temporary government-enforced monopolies. This economic policy of private ownership often competes with another policy goal that favors providing broad public access to intellectual creations to promote a competitive marketplace. Current U.S. intellectual property law strives to strike a balance between these two competing policy interests. Thus, the history of intellectual property is really rooted in an interest in economic growth.

Intellectual property encompasses several areas of law including patents, copyrights, trademarks and trade secrets. Each one of these concepts is governed by a unique set of legal principles that are not mutually exclusive and protect distinct forms of expression. A patent gives an inventor exclusive rights in an invention for a limited time period. A formal and lengthy application process is required through the United States Patent and Trademark Office ("USPTO") to obtain a patent. The USPTO employs examiners, whose job it is to review patent applications to determine if the invention is properly patentable. Patents require a showing that a process, machine, manufacture or other like improvement is newly discovered and therefore might qualify for limited protection in order to allow the inventor to develop and market the patent. At present, the limited patent term is 20 years from the date an application is first filed. If a patent is granted, U.S. law grants the patentees the right to exclude others from making, using or selling the invention.

While patents protect inventions, copyright gives the author or creator of an original work of expression protection from unauthorized use by others. Copyright protects only the expression of an idea and does not protect the idea itself. Nor does copyright protect non-original expression such as facts, titles, names or methods for performing a certain task or operation. Copyright protection applies to much more than just literary works or things written on paper. Copyrightable works may also include such works as photographs, architecture, movies, sculptures, audiovisual works, sound recordings and things saved to a disk (electronic mail, graphics and web pages). The duration of copyright is determined by a variety of factors outlined in the Copyright Act, described below.

Trademark law governs the use of a particular device (e.g., a word, phrase or logo) that is used by a manufacturer or merchant to identify the source of its goods and services and to distinguish those goods and services from those performed or sold by another party. Service marks are marks or images that are used on services rather than goods. For the most part, use of a trademark in commerce is required to obtain trademark rights. A trademark owner is afforded the greatest protection for their mark if they register the mark with the USPTO or a state government. Federal trademark registration requires a formal application and examiner review process. A trademark can only be enforceable if it is or becomes distinctive. The distinctiveness of a mark is determined on a sliding continuum from arbitrary or fanciful to generic. While patents and copyrights offer protection in limited duration, trademarks can be perpetual in duration as long as they remain in use and do not become diluted. Dilution occurs when a distinctive mark loses its distinctiveness due to a blurring or tarnishing of the mark's strength with common language and words. If at any time the mark fails to identify the source of its goods or services, trademark protection is weakened and may even be lost.

---

1 Copyright and patent protection arises from the U.S. Constitution Article I, section 8, which states, "Congress shall have power…To promote the progress of science and useful arts, by securing for limited times to authors and investors the exclusive rights to their respective writings and discoveries." Federal trademark regulation is an extension of Congress' power to regulate interstate commerce.

Patents, copyrights and trademarks all offer specific legal remedies if they are infringed. The legal remedies vary depending on exactly what rights the inventor, author or merchant hold. Legal remedies often include injunctions against use and, in some cases, monetary damages.

Trade secrets are made of confidential business information that provides an organization a competitive edge in its own market. For nonprofits, trade secrets might include confidential client lists and files, employee performance information and financial and cost structure data. Trade secrets are not registered anywhere, but instead must be protected by an organization through self-monitoring in order for it to claim trade secret protection.

Caveat: It is important to remember the subtopics in this chapter are not mutually exclusive. Although each topic fits under the broader umbrella of intellectual property, each topical area is governed by a specific set of laws that are applied in different ways. This chapter will briefly introduce patents, copyrights, trademarks and trade secrets each as separate legal topics. Although these overviews provide helpful background knowledge, considerations for nonprofits and links to resources, it is imperative to be aware that intellectual property is a very complex area of law that has many intricacies and nuances which cannot be outlined or explained in the brevity of this overview, and that appropriate use of legal counsel is necessary.

Next, this chapter will provide some considerations regarding licensing of material and social media. Finally, this chapter will provide a list of applicable resources.

Nonprofits may encounter intellectual property issues in their daily operations and programs. In an effort to better illustrate some of the technical elements of the subject areas covered, consider the example of the fictional nonprofit, the Society for Cat and Kitten Safety ("SOCKS"). SOCKS' charitable mission is to improve the lives of kittens and rescue distressed felines. In response to the perilous situation that arises when mothers die before a kitten is weaned, SOCKS developed a feeding mechanism for the kittens to provide them with nutrition and keep them alive. As a result, without much fanfare or public attention, SOCKS has been able to increase their capacity and more effectively serve its community through rescuing distressed kittens.

B. Patents

Q1. What is a patent?

A1. A patent is a right granted by the federal government that allows an inventor to prevent others from making, using, selling, offering for sale, or importing their invention. Popular inventions like the airplane and zipper were patented at one point. The patent system allows the government to give a monopoly to inventors in exchange for a full disclosure to the public of how the patented invention works. This exchange is meant to encourage inventors to share the benefits of their inventions with the public by giving them the ability to sue competitors who use their patented inventions without permission. Patents are limited to twenty years from the date the patent application was filed. After the patent has expired, the invention is part of the public domain, meaning that it may be used by anyone.

Patents do not protect mere ideas that are not "reduced to practice," meaning that the patent application has to include a complete description of the invention, and the invention must actually work. Patents are not granted for laws of nature, natural phenomena, or mathematical principles. In the fictional example from the Overview, the feeding mechanism developed by SOCKS may be patentable since it actually works and can be described and the technology can be diagrammed.

Q2. What can be patented?

A2. Patent law covers a wide range of inventions. While initially limited to mechanical inventions, industrial processes and the like, patents now cover software and methods of doing business.

There are three basic types of patents:

- *Utility patents,* which include new and useful processes, machines, manufactured articles, compositions of matter and new and useful improvements of previous inventions;
- *Design patents,* which include new and original ornamental designs for manufactured goods; and
- *Plant patents,* which include new seed or living plant varieties.

Q3. How does an organization obtain a patent?

A3. In the United States, patents can only be obtained through an application process at the U.S. Patent and Trademark Office (USPTO). The process can take several years and be quite expensive. If the USPTO accepts the application, a patent will be issued with a patent number.

The application process usually begins by doing a thorough search to see if the invention either has been patented already, or has become public knowledge in the field. If you have not yet applied for a patent, it is important to keep your invention a secret because if it becomes publicly known, it may not be eligible for protection. Any public use or sale of a product that includes the invention or any publication of the invention before filing the application will mean that the invention is no longer patentable in the United States.

Once a search has been completed and it appears there are no conflicts with current patents or public knowledge, the application begins. A patent application usually contains the filing date, an abstract that is a brief description of the invention, drawings of the invention, the patent specification that describes the invention and the claims of the patent that outline the specific scope of legally protected elements of the invention.

The claims of a patent are the essence of the patent itself. Patent claims can be expanded or narrowed during the application process, but once a patent is granted, they can only be amended to narrow the scope of the invention.

The United States Patent and Trademark Office charges various fees over the course of the patent application and maintenance periods. Under most circumstances, the PTO classifies 501(c)(3) organizations as small entities for the purposes of the patent fee schedule. As small entities, nonprofits pay reduced fees.

The process for obtaining patents is often very complicated. For many more details see the USPTO Manual of Patent Examining Procedure at www.uspto.gov/web/offices/pac/mpep/index.htm.

Q4. How can a nonprofit protect industrial processes?

A4. Other than applying for a patent on the process (see Question 3) and enforcing that patent (see Question 5), it may be possible to protect a process by keeping it as a trade secret. Trade secrets law protects any process, formula, design or compilation of information that is generally not known or reasonably found and that can give a business an economic advantage. For more on trade secrets, see Section E: Trade Secrets.

Q5. What is a business method patent and how does it apply to nonprofits?

A5. Business method patents are a controversial area of law. Some of the business methods being patented are related to complicated financial transactions performed with the aid of a computer. Nonprofit organizations that manage a large and complicated endowment or fund and use a patented method to manage those funds may be affected by the U.S. Supreme Court case *Bilski v. Kappos*, 561 U.S. 593 (2010), which held that Bilski's risk-management method was not the type of innovation that may be patented.[2] The patent application claimed that the procedure should be patented, as it instructed buyers and sellers how to protect against the risk of price fluctuations in the energy markets.[3] The patent examiner rejected the application on the grounds that the invention was not "implemented on a specific apparatus, [it] merely manipulates an abstract idea, and solves a purely mathematical problem." The Supreme Court eventually affirmed the rejection of the patent application.

According to some experts, the *Bilski* decision does not change the business method patent landscape as much as once anticipated, and the law will continue to develop in this area.

Q6. How does an organization enforce a patent?

A6. If SOCKS' feeding mechanism patent application was approved, it has the right to enforce its patent rights against any infringers. For example, if the local pet shop copied or infringed on the feeding mechanism design, SOCKS would have a few options. Enforcing a patent involves demanding the infringer stop using the patented technology (usually by a "cease and desist" letter), entering into a license agreement with the infringer or bringing a lawsuit in federal court for patent infringement.

Patent lawsuits must be filed in federal court and can be a lengthy and costly ordeal. Like other lawsuits, patent infringement suits begin with filing a complaint that lays out the case being made by the organization or person whose patent is infringed, the plaintiff. The defendant, or alleged infringer, will then file its answer and any counterclaims it might have against the plaintiff. Patent infringement cases often include a "Markman Hearing," which is a pretrial hearing where a judge will determine the precise meaning of the relevant terminology used in the claims of the patents in question.

Patent infringement litigation may be resolved by a dismissal of claims, a trial leading to a verdict or the parties entering into a settlement agreement. A verdict may result in money damages, injunctive relief or both. The terms of a settlement agreement may include cash payments or a license agreement that would allow the infringer to continue to use the patent in exchange for royalty payments.

2 *Bilski v. Kappos*, 561 U.S. 593, 611 (2010).
3 *Bilski v. Kappos*, 561 U.S. 593, 616 (2010).

Q7. What are the considerations and costs of enforcing a patent?

A7. Bringing or defending a patent infringement lawsuit can be very expensive. The costs involved usually involve a fair amount of work in discovery or reviewing documents held by the other party and the testimony of expert witnesses. Because patents usually involve very technical subject matter, expert witnesses are a necessary feature of most patent litigation. It is not uncommon for patent litigation to last several years. The amount of money awarded for damages is calculated based on what the patent owner may have lost by the infringement and not based on what the infringer might have gained. Once infringement is proved, some amount of damages is assumed to have occurred.

Q8. How does a nonprofit make sure it is not infringing on a patent?

A8. It is often very difficult to know without a doubt that you are not infringing on a patent. In fact, many large companies are unaware that they are infringing a patent until they hear from the patent owner or are sued. A thorough search of the USPTO records by a patent attorney who has knowledge of the underlying technology can often find patents that may be infringed upon or would at least pose a potential risk. If a nonprofit is considering using a particular technology, even one developed by the nonprofit itself, it may be a good idea to begin to examine what patents may be infringed by using that technology. These searches are called a "clearance search" or "freedom to operate search" and can be an expensive process but a necessary one when the costs of infringing can be much more expensive. Moreover, if a nonprofit is licensing a particular technology or method from another entity, the nonprofit should insist that the license agreement includes a provision to indemnify and hold the nonprofit harmless if a third party alleges infringement of a valid patent. Nonprofits should not assume the risks of infringement when entering into license agreements for technology.

Cross-licenses. Situations sometimes arise where two organizations are prevented from developing their products because each holds a patent needed by the other. Because patents give inventors the right to exclude others from using the patented technology, rather than an absolute right to practice their own invention, companies and nonprofits often enter in to cross-license agreements. These agreements are what they sound like—both organizations license technology to each other in exchange for the other's technology.

C. Copyrights

Q9. What is a copyright?

A9. A copyright is an exclusive set of rights given to the author(s) of works of original expression, the duration of which depends on when the author created the work.[4] Copyrights in the U.S. are protected by the federal Copyright Act. The specifics of copyright law can be technical. In general, in order for a work to be copyrightable, it must fulfill three requirements. First, the work must be original. An original work is one that was independently created by the author (i.e., it was not copied from some other source). The actual threshold for creativity is very low and almost any "creative spark" will meet the creative requirement. Second, a work must tangibly be expressed or fixed in some form. A tangible fixation may include things such as computer programs stored in memory chips, a recorded broadcast, and computer software. Third, the work must be a "work of authorship."

4 Peter B. Hirtle, *Copyright Term and the Public Domain in the United States* (Jan. 1, 2017), copyright.cornell.edu/resources/docs/copyrightterm.pdf (including a chart of copyright terms for various publications).

The Copyright Act identifies nine specific categories that are considered "works of authorship." These include:

- literary works
- musical works, including any accompanying music
- dramatic works, including any accompanying music
- pantomimes and choreographic works
- pictorial, graphic, and sculptural works
- motion pictures and other audiovisual works
- sound recordings
- architectural works
- compilations, collective works, and derivative works.

These categories should be viewed broadly and may include such things as software programs.

A copyright protects the form of expression of an author or creator against copying and distribution of the creator's expression. Literary, dramatic, musical and artistic works are all included under the protection of U.S. copyright law. Copyright protection is available for both published and unpublished works.

The owner of a copyright has certain exclusive rights. These exclusive rights include: (1) reproducing the work in copies or sound recordings; (2) making derivative works based on the original; (3) distributing copies or sound recordings of the original to the public by sales, rental, leasing, lending or licensing; (4) performing the work publicly; (5) displaying the work publicly; and (6) in the case of sound recordings, performing the work publicly by some means of a digital audio transmission. The duration of copyright protection depends on several specific factors, including when the original work was created, when the work was published and, in some cases, when the work was published and registered (prior to 1978). The entire Copyright Act is available at www.copyright.gov/title17.

Q10. How may copyright laws affect nonprofit organizations?

A10. Copyrights are very common and seemingly everywhere. Nonprofits will encounter copyright laws in their roles as both authors and as consumers of information and creative expression. Nonprofits should have a general working knowledge of copyright law and be mindful of copyright infringement both in respect to their own copyrightable content and to that of others. Nonprofits should take steps to ensure their copyrightable material is protected. Furthermore, nonprofits should be duly aware of infringement of others' copyrights. For example, the fictional organization SOCKS would probably encounter copyright issues if an instructor used Xeroxed pages from a book to distribute to students of its Care of Cats and Kittens classes without permission of the copyright holder.

Copyright law is a complex and highly technical area of the law, and it is becoming more complex as the quantity of digital content increases. Despite the complexity of copyright law, there are some fundamental principles that can guide nonprofits around this topic.

First, copyright protects only the expression of an author and not ideas or information. Of course, the distinction between what is an idea and what is an expression of that idea is blurry and often litigated. The words describing a process or idea are protectable under copyright, while the idea or process itself is not. Importantly, if there is only one way of expressing a particular idea, then there is less likely to be protection for that expression.

Second, "author" is a term that is used broadly to mean the actual creator of the work. This can be an organization or an individual. Nonprofits must be mindful of whether works are works for hire or works created as commissioned works. Only works for hire result in copyright protection for a nonprofit organization so that the nonprofit is considered the author.

Third, the author of a work has several exclusive rights, including the right to reproduce, distribute, perform and display the work. Additionally, the author has the right to create or authorize derivative works based on the original work. A derivative work is a work that is a based in large measure on the original work, for example a film production of a published novel.

Fourth, an author can assign each of these rights via exclusive and non-exclusive licenses (discussed in Section G: Licensing).

Fifth, registration of copyrights and use of the copyright symbol are not required but do provide notice to the world that the nonprofit claims a copyright for the labeled work.

Q11. What is not protected by copyright?

A11. There is often a popular notion that once something is written down or expressed in a particular form, it is copyrightable. That is not always the case. Copyright law does not protect all material. Most importantly, copyright does not protect general ideas underlying the creative expression of copyright. Similarly, copyright does not protect procedures, methods, processes, concepts and principles. These are distinguished from a description, explanation or illustration, which are all generally copyrightable.

Similarly, copyright does not protect expression that merely consists of facts, such as addresses, phone numbers and scientific data. This may affect a nonprofit that is quoting statistics or making comparisons based on general public knowledge. Such works are not protected by copyright.[5] Additionally, work that is not fixed in some tangible form of expression—for example, an improvisational speech or performance that has not been written or recorded—cannot be copyrighted.

Q12. Who is an author?

A12. Determining the author of a work seems like a straightforward task. Yet, this can be one of the most difficult questions to determine in analyzing copyright protection, especially when an employee or volunteer creates something for organization. Under copyright law, the creator of the original expression in a work is the author. The author owns the copyright, unless there has been a written agreement by which the author assigns the copyright to another person or entity.

In the case where a person or persons creates a work for its employer or other commissioning party, that work may be considered a work made for hire. Whether a work is a work made for hire is determined by the particular relationship between the parties. This can be difficult because the Copyright Act definition of a work made for hire is complex and is not always easily applied. In general, to determine whether a work is made for hire, an organization must determine whether the work was created by an employee or by an independent contractor. If the work is created by an employee and is created within the scope of the employee's employment, then the organization for which the work is prepared is considered the author of the work and is entitled to copyright. An employee in this context does not always constitute the

5 Even without copyright protection, proper attribution of the source of such data is expected as a professional courtesy.

traditional meaning of the word "employee." For example, a nonprofit may engage a volunteer to create a work for the organization. In effect, the volunteer has entered into a business agency relationship with the nonprofit, and therefore such created works may be treated as works for hire.

If a work is created by an independent contractor, and the work is specially ordered or commissioned as part of a set of defined works (a collective work, a motion picture or other audio visual work, a translation, etc.), then it is a work for hire if the parties agree in a signed agreement that the work is a work for hire. Under these circumstances, the copyright would belong to the organization, and no further assignment or licensing would be needed. On the other hand, if the work does not qualify as a work for hire, then the independent contractor, as author of the work, would need to assign appropriate rights of the work to the organization; the organization would not own the copyright in the work. When in doubt, an agreement between the organization and the independent contractor that both classifies the work as a work for hire and assigns any and all rights to the organization is recommended.

Q13. Does an organization need to do anything special to obtain a copyright?

A13. There is a common misperception that copyright is "applied for." This is incorrect. An author has a valid copyright the instant a work is put into a tangible format, such as in print, a blog, a video tape or audio CD. Since copyright is instantaneous at the moment of creation, there is no application process. However, there are actions an organization can take to protect its copyright, which include registration of the copyright and providing notice of copyright.

Q14. Is it important for a nonprofit organization to register its copyrighted materials and provide notice of its copyright?

A14. Registration of copyrighted material with the federal government is not required, but the registration system provides several benefits to copyright owners who register their works. Timely registration provides wide-ranging public notice and presumptive validity of the copyright. Registration is required before a copyright owner can sue for possible infringement and early registration provides for the potential collection of statutory damages and attorney fees if infringement is proven.

A copyright owner registers the copyrighted work with the U.S. Copyright Office. An application for copyright registration requires (1) a completed application form; (2) the filing fee is $35 if you register one work by a single author who is also the claimant and the work is not made for hire. Otherwise, the fee for online registration is $55;[6] and (3) in the case of literary works, two nonreturnable copies that will be deposited with the Copyright Office. A copyright registration is effective on the date the Office receives all the necessary elements. More information on copyright registration is available at www.copyright.gov/registration/.

A copyright notice is an identifying label placed on copies of a work to inform everyone of copyright ownership. U.S. law formerly required copyright notice. This requirement was eliminated on March 1, 1989. Historically, works created before that date required notice. The Copyright Office currently does not have a position on whether documents created before March 1, 1989, must have a copyright notice. Even though there is no official copyright notice requirement under U.S. law, providing notice of a copyright is often beneficial for the copyright owner. Copyright owners may provide notice by using the familiar © symbol or the word "copr." or "copyright" followed by the year of first publication and the name of the owner (e.g., © 2017 Minnesota Council of Nonprofits). Providing the public with notice of copyright

6 United States Copyright Office, *Copyright Office Fees*, www.copyright.gov/circs/circ04.pdf (last visited Aug. 16, 2017).

informs the public that the work is protected by copyright and identifies the owner of the work.[7]

Q15. What is copyright infringement?

A15. Generally, copyright infringement occurs when one of the exclusive rights of the copyright owner is violated. This usually occurs when a copyright worked is reproduced, distributed, performed, displayed or made into a derivative work without the permission of the copyright owner. Copyright infringers may be subject to damages and, in some cases, an injunction.

Q16. What is the public domain?

A16. Copyright protection, as outlined in the Copyright Act, is not perpetual in duration. Under the Act, most original works are only covered for a limited time, depending on the type of publication.[8] Once copyright protection "expires," the works of authorship and its content enter the public domain. Works in the public domain are not owned or controlled by anyone and can be used freely for any purpose. There are several internet-based lists for works that are in the public domain, although these lists are by no means exhaustive. For a list of public domain works, see publicdomainreview.org. Bear in mind, however, that while a particular work may be in the public domain, derivative works based on that work may still be the subject of copyright protection. Thus, while it may not be possible to infringe Lewis Carroll's 1865 book *Alice's Adventures in Wonderland*, a work may still infringe Walt Disney's 1951 film adaptation *Alice in Wonderland.*

Q17. What is "fair use" and when does it apply?

A17. Unless an organization or individual has a license or permission to use copyrighted material, actual use of such material may constitute copyright infringement and thus be actionable. The "fair use" doctrine provides a limited exception to the use of copyrighted material.[9] The doctrine is quite complex and is only explained in the simplest form here. Simply acknowledging or giving credit to copyrighted material before using it is not a substitute for actual permission to use such work or material.

The safest way to ensure there is no copyright infringement is to obtain permission, unless "fair use" clearly applies to the situational use. Over the years, the courts have developed several purposes for which use of copyrighted material is considered "fair." These include criticism, comment, news reporting, parody, teaching, scholarship and research. The law looks to four factors in determining if a particular use is fair:[10]

1. The purpose and character of the use, including whether such use is of commercial nature or is for nonprofit educational purposes;
2. The nature of the copyrighted work;

---

7 For more information, *see* 17 U.S.C. §§ 107-121 (2014).

8 Peter B. Hirtle, *Copyright Term and the Public Domain in the United States*, (Jan. 1, 2017), copyright.cornell.edu/resources/docs/copyrightterm.pdf (including a chart of copyright terms for various publications).

9 See 17 U.S.C. §§ 107 (1992).

10 Fair Use (copyright), www.smithhopen.com/glossary_term/132/Fair-Use-copyright (last visited Aug. 16, 2017). See also More Information on Fair Use, www.copyright.gov/fair-use/more-info.html (last visited Aug. 16, 2017).

3. The amount and substantiality of the portion used in relation to the copyrighted work as a whole; and
4. The effect of the use upon the potential market for, or value of, the copyrighted work.

Some cited examples of activities that courts have regarded as fair use include: "quotation of excerpts in a review or criticism for purposes of illustration or comment; quotation of short passages in a scholarly or technical work, for illustration or clarification of the author's observations; use in a parody if some of the content of the work is parodied; summary of an address or article, with brief quotations, in a news report; reproduction by a library of a portion of a work to replace part of a damaged copy; reproduction by a teacher or student of a small part of a work to illustrate a lesson; reproduction of a work in legislature or judicial proceedings or reports; and incidental reproduction."[11]

The problem remains, however, that fair use is a defense to a claim of copyright infringement. Thus, assertion of fair use may not prevent a copyright holder from filing a copyright infringement action. Moreover, copyright holders have a duty to protect their rights—lest they be accused of "sleeping on their rights"—making the threat of litigation more likely. In today's climate of heightened attention to copyright matters by copyright owners, an organization's safest means of proceeding is to communicate directly with the copyright owner and to document in writing any agreement of the parties.

Q18. Does an organization need to get copyright permission to use popular songs (like campfire songs and "Happy Birthday to You") at its events and other programs? If so, how does an organization get permission?

A18. Nonprofit organizations will need to get permission in most cases where the songs are still under copyright protection. Traditional songs may be in the public domain and not protected by copyright. There are a variety of ways a copyrighted work might pass into the public domain, but generally, if it was published before 1923, it is now in the public domain. Otherwise, you may need to have a license to use a song for your event or program.

While there are some limited exceptions for small venues and educational or religious performances,[12] most organizations will need a license to perform a copyrighted song. An organization could get permission directly from each author, but because that may be impractical or impossible, performing rights organizations have developed. A public performance license can be obtained from one of the two major performing rights societies, BMI (www.bmi.com) or ASCAP (www.ascap.com). Both have licensing programs depending on the type of organization and the type of event. Most licenses will allow the organization to perform nearly any copyrighted song. Licenses to record a musical composition for distribution are obtained from the Harry Fox Agency (www.harryfox.com).

The specific case of the copyright to the song "Happy Birthday to You" is complicated. Based on a copyright registration from 1935, Warner/Chappell music claims the copyright to the song and licenses its use. The copyright claim has been the subject of much debate and analysis regarding the traditional origins of the song. But because no court challenge has determined otherwise, the song remains subject to a valid copyright.[13]

11 *See also* Fair Use (copyright), www.smithhopen.com/glossary_term/132/Fair-Use-copyright- (last visited Aug. 16, 2017).
12 *See* 17 U.S.C § 110 (2005).
13 *See* Happy Birthday to You, en.wikipedia.org/wiki/Happy_Birthday_to_You (last visited Aug. 16, 2017).

Q19. How does an organization enforce a copyright?

A19. Copyright enforcement, particularly by means of litigation, requires that an organization first register the work with the Copyright Office. If an organization suspects their copyright is being infringed, it is important that it thoroughly investigate the matter. If the organization determines its copyright is in fact being infringed, it may first want to send a "cease and desist" letter informing the infringer of the basis of the copyright claim and asking the infringer to stop using the copyrighted material. In doing so, the organization puts the infringer on notice of the organization's rights and that continued infringing use might be deemed "willful" for the purpose of determining damages. In some cases, this will be enough to deter the infringer's actions. However, if a cease and desist letter is not enough to deter the infringer, formal legal action may be necessary. An organization may seek to protect its copyrights against unauthorized use by filing a civil lawsuit in federal district court. Through legal action, an organization may seek an award of damages and, in some cases, an injunction to stop the continued infringement. Copyright enforcement legal action—like most litigation—can be lengthy and expensive. An organization's most cost effective method of enforcing and protecting its copyrights is to diligently let the public know its material is copyrighted and to deal with infringers on a case-by-case basis.

D. Trademarks

Q20. What is a trademark?

A20. A trademark can be anything that identifies a particular person, group or business as the source or origin for a particular good or service. Trademarks exist to protect both a business' identity and goodwill and to protect consumers from counterfeit or look-a-like goods or services. A trademark is any word, name, symbol or device that identifies a particular source or origin of goods or services. Most often, trademarks take the form of a brand name (like COKE®) or logo (such as the NIKE® "swoosh"), but can be music (such as the NBC® three note chimes) or even, in rare cases, smells, the "look and feel" of a product or a particular color of product (such as pink fiberglass insulation, which is a trademark of Owens-Corning). Basically, just about anything can be a trademark, so long as it can identify a specific business, person or group as the source of goods and services.

See the U.S. Patent and Trademark Office's publication "Trademark Basics" at www.uspto.gov/trademarks/basics/index.jsp for more details.

Q21. What cannot be a trademark?

A21. There are a several things that by definition cannot function as a trademark. If the word is the generic word for a product, it cannot be a trademark for that product. For example, "apple" could not be a trademark for an apple grower, but it works fine as a trademark for a computer company.

The U.S. Patent and Trademark Office lists a number of specific exception to the general rule for what cannot be protected by trademark law, such as offensive or disparaging names or functional features of a product. See www.uspto.gov/trademarks for more information.

Q22. What is the difference between a state and federal trademark?

A22. A trademark can be registered at both the state and federal levels. At the state level, trademarks may be registered with the Minnesota Secretary of State's Office.[14] Registrants should file a Trademark Application, this form is available at www.sos.state.mn.us/media/1809/trademarkapplication.pdf, accompanied by a $50 mail filing fee ($70 for expedited service in-person).15 Once approved, state marks are effective for a term of ten years.[16] Marks may be renewed for another ten-year term. Renewal applications should be submitted within six months prior to the expiration of the ten-year term.[17] Renewal applications can be found at www.sos.state.mn.us/media/1826/trademarkrenewal.pdf and should be accompanied by a $25 filing fee ($45 for expedited service in-person). See also Chapter 2: The Nonprofit Corporation, Section B: Reserving a Name for a Nonprofit Corporation. For the federal registration process, see Question 9 in Chapter 2.

Registering marks with the state protects the marks from infringement within the state and allows the registrant to enforce trademark rights in a Minnesota district court, but the protection does not extend to enforcement in other states. State trademark laws do not supersede federal trademark rights, and federal law will preempt state law rights if there is a conflict of law.[18] Finally, it should be noted that because trademark rights are acquired through use of the mark in commerce, an organization can acquire enforceable common law trademark rights without registration. As with many other forms of registration, however, trademark registration provides notice and may constitute *prima facie* (on its face or at first appearance) evidence of the validity of the trademark.

Q23. What is the process for federal registration of a trademark or service mark?

A23. Under U.S. law, trademarks are acquired through use, meaning that you have a trademark as soon as you start using it, although there are significant limitations on the strength of trademarks that have not been registered. Federal registration makes those trademark rights much more certain and secure and gives the trademark owner additional remedies against infringers in court.

Federal trademark registrations are usually processed online through the U.S. Patent and Trademark Office's Trademark Electronic Application System (TEAS), available at www.uspto.gov/teas/index.html. The application process requires the name and contact information of the business or individual, a description of the trademark and often an image of the mark, the class of the mark as indicated by an international system of numbering categories of goods and services, a description of the particular goods or services the mark will be used on, and a specimen of the mark showing how it is being used.

The selection of a classification of the product or service on which the mark will be used is important because trademark infringement is only considered for a confusingly similar mark within the same class of goods or services. The list of classifications is online at www.uspto.gov/web/offices/tac/tmfaq.htm#Application018. The classifications cover the entire range of manufactured products, from chemicals and vehicles to toys, as well as a range of personal and professional services.

14 Minn. Stat. § 333.20, subd. 1 (2016).

15 Minn. Stat. § 333.20, subd. 4 (2009).

16 *How to Renew Your Trademark or Service Mark*, www.sos.state.mn.us/business-liens/business-help/how-to-renew-your-trademark-or-service-mark/ (last visited Aug. 16, 2017).

17 Office of the Minnesota Secretary of State, *Renewal of Trademark, Service Mark, Certification Mark or Collective Mark* (2017), www.sos.state.mn.us/media/1826/trademarkrenewal.pdf.

18 *See* Federal Registration of Your Trademark or Logo, www.mclane.com/thought-leadership/federal-registration-of-your-trademark-or-logo (last visited Aug.17, 2017).

Federal applicants have two choices for describing the mark to the PTO examiners. First, they can present the mark in typed format such as "1-2-3 GO!" or "AMTECH." Second, applicants can present the mark in stylized or design format. This would include sending a black and white computer image (JPG or GIF only) along with the application.

Last and most important, the applicant must show actual use of the mark on goods or services in interstate commerce. Interstate commerce means shipping goods across state lines or delivering services to residents of another state. This requirement is key because it is the basis for federal trademark protection. Without evidence of use in interstate commerce, the mark is not eligible for federal protection.

It is possible to file an "intent to use" application, which basically saves your place in line so that no one else can register your trademark before you do. This can be useful when a name has been chosen but is not yet being used. However, you will eventually need to start using the trademark; the fees to extend the "intent to use" time period can become expensive and are limited to three years total.

The federal application is filed with the PTO. There are three options for initial application fee for electronic filing, and each of these three options have specific requirements that impact the fee amount.[19] Organizations should be familiar with these factors before accessing the new application forms.[20] The regular initial application fee for electronic filing is $400 per class of goods or services. The application will be examined by an attorney at the PTO for the completeness of the application and the suitability of the trademark. Applications can be rejected for presenting marks that are scandalous, falsely or inadequately described or confusingly similar to other marks. After application and examination, there may be some correspondence with the PTO to verify certain aspects of the application.[21] If the PTO issues the trademark registration, indications of continued use will have to be presented every five years. Assuming all of the requirements are met, a trademark is valid as long as the mark owner continues to use it.

Q24. How does an organization protect or enforce a trademark?

A24. An organization's trademarks are protected if they are the only organization using them and if they are using them as trademarks and not as ordinary words. Because trademarks work as identifiers of organizations, businesses and people, they must be continuously protected and policed. An organization must use their trademarks consistently and continuously in a way that makes it clear they are trademarks and prevent others from using them in ways that are likely to cause confusion.

Trademark usage: Trademarks have to stand out from other words. Typically, trademarks are capitalized or written in all caps and are used with either the ™ or ® symbols or some other written notice is given to indicate the status of the mark. The ® symbol indicates that the trademark has been registered with the U.S. Patent and Trademark Office. The ™ symbol is used on any non-registered mark, whether or not the application process has been started. Minnesota adopted the USPTO classification system, and the symbols used by the USPTO also should be used in Minnesota.[22] These symbols serve to put others on notice that you are claiming these words as trademarks.

19 Trademark Fee Information, www.uspto.gov/trademark/trademark-fee-information (last visited Aug.17, 2017).
20 *Id.*
21 As part of the process for issuing a trademark, the PTO provides notice of upcoming trademark registrations. Interested parties may, upon becoming aware of upcoming marks, seek to oppose the registration, or later may seek to have the mark canceled for various reasons. These proceedings, similar to a legal proceeding in a court, take place before the Trademark Trial and Appeal Board.
22 Minn. Stat. § 333.26 (2016).

Trademark owners must also take care not to let their trademarks become generic terms. Generic terms are words that cannot be trademarks because they are the ordinary word for something and do not refer to a particular source. For example, cola is a generic word, whereas "COKE®" is a trademark. Trademarks can become generic if the public no longer thinks of that word as referring to any one source in particular. One way to avoid this is to never use your trademark as a noun or a verb. For example, rather than say "grab some BIZCOs," say "grab some BIZCO widgets."

Trademark policing: A trademark owner must prevent others from using a word or phrase that is similar enough to their own trademark that the public would be likely to be confused. When a trademark owner becomes aware of potential infringement, they must do what they can to stop it. This is because the longer two similar marks are being used simultaneously for the same class of goods or services; the less likely it is that the public will find either one of them distinctive.

Q25. The organization had received a cease and desist letter. How should it respond?

A25. As with all legal disputes, it is better to address the problem early rather than ignore it. First, the organization should read the letter carefully to see what rights are being asserted and what mark is at issue. If possible, the organization should conduct some informal research to understand the scope and context of the asserted mark. Informal research may include searching the mark on the PTO website to see when the mark was registered, for what class of goods, and whether the mark is still valid. Similarly, a visit to the Minnesota Secretary of State's website may reveal a state registration. Next, the organization should examine the conduct that is alleged to be infringing to understand the basis for the claim. The organization should have a good understanding of what changes it would need to make to cease the allegedly infringing behavior. With a good understanding of what the issues are, the organization can strategize next steps, which may include a letter or phone call laying out a response in opposition or an agreement to acquiesce to the demands of the letter. When in doubt, call an attorney to see if there is a good response to the cease and desist letter other than giving in to its demands. An early response can sometimes prevent costly litigation.

Q26. How are internet domain names or website addresses protected?

A26. Domain names are basically pointers or aliases that redirect people to a computer server that is hosting the website. For example, the domain name <google.com> is registered as a domain name, and when you enter that domain name in your web browser, your ISP knows that the domain name <google.com> should point to the computers hosting Google's website.

Domain names often contain or are comprised of trademarks. Problems arise when a domain name is registered by someone other than the trademark owner. When someone registers a domain name, they agree to arbitration to resolve any disputes between a trademark owner and the domain name registrant. The arbitration proceedings are governed by the Uniform Domain-Name Dispute-Resolution Protocol (UDRP). Arbitration can be done by any number of organizations, such as the National Arbitration Forum or the World Intellectual Property Organization. Typically, if the arbitrators determine that the registered domain name should rightfully belong to someone else and that the person registering the domain name acted in bad faith, the domain name will be transferred to the rightful owner.

The UDRP policy can be found at www.icann.org/en/udrp/udrp.htm.

E. Trade Secrets

Q27. What is a trade secret?

A27. A trade secret is information that has independent economic value for an organization values because it is not generally known, or readily ascertainable, to other persons or organizations that could obtain economic value from its disclosure or use. Trade secrets must be the subject of reasonable efforts to maintain its secrecy. Trade secrets may consist of ideas, process, formulas, marketing or campaign strategies and other similar organizational secrets. Unlike other forms of intellectual property, protecting trade secrets is essentially a do-it-yourself form of protection. There is no federal or state registration process to secure trade secrets. Trade secret protection lasts for as long as the secret is maintained. Once a trade secret is made public, trade secret protection ends.

A trade secret owner can prevent other groups or individuals from benefiting from its trade secrets or disclosing them to third parties without permission. If an organization protects its trade secrets, the law provides for injunctive relief halting any unauthorized use and dissemination of such secrets. The law also provides for damages if the trade secrets are misappropriated to third parties. Individuals who leak trade secrets can face criminal charges and civil damages with penalties of the actual cost of misappropriation and unjust enrichment.[23]

Q28. How can organizations protect trade secrets?

A28. Trade secrets are often the most difficult form of intellectual property to protect. This is due in part to the fact that the information must actually be kept secret for as long as trade secret protection is sought. Simply calling information a trade secret will not make it such. An organization must take reasonable efforts under the circumstances to protect the trade secret and to establish its desire to keep the information secret. Thus, an organization should develop internal procedures to maintain the confidentiality of anything it deems a trade secret. Some steps that can be taken to protect trade secrets might include:

- Identifying and documenting specifically what the organization deems a trade secret;
- Restricting access of files or information to essential personnel;
- Labeling all proprietary information as confidential;
- Allowing disclosure only when there is an actual need to know the information disclosed;
- Developing technology use policies;
- Maintaining a computer system that is monitored through passwords for all proprietary information;
- Requiring a non-disclosure agreement which restricts the use of the information as a trade secret; and
- Including a section in the company's employee or volunteer manual prohibiting the disclosure of proprietary information.

23 Minn. Stat. § 325C.03 (2016). Minnesota follows the Uniform Trade Secrets Act. The law is codified under the Minnesota Statutes Chapter 325C. See www.revisor.mn.gov/statutes/?id=325C.

F. Social Media

Q29. What are the intellectual property considerations from use of social media?

A29. Social media poses the same potential problems as any other kind of media. The increased risk may be because most social media is more casual, and people may be more likely to say or do things that they would not say or do on an official organization website. Keep in mind that copyright and trademark laws apply to social media, as do false advertising, libel, slander and any other laws that regulate communications. Good judgment should be your guide. If you could not do it in traditional media, you probably should not do it in social media.

Q30. What social media policies and procedures might an organization consider adopting?

A30. An organization that is going to use social media should have a written policy regarding use. This policy should include when it is appropriate to identify yourself as a spokesperson for the organization and how employees might keep their private life separate from their role in the organization; what kinds of topics should be considered confidential or inappropriate for discussing over social media; and how to deal with offensive or problematic responses received by the organization from others via social media. A social media policy should also set out goals for the organization to achieve through its use of social media.

G. Licensing

Q31. What is a license?

A31. By definition, a license is an instrument by which an owner or holder of a particular right conveys or assigns the right to do something subject to certain terms and conditions. Essentially, a license is a privilege for a licensee to do something with a patent, copyright or trademark. Licenses are contractual documents and, therefore, are legally enforceable. Licenses may be restricted in several ways, including by duration (i.e., term) and territory.

Q32. What is Creative Commons and when might a nonprofit utilize it?

A32. Creative Commons is a copyright licensing scheme that is intended to make it easier to share and use copyrighted works, particularly for non-commercial uses. There are a number of license options available and you can choose what kind of restrictions you would like to place on your works. For more details, see www.creativecommons.org.

H. Other Issues

Q33. When an employee authors a publication, creates a new program or develops a new product, who owns the end product—the employee or the employer?

A33. When an employee creates a work within the scope of their employment, the employer is the owner of the work and copyright. The challenge often arises over who is an employee. Beyond the common meaning of "employee," individuals who prepare the work under circumstances where the employer has substantial control over the work or the preparer will be considered employees for determining copyright ownership.[24]

I. Related Resources

Websites

Google Patents
patents.google.com/

Intellectual Property, Minnesota State Law Library
mn.gov/law-library/legal-topics/intellectual-property.jsp

Library of Congress Copyright Database
cocatalog.loc.gov/cgi-bin/Pwebrecon.cgi?DB=local&PAGE=First

Protecting Your Organization's Intellectual Property, Minnesota Council of Nonprofits
www.minnesotanonprofits.org

U.S. Patent and Trademark Office Pro Se Assistance Program
www.uspto.gov/patents-getting-started/using-legal-services/pro-se-assistance-program

Statutes

Copyright Law of the United States
www.copyright.gov/title17/title17.pdf

Organizations

Cornell University Law School, Legal Information Institute
www.law.cornell.edu

LegalCORPS
Inventor Assistance Program
Phone: 612-206-0780
Email: info@legalcorps.org
legalcorps.org/inventors
LegalCORPS offers pro bono legal services to small businesses and nonprofits and provide assistance to inventors with provisional and non-provisional patent applications.

24 Factors to consider to determine employment status include: source of the instrumentalities and tools; location of the work; duration of the relationship between the parties; whether the hiring party has the right to assign additional projects to the hired party; extent of the hired party's discretion over when and how long to work; method of payment; the hired party's role in hiring and paying assistants; whether the work is part of the regular business of the hiring party; whether the hiring party is in business; provision of employee benefits; and the tax treatment of the hired party. No one factor is determinative, *Cmty.for Creative Non-Violence v. Reid*, 490 U.S. 730, 109 S. Ct. 2166 (1989).

Minnesota Lawyers for the Arts
Phone: 651-292-4381
springboardforthearts.org/business-help/legal-assistance
Minnesota Lawyers for the Arts offers attorney referral for artists and a free 30 minute brief advice phone consultation in business issues including copyright and trademark issues.

U.S. Copyright Office
www.copyright.gov

U.S. Patent and Trademark Office
www.uspto.gov

INDEX

QUESTIONS BY CHAPTER

Chapter 1

FAQs about Nonprofit Organizations

Differences between Various Types of Nonprofit Organizations

Differences between 501(c)(3) Charitable Nonprofit Organizations and Other Types of Organizations

Chapter 2

Reserving a Name for a Nonprofit Corporation

The Nonprofit Incorporation Process in Minnesota

Articles of Incorporation

Bylaws

Keeping your Nonprofit Corporation in Good Standing

Dissolving a Nonprofit Corporation and Disposing of its Assets

Chapter 3

Obtaining Federal Income Tax Exemption

Maintaining Federal Income Tax Exemption

State Income Tax Exemption

Property Tax Exemption

Sales Tax Exemption

Federal and State Unemployment Tax and Payroll Taxes

Chapter 4

The Role of the Minnesota Attorney General

Registering as a Charitable Organization

Registering as a Charitable Trust

Registering as a Professional Fundraiser

Verifying an Organization's Ability to Solicit Donations

Other Registration and Notification Requirements

Chapter 5

Charitable Pledges

Donor Substantiation Requirements

Responsibilities to Funding Sources

In-kind Donations

Donations of Vehicles, Land, Buildings and Stock

Planned Giving Vehicles

Other Issues

Chapter 6

Board Structure and Composition

Board Duties and Responsibilities

Officers and their Duties

Conflicts of Interest

Board Liability

Board Meetings, Minutes and Notices

Voting Rights and Requirements

Other Issues

Chapter 7

Legal Opportunities and Limits on Lobbying for 501(c)(3) Nonprofit Organizations

The 501(h) Election: The Expenditure Test

Direct Versus Grassroots Lobbying

Lobbying Registration and Reporting at the State and Federal Level

Election Activity and Voter Education

Differences between Restrictions on 501(c)(3) and 501(c)(4) Tax Exempt Organizations

Ballot Measures

Chapter 8

Legally Sound Financial Practices

Limitations on the Expenditure of Restricted Funds

Payroll Taxes

Fiscal Agency or Sponsorship

Audit Requirements

IRS Information Return (Form 990) Requirements

Unrelated Business Income Tax (UBIT)

Private Inurement and Intermediate Sanctions

Other Issues

Chapter 9

Distinctions between Employees and Independent Contractors

Distinctions between Exempt and Nonexempt Employees

Hiring and Firing Employees

Employee Benefits

Personnel Policies and Job Descriptions

Personnel Records

Complying with Other Federal and State Employment Laws

Volunteer Personnel

Chapter 10

Risk Management

Common Coverage Exceptions

General Liability Insurance

Directors and Officers Liability (D&O) Insurance

Professional Liability Insurance

Automobile Insurance

Insurance for Special Events

Property Insurance

Workers' Compensation Insurance

Volunteer Liability and Immunity

Chapter 11

Public Inspection Requirements for IRS Filings

Sharing other Information with Members with Voting Rights, Donors and the General Public

Sharing Information about Donors

Sharing Information about Members

Sharing Information about Clients

Other Disclosure and Privacy Issues

Chapter 12

Collaborative Ventures

Mergers

Forming Related Exempt Organizations: 501(c)(3)s, 501(c)(4)s and PACs

For-profit Subsidiaries

Limited Liability Companies (LLCs)

Government Contracting

Chartered National, State or Local Organizations

Other Issues

Chapter 13

Minnesota Lawful (or Charitable) Gambling

Nonprofit Postal Rates

Parades

Other Regulatory Issues

Chapter 14

Use of Professional Legal Advisors

Use of CPAs

Use of Auditors

Organizational Policies and Procedures to Ensure Compliance

Record Maintenance and Retention

Chapter 15

Basic Elements of a Contract

Boards and Contracts

Nonperformance, Breach and Escape

Attorney Review

Contracts Checklist

Other Issues

Chapter 16

Patents

Copyrights

Trademarks

Trade Secrets

Social Media

Licensing

Other Issues